Charles William Boyce

A Brief History of the Twenty-Eighth Regiment New York State Volunteers

First Brigade, First Division, Twelfth Corps, Army of the Potomac, from the author's diary and official reports

Charles William Boyce

A Brief History of the Twenty-Eighth Regiment New York State Volunteers
First Brigade, First Division, Twelfth Corps, Army of the Potomac, from the author's diary and official reports

ISBN/EAN: 9783337126193

Printed in Europe, USA, Canada, Australia, Japan

Cover: Foto ©ninafisch / pixelio.de

More available books at **www.hansebooks.com**

A BRIEF HISTORY

OF THE

Twenty-eighth Regiment
New York State Volunteers

FIRST BRIGADE, FIRST DIVISION,
TWELFTH CORPS,

ARMY OF THE POTOMAC,

FROM THE
AUTHOR'S DIARY AND OFFICIAL REPORTS.

WITH THE

MUSTER-ROLL OF THE REGIMENT,

AND MANY

PICTURES,
ARTICLES AND LETTERS

FROM SURVIVING MEMBERS AND FRIENDS,

WITH THE REPORT OF PROCEEDINGS OF THE THIRTY-FIFTH ANNUAL REUNION
HELD AT ALBION, NEW YORK, MAY 22, 1896.

Boyce, Charles William, 1842-
A brief history of the Twenty-eighth regiment New York state volunteers, First brigade, First division, Twelfth corps, Army of the Potomac, from the author's diary and official reports. With the muster-roll of the regiment ... and ... with the report of proceedings of the thirty-fifth annual reunion held at Albion, New York, May 22, 1896. [By] C. W. Boyce ... [Buffalo, The Matthews-Northrup co., 1896?]

190 p. incl. front., illus. (incl. ports., maps) 25½cm.
1. New York infantry. 28th regt., 1861-1863. 2. U. S.—Hist.—Civil war—Regimental histories—N. Y. inf.—28th.

EDWIN F. BROWN,

Colonel Twenty-eighth Regiment New York State Volunteers,

Inspector-General United States Soldiers' Homes.

MADE IN
THE COMPLETE ART-PRINTING WORKS
OF
THE MATTHEWS-NORTHRUP CO.
BUFFALO, N. Y.

TO THE

HALLOWED MEMORY

OF THE

Gallant Dead of the Twenty-eighth New York Regiment

AND TO

The Comrades,

"WHO, DARING TO DIE, YET SURVIVE,"

THESE PAGES

ARE AFFECTIONATELY DEDICATED.

CONTENTS.

(Continued.)

PHOTOGRAPHS.

PREFACE.

THESE MEMOIRS of the gallant Twenty-eighth Regiment, New York State Volunteers, have been prepared from the writer's diary and from official records, in response to a resolution of the comrades, passed at the Reunion in 1894, and repeated in 1895.

No history of this regiment has ever been published, though a general desire for one has always been expressed.

The Secretary has consented to do the best he can. His only qualification for the work is a personal knowledge of the facts, having been "Present for Duty" with the regiment on every march and every event of its history. He hopes it will be found correct in the facts and dates given, and will be of interest to his comrades, for whom, alone, it has been prepared.

Our thanks are due to all who have aided in the work. Especially are we indebted to Mr. W. F. Goodhue, consulting engineer of Milwaukee, Wis., and Secretary of the Third Wisconsin Volunteers, for the very accurate maps used. These were made from the original drawings, kindly loaned by him for this purpose. We are under obligations, also, to Captain George K. Collins, of Syracuse, N. Y., Historian of the One Hundred and Forty-ninth New York Volunteers, and author of the interesting history of that organization, for many of the cuts used. These comrades wore the "star," and have shown this kindness to their companions of the old Twelfth Corps by freely dividing their "rations" with us, which we here gratefully acknowledge.

To the comrades and others who have furnished the fine special articles published in connection with the history, we are under great obligations;

and to all who have sent their photographs. The writer knows by experience that as we grow older, there comes a great aversion to having one's wrinkles and gray hairs made so painfully prominent. It is with great satisfaction, that we are enabled to publish the pictures of more than half the surviving members of the regiment.

The name, with the official record of every member of the regiment, is printed in the muster-roll, which has been copied with care from the war records in the Adjutant General's Office at Albany, N. Y. Doubtless, many errors will be found. Especially is the roll incomplete in the record of those taken prisoner at Chancellorsville. Many omissions in this have been noticed. The battle occurring so near the date of muster-out, the company officers had little time to complete their rolls. These omissions would have been supplied could the record at Washington have been consulted.

Where the member is known to be alive his present address is given. This roll gives the list of the heroic dead, who offered their lives in battle, that the nation might live. Of every one it can be said, " He died on the field of honor."

Here, also, are found the names of those who, surviving the trying ordeal of a two years' service, have since died; and the date of death, when known. We cherish as a sacred legacy the noble deeds of these comrades, whose memories will never be dropped from our hearts, though their names are no longer carried on our yearly rolls.

No braver body of men served in the war than the Twenty-eighth New York, and the record of their valor deserves a more worthy tribute than these pages.

C. W. BOYCE,
Secretary.

BUFFALO, N. Y., June 1, 1896.

MAP OF THE CAMPAIGNS

OF THE

Twenty-eighth New York Volunteers

IN VIRGINIA AND MARYLAND,

1861-62-63.

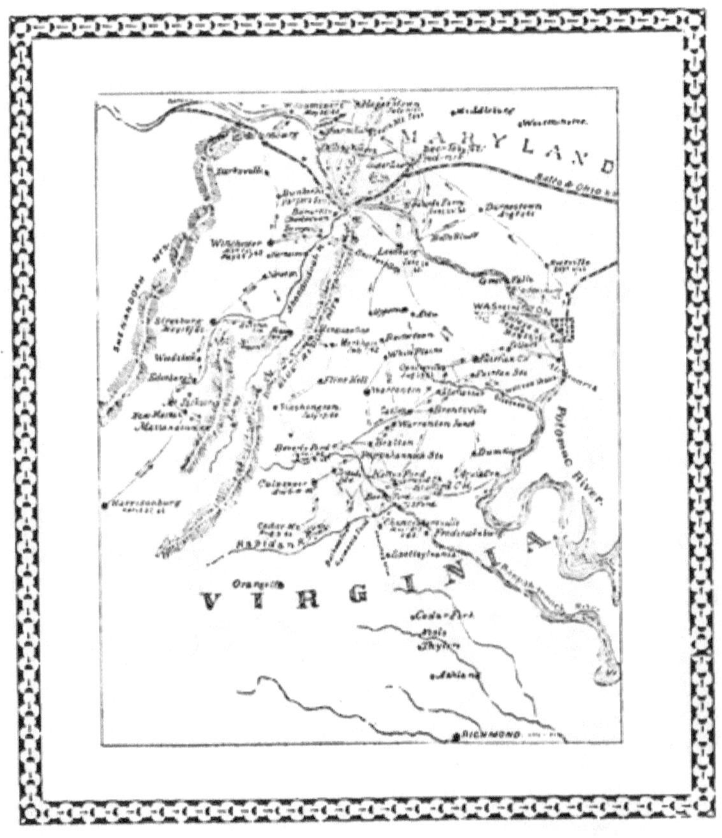

A BRIEF HISTORY

OF THE

TWENTY-EIGHTH REGIMENT,

New York State Volunteers.

CHAPTER I.

ORGANIZATION AT ALBANY.

MAY 14TH TO JUNE 24TH, 1861.

THE Twenty-eighth Regiment, New York State Volunteers, was composed principally of young men from the counties of Niagara, Orleans, Genesee, Ontario, and Sullivan, who volunteered, without bounty, at the first call of President Lincoln, for seventy-five thousand men. Many of them were among the very first in the State to enlist, having done so within three days of the assault on Fort Sumter.

It has been well authenticated that Captains E. W. Cook and W. W. Bush, in anticipation of the President's proclamation, opened recruiting offices in their respective places of business on Main Street, at Lockport, N. Y., on the day of the call, before it had been printed. The men thus enrolled became companies A and B of the Twenty-eighth Regiment.

Captain Bush, after the war, was presented with a beautiful gold badge by the G. A. R. Posts of Western New York, in recognition of the conceded fact that he was "The First Volunteer" for the war, under this call.

The other companies were also recruited early in their several localities, and as fast as accepted, and mustered, were sent to the rendezvous at Albany. They arrived there early in May, and were assigned to quarters in the Burt and other vacant buildings on Broadway, all getting their meals at the Adams House.

The accommodations at this hotel were, perhaps, as good as could have been expected under the circumstances, but were severely condemned by all then. The food was abundant, but very plain. The rattle of tin cups and plates on the bare tables, and the calls of the men for bread, coffee, etc., made an indelible impression on the memory of all participants. It has been said that no member of the Twenty-eighth New York, when traveling, ever stops at an "Adams House" if any other hotel is in the place. The name to him is a synonym of poor fare, to be shunned if possible. How often afterward those who complained the most would have enjoyed, with thankful hearts, the same substantial fare.

The first days in Albany were occupied with drills and visiting places of interest about the city. Soon all were called to pass the severe physical examination of Dr. Hutchinson, a surgeon of the regular army. Many were rejected and were compelled to return to their homes. The accepted ones soon changed their quarters to the new Industrial School building, which was a great improvement. Bunks

were built three tiers high in the large airy rooms The food consisted of beef, potatoes, coffee and bread. The large drill ground, near, was a fine one.

On the 18th of May, the requisite number of companies having been obtained, the regimental organization was formed by the election of the following

FIELD AND STAFF OFFICERS.

OFFICERS.	NAME.	RESIDENCE.
Colonel,	DUDLEY DONNELLY,	Lockport, N. Y.
Lieutenant-Colonel,	EDWIN F. BROWN,	Medina, N. Y.
Major,	JAMES B. MITCHELL,	Batavia, N. Y.
Adjutant,	CHARLES P. SPROUT,	Lockport, N. Y.
Quartermaster,	CHRISTOPHER L. SKEELS,	Lockport, N. Y.
Surgeon,	ALBERT M. HELMER,	Lockport, N. Y.
Assistant Surgeon,	MATTHEW F. REGAN,	Lockport, N. Y.
Chaplain,	CHARLES H. PLATT,	Lockport, N. Y.

The NON COMMISSIONED STAFF Officers, appointed, were:

Sergeant-Major,	CHARLES B. WRIGHT,	Lockport, N. Y.
Quartermaster-Serg't,	EDWIN A. SWAN,	Medina, N. Y.
Commissary Sergeant,	LEONARD D. SALE,	Monticello, N. Y.
Hospital Steward,	THOMAS BENTLY,	Medina, N. Y.
Drum Major,	JOHN MINOR,	Sullivan Co., N. Y.
Fife Major,	ALONZO J. MCMASTER,	Lockport, N. Y.

The COMPANY Officers were as follows:

CO.	CAPTAINS.	FIRST LIEUTENANTS.	SECOND LIEUTENANTS.	ORGANIZED.
A.	E. W. COOK.	D. R. WHITCHER.	J. A. REPASZ.	Lockport.
B.	W. W. BUSH.	A. B. JUDD.	J. C. WALSH.	Lockport.
C.	W. H. H. MAPES.	W. P. WARREN.	F. N. WICKER.	Lockport.
D.	E. A. BOWEN.	G. DAVIS.	L. CHAFFEE.	Medina.
E.	T. FITZGERALD.	W. J. BROWN.	H. PADELFORD.	Canandaigua.
F.	C. H. FENN.	W. W. ROWLEY.	G. M. ELLIOTT.	Batavia.
G.	D. HARDIE.	J. O. NICKERSON.	W. M. KENYON.	Albion.
H.	J. WALLER.	J. C. TERRY.	L. M. BROWN.	Monticello.
I.	T. P. GOULD.	J. C. WARE.	G. A. BINGHAM.	Niagara Falls.
K.	H. H. PAIGE.	V. FARLEY.	J. D. AMES.	Lockport.

The regiment was most fortunate in the selection of its Field and Staff officers. The choice of Colonels Donnelly and Brown, as commanders, could not have been bettered, and proved highly satisfactory to all. They were both men of prominence and ability at their homes, and always enjoyed the unbounded confidence and respect of the entire regiment. Colonel Donnelly was a man of military education and training, naturally a soldier, and fitted to command. He had for years filled the position of Lieutenant-Colonel of the Sixty-sixth Regiment, New York State Militia; and was a fine disciplinarian. Lieutenant-Colonel Brown, as an organizer and leader, had few superiors. Each was strict and firm, yet kind, always a friend to every true soldier, but severe on evil doers.

Major Mitchell was the oldest officer of the Field and Staff, and was a prominent and respected citizen of Batavia, N. Y. He had organized the first company in Genesee County, and when this united with the Twenty-eighth, he was elected Major, but very soon resigned on account of poor health.

Adjutant Sprout, by his genial disposition, won the respect and love of all. He was a man of sturdy, rugged nature; a fine soldier, one who never knew fear.

The position of Quartermaster could not have been filled by a more active, capable or painstaking man than C. L. Skeels. His management of the office proved most efficient, and, if the men ever lacked for supplies, they knew it was not in the power of man to get them.

Doctor Helmer was a surgeon of large practice and pronounced skill, and ranked as one of the best in the army.

The other Field and Staff, and non-commissioned Staff officers, were selected for acknowledged fitness for their several positions, and, with but few exceptions, filled them with ability.

The Line Officers of the Twenty-eighth Regiment were as fine a body of men as ever drilled recruits, or led companies into battle. They were nearly all men of education and position. A few had the benefit of previous military training in Militia companies. All soon became proficient in army tactics and made the regiment one of the best drilled of any of the volunteer organizations.

The numerical strength of the regiment was: Field and Staff eight, Non-commissioned Staff six, Captains ten, Lieutenants twenty, with twenty musicians and seven hundred and thirty-two privates, a total of seven hundred and ninety-six, officers and men.

Of the rank and file, it can be truly said, no better nor braver body of volunteers enlisted during the war. It is universally acknowledged that the volunteers of 1861 and 1862, as a class, were much superior to those of any later period, and the Twenty-eighth was composed of some of the best material in Western New York.

The organization thus perfected, the Twenty-eighth was on May 22d, mustered into the service of the United States for two years, unless sooner discharged. The occasion was a memorable one. The day was delightful, and the regiment, drawn up in line on the beautiful parade ground, in front of the barracks, made a fine appearance. The oath was administered to the companies in a very impressive manner by Captains Seaton and Sitgreaves, and was subscribed to, by all raising the right hand. It was as follows:

"All, and each of you, do solemnly swear, that you will bear true allegiance to the United States of America, and that you will serve them honestly and faithfully, against all their enemies or opposers whatsoever (for the term of two years), and observe and obey the orders of the President of the United States and the orders of the officers appointed over you, according to the rules and articles for the government of the armies of the United States, so help you God."

Eleven men, whose courage failed them, had previous to this time, refused to take the oath. Four were from Company B and seven from Company G. After having their heads shaved, and being decorated with white feathers, they had been promptly drummed out of camp to the tune of "The Rogue's March." This action did not meet with entire approval.

The succeeding days were spent in drilling, and in learning the duties of a soldier's life. Nightly, squads would visit the city. Often they were captured by the patrol, brought back to camp, and confined in the guardhouse.

The first dress parade of the regiment was held on the Washington Parade ground, May 30th; this became, thereafter, a daily occurrence.

Many a homesick boy, away for the first time, was made happy by receiving boxes of good things from home, which were always shared with other comrades. Literary and musical societies were organized, and served to pass the time more pleasantly. The companies contributed towards the purchase of musical instruments.

Governor Morgan, riding a beautiful white horse, often visited the regiment, giving the officers words of praise and commendation.

June 1st came the welcome order to move to Camp Morgan — about three miles from the city and one from the river. This was the regiment's first march, and was not long, but many of the men think they never had a harder one. They were unused to the march, and especially not yet accustomed to moving in light marching order. They had yet to

THE REVEILLE.

I can't get 'em up,
I can't get 'em up,
I can't get 'em up in the morning,
I can't get 'em up,
I can't get 'em up,
I can't get 'em up at all.

The corp'ral's worse'n the private,
The sergeant's worse'n the corp'ral,
The lieutenant's worse'n the sergeant,
The captain's the worst of all.

learn how few things are absolutely necessary, and all were burdened with articles supposed to be essential. These were very soon reduced in number, or cast aside altogether. The day was hot and dusty, and many stragglers were brought up by the rear guard.

The camp was adjoining the Sixteenth New York Regiment, which had just been organized and was in command of Colonel Davies. Here commenced the life in tents, which continued throughout the entire service, except, when houses were occupied at Hancock, for a short time, the next winter. This was a welcome change from the irksome barracks' life of the last few weeks.

The experience at Camp Morgan was varied, and these should have been the happiest days of the regiment, but were, without doubt, the most discontented ones. Here the men found it much more difficult to steal past the guards than at the barracks, but passes were issued, and frequent visits were made to the city.

The following was the daily routine: Reveille at five A. M. Roll Call at five-thirty. Drill five-thirty to six-thirty. Breakfast, seven. Guard Mount, eight. Sick Call, nine. Drill, ten to eleven thirty. Dinner, twelve. Drill, two to three-thirty. Dress Parade, five. Supper, six. Roll Call, nine. Taps and Lights Out nine-thirty.

The Bethlehem cook-house was situated outside the camp, and the men marched there for meals. The food was substantial, and had it been better served no complaints could have been justly made. Dissatisfaction was often shown by drumming on tin cups, when passing near Colonel Davies' tent. This was soon stopped, by the offenders being put in the guardhouse.

June 15th the first issue of clothing was made, and proved very acceptable to many. On leaving home, the men had been told not to bring extra clothes, as uniforms and clothing would be drawn on arriving at Albany. But the days and weeks passed, and the old garments were getting not only threadbare but in many cases in rags. This occasioned much merriment as well as discomfort. An organization, known as the "Ragged Cadets," was formed. No person was eligible to membership, whose clothing was not badly worn. While to be an officer, required more holes than cloth. These "R. C.'s," as they were styled, had daily parades, causing much laughter and fun. As soon as the men drew their overcoats, the companies paraded, presenting the comical sight of regulation coats of blue, covering trousers of nearly every color.

On the 21st, knapsacks, canteens and haversacks were furnished, and on the 23d, guns and accoutrements. The guns were the Remington Rifles, with sabre bayonets, and were greatly admired. The canteens were generally marked by the men with their names, to distinguish them. Often they were misplaced and lost. It is said, the practice was so general of appropriating a canteen, and marking one's name on it, that an Orderly Sergeant could take almost any canteen in his company and call from it the complete roll of his men.

The drills and dress parades improved daily, and seemed fine to raw recruits, but they were simply a burlesque on subsequent attainments.

The sick call soon became an important one, as the mumps broke out in camp, and many were taken ill. Every member of the regiment was vaccinated; the surgeon remarking that this was the first blood the men had shed in defense of their country.

Boxes of delicacies from home continued to arrive, and were always received with great pleasure. The Debating Society, organized at the Barracks, was continued in a large tent, loaned by citizens of Albany, through the influence of N. Ward Cady, a member of Company D.

Other meetings, religious, temperance and social, were held in the tent, and were of much interest, being always well attended. One of the questions before the debating society, remembered still with a smile, but which seemed serious enough, was the following: Resolved, "That the members of this regiment, have no just cause for insubordination, at the lack of clothing, supplies and money due the members." This shows the state of mind existing then. Relief, however, soon came, in an issue of necessary clothing. On the 18th the paymaster made his first appearance, paying the amount due from the State. At this time the privates received the munificent sum of eleven dollars per month. Even this was very acceptable, as the sutler, the convenient access to the city, and the universal habit of borrowing from each other, had drained nearly all the pocket-books in the regiment.

On June 12th one of the happiest experiences of Camp Morgan life occurred: when a beautiful flag was raised at the colonel's tent, with speeches and patriotic songs.

Chapter II.

TO WASHINGTON — UNDER PATTERSON.

June 24th to July 28th, 1861

ON JUNE 24th the long expected and welcome order came to be "off for the war." At one o'clock tents were struck at the firing of a cannon, and, with the cheers of the Sixteenth New York Regiment, the members of the Twenty-eighth left camp, and marched in the heat and dust, through the city to the steamboat landing, where they embarked on two barges, lying at the wharf in waiting.

All along the route the line was greeted with enthusiasm, and the waving of handkerchiefs, by the crowds in waiting to see the departure. Drawn by a propeller the barges started down the Hudson River, stopping at New York several hours; then across the harbor to Elizabethport, where the regiment took cars for Washington. The citizens of Western New York had provided a liberal lunch and, by this thoughtful kindness, the long and tedious journey was made with comfort. A royal greeting was given by many towns in Pennsylvania. Hot coffee and sandwiches were supplied in abundance, while cheers and encouragements were received along the entire route.

On the afternoon of the 26th, previous to arrival in Baltimore, the guns were loaded for the first time with ball cartridges. The riot and attack on the Sixth Massachusetts troops, April 17th, had caused apprehensions that the Twenty-eighth might also be molested, but no hostile demonstration was made. Many groans were heard, and several cheers for Jeff Davis, to which no attention was paid.

On the march across the city from station to station, a very severe rainstorm occurred, and all were drenched. After much excitement and delay, the regiment left the city early in the evening loaded in cattle cars, and arrived in Washington at midnight, occupying houses in the vicinity of the Capitol building.

Such was the confusion and haste in bringing troops to Washington at this time, that the Senate Chamber and House of Representatives were used as quarters for regiments; and the basement was extemporized into a bakery to make soft bread for the soldiers. No better arrangements could be made in those first days of the war.

The Twenty-eighth went into camp about one mile north of the city, on New York Avenue, where it remained ten days. This camp was named in honor of Senator Harris, of New York State. On July 4th, the regiment participated in the first Grand Review of the war. This was the largest demonstration many had ever witnessed, and consisted of all the troops, in Washington at the time, marching at

company front before President Lincoln, Gen. Scott, the Cabinet and other notable personages. The reviewing stand was situated on Pennsylvania Avenue, in front of the White House. This was the first time that many had seen the President: and proved to be the last they ever saw of Lieutenant-General Scott, who soon after was retired on account of his advanced years. It was a grand pageant, and all thought this splendid body of troops would alone prove sufficient to put down the rebellion in three months, so little did any one then know the magnitude of the task before the country.

The regiment had frequent drills on the flats, and the men improved every opportunity possible of visiting public buildings and places of interest. Washington was not then the fine city it has since become; the Capitol building was not completed: huge cranes were seen projecting from the unfinished dome: the Statue of Liberty was standing on the ground, ready to be placed in position and acres of uncut stone were strewn about.

On July 6th the Twenty-eighth left the city to join General Patterson's army at Williamsport. Again the regiment was loaded on cattle cars, and started "for the front,—*by the rear*," as an Irish private remarked. After an all-night's ride, Harrisburg, Pa., was reached Sunday morning, amid the ringing of church bells. But another kind of "service" claimed the attention of the men, and they left at once for Hagerstown, where they arrived, tired and dusty, early in the evening Here they left the cars for the last time, ever after marching on all occasions until starting for home, two years later.

The citizens of Hagerstown showed many attentions that will always be remembered with pleasure. They brought to the roadside, where the regiment was halted, lunches, water, soap and towels. Hungry and dusty travelers never have been offered anything more acceptable. With three hearty cheers for this kindness, the regiment started for Williamsport, a distance of eight miles, which place was reached at midnight.

For the first time in its experience, the command bivouacked on the ground, without tents, as the wagons did not arrive until the next morning.

July 8th, at sunrise, the Potomac was forded. This novel sight caused much merriment among the men. The water was not cold, but clear as crystal, with a smooth sandy bottom, and only two or three feet deep. The crossing effected, the regiment started for Martinsburg, a distance of fourteen miles. This march was on that smooth pike, which was to be such an important factor in the history of the war, and over which, the Twenty-eighth tramped many a weary mile. The regiment was now on the soil of Virginia for the first time, and the men were full of confident enthusiasm.

"MANY A WEARY MILE."

General Patterson's army of some fourteen thousand men had crossed the river July 2d. After a sharp skirmish at Falling Waters, by the brigades of Colonels Abercrombie and Thomas, the enemy was driven beyond Martinsburg. This Colonel Thomas was George H. Thomas, who was soon after promoted general, and obtained such great distinction later in the war in the western army. He is often spoken of as the "Rock of Chicamauga," and known by his soldiers as "Pap Thomas."

The Confederate forces were the Second, Fourth, Fifth and Twenty-seventh Virginia, and General J. E. B. Stuart's Cavalry with Captain Pendleton's Battery of four guns. This brigade was led by General Jackson, soon to be known as "Stonewall Jackson."

The men of the Twenty-eighth New-York have reason to remember this daring Southern leader, whose fame is unsurpassed by any other Confederate General of the war. He commanded the forces opposing them on this their first entry into

Virginia, and it was the singular fortune of war that placed him and the old Stonewall Brigade in the front of this regiment in every engagement of its two years' service. The term of enlistment of the Twenty-eighth, and the life of this intrepid commander, both ended at Chancellorsville, two years later.

As the march continued toward Martinsburg many evidences of the recent skirmish were seen, and all realized they were now in an enemy's country, and the severe duties and trials of a soldier's life had commenced. The day was extremely hot, the march a long and dusty one, and when camp was reached, at Martinsburg, all were weary and foot sore. The camp was in a piece of woods and was named after the Hon. Burt Van Horn, a member of Congress, and a distinguished citizen of Western New York.

The destruction of railroad property here by the Confederates had been very great. Seventy-two engines and many cars and bridges, belonging to the B. & O. R. R. Co., which had their headquarters here, were burned or ruined, to prevent them falling into the hands of the Union forces.

This first night in Virginia will never be forgotten by any member of the regiment. The pickets, from fright, at the strange feeling of being in an enemy's country, commenced firing at imaginary foes in the darkness, and this was kept up nearly all night. Many amusing stories of this occurrence are told. How one soldier fired thirty rounds of cartridges at one stump and hit it every time, being a good shot. How another left his post to tell Colonel Donnelly that he had "an enemy up a tree," and the colonel, with serious face, directed the guard to watch him "till morning, and don't let him down." The officer of the day, it is said, did not make his rounds from danger of being shot by his own pickets.

But the night passed away, and with it the fears of the men, whose nerves were soon to be tried by something more serious than darkness.

It was here at Martinsburg that the severe thunder storm, at night, came on so suddenly, and with such force, that many thought the enemy had made an attack on the camp. It proved to be Heaven's Artillery instead, and was a terrific storm.

On the 10th, Captain Cook with Company A, and Captain Mapes with Company C, in connection with four companies of the Nineteenth New York, all under the command of Colonel Clark, went some five or six miles north of the town, as a guard to the forage train of Captain Skeels. Co. A of the Twenty-eighth was ordered on in advance, while the wagons were being loaded at a barn Lieutenant Whitcher, with a platoon of the company, marched about half a mile farther to the front, to prevent any surprise from the enemy, known to be scouting in the vicinity. Captain Cook soon joined these men, where they were posted in squads about forty rods apart. The advance consisted of Lieutenant Whitcher and Privates Davis and Sly. Soon after, a company of about fifty Confederate cavalry dashed upon them, when firing on both sides commenced. Captain Cook always carried a fine Maynard rifle, and was one of the best shots in the regiment. He emptied the first saddle, and then with the men retreated over the fields to a skirt of woods near by, all firing as they fell back. The Confederates returned their fire, and charged down the road to within ten rods of them. Before reaching the woods, while in the act of taking aim, Private Sly received a ball in the chin, passing through the spinal column and killing him instantly. The reserves were now hurried forward by Captain Skeels, when the enemy retreated. Lieutenant Whitcher had a close call, having the snap of his sword belt cut off by a ball. In the skirmish three of the Confederates were killed and several wounded.

Comrade Sly's body was brought back to Martinsburg and was buried on the 11th, with military honors, the entire regiment being present. After a very impressive service, a detail of his comrades fired a salute of three volleys over his grave. This was the first life taken by an enemy's bullet; the first offered by the Twenty-eighth New York in the war for the Union. He deserves an enduring monument to his memory.

When the regiment left Washington, thirty-five baggage wagons were allowed; and even this was thought to be a small number. Many of the officers could not see how they could get along with such limited means of transportation. Soon, however, they learned the important lesson, that a long wagon train greatly burdened an army. At times, later in the war, but one wagon to an entire regiment was allowed. At Martinsburg each

company was cut down to one wagon. This seemed a great hardship, and many stores and much private property had to be abandoned or destroyed. The men piled their surplus baggage in the company streets and set it on fire, preferring to see it burn rather than fall into the hands of the Confederates. One company threw away a lot of bacon which, being a trifle mouldy, was thought to be unfit for use; but the wagon master, thinking it might be wanted, carried it along, and subsequently, when company provisions became short, and the men hungry, sold the bacon again to the same company.

JOHN BROWN'S FORT.—HARPER'S FERRY.

The regiment remained at Martinsburg about a week, when on the 15th the order came to move twelve miles to Bunker Hill.

On July 17th the direction was changed to the left and rear, and the army marched thirteen miles to Charlestown, where it remained until the 21st.

This was a great surprise and disappointment to the men. All had expected a march to Winchester and an encounter with the enemy. When the order came to march to the rear, the indignation was outspoken on all sides. General Patterson was called a traitor, and the men felt the disgrace that this withdrawal, without an engagement, implied. They did not then know that Johnston left their front on the 18th, and on the 21st was leading his troops on the battlefield at Manassas. In response to an urgent call from Richmond, this general had withdrawn his forces from Winchester, and had joined the forces of Beauregard, at the opportune time to turn the tide of battle there from a promised victory, to a Union defeat and rout.

The Confederates had completely eluded Patterson, whose defense for this retrograde movement was, that the term of service of so many of his troops had nearly expired, that his base of supplies from Harper's Ferry would be much nearer than from Williamsport, and that the 18th, the day arranged for the advance on Manassas, had passed and, therefore, the necessity to hold Johnston in the valley, was over. But the extent of Patterson's responsibility for the Union defeat at the first battle of Bull Run is left to the student of history. He was honorably discharged the service on July 19th, and made application for a court of enquiry into his conduct of the campaign. This was refused by the Secretary of War.

The following is from the New York *Tribune's* account of General Patterson's withdrawal. It shows very clearly the feeling at the time: "The Twenty-eighth New York (Colonel D. Donnelly), which is the pride of the whole division, is one of which the Empire State may feel justiy proud. It is one of the regiments from which no complaint was heard so long as we were in pursuit of General Johnston's army toward Winchester, but when they were commanded to turn their backs upon the enemies of the country at Bunker Hill and Charlestown by general Patterson they began to show dissatisfaction and even complain of being too unwell to travel. Colonel Donnelly was so displeased with the order that he commanded the Stars and Stripes to be rolled up and put in a wagon. When asked by Colonel Butterfield why he did not carry his colors he replied that 'he would not show his flag in a retreat.' His officers sympathized with him."

On the march to Charlestown a false alarm was given that the enemy was occupying a piece of woods in advance on the

right. For a short time an attack was expected; the regiment was drawn up in line of battle at a fence. A reconnoitering force soon discovered that no enemy was present, and the incident is referred to as "the charge on the rail fence."

While in camp at Charlestown many pieces of the tree under which John Brown was hung and of the scaffold then preserved in the jail were gathered and sent home as relics.

The march on the 21st was to Bolivar Heights, above Harper's Ferry, where the regiment remained several days. The last night there, owing to the report of the disaster at Bull Run, having reached the division, with all its attendant alarm, the men lay in line of battle, open order, under arms, on the ground, without tents.

General Patterson's successor was General N. P. Banks. Under his leadership the Twenty-eighth served more than half its term of enlistment. Whatever may be said of his abilities as a commanding general, he won the respect of the men of his division, by his kindness. Any soldier could approach General Banks, and all felt in him they had a friend.

Chapter III.

IN MARYLAND—BERLIN TO HANCOCK.

July 28th, 1861, to March 1st, 1862.

JULY 28th, the regiment left its position on Bolivar Heights, marched down the long hill, through the half-destroyed, historic town of Harper's Ferry, passed the engine house of John Brown fame, and crossed the river near the abutments of the railroad bridge burned by the Confederates on June 14th.

The famous bridge was destroyed and rebuilt during every year of the war. In 1861, as stated above, again in August, 1862, by the enemy, then in June, 1863, by the Union cavalry under Major Coles, and the last time, by the Confederates in 1864.

After a delay of one day at Sandy Hook, two miles down the river from Harper's Ferry, the march was continued on the 29th four miles to Berlin, where Camp Granger, named for John A. Granger, a patriotic citizen of Canandaigua, was formed in a beautiful grove, half a mile from the river.

Here the regiment remained a month, engaged at picket duty; guarding the river from Berlin to near Point of Rocks, a distance of ten miles. The Confederate pickets performed similar duty on the opposite side of the river.

Meanwhile, several raids into Virginia were made. On the 8th of August, Company D of the Twenty-eighth Regiment, and a company from the Nineteenth New York, stationed at Point of Rocks, formed a scouting party and went over the river to Lovettsville, Va., guided by a loyal Virginian named Simons. A company of Confederates, before they could be surrounded, escaped from the town. Mr. Simons, whose life had been threatened, was brought, with his family and goods, back to Berlin. On the 12th, the paymaster arrived, paying the men, in gold, for their first two months' service in the army.

DESTROYED RAILROAD BRIDGE AT HARPER'S FERRY.

Company D of the Twenty-eighth was stationed on a large, densely wooded island situated about midway in the river. The men seemed quite contented with their lot until a Virginian, in looking for his cows, discovered them confined on the island guarded by this company. The cattle had forded the shallow river to graze in the shade, and had been captured and kept unknown (?) to the officers. When reprimanded by the colonel the men claimed they had kept the cows for fear they would be lost, and had only milked them for their care.

Another scouting party, organized and commanded by Colonel Brown, consisting of companies B and F, led by Captains Bush and Fenn, guided by a Unionist named Means, crossed the river on the night of August 15th, at Berlin, and surprised a body of Confederate cavalry, opposite the Point of Rocks, killing one, capturing nine and securing twenty-one splendid horses. One of the best, a blooded black mare, was used by Colonel Brown and proved to be a very fine animal. She was constantly ridden by the colonel, and was shot while carrying him into the battle of Cedar Mountain, one year later.

The regiment left Camp Granger August 21st, passed through Jefferson, Buckeystown and Urbania, and on the 22d camped at Hyattstown, twenty miles from Berlin. On the 29th the march was continued thirteen miles to Darnestown, where the main force of General Banks was encamped. This division contained some of the finest regiments that served in the war. Among these were the Fifth Connecticut and Forty-sixth Pennsylvania, which were brigaded with the Twenty-eighth New York after this during the remainder of its term of service. The men were congenial companions in camp and on the march. Many lifelong friendships were formed with the members of these regiments. In line of battle they were always brave, true and reliable. The Twenty-eighth knew that with such regiments on its flanks they could not be turned by the enemy unless greatly outnumbered. The Second Massachusetts, Third Wisconsin, Twenty-eighth and Twenty-ninth Pennsylvania regiments were also in the division. These were all splendid organizations, with records of which any in the army might be proud. The Second Massachusetts had the unusual good fortune to be commanded by men of military education and training. The colonel and lieutenant-colonel were both graduates of West Point. This was Boston's crack regiment, and undoubtedly one of the best in the division. The men were soldierly in bearing, good neighbors, and in drill and discipline equal to a regular army organization.

The Third Wisconsin had an eventful history. Few regiments in the War saw more varied phases of military experience. The record of this regiment, extending from Winchester to Gettysburg in the Army of the Potomac, is one of distinction and honor. In August of 1863 it, with the Second Massachusetts, Twenty-seventh Indiana, and other picked regiments, was sent to New York City to suppress the draft riots. Later with the Twentieth Corps it joined General Sherman's army in the West, and marched with that army to the sea.

The Twenty-eighth Pennsylvania was the largest regiment in the division. It numbered twelve companies of infantry with one company of artillery, in all about fifteen hundred men, and was commanded by Colonel Geary, who became, after the war, Governor of Pennsylvania.

These regiments were always a credit to the "old First Division"; they always fought well, both in the Army of the Potomac, and under General Sherman in the West. The record of their noble achievements is written on every page of the history of the Twelfth and Twentieth Corps, and reflects honor upon them all, and the cause for which they fought. The First Maryland, Nineteenth New York, and other good regiments were also in the division, but the Twenty-eighth's acquaintance with them was less intimate than with those mentioned.

The Twenty-eighth New York remained at Darnestown nearly two months in Camp Shaler. This was named in honor of the colonel of the Sixty-sixth New York State Militia of western New York. In this organization Colonel Donnelly had held the position of lieutenant-colonel, previous to his connection with the Twenty-eighth. Many members of the regiment had been with him, in the old Sixty-sixth.

Company and regimental drills, inspections, reviews, court-martials and the usual routine, filled the time at this camp The band was organized here, and always proved a very enjoyable feature of the

regiment. Its history with the Twenty-eighth is well told in the article by Comrade Whitmore.

The wives of several officers of the regiment arrived at this time, and were most heartily received. The sight of a lady from New York State was a welcome one, indeed.

A grand review was held on the 26th of September in honor of the proclamation by the President, appointing a Fast Day. The entire division was present, and marched with bands playing, banners waving, and in full uniform. It was an impressive sight. The exercises were held in a field, on a stand, around which the troops closed in solid column, the cavalry and artillery on either side. The united bands led the soldiers in singing "My Country, 'Tis of Thee." The Chaplain of the Second Massachusetts preached the sermon, this was followed by prayer; and the exercises closed by the division uniting in singing a hymn to "Old Hundred."

On the 1st of October the division was again reviewed, marching at common time, and then at quick time, past General Banks and Staff.

October 18th, immediately after dress parade, Adjutant C. P. Sprout was presented with a beautiful sword, hat, sash and spurs by the non-commissioned officers and privates of the regiment, as a testimonial of their high esteem and regard. The presentation speech was made by Sergeant Maxwell of Company B. The adjutant responded in a feeling manner, acknowledging the gift, and expressing the hope that the pleasant relations existing between the officers and men would long continue. Rousing cheers followed his remarks, showing he held a very warm place in the hearts of all.

The quiet of the long stay at Darnestown was broken on the 21st of October, when orders were suddenly received and the regiment made an all-night's march of twenty miles through Poolsville to Edwards Ferry, arriving there early the next morning. The bloody battle and repulse at Ball's Bluff had been fought the day before. On all sides were seen the horrible evidences of the engagement. Ambulances were loaded with the wounded and dying soldiers. Men were lying on the ground unprotected from the cold rain that was falling upon them. Great suffering was experienced, many having lost nearly all their clothing while swimming the river in the retreat from the battlefield. The Twenty-eighth was marched down to the landing, expecting to cross, but the order was countermanded. In the evening it was again ordered to cross. This also was countermanded. The regiment remained here two days, during which time General McClellan made his appearance, and was heartily cheered by the men. In the distance across the river the Confederate pickets were plainly seen watching any attempt at a further movement on the part of the Union forces, but none was made. Having seen something of the fearful results of war, the Twenty-eighth, passing the house where lay the body of Col. Baker, marched away from the scene of this wicked sacrifice and criminal blunder.

October 26th, the regiment marched twelve miles to Muddy Branch and went into camp in a grove of second growth pines. The men commenced building log houses, with the expectation of passing the winter here. Great skill was shown in this work, the companies vying with each other to have the best. The houses were oblong in shape and covered with small tents; the cracks were filled with mud, often with moss, and this gave them a neat appearance. The bunks were placed on the sides. The door was at one end, and fireplace in the other. The chimneys were decorated at the top with barrels or boxes. Often these took fire, causing alarm to the owners and much excitement in the adjoining tents.

It was at this camp that the following story is told of Col. Donnelly. He was full of good humor and enjoyed a joke as well as anybody, even when he was the subject of it.

The colonel, on returning to camp one night, was halted by the sentinel on guard in the usual manner of "Who goes there?"

It was somewhat dark, and just as the sentinel's challenge was made the colonel stubbed his toe and exclaimed in a decided tone: "Michael and all his lost archangels!" — a favorite expression of his.

The sentinel, who knew the colonel well, was a bit of a wag, and comprehending the situation, brought his piece to the proper position, and returned, in a heavy voice: "Halt, ye lost archangels! Advance, Michael, and give the countersign."

The colonel always took much pleasure in telling the anecdote.

CAMP WHITE, NEAR FREDERICK, MD.

The time here was devoted to drills and guard duty on the river. While in camp at Muddy Branch the ladies of Batavia, N. Y., presented the regiment with a beautiful flag at the hands of Captain Fenn of Company F. Sergeant Geo. Hamilton was appointed to carry this flag, and with much pride the regiment marched over to brigade headquarters and showed it to General Williams, who seemed greatly pleased and honored by the call.

November 28th, Thanksgiving services were conducted by Chaplain Platt. The paymaster also made a visit, which proved a source of thankfulness not mentioned in the Chaplain's address. At this and all subsequent occasions the payment was made in paper instead of gold.

Cold weather had now commenced, and all had expected the log houses built with so much care would be the winter quarters of the regiment. But on December 4th the unwelcome order came to pack up and go to Frederick; leaving the houses for other regiments who might occupy the camp when the Twenty-eighth had gone. Some members of the regiment were determined that these snug quarters should not be enjoyed by others; and by some means, unknown to the officers, the entire camp was in a blaze as the men fell in line and marched away. This movement occupied three days, and was thirty six miles; via Clarksburg. Hyattstown, and across the Monoccacy River. On December 7th, they encamped three miles west of Frederick City. Above is given a sketch of this camp, which was in a beautifully situated maple grove at the foot of the mountains, on an elevation overlooking the city. The comrades will recognize this is but a poor representation of this fine location. During the month the Twenty-eighth remained at Camp White the men often visited the city on passes, the mail and papers were daily received, and many boxes of good things came from kind friends at home.

Here John Lanahan, a private of Company I, Forty-sixth Pennsylvania, was executed for the murder of Major Lewis of the same regiment. The shooting occurred in September on the march to Darnestown, while Lanahan was under arrest for bad conduct. He was tied to the rear of a wagon, and while halting at a ford, being intoxicated, seized a gun and shot the major, who died instantly, falling from his horse into the stream. Lanahan was condemned by court-martial to be hung. The order was executed on December 24th. Many would have preferred not to witness the revolting sight, but the entire brigade was marched in hollow square about the scaffold. It was a solemn and impressive occasion, and took place

during a severe snowstorm. The body, swaying in the wind, was entirely covered by the snow as the regiments filed past, returning to their camps.

January 6, 1862, in a heavy snowstorm, which had continued for two days, the Twenty-eighth left its pleasant camp and marched twenty-four miles to Hagerstown, where it was quartered in churches for the night. The next day the command moved on to Clear Spring, and again occupied churches and houses. The third day marched within three miles of Hancock, taking shelter from the storm in barns. Reaching Hancock, January 9th, the men of the Twenty-eighth were assigned to vacant houses in the place.

The sudden call here was due to the Confederate forces under General Jackson having made a demonstration on the town, threatening to shell it. This raid on the part of the enemy, however, was a failure; the severe storms and bad roads made any movement very difficult. General Jackson was compelled to return to Winchester with no result, except the demoralization of his command.

For two months General Williams' Brigade remained at Hancock, doing picket duty on the river. The familiar report of "All quiet on the Potomac" could be made for the entire time. The days dragged very heavily. The monotony was broken only by the nightly pranks of the mischievous ones, playing practical jokes on their companions, by drills and parades, and frequent trips into Pennsylvania, which was but two miles distant. The quality of the milk, and the liberal, kind-hearted hospitality of the farmers there, was often tested, by the men.

On February 17th, a celebration was held that will easily be recalled. At five o'clock the regiments were in line with the general and staff in the center, when the adjutants of each regiment came to the front and read the news of the capture of Fort Donaldson, with 15,000 prisoners. The men cheered loudly, the artillery fired a salute and all passed in review as they marched back to quarters. But the celebration of the victory was not yet over. It had just commenced. To say the men were jubilant would express it too mildly. Officers and men were wild over the glorious event; and the rumor was current that orders from Brigade headquarters were given, that "any officer or soldier found sober after ten o'clock should be put in the guard house." That the occasion was properly celebrated is attested by the fact that there is no record of any arrest having been made.

Washington's birthday was observed by the entire brigade forming a hollow square about General Williams and staff. The ceremonies were conducted by Chaplain Platt of the Twenty-eighth New York, who offered prayer and read Washington's Farewell Address. This was followed by the regiments marching in review before General Williams. The succeeding day a battalion drill with knapsacks tried the muscles, if not the courage, of the men. Many scouting parties made trips over the river into Virginia, but these proved uneventful.

CHAPTER IV.

THE SHENANDOAH VALLEY.

MARCH 1ST TO MAY 23D, 1862.

THE time for the Virginia campaign had now arrived, and on March 1st, with three days' cooked rations, the Twenty-eighth, with no regrets, started for Williamsport. All were anxious that the forward movement, so long contemplated, should begin. General Banks' corps now consisted of two divisions in command of Generals Williams and Shields. These commanders were each veterans of the Mexican War, and were among the best in the country. General Williams had the unlimited confidence and love of the men of his division, and also of the general officers. He was often placed in command of the Corps, which position he always filled with distinction and ability.

General Shields was also an able officer, and the opportunity came within the month for him to show his fighting qualities. At Winchester, on the 23d of March, he won the rare distinction of being the only general that ever defeated Stonewall Jackson. This General Shields decisively accomplished, ably assisted by Colonel Kimball, upon whom the command devolved, when he was wounded.

The first day's march the brigade moved twenty-three miles to Clear Spring, and on March 2d crossed the Potomac at Williamsport, at the same place forded eight months before, under General Patterson. The water was deeper now, and very cold, and the weather extremely unpleasant, a snowstorm coming on during the morning. Greatly to the men's relief, the crossing was effected by a rope ferry, propelled by the current. It was an interesting sight to see the boat cross and recross with no visible power, but proved very satisfactory, carrying one hundred men over every ten minutes.

The forces opposed to the Twenty-eighth on this advance were those of General Jackson again, with his brigade.

The only resistance encountered the first day was the enemy's pickets firing on Company B of the Twenty-eighth, which was acting as advance guard. With the aid of the cavalry, five Confederates were captured, the others making their escape. The march was continued thirteen miles to Martinsburg, where a part of the army was quartered in houses: the rest occupied tents.

Here the regiments of General Banks' division remained until the 5th of March, when they moved twelve miles to Bunker Hill, where they remained one week. March 12th the advance to Winchester was continued, the Confederates retiring, Captain Ashby, with his cavalry, commanding their rear guard. This noted leader was one of great daring, and his loss, which occurred on June 6th, in the upper valley near Harrisonburg, was a severe one to his cause. General Jackson was very reluctant to retreat from Winchester without a battle, and had assured the citizens "they should not be abandoned to the enemy." But his command was not strong enough to warrant an engagement and he withdrew up the valley, followed by the division which entered the city with bands playing and banners waving. This was the principal town in the Shenandoah Valley, and the county seat of Frederick County.

The position of Winchester was unfavorable for defense, and made its occupation by either army a difficult task. It was captured and recaptured more than thirty times during the War. The town, itself, was not a fine one. With but few exceptions, the residences were very poor in appearance. It contained a medical college, a young ladies' institute, several churches and hotels, and many business places. The streets were roughly paved with cobble stones.

The surrounding country was most delightful. The scene, in all directions, was one of rolling land, surrounded by wooded mountains. The Shenandoah Valley has been justly called the Garden of Virginia, its rich farms producing the finest wheat in the country.

To see this valley before it had been devastated by the hand of war was the

special privilege of General Banks' division on this campaign. Its well fenced fields of grain and meadow were now in their beautiful green. Its orchards were full in lovely bloom. On its hillsides were many cattle and sheep grazing in undisturbed quiet. Its barns were well filled with the result of the husbandman's labors. All was soon to be changed. This beautiful valley never appeared so charming again during the War, as on this first entry of the army in the spring of 1862.

The citizens of Winchester were very pronounced in their Southern feelings. They exhibited their hatred to the Union soldiers on all occasions. The colored people, however, here as everywhere, greeted the advance with cheers. The regiment went into camp about one mile north of the city, the brigade camping near. The weather at first was cold with occasional snow flurries. At this time, a box of clothing and supplies from the ladies of Western New York came very opportunely, which was acknowledged by Colonel Donnelly. The following extract from his letter will be of interest:

WINCHESTER, March 21, 1862.

"If the ladies could see the distress that I have among the soldiers, and which has been relieved by their kind donations, if they could witness, as I have, the tear of gratitude trickle down the cheeks of some unfortunate, frost-bitten volunteer, as he looked at the comfortable mittens sent by them, and which are not provided by the Government, they would be amply repaid for all they have done. God bless the ladies! They have done more by their sympathy and timely aid to encourage and cheer the volunteers in the performance of their duties than all others combined. Remember me to them all and tell them that when we come to the hour of trial the Twenty-eighth will strike a blow at this rebellion, which will make them proud of their charities."

The Twenty-eighth remained at Winchester ten days when an order came to General Banks to march with General Williams' division through Snicker's Gap, and unite with the army at Centerville, leaving General Shield's division to occupy the valley. General Banks started March 22d, and passed through Berryville to Snicker's Ferry, and had commenced the crossing of the Shenandoah river at that place, when the breaking of the bridge delayed the movement. While halting for it to be repaired, the entire force was ordered to return to Winchester, as General Shields had been attacked there soon after General Williams left. General Jackson, with his usual vigilance, was informed that General Banks had left the valley, and, deeming it a good opportunity to strike a blow, suddenly approached Winchester with the expectation of annihilating the little army there before help could reach it. But General Shields was ready, and, after a desperate battle, fought before General Banks' forces could return, General Jackson,— severely punished,— withdrew from the field.

The First Division returned and started in pursuit through Winchester, passing the battlefield of the day before. The men made a very severe night march on the 23d to reach the battlefield, having marched thirty-seven miles in the three days. The pursuit was continued to Newtown on the 24th.

Company I of the Twenty-eighth had been detailed with a company from each of the following regiments, the Fifth Connecticut, the Forty-sixth Pennsylvania, and the First Maryland to act as train guard for the large brigade supply train, consisting of about two hundred wagons. This train was to follow over the mountain to Manassas on the next day. The guards were in command of Major Mathews of the Forty-sixth Pennsylvania. They were with the train south of the town, near the Strasburg pike, and ready to start when Jackson's attack on Shields became known. These companies were the only forces that could immediately be used, as they were, fortunately, in line, and could be at once deployed on the field. The train was sent to the rear and the companies instantly moved forward at double quick as skirmishers, and held the advance cavalry of the enemy in check until the main command could be brought to the front. This prompt action undoubtedly saved the train and was of material assistance to General Shields, whose regiments were encamped north of the town. The boldness of this skirmish line impressed the enemy that a much larger force was on the ground. The companies soon were relieved by a brigade of infantry. In the next day's engagement Company I rendered material assistance as support to a battery, and in different positions on the field, but was not actively engaged in the front line of battle, and, consequently, suffered no loss. These companies of General Banks' division deserved some recognition in the reports of the engagement, but none was made.

That the members of Company I of the Twenty-eighth may have the credit due them, it is referred to here.

A singular fact occurred in connection with this supply train. From some unaccountable blunder, the order countermarching the division of General Williams did not reach the officer in charge of the train, and the day after the battle it started over the mountain to Manassas, many miles away. The entire journey was made before the mistake was noticed. Then, orders were received to return, and, after a weary march of many days in the storm and mud, it rejoined the division at Strasburg.

The Twenty-eighth halted at Newtown for one night, continuing on the 25th, five miles to Strasburg, where it remained about one week. The round "Sibley" tents, in use this year, made the camps resemble Indian villages. These had a sheet iron stove in the center, the pipe extending through the top, and were very comfortable. Fires not infrequently occurred by the tent coming in contact with the pipe. These accidents caused much anxiety in camp, and often destroyed the tents.

April 1st General Bank's division continued up the valley, a distance of twelve miles, to Woodstock, the enemy's rear guard, consisting, as usual, of Ashby's cavalry, falling back. Here the Twenty-eighth remained two weeks, changing camp on the 6th, to obtain a better location. On the 14th the news of the victory at Island Number Ten, caused great rejoicing.

While at Woodstock, Captain Fitz Gerald was sent with his own command and companies from the Fifth Connecticut and Forty-sixth Pennsylvania to Columbia Furnace. On the night of the 15th detachments from the companies of the Fifth Connecticut and Twenty-eighth New York, supported a detachment of Ringgold's cavalry under Captain Greenfield and marched thirteen miles, capturing Captain Harper's entire company of Ashby's cavalry. This took place at a small cross roads named Hudson's Corners. The Confederates were completely surprised, and all surrendered without firing a shot. The few who tried to escape were overtaken. Captain Harper was absent, but his three lieutenants and sixty men were secured with their horses, equipments and stores. In the notes, Major FitzGerald has given a fine description of this raid.

April 16th the march was resumed to New Market, a distance of twenty-three miles. On the 17th, Ashby's cavalry, which was constantly disputing the advance, set fire to a large covered bridge near Mount Jackson. Companies D and F of the Twenty-eighth doublequicked in time to save it from destruction. This allowed the troops to cross and enter the town of Mount Jackson, the terminus of the Manassas Railroad, where a scene, similar to that at Martinsburg the year before, met the gaze. Buildings, engines and cars had been destroyed by the enemy before retreating and were left a smoking heap of ruins.

The following report to the War Department, on this day's operations, will be of interest:

MOUNT JACKSON, April 17, 1862.

To Honorable E. M. Stanton, Secretary of War:

"Our troops occupied Mount Jackson at 7 o'clock this morning and are now in front of Rude's Hill, where the enemy appear to be in force. The people report that they intend battle there. They resisted our advance in order to gain time for the burning of bridges and railway cars, engines, etc., that had accumulated at the terminus of the road; but our movement was so sudden, and the retreat of the rebels so precipitate, that we were enabled to save the bridges, two locomotives and some cars. All these had been prepared with combustible materials for instant conflagration. Many prisoners have been taken, and several fine horses captured from the enemy. The troops have acted admirably. They were in motion at one o'clock A. M.

N. P. BANKS,
Major General Commanding.

The following congratulatory order was returned:

WAR DEPARTMENT,
WASHINGTON, April 17, 1862.

To Major-General Banks, Mount Jackson:

To you, and to the forces under your command, the Department returns thanks for the brilliant and successful operations of this day.

EDWIN M. STANTON,
Secretary of War.

The command remained at Mount Jackson until April 25th, when the advance up the valley was continued to Harrisonburg. The Twenty-eighth marched on some five miles to Keezeltown, where it went into camp, leaving Captain Bowen to act as Provost Marshal; and his company, which had been the first Federal infantry to enter Harrisonburg, was appointed Provost Guard of the town. Captain Bowen's office was in the Court-House. General Williams occupied the

beautiful building of the Bank of Rockingham. The keys to the doors of this bank could not be found. After some delay an officer unlocked this supposed burglar-proof establishment with a rusty nail. Other officers had their headquarters near. The Court-House was in the center of the public square, a beautiful park, well shaded with trees. Here was situated a mammoth spring, one of the finest in the valley, noted for its beautiful springs. It was covered with a dome-shaped roof and had stone steps descending to the water. A large stream, pure as crystal, which many a thirsty soldier found delightfully cool and refreshing, was constantly flowing from it.

COURT-HOUSE AND SPRING AT HARRISONBURG, VA.

Under the able management of Captain Bowen, the streets were cleaned, the post-office was opened, the printing press was started, saloons were closed, and the best of order was preserved. The citizens all acknowledged that the good order was fully equal to that maintained in times of peace.

The selection of the captain, and his conduct of the office, proved very satisfactory to the inhabitants and creditable to himself and the army. The result from this appointment was very unusual and interesting. By many acts of kindness the people were shown that their rights as citizens would be protected, and that the army was not one of invasion for plunder and murder.

When the command moved from Harrisonburg, soon afterwards, Captain Bowen left there many true friends. He was a prisoner of war at Libby Prison, within four months; having been taken at Cedar Mountain on August 9th, and, owing to retaliatory measures, was treated, as were all General Pope's officers, as felons, not as prisoners of war. This was on account of this commander's severe orders, that citizens living near a railroad were to be held responsible for any damage done to it, those not taking the oath to be sent South, and others of a like character. Captain Bowen's friends at Harrisonburg, learning of his condition at Richmond, at once made efforts for his release, and secured from Jefferson Davis the following order:

HEADQUARTERS DEPARTMENT,
HENRICO-RICHMOND, VA., Sept. 11, 1862.

Captain Erwin A. Bowen, C. S. Military Prison:

SIR: I am instructed by the general commanding this department to inform you that, in consideration of your kind treatment of our citizens while acting as provost marshal at Harrisonburg, the Secretary of War has directed that you be treated as a prisoner of war, to be exchanged at an early day. Respectfully,

W. S. WINDER, A. A. G.

This resulted in his immediately being granted the freedom of the city, on his parole, and his exchange soon followed.

Twenty years later, when the Twenty-eighth paid a fraternal visit to the Fifth Virginia regiment a halt was made at Harrisonburg, and in the Court-House square Captain Bowen was given a public reception, which showed the grateful feelings of his Southern friends that had survived for more than a score of years.

The regiment did not remain long in camp at Keezeltown, on account of the difficulty in getting supplies over the bad roads. Soon it was recalled near Harrisonburg, where it remained until May 5th. The men were sorry to leave that beautiful city, and especially sorry when the order came, not to march on toward Staunton, but to commence a retrograde movement down the valley. General

Banks had been ordered by General McClellan, to advance on Staunton as soon as railroad communication from Manassas had been re-established, on condition of his being able to concentrate a force of thirty thousand men. As this was not possible, the withdrawal to Strasburg was ordered from Washington.

The difference in the feelings of the men when entering the town and now was very apparent. With regret they moved back to New Market, nineteen miles, and went into camp.

The small army corps of General Banks was here divided, General Shields' division being ordered to join the army of General McDowell at Fredericksburg. This withdrawal left General Banks with only the division of General Williams, of about five thousand infantry to hold the valley against an active enemy who could attack his flank at any time by way of the many gaps in the mountains on the east. This fact General Jackson at once perceived and made his plans for a descent on General Banks' forces.

May 9th, the Twenty-eighth was sent as support to cavalry into the Luray Valley. It marched over the Peaked Mountains, through Swift's Gap to the south fork of the Shenandoah River, a distance of over twenty miles, and returned on the 10th with no result. This march was ordered on the report that General Jackson was in the Luray Valley with a force of infantry. The road over the mountains was beautiful indeed, being smooth and firm, making the ascent a gradual one by a zigzag course. But the fine road, the magnificent scenery, the woods afire, the fact of being in the vicinity of the famous Luray caves, had no interest to foot-sore, weary soldiers when they learned it was only a false alarm.

The regiment remained at New Market several days. On May 7th the news of the evacuation of Yorktown was received. The batteries fired national salutes. Best's battery, under the personal direction of General Banks, fired at a target. The combined bands of the First Brigade joined in the celebration, visiting each regimental headquarters, playing national airs. They were accompanied by Colonel Donnelly, who was in temporary command of the brigade, and other officers. Colonel Brown was serenaded at his tent, and responded with a fine speech, saying "he thought we would soon be permitted to return to our homes." Colonel Donnelly replied that he was "only in command of the brigade by an accident." "Three cheers for the accident," cried Lieutenant-Colonel Selfridge of the Forty-sixth Pennsylvania, and these were given with a will. Colonel Donnelly continuing, said: "When General Williams shall return to take command again, I am thankful I have so good a regiment to go to. I am proud of the Twenty-eighth New York, and proud of the First Brigade. Let us give three cheers for Old Alf Williams, one of the best men the world ever saw." The enthusiastic response indicated that the men agreed most heartily with the colonel's opinion of the Brigadier-General.

On the 13th of May the regiment marched through Mount Jackson and Edenburgh to Woodstock, a distance of twenty miles, and went into camp for the night in a large field of wheat. The next day's march was fifteen miles, to Round Hill, near Strasburg, where the command remained ten days

On May 22d occurred the first anniversary of the regiment's muster into the United States service at Albany. This was celebrated by the officers at headquarters, where speeches were made in honor of the event. The men had now been in the service one year, and while they had been in no general battle all felt that in skirmishing, marching and campaigning they were veterans. Soon, however, the Twenty eighth was destined to take part in the realities of war in bloody engagements, with severe losses, seldom exceeded in a regiment's history.

CHAPTER V.

THE BATTLE OF WINCHESTER, AND BANKS' RETREAT.

MAY 23D, 24TH AND 25TH, 1862.

STONEWALL JACKSON, learning of the small force left in the valley, after the withdrawal of Shields' Division, determined on General Banks' destruction or capture. He had been joined by the divisions of Generals Ewell and Edward Johnson, and had now an army of seventeen thousand five hundred men to hurl upon Banks' small command of four thousand infantry and fifteen hundred cavalry.

That this force was not defeated or captured, and that the immense trains of over five hundred wagons were conducted across the Potomac with but small loss, was a "source of gratification" to General Banks and speaks well for the soldierly qualities of the regiments composing his division.

General Banks wisely had determined that "to remain at Strasburg was to be surrounded and destroyed," and the only course left to him, with his little division, was "to enter the list with the enemy in a race or a battle, as he should choose, for the possession of Winchester."

May 23d, Colonel Kenly's First Maryland regiment, which had been assigned by General Banks the duty of guarding Front Royal and vicinity, was suddenly surprised and defeated by the overwhelming forces of General Jackson, who approached by the Luray Valley. This position was eighteen miles distant from Strasburg, where the division of General Banks was encamped. Colonel Kenly was surrounded, but made a stubborn resistance, losing nearly his entire command. This was the beginning of the famous "Banks' Retreat," in which the Twenty-eighth bore an important part.

On the morning of the 24th, the small division, consisting of the First Brigade commanded by Colonel Donnelly, the Third commanded by Colonel Gordon, and the cavalry under General Hatch, started at one o'clock from Strasburg for Winchester, on what proved to be *both* "a race and a battle."

The details of this march, the battle of Winchester, and the retreat which followed are well told in the official reports of Colonels Donnelly and Brown. They show in full the part taken by the Twenty-eighth regiment in these historic events.

REPORT OF COL. DUDLEY DONNELLY, TWENTY-EIGHTH NEW YORK INFANTRY, COMMANDING FIRST BRIGADE, OF OPERATIONS MAY 24TH TO 26TH.

HEADQUARTERS 1ST BRIG., 1ST DIV.,
DEP'T OF THE SHENANDOAH,

WILLIAMSPORT, MD., May 29, 1862.

General,— In obedience to orders received from you, on the morning of the 24th of May instant, at 1 o'clock, the First Brigade, comprising the Forty-sixth Pennsylvania, Twenty-eighth New York, and Fifth Connecticut Volunteers (the First Maryland being at Front Royal on detached service), and Best's battery of Fourth U. S. Artillery, broke up their encampment at Round Hill and marched to Strasburg, at which place we halted for one hour. I was then directed by Major General Banks to march to Middletown on the road to Winchester, a large portion of our train having preceded us in that direction.

As the head of the column approached Middletown a portion of the train was met returning in great confusion and disorder, the guards reporting that they were attacked by the rebels in front. The trains were ordered by me to move into a field. The brigade advanced rapidly through the village, when a large body of the enemy's cavalry appeared on the right, half a mile distant, partially covered by woods. The brigade was halted, and two companies of the Forty-sixth Pennsylvania Volunteers were thrown forward as skirmishers, and a section of Battery M, First New York Artillery, supported by the Forty-sixth Regiment Pennsylvania Volunteers, under Col. J. F. Knipe, were advanced in that direction. Five companies of the rebel cavalry appeared in an open field immediately in front of a piece of woods, and our artillery opened upon them. The enemy retired, after receiving a few well-directed shots, to the woods in their rear. The skirmishers advanced and drove the enemy from the woods into and across another open field, where the artillery and the Forty-sixth Pennsylvania Volunteers advanced and occupied the position. The artillery again opened upon them. Our line advanced, the rebels retreating, notwithstanding re-enforcements of cavalry were observed to join them.

At this point, having driven them back two miles from the pike, the troops engaged returned to the main road by your order, and our march was continued toward Winchester, the train following in the rear. When within five miles of Winchester I detached the Twenty-eighth New York Volunteers

and a section of artillery to return to Middletown, by your order, to support General Hatch, an attack having been made in the rear of the train. With the remainder of the force under my command I marched forward, and, by your direction, took a position on the Front Royal road one mile from Winchester.

It being dark we could not select our position with care. The Forty-sixth took position on the right of the road, the Fifth Connecticut Volunteers on the left, Best's battery on the hill immediately in the rear. Ascertaining that the hills in front were picketed by two companies of the Tenth Maine and some cavalry the men were allowed to bivouac, but could not rest, being without blankets, overcoats, or knapsacks, and having little or no food.

During the night the enemy kept continually firing on the pickets, but met with such determined resistance that our line remained undisturbed till soon after daylight, when the Twenty-eighth New York Volunteers arrived on the ground. Before the men had prepared their breakfast the enemy drove in the pickets with a large force of infantry and artillery. The regiments rapidly formed in line, the Fifth Connecticut Volunteers deploying from column of companies in the face of a severe fire. The enemy attacked the center, pouring in upon it a storm of shot and shell, and at the same time moved three regiments to the left, menacing our left flank. They were met firmly by the Fifth Connecticut and Forty-sixth Pennsylvania Volunteers at the center, and after a short but decisive conflict fled in disorder, leaving a large number of dead and wounded on the field. As they retired a section of Best's battery, under Lieutenant Cushing, poured in upon them a deadly fire of grape and canister, mowing them down at each discharge. They attempted to rally again as they moved toward the left, but received a volley from the Twenty-eighth New York Volunteers, which completed their entire rout.

Lieutenant-Colonel Brown, with the Twenty-eighth New York, moved rapidly to the left, and by skillfully disposing of his force effectually prevented our flank being turned. The rebel infantry withdrew to their original line on the hill, and made no further attack or demonstration on our position.

A heavy fog having settled over the ground the firing ceased on both sides for almost half an hour. As the mist cleared away the enemy opened upon us from two batteries, which was promptly responded to by our batteries, re-enforced by a section of Battery M, First New York Artillery, under command of Lieutenant Peabody. At the same time we became aware that the right wing of the division was attacked. The rebel batteries continued to shell the left wing, and although their pieces were well served our men stood firm.

I received orders from General Banks through Captain d'Hauteville to retire, as the right of our division was turned. I immediately gave orders to retreat. The brigade retired in good order, taking the right of the pike and a half a mile distant therefrom toward Martinsburg, the head of the column being opposite the rear of the other wing of our division.

We continued to march in this order to Bunker Hill, pursued by the artillery and cavalry of the enemy, near which place the Forty-sixth Pennsylvania fell into the rear of the right wing on the pike.

At this point the sick men and stragglers, who numbered about fifty, while resting on the ground, were suddenly surrounded by three companies of cavalry and called upon to surrender, but falling quickly into line they delivered a galling fire into their midst; then, fixing bayonets, they charged and drove them out of the woods. The rebels left six dead on the field and we captured one prisoner. We were not pursued any farther by the enemy.

On arriving at the Charlestown road opposite Martinsburg I communicated with Major-General Banks, and received orders to move on. We took the road to Dam No. 4, at which place we arrived about 10 o'clock P. M. Finding the river too high to ford we marched three miles up the river to Jameson's Ferry, where a boat was found capable of crossing thirty men. After throwing out a strong rear guard, I allowed the men to lie down and sleep, only awaking sufficient numbers to keep the ferry busy.

I am much indebted to Lieutenant Colonel Chapman, Fifth Connecticut Volunteers, and Captain Bowen, Twenty-eighth New York Volunteers, for their untiring exertions in assisting me in crossing the men with the small means at our command.

At 4 A. M., the entire force having been crossed, the field officers of the regiments, accompanied by the brigade officers, passed the river. The entire crossing was effected without accident or panic after a march of forty-three miles without rest or food for twenty-four hours.

The commanders of the regiments, Colonel J. F. Knipe, Forty-sixth Pennsylvania Volunteers, who was slightly wounded; Lieutenant-Colonel E. F. Brown, Twenty-eighth New York, and Lieutenant-Colonel George D. Chapman, Fifth Connecticut Volunteers, and the officers and men of their commands, are entitled to great credit for the courage and coolness displayed by them in the face of a superior force.

Owing to the untiring exertions of the officers and coolness and good discipline of the men I was enabled to conduct the retreat in good order and without loss.

I would particularly mention the gallant conduct of Captain E. A. Bowen, Twenty-eighth New York Volunteers, who commanded the rear guard and effectually protected our retreat. Lieutenant E. L. Whitman, of the Forty-sixth Pennsylvania, attached to my staff, alone carried the orders to the different regiments through the thickest of the fight, and is entitled to my warmest approbation. Captain W. D. Wilkins, assistant adjutant-general First Division, who brought the order to retreat, was unable to rejoin the right wing, and remained with the First Brigade. By his coolness and personal bravery he encouraged the officers and men and rendered valuable assistance, as I had but one staff officer present.

The train of the entire brigade, numbering over 100 heavily loaded wagons, was brought safely through with small loss by the untiring energy and skill of Lieutenant C. L. Skeels, acting brigade quartermaster. The whole force of the First Brigade amounted to less than 1,700 men. The reported loss up to this time in killed is three; wounded, forty-seven; missing, two hundred and fifty-one. This will be materially lessened, as numerous parties have been heard from who crossed the river at different points above and below this place. The force of the enemy opposed to the left wing was nine regiments of infantry and two batteries of artillery.

I hope the First Brigade has done no discredit to the discipline attained while under your command.

I am, respectfully, your obedient servant,

D. DONNELLY,

Colonel, Twenty-eighth New York Vols., Commanding.

Brig.-Gen. ALPHEUS S. WILLIAMS,

Commanding First Division.

REPORTS OF LIEUT.-COL. EDWIN F. BROWN, TWENTY-EIGHTH NEW YORK INFANTRY, OF OPERATIONS MAY 24TH AND 25TH.

HEADQUARTERS TWENTY-EIGHTH REGIMENT, NEW YORK VOLUNTEERS.

CAMP NEAR WILLIAMSPORT, MD., May 25, 1862.

Sir,—I have the honor to report that on the morning of the 25th instant the regiment under my command took up its position in line of battle on the extreme left of the brigade at about 4 o'clock. A brisk fire from the rebel batteries was soon opened upon us with shot and shell. Our ambulances immediately moved to the rear and the position of our regiment was somewhat altered. Immediately after this a strong column of infantry was seen advancing, and was, when discovered, within 200 yards of us.

At this time the Twenty-eighth was standing in line of battle directly behind a stone wall, and about ten rods in rear of the Fifth Connecticut Volunteers, who were standing in column by companies, the men making coffee. A moment later the head of the column of rebels opened fire on the Twenty-eighth New York and the Forty-sixth Pennsylvania, not yet having seen the Fifth Connecticut, who were stationed on low ground. This fire we immediately returned over the heads of the Fifth Connecticut. We continued firing until the Fifth deployed in line of battle, when we immediately moved by our left flank some distance farther to the left, intending to occupy an orchard. We advanced for this purpose, so that the line of battle of the brigade was crescent-shaped, the Fifth Connecticut occupying the center, the Forty-sixth the right.

When the left of the regiment was within about ten rods of the orchard the enemy were seen moving to their right, and at this short range we poured a volley from the left wing of the regiment with tremendous effect. At this time the fog and smoke were so dense as to make it impossible to see over a few rods. Captain Bush was ordered by Major Cook to advance a platoon as skirmishers on our left to find the enemy. While the skirmishers were advancing Private Bartram, acting as my orderly, being mounted, rode to the top of the hill behind which the rebel column had retreated. Owing to the smoke and fog he was unable to see them until within less than six rods. A volley was fired at him, and strange to say only one ball took effect, wounding the horse slightly. Bartram reported the enemy as no doubt trying to outflank us on the left wing (their right). The position of the regiment was again changed to counteract this movement. A strong position was taken behind a stone wall, where we waited, expecting the advance of the enemy every moment, but he, taking advantage of the fog, and no doubt being satisfied with the morning's work, withdrew to a safe distance. When the fog lifted they were seen in great force about a half or three-fourths of a mile from us, near their batteries, with a line of skirmishers in front, coming on with great caution.

About this time, the right wing of our army having given way, we were ordered to retreat, which order we obeyed in good order under a heavy fire of shot and shell. The aim of the rebel batteries was wonderful, but not more so than the escape of the men, who seemed to bear charmed lives, only one man being wounded. We continued our retreat, keeping to the right of the pike. The rebels, being considerably in advance of us on the pike, kept up a brisk fire with their artillery, as opportunity offered for several miles. When near Bunker Hill their cavalry made a dash at our rear, but were handsomely beaten off and so badly used that they troubled us no more during the day.

We continued our march, reaching the Potomac at Dam No. 4 about dark, a distance of 45 miles from Winchester. Here we hoped to be able to ford the river, but found it impracticable. We again resumed the march, proceeding up the river about one and one-half miles, where we found a ferry boat capable of carrying about 30 men. With this and a small boat by daylight on the morning of the 26th we were all crossed over without panic, confusion, fear, or loss of life.

Owing to the scarcity of commissioned officers Sergeant Casey, of Company A, had command of the rear guard of skirmishers, which duty he performed most admirably and with great credit to himself, as did most of the detail and several volunteers. We were the last regiment on the field, and the pursuit on the pike was pushed with such vigor that we found ourselves considerably in the rear of those on the pike, which made it necessary for us to avoid Martinsburg, which was done under your immediate direction with consummate skill.

Officers and men behaved with admirable coolness during the entire engagement, and during the retreat with wonderful and deliberate energy. Many instances of complete exhaustion occurred, and in several cases the men have shown great skill in eluding the scouts and in many cases made a defense successfully.

I would be delighted to make a special mention of some cases of valor and skill, but my heart is too full of gratitude to all, both officers and men, to disparage one by a more favorable mention of another. The men who were compelled to drop to the rear from exhaustion are coming in singly and in squads.

The reports at the present time show: Killed, none; wounded, 2; missing, 79; and there are strong hopes of reducing this number considerably. About 60 men have crossed at Harper's Ferry, and all have not yet reported.

We have great reason to be grateful to kind Providence and applaud the skill and energy of our commanding officers for the miraculous escape of our men from utter annihilation.

WILLIAMSPORT, MD., May 29, 1862.

Sir,—In addition to my former report of the battle at and retreat from Winchester I beg leave to submit this additional report of the skirmish with the rebel artillery and cavalry on the afternoon and evening of Saturday:

About 4 o'clock I received orders to countermarch and return to Newtown from near Kernstown and report to General Hatch. This we did cheerfully, accompanied by the Second Regiment Massachusetts Volunteers and two sections of

artillery, one of Best's and one of Cothran's and the Twenty-seventh Indiana Regiment. Two companies (B and G), under command of Captain Bush, were deployed on the right as skirmishers, and two on the left (D and C), under command of Captain Bowen. When about one mile from Newtown a brisk firing of artillery was commenced by the rebels, which was promptly responded to by ours. They (the rebels) were soon driven from their position and retired beyond Newtown. We followed them up, and the rebels planted a battery about half a mile beyond the town. One section (Cothran's) took position on the right of the town, supported by Captain Bush and Captain Hardie, and one section on the left, supported by two companies of the Twenty-seventh Indiana. Captain Bowen extended his line of skirmishers nearly a mile on the left and discovered a body of cavalry in the woods, with whom they exchanged several shots. The cavalry concluded it better to keep proper distance and retired. The main body remained in the town. The artillery practice was vigorously kept up till dusk, when we were ordered to retire toward Winchester. Our skirmishers were deployed as before, and we retired in column by platoon. As we passed the wagons which were disabled and the pontoons left in the highway, I detailed Lieutenant George Ellicott, Company F, and ten men to burn and destroy them. This was successfully done, though frequent shots were exchanged.

We arrived safely at Winchester at 11 P. M., considerably wearied by our day's march, and at 4 o'clock on Sunday morning we took our position in line of battle, as per report previously sent forward.

Very respectfully submitted,

E. F. BROWN,

Lieut.-Col., Comdg. Twenty-eighth Regiment New York Vols.

Col. D. DONNELLY,

Twenty-eighth N. Y. Vols., Comdg. First Brig., First Div., Dept. Shenandoah.

General Banks has been blamed for making a stand at all, with a force of only about one-fourth of the enemy's. But, had he retreated without a battle, he would have been censured also. That he made a plucky fight and a masterly retreat has always been conceded.

General Jackson was greatly mortified that Banks' army had escaped him. He attributes it to his cavalry stopping to pillage instead of joining in the pursuit. The following extract from his official report will show this fact:

HEADQUARTERS 2D CORPS, ARMY OF WESTERN VIRGINIA,

April 10, 1863.

* * * * * * * "From the attack upon Front Royal, up to the present moment, every opposition had been borne down, and there was reason to believe if Banks reached Winchester it would be without a train, if not without an army, but in the midst of these hopes, I was pained to see, as I am now to record the fact, that so many of Ashby's command, both cavalry and infantry, forgetful of their high trust as the advance of a pursuing army, deserted their colors, and abandoned themselves to pillage to such an extent as to make it necessary for that gallant officer to discontinue further pursuit. The artillery, which had pushed on with energy to the vicinity of Newtown, found itself, from this discreditable conduct, without a proper support from either infantry or cavalry. The Federal forces, upon falling back into the town, preserved their organization well. In passing through its streets, they were thrown into confusion, and shortly after, debouching into the plain, and turnpike to Martinsburg, and, after being fired upon by our artillery, they presented the aspect of a mass of disordered fugitives. Never have I seen an opportunity, when it was in the power of cavalry to reap a richer harvest of the fruits of victory. Hoping that the cavalry would soon come up, the artillery, followed by infantry, was pressed forward for about two hours, for the purpose of preventing, by artillery fire, a reforming of the enemy; but, as nothing was heard of the cavalry, and as little or nothing could be accomplished without it, in the exhausted condition of our infantry, between which and the enemy the distance was continually increasing, I ordered a halt."

T. J. JACKSON,

Lieutenant-General.

After crossing the river, May 26th, it was found that the loss sustained by the regiment was but sixty-two captured, instead of seventy-nine, as first reported by Colonel Brown. The others crossed the river at different points, and arrived in camp during the day. This loss by companies was as follows: Company A three, B four, C eleven, D nine, E four, F six, G ten, H four, I four, K seven; total sixty-two. Some of these were wounded, and all were taken prisoners. After a four months' experience in Libby Prison or Belle Isle, at Richmond, Va., they were all exchanged, rejoining the regiment in October.

The men lost their knapsacks, containing all their clothing, and many officers also lost a portion of their baggage. That there was no loss of life was a cause for thankfulness.

General Banks' first report of the retreat to the President was as follows:

WILLIAMSPORT, May 26, 1862, 4 P. M.

I have the honor to report the safe arrival of command at this place last evening at 10 o'clock, and the passage of the Fifth Corps across the river to-day with comparatively but little loss. The loss of men killed, wounded and missing in the different combats in which my command has participated since the march from Strasburg on the morning of the 24th inst. I am unable to report, but I have great gratification in being able to represent it, although serious, as much less than might have been anticipated, considering the very great disparity of forces engaged and the long-matured plans of the enemy, which aimed at nothing less than entire capture of our force. A detailed statement will be forwarded as soon as

possible. My command encountered the enemy in a constant succession of attacks and at well-contested engagements at Strasburg, Middletown, Newton, at a point also between these places and at Winchester. The force of the enemy was estimated at from 15,000 to 20,000 men, with very strong artillery and cavalry supports. My own force consisted of two brigades, less than 4,000 strong, all told, 1,500 cavalry, ten Parrott guns and six smoothbores. The substantial preservation of the entire supply is a source of gratification. It numbered about 500 wagons on a forced march of 53 miles, 35 of which were performed in one day, subject to constant attack in front, rear and flank, according to its position, by enemy in full force. By the panics of teamsters and the mischances of river passage of more than 300 yards with slender preparations for ford and ferry, it lost not more than 50 wagons. A full statement of this loss will be forwarded forthwith. Very great commendation is due to Captain S. B. Holabird, assistant quartermaster, and Captain E. G. Beckwith for the safety of the train. Our troops are in good spirits and occupy both sides of the river.

N. P. BANKS,

Major-General, Commanding.

The President.

CHAPTER VI.

AGAIN IN THE VALLEY—CULPEPER.

JUNE 2D TO AUGUST 7TH, 1862.

NECESSARY clothing was soon furnished, and within a week the regiment again crossed the Potomac for another advance up the Shenandoah Valley. This was the third and last crossing at Williamsport into Virginia. This time, as in March, the crossing was made by ferry. The march the first day, June 2d, was to Martinsburg, led by the Twenty-eighth New York, the second day on through Winchester, where the command went into camp, about two miles south of the city. On this return a very bitter feeling was shown between the soldiers and the inhabitants of Winchester. Reports were general that many citizens had fired shots at the men on the retreat, and this was believed to be the case. The commanding officers, fearing that encounters would result, placed guards all along the route through the city, to prevent the men from leaving the ranks.

The sick and convalescents left in the hospital had been paroled by the Confederates, and were very glad to see the Stars and Stripes again. They crowded to the doors and windows, waving and shouting their welcome as the regiments marched through the city.

The division remained in camp near Winchester several days. The Tenth Maine, a splendid regiment, was now brigaded with the Twenty-eighth. The men were always good comrades, and the two regiments became very neighborly. Both were mustered out of service on the expiration of their time, about one year later. Many of the recruits of the Twenty-eighth, subsequently joined the Tenth Maine Battalion.

June 9th the army marched to Front Royal. Here, on all sides, were the evidences of the recent severe engagement of Colonel Kenly's forces, and these showed he must have made a good resistance before he was overpowered.

On the 10th, camp was changed nearer the river, to one of the most lovely spots ever occupied by the Twenty-eighth. It is remembered for the beauty of its location. Front Royal is charmingly situated at the foot of the Blue Ridge Mountains. The scenery here is unsurpassed, and while the regiment remained the weather was most delightful.

Belle Boyd, who later obtained such notoriety as a spy, resided at Front Royal. Many officers made her acquaintance. How many of them, unwittingly, gave her, in exchange for her sweet smiles and brilliant wit, valuable information of Federal movements and numbers, to be at once sent into the Confederate lines, will never be known.

June 29th, the brigade left camp at Front Royal, passing through Chester Gap, on a reconnoissance to Luray, and returned the next day, having marched over twenty miles. This movement into the Luray Valley, the same as the one on May 9th from New Market, was unproductive of results, except in the wear on the muscles, *soles* and patience of the men. It was another "Jackson scare," and, as usual, he was not found where he was expected.

July 6th the regiment took its last look at the beautiful Shenandoah Valley, the scene of operations for so long a time; the Twenty-eighth having entered it just a year before. The river was crossed by a rope ferry, and the men marched over the Blue Ridge Mountains, through Chester Gap to Amisville, where they encamped in an orchard, and remained several days. On the 11th, General Banks' forces moved on and went into camp three miles from Warrenton, joining General Pope's army, which was encamped near this place. On the 14th of July the First Brigade marched toward Culpeper, fording the Hedgeman River, which was nearly waist deep. The second day the men passed through Sperryville and Woodville, reaching Culpeper Court House on the 16th of July, and camping near the town.

The citizens were very outspoken in their hatred of the Northern army and in exhibiting their Southern sympathies. Women went out of their way to cast indignities on the soldiers. One, standing prominently on a veranda, glared at the moving column, uttering the single word "Scum," through her closed teeth. To the credit of the regiment it can be said her derision received no response.

On the 17th the brigade left Culpeper as support to General Hatch's cavalry, which was making an armed reconnoissance to Madison Court House. This force returned on the 21st, having marched over seventy miles through mountainous and unfrequented routes, encountering rainy weather nearly all the time. The regiments returned to Culpeper and occupied the same camp ground left a few days previous; and here they remained about two weeks.

A large field of corn was adjoining this camp. The men found that the ears of the corn were in fine condition to be used for roasting, and were not slow in appropriating some for their suppers, as the supply train with the rations had not arrived. The owner at once paid a visit to Colonel Donnelly, remonstrating at the action of the men. The interview was long and interesting; the guard at the headquarters tent, who overheard the conversation, reports only the final words of the colonel to the Loyal Virginian, which were as follows:—

"If, as you say, you are a Union man, you ought to be willing to give a few ears of corn to half-starved soldiers, fighting to preserve the Union; and if, as I suspect, you are a rebel, you deserve to lose your entire crop."

The members of the Twenty-eighth look back to this camp with sad thoughts as the last one occupied as a full regiment. Here they were, strong in numbers, in vigor and in confidence, veterans that had seen service. The Twenty-eighth was soon to be left but the skeleton of the organization as it existed at this time.

General S. W. Crawford now commanded the brigade, consisting of the same tried and true regiments which had served in the Valley campaign. These were the Fifth Connecticut, Forty-sixth Pennsylvania, the Tenth Maine, but lately assigned, and the Twenty-eighth New York. These formed the First Brigade of the First Division. The best feeling always existed among these four regiments. It is seldom the experience of soldiers of different organizations to become so intimate and friendly as did this brigade on all occasions.

General Williams, the old brigade leader, now commanded the division. The corps was commanded, as heretofore, by General Banks, and designated the Second Corps, Army of Virginia. This was changed within a month to the Twelfth Corps, Army of the Potomac, which number it retained until the fall of 1863, when the Eleventh and Twelfth Corps were consolidated and numbered the Twentieth; much to the regret and indignation of the men of the old Twelfth, who felt they had made a name and record of which any corps could be proud. And they have never forgiven the cruel order that took from them the number they loved so well and had made illustrious in the record of the War.

The army was now in command of a new general, who had come from the West with great promise. All sincerely hoped he would be successful. General Pope had been singularly unfortunate, however, in his introduction to the soldiers on taking command. The bombastic tone of his general orders, beginning with "Headquarters in the Saddle," had not been received with favor. He had said that he "desired the troops to dismiss from their minds certain phrases much in vogue;" under his leadership "only the backs of the enemy should be seen;" his "policy should be one of attack, and not of defense;" "all ideas of lines of retreat and bases of supplies must be discarded," and others of a like character. These soon became the jest of the soldiers, and were considered unjust and cruel reflections on the conduct of previous commanders.

CHAPTER VII.

THE BATTLE OF CEDAR MOUNTAIN.

AUGUST 9TH, 1862.

THE large Army of Virginia was organized by the union of the forces of McDowell, Sigel and Banks, and placed under the command of General Pope. This proved such a menace to the enemy that General Jackson, with Ewell's, Winder's and A. P. Hill's divisions, started from Gordonsville on August 7th, hoping to strike General Banks' corps, which was apart from the main force, at Culpeper before he could be reinforced from General Pope's army at Warrenton.

General Bayard's cavalry had a collision with the enemy August 8th at Orange Court House, and the First Brigade was suddenly called from the camp ground near Culpeper to support them. The men were full of enthusiasm, never in better spirits or condition. Conscious of their strength, they proudly started out, expectant and ready to meet the enemy. General Strother (Porte Crayon), an officer on General Banks' staff, has written the following as to their appearance at this time: "As we entered Culpeper, Crawford's brigade was moving to the front, with drums beating and colors flying. It was the most inspiriting sight I ever beheld. There were four regiments of infantry and two batteries. The regiments were the Forty-sixth Pennsylvania, Fifth Connecticut, Tenth Maine and Twenty-eighth New York, with Roemer's and Knapp's batteries."

The day was extremely hot and the march a very hard one. Many cases of sunstroke occurred. The regiment moved to the vicinity of Cedar Mountain, where they went into bivouac for the night.

The Confederates call this the battle of Cedar Run, instead of Cedar Mountain, from the small stream of that name near which the engagement took place. The mountain itself is nearly a mile distant, and was occupied only by the artillery of the Confederate army. From its commanding site a destructive fire was thrown into the Union lines. Here, also, General Jackson saw the entire movements of both armies.

It is also known as Slaughter's Mountain, the name of a prominent minister, Rev. Philip Slaughter, whose farm extended far up its side.

The advance of the enemy's cavalry had been encountered beyond Cedar Mountain and held in check by Bayard's Cavalry Division, which had moved back to this place and now reported the enemy approaching in force.

Orders were received from General Banks to hold the position until the arrival of the remainder of the corps. The entire force of the enemy was not yet on the field, and no attack was made during the night.

The morning of August 9th proved to be as hot as the preceding one had been. The artillery opened with occasional shots, while both armies were coming on the field and getting into position. Generals Banks and Williams arrived during the morning with the entire corps. The First Brigade was ordered to the right of the Culpeper road, in a piece of woods, facing a cleared wheat field, in which the grain was standing in shocks. Across this field was another skirt of woods, near which batteries of the enemy were posted. These kept up a scattering fire during the day.

For several hours the action was between the artillery, with occasional skirmishing. The sounds of occasional musketry and the batteries on the mountain, firing grape and canister, were heard by the regiments lying in position behind the rail fence in the edge of the woods waiting the order to advance.

The enemy could be seen in the opposite woods across the field in the front by those who went forward to reconnoiter, and great anxiety was manifested to capture the battery that was constantly firing from a position near these woods. This fire was directed to the forces of the Second Division on the left. At this time a council was held in the woods by

Generals Williams and Crawford, at which the commanding officers of the regiments in the First Brigade were present. At this meeting Colonel Knipe of the Forty-sixth Pennsylvania was very anxious to charge on the battery previously referred to, insisting that it could be easily captured.

This action was opposed by some officers as a very unwise movement until the enemy's forces were more fully ascertained, but it was finally decided to be done, by the commanding general.

And, as the result of this decision, at about five o'clock General Crawford was ordered to advance. He formed the Fifth Connecticut, Twenty-eighth New York and Forty-sixth Pennsylvania in line of battle and, unfortunately, left the strongest regiment, the Tenth Maine, in reserve in the woods.

Preparatory to the movement he sent a staff officer for a section of artillery to shell the woods in the front, where the enemy was known to be in force.

Before the officer could return General Banks ordered the movement to be made at once, and, following the colors of the regiment, borne by Sergeant Lewis of Company D, the men, throwing down the fence or leaping over it, with loud cheers, started across the open field, with fixed bayonets, at double quick, on that memorable charge, that has no superior for valor, and but few equals in the losses sustained in proportion to the numbers engaged of any battle of the War.*

THE BATTLEFIELD OF
CEDAR MOUNTAIN.
August 9, 1862.

The entire line was instantly met with a murderous fire from the front, and also from the right flank, where six companies of the Third Wisconsin had been ordered in after the First Brigade had started, but had met with such resistance from the enemy and the nature of the ground that they could not keep pace with the advancing regiments. They encountered the Stonewall Brigade, consisting of the Second, Third, Fourth and Fifth Virginia regiments, which was moving forward. This handful could not withstand the force of these overwhelming numbers, and after a brave resistance broke and retired to the rear. Their losses were very heavy, Lieutenant-Colonel Crane, the commanding officer, was killed and more than one fourth of their number was either killed or wounded. This left

* See Official Report, page 44.

the right flank of the First Brigade entirely unprotected, as the Third Brigade (General Gordon's) on the right had not advanced with the first; greatly to the surprise of General Crawford, who had expected it to move forward with him in the charge. The Confederates poured into the ranks their deadly fire, but the Twenty-eighth New York, with the Fifth Connecticut and Forty-sixth Pennsylvania, pressed on to the woods, and met the enemy in force, consisting of Campbell's Brigade of the Twenty-first, Twenty-second and Forty-eighth Virginia regiments, the First Virginia Battalion, Taliaferro's Brigade of the Tenth, Twenty-third and Thirty-seventh Virginia, and the Forty-seventh and Forty-eighth Alabama regiments.

Here occurred a most desperate hand to hand conflict. The Confederates could not withstand the onslaught, and they and their batteries were entirely routed and driven back on the reserves. The day seemed lost to the South. Jackson personally hastened to the front "amidst this fire of hell," as it has been called by a Southern writer.

The situation at this juncture, described by Confederate historians, was a desperate one. They freely admit that the brigades of Taliaferro, Campbell and part of Early's line were driven back in confusion, their left turned, the artillery and the rear of their position entirely exposed.

General Jackson, in his official report, designates this charge of the First Brigade as "the *main body* of the Federal infantry," and states, "they moved down from the wood through the corn and wheat fields, and fell with great vigor upon our extreme left, and by the force of *superior numbers*, bearing down all opposition, turned it and poured a destructive fire into its rear. Campbell's Brigade fell back in disorder. The enemy pushing forward, and the left flank of Taliaferro's brigade being by these movements exposed to a flank fire, fell back, as did also the left of Early's line, the remainder of his command holding its position with great firmness. During the advance of the enemy, the rear of the guns of Jackson's division becoming exposed they were withdrawn."

Had the three regiments been properly supported, the result of the battle of Cedar Mountain would have proved a Union victory. In vain do they look for reinforcements. Starting with about 1,200 men, they had wasted themselves in their super-human effort. Assailed by two fresh brigades in front, flank and rear, the men were compelled to cut their way back across the field over which they had advanced.

Colonel Donnelly was mortally wounded before he reached the woods, and was taken from the field by his orderly supporting him on his horse. Colonel Brown had his left arm shattered and was taken prisoner. While being conducted to the rear, a wounded man of the Fifth Connecticut lying on the field was brutally ordered by the soldier who had the colonel in charge to go with them. This he was unable to do as he was wounded in both legs; the Confederate proceeded with his prisoner, when suddenly the colonel heard the sound of a bullet close to his head and his captor fell at his feet, having been shot by the wounded man just left. The colonel started at once to recross the field, but, weak from the loss of blood, he would have been unable to reach the lines had not Colonel Andrews of the Second Massachusetts, which was drawn up in line, sent a corporal from his regiment to assist him. Colonel Brown was removed to the field hospital for the night, and the next day sent to Culpeper, where his arm was amputated.

Major Cook was taken prisoner. Adjutant Sprout was killed, his body being found in advance of the farthest point reached by any of the men, surrounded by several Confederates, who had, undoubtedly, fallen by his hand.

Of the eighteen officers of the Twenty-eighth, who started to cross that bloody field, seventeen were either killed, wounded or captured. Of the three hundred and thirty-nine enlisted men, who went into the action the loss was one hundred and ninety-six; more than half the number engaged.

The Tenth Maine and Third Brigade was now advanced, only to share the same fate. The remnants of the division retired to their original positions, until ordered from the field with the corps, which movement was made after dark.

The action on the left by Augur's division had been a desperate battle, but overpowered by numbers, it had been withdrawn, and the entire army fell back, leaving the field covered with the dead. The enemy followed cautiously and

maintained a fearful cannonading during the night.

The result of the battle of Cedar Mountain was to both armies a costly sacrifice of human life. The enemy had possession of the battlefield, and have always claimed the victory. The forces under General Jackson, by the best authorities, were twenty-seven thousand men of all arms, of which twenty-five thousand were present in the action.

General Banks' forces, as officially stated, were six thousand two hundred and eighty-nine infantry, thirty guns and twelve hundred cavalry, aggregating less than eight thousand, or one-third the force of the enemy. The losses of General Banks' corps in this battle were two thousand two hundred and sixteen killed, wounded and missing, of which the First Brigade lost eight hundred and sixty-seven.

The loss of officers in the three regiments making the charge was seldom equaled in the history of the war. Every field officer was either killed, wounded or captured; and all but seven of the line officers. "This loss speaks better than words of the heroism of the charge," wrote General Williams in his official report. The enemy acknowledged twelve hundred and seventy-six killed and wounded, and gave no report of the missing; hence, the generally accepted estimate that the losses of the Southern army were fully equal to those of the Union is undoubtedly correct. Fox, in his "Regimental Losses of the War," writes: "The Battle of Cedar Mountain was fought by General Banks' corps alone and unassisted, and the record shows that the two divisions did there some of the best fighting of the war."

Colonel Packer, of the Fifth Connecticut, says of the battle of Cedar Mountain:

"About 2 P. M. the regiment moved into position, and at 4 P. M. we commenced that fearful charge, which cost us so many lives, and maimed so many brave heroes for life. Pen and thought combined cannot do this subject justice. It was as if the men had deliberately walked into a fiery furnace, and I only wonder how any escaped from certain death upon that field."

The responsibility of throwing this little army corps, with no reserves at hand, against an enemy well posted, and of three times its number, when an army of over twenty thousand men was within easy marching distance, is one that has always been in question. Cedar Mountain has been called "one of the greatest blunders, and one of the most wicked, useless, and unnecessary sacrifices of human life that the history of the war affords."

General Banks justifies the battle by the order received from General Pope, that he was to "attack the enemy as soon as he approaches, and be reinforced from Culpeper." That he was not so reinforced, and that General Pope remained at Culpeper during the day, until too late to render any assistance, is a matter of history. No doubt, neither of these generals thought the enemy had so large a force on the field. General Pope had told General Banks that "there must be no backing out this day, and also that the policy was to be one of attack, and not defense."

He undoubtedly forced the battle on the impulse of this sting, instead of his better judgment. If he wished to show to the country that his division, which had retreated in the Shenandoah Valley — by his order — would as readily obey an order to fight, he must have been greatly elated "For upon the order to attack they burst upon the foe with a valor so splendid and devoted, that criticism is silenced in admiration, and History will mark the day at Cedar Mountain as one of the proudest upon her illustrious record."

General Pope, in a report to General Halleck on the 11th, said, "The fight was precipitated by Banks, who attacked instead of waiting, as I directed him." General Crawford states in regard to this controversy between Generals Pope and Banks that "it was evidently Pope's intention that the enemy should be checked until he was ready to attack, and that no general battle should be fought until his forces were in hand. But Jackson would not wait, and Banks could do no more than he did" Also "that General Gordon, on our right flank, did not move up the Third Brigade promptly in line, and make the attack with him."

In regard to the fighting of the brigade, General Pope writes to the War Department, "No greater gallantry and daring could be exhibited by any troops." General Halleck responded in the following congratulatory address, which was read to each regiment in the army: "General

Pope, your telegram of last evening is most satisfactory, and I congratulate you and your army, and particularly General Banks and his corps, on your hard earned but brilliant success against vastly superior numbers. Your troops have covered themselves with glory, and Cedar Mountain will be known in history as one of the great battlefields of the war."

Signed, H. W. HALLECK,
General in Chief.

General Pope added that he was "delighted and *astonished* at the gallant and intrepid conduct of General Banks' Corps." He does not state the grounds for his "astonishment."

No soldier of the Twenty-eighth New York can refer to Cedar Mountain without feelings of sadness, as every member of the regiment here lost a personal friend or close companion.

The list of the dead and wounded contains some interesting facts. In Company D were three pairs of brothers who fought side by side, and in each, one fell and the other escaped death, but suffered wounds or capture. David Sanderson was killed and his brother Frank escaped. Perry Gilbert was shot and Martin was desperately wounded. Royal White also met a hero's death, while Newton was captured and sent to Richmond.

On the second day after the battle, under a flag of truce, details of men who were sent to bury the dead, were amazed to find the Union wounded not yet cared for. They had lain on the field, in the terrible heat, with little shelter, and no medical attention or food for more than thirty-six hours. The sufferings and horrors of this time before relief came cannot be described nor fully realized.

The enemy had possession of the battlefield and had cared for their own wounded, but left the Union men lying where they fell. Some humane Confederates had brought water, and built shelters of boughs to protect a few of the wounded from the hot sun. While others, more ghouls than human, had robbed both dead and wounded of all their valuables, shoes and clothing, leaving many nearly naked.

It is hoped this was not done with the knowledge of the Confederate officers. They must have known, however, the Union wounded had not been cared for, and the only excuse for this criminal neglect is that a large portion of the Southern army had withdrawn from the field the day after the battle, and had left only sufficient numbers to maintain a show of force in front of the Union lines.

Under the truce, the wounded were cared for and removed to the hospitals at Culpeper. The dead were buried in one large grave. Many of them had become so discolored by the intense heat that they could not be recognized. Instances of mistaken identity occurred here. The members of Company G, who were looking for Lieutenant Kenyon, found a body supposed to be his, and buried it, marking the grave with his name. Later he returned with the paroled prisoners, and it was found the body was that of Lieutenant Dutton of the Fifth Connecticut, son of Judge Dutton, who had the remains removed to his native State. In this manner many absent comrades were sought for among the wounded and dead, and when not found were supposed to be prisoners. But when the months passed away, and the missing ones did not return, the sad truth that had been feared from the first was forced upon all, that they had fallen on the field of their heroism, and were buried with the unknown.

"Alas! how few came back
From battle and from wrack!
Alas! how many lie
Beneath a Southern sky,
Who never heard the fearful fight was done,
And all they fought for won.
Sweeter, I think, their sleep,
More peaceful and more deep,
Could they but know their wounds were not in vain."

With saddened hearts and thinned ranks the regiment retraced its steps to its old camp ground north of Culpeper Court House. Here the wounded were gathered in the churches and other buildings, used as hospitals, and here Colonel Donnelly died from his wounds on August 15th. His body was escorted to the station by the few who remained of the regiment. Only sixty-four were left to perform this sad duty to their loved commander. He was buried in Lockport three days later, in the beautiful cemetery where subsequently the survivors of the regiment erected a suitable monument to his memory.

When the army fell back from Culpeper, Colonel Brown, Captain Warren and many other wounded of the Twenty-eighth, unable to be moved, were left in the hospital, with the severely wounded of the

division in charge of Surgeon Helmer. When the Confederate army occupied this place, they were taken prisoners and later sent to Richmond.

Among the few army surgeons was the patriotic and noble citizen, Dr. S. F. Benjamin, who had left his home at Medina, N. Y., to care for the wounded. He voluntarily remained with them, and was also taken to Richmond as a prisoner. He had a severe experience there, being tried as a civilian prisoner under suspicion of being a spy, but was finally released.

The following reports of the engagement are printed from the official records of the War Department.

REPORT OF BRIG.-GEN. ALPHEUS S. WILLIAMS, U. S. ARMY, COMMANDING FIRST DIVISION, SECOND CORPS.

HEADQUARTERS 1ST DIVISION, 2D CORPS,
ARMY OF VIRGINIA.

NEAR CEDAR RUN, VA., August 16, 1862.

Major,— I have the honor to submit the following report of the operations of the division under my command in the action at this place on the 9th instant:

My division, since the transfer of Geary's brigade, is composed of the brigade commanded by Brigadier-General Crawford (Twenty-eighth New York, Colonel Donnelly; Forty-sixth Pennsylvania, Colonel Knipe; Tenth Maine, Colonel Beal, and Fifth Connecticut, Colonel Chapman), and of the Third Brigade, commanded by Brigadier-General Gordon (Third Wisconsin, Colonel Ruger; Second Massachusetts, Colonel Andrews, and Twenty-seventh Indiana, Colonel Colgrove). The Twenty-ninth Pennsylvania, nominally attached to this brigade, has been on detached service some months. A battery of artillery is attached to each brigade, and on this occasion Crawford's brigade, which had been some time in advance at Culpeper, had, in addition, four pieces (Parrott's) of Knap's Pennsylvania battery.

With Gordon's brigade I reached Culpeper about midnight on the 8th instant, and on the following morning received orders to move to the front without trains, and unite my division in the position taken up by General Crawford the previous evening. I arrived on the ground about 12 M., at the moment that the enemy opened with his artillery, which was speedily silenced by the fire of Knap's battery. I dispatched a messenger at once to the major-general commanding the corps, with a brief account of the condition of affairs and of the nature of the position held. From this time to 3 o'clock P. M. there was very little demonstration on the part of the enemy, except some cavalry movements toward his right and an occasional interchange of shots with the cavalry under Brigadier-General Bayard.

In the meantime Gordon's brigade had arrived with Cothran's New York battery, and taken a strong, elevated position on our extreme right, from which, through the open field, any movement of the enemy in that direction could be observed and checked. The major-general commanding the corps also came up and assumed command. The arrival of Gen. Augur's division, taking up position on the left of the main road, relieved two regiments of Crawford's brigade, supporting batteries, and they were transferred to the right.

At this time (soon after the enemy had renewed his artillery firing) my division occupied nearly a continuous line along the bottom-land of Cedar Run, from the road to the elevated ground spoken of as the position of Gordon's brigade, a distance of from 800 to 1,000 yards. A densely wooded ridge in front masked the whole line from observation, and the entire division lay almost without loss during the heavy cannonade which preceded the infantry attack. Skirmishers from both brigades occupied the wood in front and on the right flank.

About 5 o'clock, by direction of the major-general commanding the corps, I ordered Crawford's brigade to occupy the woods in front, preparatory to a movement which it was thought might relieve the left wing, severely pressed by the enemy, especially by a heavy cross-fire of artillery, one battery of which would be exposed to our infantry fire from the new position. Five companies of Third Wisconsin, deployed as skirmishers, were by same orders attached to General Crawford's command for this advance. The remainder of Gordon's brigade was held in the original position to observe the right flank, and especially some woods a half mile or so on the right (which it was thought was a cover for rebel cavalry), as well as to be in readiness to re-enforce Crawford's brigade in case of necessity. Observing horsemen moving out and into these woods, I dispatched my personal escort (Company M, First Michigan Cavalry, Captain Dennison) to report to General Gordon, to be used in reconnoitering in that direction. Receiving urgent directions to hasten the movement of Crawford's brigade, I dispatched Captain Wilkins, assistant adjutant-general, with orders to General Crawford to begin his advance as soon as the brigade was in line.

At this time this brigade occupied the interior line of the strip of woods in front of its original position. A field, varying from 250 to 500 yards in width, partly wheat stubble and partly scrub-oak underbrush, lay between it and the next strip of woods. In moving across this field the three right regiments and the six companies of the Third Wisconsin were received by a terrific fire of musketry, both from the underbrush, from the wheat field, and from the woods. The Third Wisconsin especially fell under a partial flank fire from the underbrush and woods, which swept its right companies with great destruction, and under which Lieutenant-Colonel Crane fell, pierced with several fatal wounds, and the regiment was obliged to give way. The enemy was, however, driven out of the open field by the other regiments and some distance into the woods, where, being strongly re-enforced, their fire became overwhelming. No better proof of its terrific character can be given than the fact that of the three remaining regiments which continued the charge (Twenty-eighth New York, Forty-sixth Pennsylvania, and Fifth Connecticut) every field officer and every adjutant was killed or disabled. In the Twenty-eighth New York every company officer was killed or wounded; in the Forty-sixth Pennsylvania all but five; in the Fifth Connecticut all but eight. A combat more persistent or heroic can scarcely be found in the history of the war; but men of even

this unequaled heroism could not withstand the overwhelming numbers of the enemy, especially when left without the encouragement and direction of officers.

While the regiments were thus engaged, the Tenth Maine, Colonel Beal, had advanced across the fields nearer the road, and engaged the enemy with great vigor. Though suffering less in loss of officers than regiments farther to the right, its list of killed and wounded abundantly testifies to the persistent gallantry with which it fought, as well as to the outnumbering forces of the enemy it had to encounter. Anticipating the necessity of using Gordon's brigade in support of Crawford's, and yet reluctant to move it from its strong and most important position until the necessity was apparent, I had arranged with General Gordon a signal for his advance, and with a staff officer of the major-general commanding to await orders before giving the signal.

This signal was given as soon as orders were received, but observing some preparatory movement at the time, I dispatched two staff officers to hasten up the brigade. General Gordon put his brigade in movement at double-quick as soon as the order was communicated. I had myself moved toward his position, but on my way, finding Colonel Ruger, Third Wisconsin, rallying his broken regiment, I joined him in the effort, and had soon the satisfaction of seeing his command united to Gordon's brigade, and the whole moving promptly and gallantly to the support of their overpowered companions of the First Brigade.

As Gordon's brigade reached the interior edge of the first wood it was received by a tremendous fire of the enemy from the opposite woods and from the undergrowth to the right and front. It was evident that the enemy had been strongly re-enforced, and greatly outnumbered us. The brigade, however, firmly maintained its position and checked the farther advance of the enemy, with a terrible loss, however, in officers and men, especially in the Second Massachusetts, Colonel Andrews, which fell under the heaviest fire of the enemy, and maintained its position with marked coolness and courage. Satisfied that it would be impossible to hold, especially after dark, our advanced position, which was exposed to be outflanked by the greatly superior numbers of the enemy, I went in person to the major-general commanding the corps with explanations, and receiving his instructions, I ordered the brigades to withdraw.

It was already dusk. General Gordon brought off the remnant of his brigade and took up his original position, which he held until relieved by General Ricketts' division. General Crawford's brigade, having lost in three regiments every company officer, necessarily withdrew in broken ranks, ... and without officers, rallied and fought with a heroism hardly found in the records of war. The commander of the brigade was amongst the last of his command to leave the field. He subsequently collected the thinned regiments of the brigade in rear of its original position, and afterward by superior order took post for the night in rear of the re-enforcing column.

I inclose herewith a list of casualties in the division, and a tabular statement of the number taken into action, showing a loss of 78 officers and 1,144 enlisted men, nearly one-third of the number engaged. This record is the strongest commendation that can be presented of the gallantry and good conduct of both officers and men. Among those reported missing some wounded probably have fallen into the hands of the enemy. Most of them, I regret to be compelled to believe, must be numbered with the killed.

Upon reoccupying the field of battle it was found necessary from the intense heat to hurry the burials, and most of the dead were interred by details of men who did not know or could not recognize them.

I refer to the reports of commanders of brigades and regiments and to that of Captain Best, U. S. Army, chief of artillery, for further details of the action, as well as for such commendation of officers and men as especial instances of good conduct merited. The prompt, ready and zealous co-operation of Generals Crawford and Gordon, commanding brigades, demanded especial commendation.

I beg leave also to bring to the notice of the major-general commanding the corps the efficient and valuable aid of my personal staff—Captain William D. Wilkins, assistant adjutant-general, who, I regret to add, was taken prisoner near the close of the action; of Captain E. C. Beman, commissary of subsistence; of First Lieutenant Samuel E. Pittman aide-de-camp; of Captain B. W. Morgan, Forty-sixth Pennsylvania Volunteers, division provost-marshal and volunteer aide—all of whom were untiring in their efforts to forward promptly my orders. I desire also especially to bring to your notice the very valuable services of Surgeon A. Chapel, division medical director. At the commencement of the action he selected and prepared as far as possible a general depot for the wounded at a house near General Gordon's position. At this depot were collected several hundred of our wounded, who received during the night the able professional services of Surgeon Chapel and his assistants, and early the following morning were carefully sent back to the hospitals in Culpeper. The prompt and judicious conduct of Surgeon Chapel has been the subject of praise by officers and men.

Nor can I close my report without a reference to the sad record of the killed and wounded of the field officers engaged. In the Twenty-eighth New York Volunteers, Crawford's brigade, Colonel Donnelly is mortally wounded, Lieutenant-Colonel Brown severely wounded, Major Cook severely and a prisoner. In the Forty-sixth Pennsylvania Colonel Knipe severely wounded, Lieutenant-Colonel Selfridge twice slightly though not reported, Major Mathews severely. In the Fifth Connecticut Colonel Chapman wounded and a prisoner, Lieutenant-Colonel Stone dangerously and a prisoner, Major Blake wounded and a prisoner. In Gordon's brigade Lieutenant-Colonel Crane, Third Wisconsin, killed, and Major Savage, Second Massachusetts, wounded and a prisoner. More faithful and valuable officers no service can boast of. The loss, temporarily, it is to be hoped, in the cases of wounded and prisoners, will be severely felt in the divisions. Of the subordinate officers who have fallen or suffered from wounds a record will be found in the reports herewith forwarded. Many of the wounded are disabled for life. It is to be hoped that a grateful country will not forget their services nor their sufferings.

In conclusion, I congratulate the major-general commanding the Second Corps on the substantial success which followed the efforts of his gallant

command to arrest and hold in check the confident advance of a greatly superior force of the enemy.

I have the honor to be, with great respect, major, your obedient servant,

A. S. WILLIAMS,

Brigadier-General, Commanding 1st Division.

REPORT OF BRIG.-GEN. SAMUEL W. CRAWFORD, U. S. ARMY, COMMANDING FIRST BRIGADE.

HEADQUARTERS 1ST BRIGADE, 1ST DIV., 2D CORPS, ARMY OF VIRGINIA.

August 14, 1862.

Major.—I have the honor to submit the following report of the operation of the force under my command in the recent engagement with the rebel forces near Cedar Mountain, Va.:

At noon on Friday, the 8th instant, while encamped with my command at Culpeper Court House, I received an order from the major-general commanding the Army of Virginia to proceed immediately to the support of Brigadier-General Bayard, whose small force was retiring before the enemy. My command consisted of four regiments of infantry (the Twenty-eighth New York, Colonel Donnelly; the Forty-sixth Pennsylvania, Colonel Knipe; the Tenth Maine, Colonel Beal, and the Fifth Connecticut, Colonel Chapman), together with Roemer's battery of six 3-inch rifle guns, and two sections of Knap's battery of 10 pounder Parrotts.

My brigade was soon under arms and on the march, and passing through Culpeper took the road leading toward Orange Court House. By four o'clock in the afternoon I came up with General Bayard's force between Colvin's Tavern and a small stream, known as Cedar Run, and which crosses the road in advance of a belt of woods running east and west. Passing to the front I discovered the enemy's pickets, and beyond, on the road to Crooked River, a portion of his cavalry.

Selecting, with the assistance of Major Houston, U. S. Engineers, of General McDowell's staff, a suitable position, I brought up my artillery, drawing up the infantry regiments in close supporting distance on the low ground of the run, completely concealed from the view of the enemy. Knap's battery, with two pieces from Roemer, was supported on the left by the Tenth Maine and the Fifth Connecticut Regiments, while the Twenty-eighth New York and Forty-sixth Pennsylvania supported Roemer's remaining guns on the right. The cavalry were ordered to the front and flank to watch the enemy. Strong pickets were thrown out within a short distance of those of the enemy, and the command bivouacked for the night.

Early next morning General Bayard reported to me that the enemy were advancing. The command were immediately under arms. It proved, however, to be a maneuver upon the part of the enemy toward our left flank. His cavalry were moving in the direction of a range of elevated hills on our left, known as Cedar Mountain. The movement was intended to conceal the passage of three pieces of artillery, which he succeeded in placing in position at the foot of the slope. Our cavalry were drawn up in our front across our position.

At 11 o'clock the enemy, being established upon the slope of Cedar Mountain at the skirt of the timber near the base on our left, opened fire upon our cavalry. Several shots were fired, when another battery opened a short distance in the rear. I directed Captain Knap to reply, which he did so effectually, that at the third shell from his guns the enemy's battery ceased to fire and shortly afterward withdrew.

An order now reached me from the major-general commanding the Army of Virginia directing me to resist the advance of the enemy, and that General Banks was advancing to my support. Lieutenant Muhlenberg, of Fourth U. S. Artillery, with Battery F of that regiment, now arrived upon the field, and was assigned position upon the right and left. The artillery fire was kept up occasionally at long range for some time, when at 12 o'clock Brigadier-General Williams arrived on the field with Gordon's brigade, of his division. Between 1 and 2 o'clock Major-General Banks arrived upon the field with the division of Augur and assumed command.

I reported to General Williams my position, and soon after received an order to move my entire brigade upon the right of the road, that position having been assigned to Williams' division. The brigade of Brigadier-General Gordon was directed to occupy my right. Upon receiving the order I directed the Tenth Maine and Fifth Connecticut regiments, who were supporting Knap's battery, to move by the flank across the road to the right of the other regiments of the brigade, supporting Muhlenberg's and Roemer's batteries. The movement had not been accomplished when an order was received to deploy one of my regiments on the right as skirmishers into a thick woods directly in advance of our right wing. The Tenth Maine Regiment was halted to support the center. Roemer's battery was advanced to a position on the left of the road. The Fifth Connecticut Regiment had passed to the right, and with the Twenty-eighth New York and Forty-sixth Pennsylvania had advanced into the woods.

The enemy at this moment opened with all his batteries, one of which he had established in an open field on our left. We had thrown forward our center, and had advanced a regiment of infantry, which deployed as skirmishers, were lying upon the ground and supporting the battery in the field on the right of his position. Just at this period I received an order from the major-general commanding the corps to advance my brigade through the woods and prepare to move upon the left flank of the enemy, and that the movement would be supported by the brigade under Brigadier-General Gordon.

In passing to the right I received from Brigadier-General Williams, commanding the division, additional instructions in regard to this movement, and passing forward, I formed my regiments into line of battle directly opposite to the enemy's left. A thick belt of woods skirted an open wheat stubble field on three sides; a road running across formed the fourth. To the right a thick undergrowth of scrub oaks and bushes covered the space. In front of the line the field sloped downward toward the woods directly opposite, the point of which terminated at the road.

Beyond this point, and concealed by it, the enemy had established a battery which stood in echelon near the road. After examining the position and finding that a space of nearly 300 yards had to be passed over by my infantry before we could reach

the opposite woods. I sent a staff officer to the general commanding, requesting that a section of the battery of Napoleons under Muhlenberg might be sent to me to clear the woods in front and on my flank. Before the officer could return Captain Wilkins, assistant adjutant-general of the general commanding the division, came up and urged the movement at once as the decisive one of the day. An order was given by him also to Colonel Ruger, commanding the Third Wisconsin Regiment, to join his command to mine and move with it upon the enemy.

My regiments were immediately formed, the Forty-sixth Pennsylvania on the right, the Twenty-eighth New York and Fifth Connecticut in line to the left The Tenth Maine was advanced through the woods on my extreme left, under the immediate direction of a staff officer of the major-general commanding the corps, and was some distance from the other regiments I then gave the order to advance to the edge of the woods, to fix bayonets, and to charge upon the enemy's position. Steadily in line my command advanced, crossed the fence which skirted the woods, and with one loud cheer charged across the open space in the face of a fatal and murderous fire from the masses of the enemy's infantry, who lay concealed in the bushes and woods on our front and flank. Onward these regiments charged, driving the enemy's infantry back and through the woods beyond. The Twenty-eighth New York, Fifth Connecticut and part of the Forty-sixth Pennsylvania entered the woods and engaged in a hand-to-hand fight with vastly superior numbers of the enemy, reaching the battery at the heart of his position; but the reserves of the enemy were at once brought up and thrown upon their broken ranks. Their field officers had all been killed, wounded or taken prisoners, the support I looked for did not arrive, and my gallant men, broken, decimated by that fearful fire, that unequal contest, fell back again across the space, leaving most of their number upon the field.

The slaughter was fearful. The field officers of the regiments which had driven the enemy back were killed, wounded or prisoners. Most of the company officers had fallen by the side of their men, and the color guards had been shot down in detail as they attempted to sustain and carry forward the colors of their regiment. The Wisconsin regiment which advanced on my right, unable to sustain the terrible fire from the bushes and woods retired to the woods in rear, where it was reformed some distance beyond and brought again into action. The Tenth Maine Regiment of my brigade, acting under direct orders from the commanding general, through one of his staff, advanced to the middle of the open space, and sustained a most severe and galling fire from the concealed enemy beyond.

In the Twenty-eighth New York its colonel (Donnelly) had fallen mortally wounded, and was borne from the field. Lieutenant-Colonel Brown had his arm shattered. Major Cook, after being wounded, was made prisoner by the enemy. Out of the 14 company officers in action there is not one remaining able to do duty. All are either wounded or prisoners. Of the Forty-sixth Pennsylvania its Colonel (Knipe) was twice wounded and carried from the field, Lieutenant-Colonel Selfridge had his horse shot under him, and Major Mathews fell dangerously wounded. Of its 20 company officers who went into action 17 were killed, wounded, or missing, and 226 of its rank and file. Of the Fifth Connecticut, Colonel Chapman, Lieutenant-Colonel Stone and Major Blake are gone. The first is reported a prisoner in the hands of the enemy. The latter two were seen to fall, and have not since been heard from. Out of 18 company officers who went into the action 10 are killed, wounded or missing and 224 of the rank and file. Out of 88 officers and 1,679 men taken by me into action 56 officers and 811 men are killed, wounded and prisoners. The batteries attached to my brigade did most excellent service. Knap, Roemer and Muhlenberg directed their operations in person, and their fire was most effective. A special report of the operations of their batteries was made to the chief of artillery. In Muhlenberg's regular battery (Best's) of the Fourth Artillery, one non-commissioned officer was killed and two non-commissioned officers and two privates wounded.

It is customary at the close of a report like this to mention those whose conduct has merited commendation, but I point the general commanding to the vacant places of my officers and the skeleton regiments of my brigade to speak more earnestly than I can do of the part they played in that day's contest. Colonel Donnelly of the Twenty-eighth New York; Colonel Knipe of the Forty-sixth Pennsylvania, and Colonel Chapman of the Fifth Connecticut, sustained by the field officers of their regiments, led them into the action. These regiments alone and unsupported reached the opposite woods, and fought hand-to-hand with the enemy. Lieutenant Sprout, adjutant of the Twenty-eighth New York, was killed at the side of the enemy's battery, and the gallant conduct of the men was sufficiently attested by one of the generals of the enemy himself, as we stood together upon the battlefield twenty-four hours after the action amid the mingled bodies of the dead of both sides The conduct of the color guards of these regiments is beyond all praise. The colors of the Fifth Regiment from Connecticut were three times shot down, and as often raised again and borne on into the fight. Of the Maine regiment but one, the color sergeant, who bore the colors from the field, remains.

I remained upon the battlefield until dark, directing the removal of the wounded, when I returned and reported to the general commanding, who directed me to move with the remnant of my command to the rear of the woods on Cedar run, at the center of our position. Moving up to it with my staff, I found it occupied by the enemy's cavalry, who open fire and charged upon us, killing two of my escort. I then reformed my regiments in the neighborhood of Colvin's Tavern, north of the battlefield.

Of the officers of my personal staff who accompanied me on the battlefield I would mention Captain F. De Hauteville, assistant adjutant-general, who from the first rendered me especial and important service, attended with great personal exposure.

Captain Cogswell, Fifth Connecticut, and Captain Duggan, First Michigan Cavalry, acted as my aides during the entire day, and rendered me great assistance. First-Lieutenant A. M. Crawford, aide-de-camp, was left by my order in charge of the camp of the brigade, and in forwarding supplies to the

command, which had been without rations thirty hours, aid in the organizing and sending to their regiments detachments who came in from the field, rendered important service to the brigade.

Brigade Surgeon Helmer also remained with me upon the field until a call was made for his professional services, since which time he has been unremitting in his attention to the wounded.

The complete list of killed, wounded, and missing is respectfully submitted.

The greater proportion of those reported missing are supposed to be killed. The bodies found on the field were so much disfigured that recognition was impossible. This report imbodies positive information only.

I am, sir, very respectfully,

Your obedient servant,

S. W. CRAWFORD,

Brigadier-General, Commanding First Brigade.

Maj D. D. PERKINS,

A. A. A. G., Second Corps, Army of Virginia.

F. DE HAUTEVILLE,

Captain, Assistant Adjutant-General.

OFFICIAL REPORT OF THE LOSSES IN THE FIRST BRIGADE.

COMMAND.	KILLED.		WOUNDED.		TAKEN PRISONERS.		PRESENT IN ENGAGEMENT.		PER CENT OF LOSS TO NO. ENG'D.
	Officers.	Enlisted Men.	Officers.	Enlisted Men.	Officers.	Enlisted Men.	Officers.	Men.	
28th New York......	1	20	6	73	10	103	18	339	59%
5th Connecticut......	3	18	8	63	2	143	21	424	53%
46th Pennsylvania.....	2	28	8	94	8	104	23	481	48%
10th Maine	2	22	5	140	1	3	26	435	37%
Total.............	8	88	27	370	21	353	88	1,679	52%

CHAPTER VIII:

POPE'S RETREAT — ANTIETAM.

AUGUST 13TH TO SEPTEMBER 19TH, 1862.

COMPANY E, of the Twenty-eighth regiment, which had been Provost Guard at Culpeper, returned to the regiment soon, and still but a battalion was present. The men were consolidated into four companies, some of which had to be commanded by sergeants.

On the 13th all that was left of the brigade was reviewed by General Crawford, the Twenty-eighth mustering only seventy-eight men. The general made an address on the heroism displayed by the brigade in the recent battle, and did not deem it unsoldierly nor unmanly to shed tears, in speaking of the dead.

Division review followed the next day, and on the 18th with three days' cooked rations the regiment left Culpeper, with the Army of Virginia, in Pope's retrograde movement toward Washington.

On this campaign the Twelfth corps was in reserve, or guarding immense baggage trains, and consequently was not engaged in any important battle. Part of the forces, however, had several skirmishes while supporting General Sigel's Corps.

On the 19th the regiment crossed the Rappahannock, and for many days moved up and down that river. On the 23d, while halted in a field, General Sigel's troops passed. It was a very amusing sight to see his "Jackass Batteries." There were "Jacks" of all sizes and colors, each had a curious device that looked like a saw-buck strapped to his back, on which was the gun of some two pounds calibre. These did not prove very successful, and were not generally used by the army.

From a German, who was leading one of the animals, on inquiring if this style of artillery was effective, was learned that it was, "If de tam mule did not go off before de gun did."

August 24th the command moved to Sulphur Springs, and the next day to

Waterloo Bridge. Soon the march was continued via Warrenton Junction and Catlets Station to Manassas, which place was reached August 30th. The weather during this march was exceedingly hot, and the suffering was great.

On arriving at Manassas, the regiment was ordered back to Bristoe Station to protect the cars there. Sounds of the heavy firing at the battle of Second Bull Run, but three miles away to the north, could be plainly heard, and the news came that a severe engagement was in progress.

The next morning came the order to fire the trains and destroy all regimental wagons, except two ambulances. This action told too plainly the result of the desperate battle fought the day before The goods destroyed were greatly needed, still the command must be obeyed.

Many locomotives, a hundred loaded cars, extending down the track for half a mile, with all their contents of army provisions, ammunition, and hospital supplies, costing the Government millions of dollars, were consigned to the flames. When the fire reached the cars of ammunition, the explosion could be heard for miles. The burning of the railroad bridge over the Broad Run by the enemy on the 27th had prevented the withdrawal of these stores. A force of engineers had been busily engaged rebuilding this bridge, but had not yet completed it.

Undoubtedly the Confederates secured much from the half-burned cars, as they were wet from recent rains and it was difficult to destroy them. Even after the cars were on fire, many of the soldiers climbed into them and by using their bayonets, opened boxes, and carried from the wreckage many articles of clothing. It was a comical sight to see the cavalry use the government trousers as saddle-bags, which they stuffed full, and carried away astride their horses.

Leaving this scene of destruction, the regiment marched to Centerville, where the defeated army of General Pope was concentrated. The next day, September 1st, the retreat continued to Fairfax.

At Chantilla, during a terrific thunder-storm the left wing of General Pope's army had a severe engagement with the Confederates, who were following closely.

It is said this battle was stopped for a time when the guns could not be discharged on account of the rain. When one of General Jackson's officers sent for permission to retire, saying, "The guns of his men would not go off," the answer was returned, "Neither will the enemy's; give them the bayonet."

Here the gallant and lamented General Phil. Kearney lost his life. The Twelfth corps being in reserve was not called into this engagement.

September 2d the army marched from Fairfax to Alexandria, and the Twenty-eighth New York camped at Fort Albany. The men experienced on this retreat more of the hardships of a soldier's life than ever before. It would be difficult to describe their sufferings. Often they were destitute of rations, subsisting entirely on green corn. Much of the water to drink or for coffee was obtained from stagnant puddles. The men were forced to sleep on the ground, without covering. Most of the time they were under arms, doing the same duty as large regiments.

After two days rest at Fort Albany, on September 4th, the Twenty-eighth crossed the aqueduct bridge to Georgetown, and moved to Tennallytown, Maryland, a distance of eight miles. On the 6th the march was continued ten miles to Rockville, where the regiment remained four days

Changes were made in the commanding officers, both of the army and of the regiment. To the great joy of the men General Pope had been superseded by General McClellan. From the day of General Pope's unfortunate order of July 14th in taking command, he had lost the confidence of the men, and, whatever military critics may now say of General McClellan, the army was perfectly wild with joy, and the men shouted themselves hoarse when they learned that "Little Mac" was again in command.

General Banks was assigned to the command of the troops in the immediate defences of Washington, his successor in command of the corps being General Mansfield, who was appointed on the 15th and within two days lost his life in sight of the regiment at Antietam.

Several officers of the Twenty-eighth, who had been on detached service, now returned, the ranking one, Captain Mapes, having been on recruiting service, assumed the command, which position he occupied from September 4th to November 1st. The four companies into which the regiment had been consolidated, were commanded by Captains FitzGerald, Fenn, Waller and Judd.

General Crawford made an effort at this time to have the Twenty-eighth and the other regiments of his brigade, "sent to the rear to be rested, recruited, and reorganized." He stated "that the very existence of the organizations demanded it. That captains were commanding regiments, and corporals, companies, that the severe service endured, the exposures suffered, and the deprivation of proper food the men had been subjected to, had sent many to the hospital. That men never known to fall behind on previous marches, were compelled to now from absolute want of muscular tone." The request was forwarded to the General-in-Chief, but no "*rest*" ever came to the Twenty-eighth except that given to the other regiments in the army.

A feeling of confidence soon pervaded, order was restored, and needed supplies of all kinds were furnished. September 10th the march was resumed to Damascus, sixteen miles, and on the 12th and 13th to Frederick City. The Confederate army had passed through the city two days previous, and an encounter with it was daily expected. Many "Barbara Fritchies" were found who showed the Stars and Stripes, as the Union army marched through. Whether they had been as bold in the presence of the enemy as she is not known. Undoubtedly a better Union feeling prevailed than the year before, when the regiment encamped near this place.

On the 14th the command started very early and marched through the fields—that the ammunition trains might have the roads—to South Mountain, where General Burnside, with Generals Hooker's and Reno's corps, was engaged nearly all day. As the men pressed forward, over fences and brooks, and through fields and woods, they could see and hear the engagement up the mountain side. They halted late at night after a long and very severe march.

The enemy retreated, abandoning the mountain during the night, and the next morning the pursuit was continued, passing the scene of Burnside's fight of the day before, where the brave General Reno was killed, and where the dead of both sides covered the ground. On over the mountain, strewn with articles abandoned by the retreating enemy, the Union forces followed to Boonsborough, where on the 15th they bivouacked, and on the 16th marched to the vicinity of Antietam. Here was heard the news of the disgraceful surrender at Harper's Ferry, but none believed it.

During the night the Twenty-eighth New York, in command of Captain Mapes, moved with the corps, into position on the right of the army near the Poffenberger farm, in the rear of the Dunker church. The Twelfth Corps was held in reserve to General Hooker's forces which were in line of battle confronted by the enemy. Early on the morning of September 17th the engagement opened.

The wounded were seen coming from the front. Soon the regiments of General Hooker's corps, which had forced the enemy back, were in turn forced back themselves, calling for help. The Twelfth Corps was formed in close column, and moved forward, pouring a steady fire into the enemy's lines.

General Mansfield in command, was a conspicuous figure as he rode his horse rapidly about the field. His actions were nervous and excited like those of a young man rather than one far advanced in life. He wore a bright new uniform, and his long white hair was streaming behind as he fearlessly reconnoitered the position of the Confederates. He soon became a target for the enemy and fell, mortally wounded, in front of the First Brigade, and was carried to the rear. A few members of the Twenty-eighth were wounded at this time.

General Williams' brigade had the right and extended to the Sharpsburg Pike. After a long struggle for the woods and cornfield, in which the musketry fire was very severe on both sides, the corps was relieved by General Sedgwick's division of General Sumners' forces, which filed into position, and the Twelfth Corps withdrew to Miller's woods, the position held in the morning. Here ammunition was replenished and the men rested on their arms. About noon the enemy made an advance to gain possession of the woods, but was driven back and the regiment was not again called under fire. The Twenty-eighth suffered a loss in this engagement of two killed, nine wounded and one prisoner. This seems a small loss, but only sixty-five men were in line, and in comparison to the numbers engaged, it was fully equal in proportion to the loss of other regiments in the brigade. The men did their duty nobly and well and

responded promptly to every call made upon them.

The enemy in front of the Twelfth Corps was again Stonewall Jackson and his forces. The Twenty-eighth was ever fated to meet them in battle.

September 18th the Twelfth Corps lay in the woods in line all day expecting the battle to be renewed. But except the picket firing and the boom of artillery on the left, there was no engagement. A truce to go between the lines and bury the dead was arranged. The scene was a horrible one, indeed. Nearly four thousand men had fallen, and in the cornfield they lay so thick that for rods the ground was entirely covered. While in the rear, lying on straw, in the open fields, awaiting removal to hospitals, were nearly twenty thousand Union and Confederate men suffering from wounds.

In the afternoon orders came for an attack the next morning, but when the morning of the 19th dawned, the enemy was gone; and the country was asking the serious question why General McClellan had allowed the Confederate army to escape.

Two of the best corps of the Army of the Potomac, the Fifth and Sixth, numbering 25,000 veterans, were held in reserve and took but little part in the engagement.

Could they have been thrown in at the proper time, they would have achieved results that would have been more worthy the heroic devotion exhibited by the other corps.

The entire command was greatly disappointed. In later years of the war, under other generals, the result would possibly have been different. The losses in this battle were very heavy. The official report shows twelve thousand four hundred and ten as the entire Union loss. The Confederate reports give their killed and wounded as ten thousand two hundred and ninety-one. This does not include the missing, which would undoubtedly make their loss the greater. Fox, in his "Book of Losses in the War," an acknowledged authority, says: "Antietam was the bloodiest battle. More men were killed on that day than on any other one day of the war. There were greater battles with greater loss of life, but they were not fought out in one day as at Antietam." The desperate fighting here may be instanced by reference to the losses of a few Confederate regiments. The First Texas lost eighty-two per cent. The Sixteenth Mississippi sixty-three per cent.; the Twenty-seventh North Carolina sixty-one per cent. The Fifteenth Virginia fifty-eight per cent. The Eighteenth Georgia fifty-seven per cent. The losses in a few of the Union regiments in the Twelfth corps were as follows: The Twenty-eighth Pennsylvania, two hundred and sixty-six. The Twenty-seven Indiana, two hundred and nine. Third Wisconsin, two hundred. The regiment in the Union army suffering the greatest loss was the Fifteenth Massachusetts, which lost in this battle three hundred and forty-four killed, wounded and missing.

CHAPTER IX.

ANTIETAM TO CHANCELLORSVILLE.

SEPTEMBER 19TH, 1862, TO APRIL 27TH, 1863.

ON SEPTEMBER 19th the Twenty-eighth New York left the scene of carnage at Antietam, and moved towards Harper's Ferry, camping on the way. On the 20th the march was continued to Pleasant Valley. Here the regiment remained two days, and then moved on Maryland Heights. Returning, September 26th, to Pleasant Valley, the men commenced to build log houses. October 2d they again marched to Maryland Heights and started a fine camp, which was named in memory of the late Colonel Donnelly.

The regiment did heavy picket duty on the river, and fatigue duty on the mountain. The men were soon quartered in log houses of their own construction. Great rivalry was shown in building them. It was generally conceded that Sergeants Coleman of Company G, and Palmer of Company D, had the finest in the camp.

The historic school house, where John Brown had stored his guns, was on the mountain side, near this camp, and was nearly destroyed by the men, who used the material in the construction of their houses. The usual scramble to appropriate anything that would add to their comfort was thus exhibited.

At Camp Donnelly a long needed rest of several weeks was enjoyed. The itinerary of the regiment showed a march of over a thousand miles since leaving the cars at Hagerstown, Md., July 7, 1861.

Here, too, the regiment regained something of its old-time strength of numbers; the paroled prisoners from Winchester and Cedar Mountain rejoined, led by Colonel Cook and other officers. Their arrival was the occasion of great rejoicing; — a happy meeting of old comrades, relating their experiences and hardships. The anxiety of many was relieved by the return of some comrades who had been marked missing.

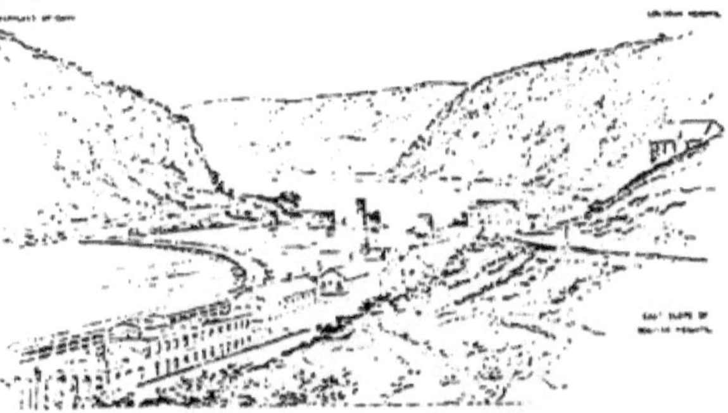

HARPER'S FERRY AND THE SURROUNDING HEIGHTS.

Captain Bowen was one of the officers who here returned, but he soon left the Twenty-eighth, having resigned to take the position of Lieutenant-Colonel of the One Hundred and fifty-first New York Volunteers. He carried with him, not alone the respect, but the love and best wishes of the regiment.

Colonel Brown was often in camp, but did not take active command, owing to his wound not being healed. He could not stand the exposure of camp life, but stood by the members of his old regiment to the last.

Many visited the Signal Station above the camp on the highest point of the mountain. This was fourteen hundred feet above the sea and one thousand above the Potomac. From the place of observation, on a clear day, could be seen without a glass all the towns in the Shenandoah Valley as far as Winchester; up the Potomac River, to the Antietam Iron Works; Sugar Loaf Mountain toward the east, and many other places; a circle of forty miles in diameter. Just below was Pleasant Valley, five miles long and two miles wide, full of camps. The regiments could be plainly seen as they marched out to dress parade, or on drill. The Potomac and Shenandoah rivers were below like threads of light, while the opposite Heights of Loudon and Bolivar, with the old town of Harper's Ferry nestled on the side and at the foot of the latter, seemed but a stone's throw away. It was a panorama of great extent and beauty.

The regiment remained on the mountain until October 31st, when the men reluctantly left their fine houses, and again changed camp to Pleasant Valley. This made the fifth march within six weeks, either up or down that long, winding road to Maryland Heights. But they could not have been sent to a more "*pleasant* valley." Here the Twenty-eighth went into camp in an orchard,—the one occupied on the first camp at this place. It had since been used by the Twentieth Connecticut. After cleaning the grounds, and a few days' delay, to see whether the regiment was likely to remain long enough to warrant the labor, log houses were again built. These proved very serviceable, as the weather was cold, and many snow storms occurred before the command started into Virginia.

Professor Lowe's balloon made daily ascensions from Bolivar Heights, and created much interest among the soldiers in the vicinity.

The other corps of the Army of the Potomac had entered Virginia. The Twelfth was left for a time to guard the upper Potomac. Major General Henry W. Slocum was assigned to the command of this

corps on the 15th of October, and assumed the duties on the 20th. By his kindness and consideration, he soon won the affection of every organization in the corps. He was a distinguished general, and later in the war was one of General Sherman's most trusted officers. General Williams, who had been in command since the death of General Mansfield at Antietam, returned to the division to the great joy and satisfaction of the men.

While at this camp Lieutenant-Colonel Brown was promoted to colonel, Major Cook to lieutenant-colonel, and Captain FitzGerald of Company E to major.

The regiment daily sent details of men on the mountain above the camp to build fortifications. This, with drills and other duties, filled the time until December 10th, when the corps was called into Virginia to join the Grand Reserve Division of the Army of the Potomac.

With many regrets at leaving Pleasant Valley, and especially at leaving the comfortable winter quarters there, the Twenty-eighth started on December 10th, and for six days marched in the mud, rain and sleet, on what proved to be its last entry into Virginia.

Crossing first the Potomac, into Harper's Ferry, then the Shenandoah on pontoon bridges, up over Loudon Heights, and down on the east side, through Hillsborough, Leesburg, Centerville, Fairfax Station, and Occoquan River, the regiment arrived at Dumfries December 16th.

The weather was cold and the march a disagreeable one, made doubly so, by the news of General Burnside's bloody repulse at Fredericksburg.

On the next day the command countermarched to Fairfax Station, as the Confederate cavalry, on a raid in this vicinity, threatened the depot of supplies there. Here the Twenty-eighth went into camp in the pine woods. The severity of the weather necessitated the building of log houses again. These had just been completed, when, on December 28th, suddenly orders came to move, and leaving the camp in charge of a guard, the regiment, in light marching order, left for Dumfries.

The object of this march was to intercept the Confederate General Stuart in his raid around the Union army.

This proved unsuccessful, and on the 29th, the men, tired and disappointed, returned to their log houses in the pines, at Fairfax. During their absence, a scare had caused the few sick and convalescent ones, left at the camp, to be ordered under arms, but the enemy's cavalry had moved several miles away, and they were not molested.

The Twenty-eighth remained at Fairfax about three weeks, during which time reviews were held before Generals Williams and Slocum.

While at this camp Colonel Brown came from Washington. The paymaster also arrived; but before the regiment could be

Fairfax Station, Va.

paid the entire corps started for Stafford Court-House on January 19, 1863, marching ten miles the first day, and the second on to Dumfries. This place was left on the morning of the 21st, during a furious rain storm, that swelled the creeks to overflowing. The command marched five miles to Choppowamsic Creek. This could not be forded, and a detail of men at once commenced a bridge, on which the troops could cross. Halting for the night, they moved on the next morning across the Aquia Creek to Stafford Court-House. The elements, on this march, conspired to prevent the progress of the army, and no soldier of the Twelfth Corps will ever forget the mud march to Stafford.

This march occupied five days, amid rain and snow, which soaked clothing and blankets thoroughly. The men literally wallowed in the red mud, a sticky paste like glue, that covered their feet and clothes. They fastened their trousers about their ankles, wading on with their shoes firmly tied to their feet, to prevent them being lost in the mud.

With the wagons it was even worse than with the men. It was with great difficulty that ambulances, trains, or artillery could be moved at all. "For three days the rain poured. For three days the army floundered."

This was the Twelfth Corps' part in the "Mud Campaign," which has gone into

history by this name. General Burnside's army had a similar experience at Falmouth. A story is told, that, when returning to camp, a private in one regiment, who was standing knee-deep in the mud, while General Burnside rode by, saluted him very politely, and exclaimed: "General, the auspicious moment has arrived!" which was the sentence the general had used in his address to the army, when

ordering the movement. The ludicrous situation was so apparent that the general returned the salute and passed on.

The regiment arrived at Stafford Court-House, January 23d, and went into camp on very uneven ground, which was covered with large pine trees. These were soon felled for use as fuel and in constructing log houses, which were greatly needed, as the weather turned very cold, and snow fell to the depth of many inches. The Twenty-eighth, surrounded closely by other regiments of the First Brigade, occupied this camp for three months; the longest time it ever remained in one place.

Stafford Court-House is situated on a desolate waste, and then consisted of a dozen dilapidated buildings and a small brick court house and jail. It was the county seat of Stafford County. The surrounding country, seen by the Twenty-eighth, was fully in keeping with it. The few farms were poorly cultivated, the land worn out. There were no good roads, and much of the country was covered with swamps and scrub pine trees.

Here the army prepared for the spring campaign. General Hooker succeeded General Burnside and was loyally received. The Army of the Potomac fought equally well under McClellan, Burnside, Hooker or Meade. It had been "all fought to pieces, but never whipped," and yielded prompt obedience to any general placed in command. "It fought just as well after Fredericksburg as before. There never was a day nor an hour, in victory or defeat, that it would not fight to the best of its ability." This is attested by the fact that the losses of the Army of the Potomac during its history, were two thirds of all the losses of the entire Union Army throughout the war.

Fredericksburg was but twelve miles distant, and many visited the place by passes. From the position on the high bank of the river, near the deserted Lacy mansion, whose terraced garden bristled with Union cannon, one could look down on the city across the river. It was still occupied by the Confederates, and all the surrounding heights, on some of which workmen were busily engaged fortifying, could be plainly seen. It was to these heights that so many Union heroes had been led, only to be slaughtered, in their vain attempt to carry them.

Under General Hooker's careful attention the army was never better provisioned. Rations of fresh beef, soft bread, and vegetables, were issued for the first time in the experience of the Twenty-eighth.

General Crawford, having been wounded at Antietam, did not return. He was undoubtedly a good general, but was never a popular one in the brigade.

Colonel Knipe of the Forty-sixth Pennsylvania was promoted a Brigadier General, and assumed command of the First Brigade. Colonel Donnelly, being the ranking Colonel, would have received this promotion had he lived.

The Forty-sixth Pennsylvania, Fifth Connecticut, Tenth Maine and Twenty-eighth New York, composing the First Brigade, here had the addition of a new regiment—the One Hundred and twenty-eighth Pennsylvania. This regiment was commanded by Colonel Mathews, formerly major of the Forty-sixth Pennsylvania.

Much sport was made of these new recruits by the men of the older regiments, asking them why they did not draw rations of butter, milk, etc. A "brigade snow ball" occurred one night after dress-parade, when the veterans and recruits had a tussle, the old regiments uniting in a charge on the One Hundred and twenty-eighth Pennsylvania. This was stopped by the interference of officers, who saw that the men were getting too serious with their play.

General Knipe mounted a stump and tried to make a speech, to quiet the disturbance. He was compelled to beat a hasty retreat amid the shower of snow balls that assailed him from all sides.

The excitement finally was quieted, and the men returned to their camps, carrying with them many evidences of the scrimmage.

Details were made from the regiment to build corduroy roads, which consisted of small trees laid closely together for a foundation, and covered with brush and dirt.

During this work, rations of whiskey were daily issued to the men. In the regiment were several temperance advocates,

THE SICK CALL.

who insisted on drawing their gill a day and pouring it on the ground to prevent others having it. This caused much feeling: many thought the liquor "too good to be wasted."

The laurel shrub was very abundant near Stafford. The soldiers became very skillful in carving pipes and other ornaments from its roots. These, with specimens of petrified wood and shells found in the vicinity, were frequently sent home as mementoes.

The wood for use soon became so scarce that daily details were made from each company to cut and back it into camp, a distance of half a mile or more.

Regimental inspection was held weekly, and brigade and division reviews often. On March 10th, a review of the entire corps was held before General Hooker and staff. April 10th, it was repeated at Kanes Landing, on the Potomac River, before President Lincoln, General Hooker and other prominent officers. President Lincoln was accompanied by his wife and son. The day was a delightful one, and the troops were in line many hours before the President arrived.

The officers were in full dress, the arms and clothing of the men in excellent condition, and the marching was never better.

The President sat his horse awkwardly, and his tall figure seemed even taller by the stove-pipe hat he wore. His appearance was in striking contrast to the fine, soldierly bearing of General Hooker, at his side, who rode a beautiful white horse. "Fighting Joe" had but one rival in the army for fine appearance on horseback—this was Hancock—"The Superb."

As the President took position in front of the line the bands played "Hail to the Chief," the colors of all the regiments and batteries saluted, and the officers and men came to present arms.

During the firing of minute guns by the artillery the general and staff accompanied the President in riding down the front of the first line, which was in open order, and up the second, and so on until the entire corps of infantry, cavalry and artillery had been inspected.

President Lincoln, with General Hooker, then took position in the center, while the troops in column by companies marched in review before him; the bands and drum corps playing, and the officers saluting as they passed. It was an imposing sight, and all felt that the Twelfth Corps would make a record that would be a credit to itself and to the country.

Four days after, marching orders came. Reserving only one blanket and one change of underclothing, all extra baggage was shipped to Washington for storage. Eight days' rations were to be carried—five in knapsack and three in haversack; each man was to carry sixty rounds of cartridges, the wagons one hundred more. Rain delayed the movement, and the date was changed to the 24th.

Though the Twenty-eighth was mustered in for two years, many rumors had been circulated that the men were to be held for a longer time. These reports, however, were effectually silenced by a general order, on April 21st, that all should be mustered out on the expiration of the term of their enlistment.

CHAPTER X.

CHANCELLORSVILLE.

MAY 1ST, 2D AND 3D, 1863.

APRIL 27th the Twenty-eighth started on its last campaign in good spirits, despite its small numbers. But four companies were in line. Company D, Captain Chaffee; Company H, Captain Terry; Company G, Lieutenant Kenyon; Company E, Lieutenant Padelford. The other companies were on detached service as follows: A and C as Provost Guard, under Captain Skeels, the Division Provost Marshal, and Companies B, F, I and K were guarding supply and ammunition trains under the command of Major Fitz-Gerald.

The first day's march was to Harwood Church, ten miles, encamping in the woods. April the 28th, twelve miles further, again encamping in the woods. On the 29th the regiment crossed the Rappahannock River on a pontoon bridge at Kelly's Ford, and the next day moved to the Rapidan River.

When the advance reached Germania Ford on this river, three companies of Confederates were found constructing a bridge on the opposite side. These were surprised and captured. This incident was one of amusing interest. The Third Brigade was the advance guard of the corps.

The situation at this ford was very peculiar. The bluff on the north bank of the river commanded the opposite side, which arose to a steep hill, leaving the only escape by the road following close by the river. The regiments came on this bluff so suddenly that the unlucky Confederates could not escape. They were hailed and ordered to surrender. The skilled marksmen of the Third Wisconsin picked off any who attempted to climb the hill in the rear.

A very few minutes were sufficient for the Confederates to see the hopelessness of escape, and they soon hung out the white flag as a token of surrender. They were ordered to come across the river. Reluctantly they obeyed, and one by one, they answered the yells of the men to "get in there and come over," preferring the risk of a watery grave to certain death where they were. Altogether it was a very unique capture; the men laughed at the antics of the Confederates in the water. But soon the First and Third brigades found, by personal experience, that it was no fun to ford the river. They were ordered across to hold the position on the opposite bank, while the pontoon bridge was being laid. The water was cold and deep, and the current very rapid, which made the fording a most difficult and dangerous one. The men, however, put their clothes and equipments on the end of their guns and waded, waist deep, across the rocky bed.

Though a force of cavalry was stationed below to rescue unfortunates who lost their footing, three of the Twelfth Corps men were drowned. The bridge was soon finished, on which the Second Division and Eleventh Corps, which was following, crossed. The men moved but a short distance from the river and went into camp: the Twenty-eighth regiment going on picket in advance of the army.

April 30th, the column marched to Chancellorsville, halting in the heavy woods in line of battle on the right of the road, the advance coming up with the enemy. The men of the Twenty-eighth bivouacked for the night in line where they lay, having built log works in their front. Trees were felled, piled on top of each other, the dirt was dug from the rear side and thrown over in front

On the morning of May 1st, at 11 o'clock, the First Brigade was called to make an advance toward Fredericksburg. It passed General Hooker's headquarters at the Chancellor-house, and moved out some distance, where General Knipe, in command, formed the regiments in line of battle, in which position they advanced through the fields for nearly a mile, and halted in a piece of woods, beyond which a battery of the enemy was posted. The Twenty-eighth, consisting of companies D,

CHANCELLORSVILLE.

E, G and H, was detailed to go through the woods as skirmishers, under command of Colonel Cook, to relieve two companies of the Forty-sixth Pennsylvania, and to engage the enemy.

The Confederates opened with the battery on a rise of ground beyond the woods, and also from a line of skirmishers, who were driven to the farther edge of the woods. The four companies kept up a constant skirmish fire for more than an hour, seeking such protection as they could from behind trees as they advanced in line. The shells and grape from the battery passed over their heads, cutting off the tree tops, which fell all about them. The brigade was ordered to lie down, and General Knipe sought permission to capture the battery. Instead he was ordered to fall back. Early in the action, private John H. Hogle, of Company E, received a ball in his head, killing him instantly. This proved to be the only death, although six men were wounded, four of whom were from Company D.

The loss of the enemy could not be ascertained, as the brigade was ordered from the field, having accomplished all that was desired in uncovering the position of the enemy. The withdrawal was made in perfect order. The Confederates closely followed the retiring brigade. The companies brought off their wounded in blankets across the fields until the ambulances could be reached in the rear. The Twenty-eighth resumed its position in the woods, behind the log works, and was not called into action again during the day. The men lay on their arms all night.

The morning of May 2d dawned bright and beautiful. Heavy firing was heard from different parts of the field, coming through the almost impenetrable woods in which the regiment lay. Early in the afternoon the corps was called to move to the left, in line with the Third Corps, in an advance on the enemy. These two corps sustained the severest part of the battle of Chancellorsville. The line had moved but a short distance when the four companies of the Twenty-eighth New York were ordered back to the log works by General Williams, who from the kindness of his big heart, thought, in consideration of their past services and the fact that their term of enlistment had nearly expired, they were entitled to some immunities from hard service, and intended to give them the easiest position possible. He did not foresee that he was sending the majority of them to Libby Prison by this movement. It was the last order he ever gave Colonel Cook and these companies, and they take "the will for the deed," and remember the dear old general with tender regard and love.

The men returned to their position behind the works, where Colonel Cook deployed the four companies, consisting of less than one hundred men, to cover the space previously occupied by the entire brigade. They heard the firing on their left and in their front more or less distinctly during the day. No other troops were in sight. The Eleventh Corps was so far to the front that none of its forces could be seen from this position in the dense woods, which was on the extreme right of the line.

About 5 o'clock, suddenly in the front, was heard the sound of battle, and soon a scene, never to be forgotten, broke upon the view. A panic-stricken mob, fleeing in disorder and rout, thoroughly demoralized and wholly without organization, came tumbling down the road on the right.

This was the Eleventh Corps, occupying the entire right of the Union line, about a mile in advance of the position held by the men of the Twenty-eighth. Both the Eleventh and Twelfth Corps had been cautioned by General Hooker to look well to the right flank, as the enemy was moving across the front in that direction. But, strangely enough, no precautions had been taken by the Eleventh Corps, and it was entirely surprised, and not prepared for this sudden attack.

These same troops before, and many times af er, ought bravely and well. Assailed from a quarter that was unexpected, and even unpicketed, it is not surprising that they retreated in disorder. Any corps in the army would have fallen back under the same circumstances, but most corps would not have allowed themselves to be surprised in this manner.

Stonewall Jackson had made another of his famous flank movements, and this one, the most successful of all, proved to be his last, as he was here mortally wounded, and died eight days later. Chancellorsville proved no exception to all previous engagements with the enemy. As usual in the history of the Twenty-eighth, Jackson was in its front.

The regiment's duty was to hold the log works, and, if possible, to rally the retreating forces. Colonel Cook ordered the companies to close upon the right, near the road. In vain did they halt the fleeing men, and, sometimes, at the point of the bayonet, force them to make a stand behind the log works. Many officers of the Eleventh Corps assisted. General Carl Schurz, on horseback, excitedly fired his revolver in the air, crying, "Halt! Halt!" This seemed but to add to the panic and confusion.

At the first appearance of the enemy in the front, the terrorized men again stampeded, and left the Twenty-eighth to hold the works alone. It is surprising that the panic did not take possession of the four companies also. No men from the Twenty-eighth retreated with the Eleventh Corps. The orders were to hold the works, and, if Colonel Cook erred at all, it was in holding them too long.

The Confederates, undoubtedly, had observed that the log works were not manned except on the extreme right, where the companies were posted, and evidently saw that this position could easily be taken by getting in the rear and cutting off the escape of the men.

Darkness was now coming on, and as no troops were on the right, the enemy was enabled to swing around in the rear, and, before its presence was observed, the few men of the Twenty-eighth were surrounded by the Fifth Alabama Confederate Regiment.

It would have been folly to have continued the unequal fight, and, as no reinforcements were near, and escape seemed impossible, Colonel Cook surrendered, ordering the men to cease firing and lay down their arms. A few from the left companies escaped before they were marched to the rear. Lieutenant Seeley, as acting adjutant, was among the number. Being mounted, he put spurs to his horse, and, lying close, rode rapidly back in the darkness, amid a shower of bullets.

Of the Twenty-eighth, sixty-seven men surrendered. These were marched to the rear through the lines of the Confederate army. The Union guns now opened, and, with good range, the shots and shells were falling on all sides. Great gaps were cut in the ranks of the Confederates, who were moving rapidly forward in solid columns. With a feeling of great relief, the prisoners passed beyond the range of the Federal guns.

A short time before the Twenty-eighth left Stafford the men had been paid, but all did not have time to send their money home when the order came to march. When the companies went into the battle, many fearing they might fall or be taken prisoners, gave their money to Sergeant W. L. Hicks, of Company E, for safe keep-

ing, as he was the regimental clerk, and was not supposed to be at the front. But the sergeant was with the men and was also taken. These funds, amounting to nearly seven hundred dollars, entrusted to his keeping, he carried safely to Richmond, secreting them from the Confederates, who took all watches and valuables from the

SERGT. W. B. HICKS, CO. E, REGIMENTAL CLERK.

prisoners. When Hicks arrived at Lockport to be mustered out, he returned to the men every dollar confided to his care. The members of the regiment knew that "Wash Hicks" could be trusted with money uncounted.

As the majority of the men captured in the works were taken prisoners, we will follow them to Richmond. They were marched some five or six miles to the rear and halted near a barn for the night. The next morning, May 3d, at daylight, they were started towards Richmond, guarded by the Twelfth South Carolina Cavalry, marching thirteen miles to Spottsylvania Court-House, where they, with others, were crowded into the court yard.

On May 4th, the march was resumed to Guinney's Station, fifteen miles, camping by the side of the railroad in a large field. The next two days the rain poured down in torrents, and the men did not move. On a hill, near here, was the fine, large house of Mr. Chandler, where General Stonewall Jackson was lying desperately wounded from the battle of the 2d inst., and where he died on the 10th.

May 7th, the column proceeded fifteen miles through Bowling Green and Milford, fording the Mattapony River, camping in the woods. Unusual vigilance was used by the guards, and the route did not seem to be a direct one. Later it was learned that the Federal cavalry, under General Stoneman, was making a raid in the rear of the Confederate army, and the march was made on byroads to elude the cavalry, for fear the captured men would be retaken. On the 8th they were pushed on eighteen miles, crossing the Pamunky and North Anna rivers, to near Hanover Station. May 9th, the balance of the trip to Richmond was made. After the crossing of the Chickahominy River, the first fortifications were passed some five miles out from the city, reaching Libby Prison about sundown, marching through the principal streets amid the jeers of the crowds on all sides. The following account of their arrival was published in the Richmond *Sentinel*. The more severe language is cut out; sufficient only is used to show its character. By such intemperate articles as this the minds of the Southern people were embittered against the Union soldiers and the sectional spirit aroused and kept alive. It is a cause for thankfulness that this spirit has passed away, and both the North and South are in favor of a more perfect union between the citizens of this united country:

"Saturday, the 9th of May, 1863, will long be remembered by the citizens of Richmond. Late in the afternoon, the head of a long column of Yankees, said to be one thousand strong, appeared on the upper part of Main Street. These were clad in the uniform of the United States service. They had no arms. For two years they had been trying, by dint of bayonet and ball, to reach this place; but not until they had laid down their arms, and surrendered themselves prisoners of war, were they enabled to accomplish their object. * * * * The procession, though not unusual, of late, was a strange one. A thousand captured, but not humiliated warriors of the North, walking sternly down the principal thoroughfare of a Southern city, guarded by less than one-third their number of Confederate soldiers, is no ordinary spectacle. Here were the men, who, night after night, and day after day, during many months, had gloated over the fancied prizes of gold, silver, household stuffs, which were to be theirs, when they had conquered the city, through which they were now passing as captives. * * * *

"Silently the Yankees marched along, watched by the countless throng of lookers-on. They stared back at the crowds that gazed from the sidewalks, and showed no shame, no remorse, nothing but impudence — brutish, cold, hard and brazen impudence. So many mean faces we never saw before."

The men were searched on entering the prison, and valuables of all kinds, even writing paper and other articles, were taken from them. Everything except their clothes was taken, with the assurance they would be returned on their release, but this was never done

The men of the Twenty-eighth were put in a large room on the second floor, with about four hundred other prisoners, and

lay so crowded on the floors that it was impossible to move without stepping on a comrade. The windows were barred, and none were allowed to go near them. The day before their arrival a prisoner had been shot through the head by a guard outside the building while he was looking from the windows. The food was bread and meat, with bean soup occasionally. The severe privations that prisoners later had to endure were not then general.

Daily papers were bought by the men who had money, and were read with great interest.

Stonewall Jackson's funeral occurred on the 12th of May, while the men were confined in Libby Prison, and the *Sentinel* gave the following account of the funeral procession :

"The long procession passed up Main Street, consisting of artillery, cavalry, infantry and bands of music. The arms of the soldiers were reversed, their banners were draped in mourning. The drums were muffled, and the notes of trumpet and horns were funeral. The tolling bell and the cannon booming at long intervals, told a mournful story.

"The war worn veterans of Pickett's division, led the soldiers, Ewell, brave, modest and maimed, rode close to the hearse of his great commander. The President of the Confederate States, pale and sorrowful, was there. The good Governor of Virginia, stricken with grief for the loss of his noble townsman, was there. The heads of departments, the State and Metropolitan authorities, and many citizens, walked humbly and sadly behind the coffin, decked with spring flowers and enveloped in the folds of a flag which the nations of the earth have never beheld. A great multitude of all ages, classes and conditions, stood by to see this procession pass. All was hushed while the mortal remains of the best, and best beloved chieftain, in all the land passed onward to the capitol of the State and the Confederacy, which he had so heroically defended and died to save from pollution. The body of Stonewall Jackson was in the hearse, and this great procession was in his honor."

Often in the middle of the night, when any loud talking or laughing was heard, the guards would come to the top of the stairs, and order the men to be quiet. To annoy them in return by a prearranged plan, a score or more of voices would awaken their sleeping comrades by singing "Yankee Doodle" or "The Star Spangled Banner." The rush of the guard up the stairs would find all apparently sleeping soundly.

May 11th, all were paroled and told they would soon regain their liberty. On the 13th they left Libby Prison, marching across the long bridge to Manchester and started for Petersburgh. A heavy rain and darkness came on before many miles had been made and a halt was ordered in the woods.

Early on the 14th the march was continued through Petersburgh on to City Point. Long before this place was reached the men commenced to break away from the column and double quicked to the river's bank to get a view of the fleet of transports laying anchored waiting to take the prisoners to Annapolis. The boats nearly all had the stars and stripes floating from their masts, and at the first sight of "Old Glory" the men shouted until they could cheer no more. The river has a high bank here and the released prisoners, as they reached the top, would roll over and over to the water's edge in their great joy at being released from prison and seeing the old flag again.

Soon the arrangements for the embarkation of the men were made, and one by one they were counted off as they walked the single plank to the vessels that started down the James River at noon bound for Fortress Monroe, which was passed on the 15th, arriving at Annapolis on the 16th.

Here new clothing was provided and the shore of the bay, near the parole camp where the men were quartered, was turned into a mammoth bath. The diary, from which these dates have been taken, contains the very significant word "*cleaned*," which is *underscored*. Whatever that may mean, it is still in the memory of all that fires were built along the shore on which all the clothing brought from Libby was carefully burned. On the 19th the start for home was made, the men reached Lockport the evening of the same day the regiment arrived, and all were mustered out together.

We will now return to the battlefield at Chancellorsville.

The few who escaped from the woods when the Twenty-eighth was surrounded and captured formed on the hill in the rear and joined the brigade in line of battle. Being so few in numbers, they were soon ordered to join companies A and G of the regiment, which were acting as provost guard. They were not again called into action, and, with the rest of the brigade, recrossed the river on May 5th.

The Twelfth Corps was the last to cross the Rappahannock, as it had been the first to cross the Rapidan at the beginning of the

campaign. This corps, with the Third, had borne the heaviest fighting of the battle. These two corps lost more men killed, wounded and missing than the other four corps combined. The Twelfth Corps sustained a loss of two thousand eight hundred and twenty-two, of the less than ten thousand men in line. The First Division, General Williams, the "best, sturdiest and toughest in the army," lost one thousand six hundred and twelve. It is said that many prisoners taken in front of this division asked, "Who were those fellows with red stars on their caps that fought like devils?"

The Twenty-eighth Regiment returned to its old camp, near Stafford Court-House, on the 6th, and on the 7th, the "Present for duty" numbered two hundred and twenty-seven men. During the week that followed preparations were made for the journey home.

Chapter XI.

HOMEWARD—MUSTERED OUT.

May 11th to June 2d, 1863.

May 11th the Twenty-eighth made its farewell visit to the corps, division, and brigade headquarters, and to the other regiments of the brigade. Generals Slocum, Williams, and Knipe, each addressed the regiment, congratulating the men on their good record in the service, and on the prospect of soon seeing their homes again.

In the camps of the several regiments of the Brigade speeches were made by the commanding officers, all of which were congratulatory and eulogistic; and were responded to by officers of the Twenty-eighth. The regiment was everywhere received with cheers, and the occasion showed the kind feeling and interest existing among the men of the old brigade.

It was a joyous time, yet tinged with a feeling of sadness at parting with comrades who the men had learned to regard with a brotherly feeling. They had faced death together on many fields of battle, endured the long weary marches, in summer's heat and winter's storm, and literally had "drank from the same canteen." But the thought of again seeing loved ones at home outweighed all other feelings, and after hand-shakings and good-byes, the regiment returned to its tents, and passed its last night in camp.

On the morning of May 12th, amid the cheers of the old First division—"first of the Twelfth Corps, and second to none,"—the Twenty-eighth left Stafford Court House, and started for HOME.

Arriving at Aquia Creek landing, the regiment took the steamer for Washington,

WHAT WAS LEFT AT STAFFORD COURT HOUSE.

which place was reached on the 13th, New York on the 14th, and Albany on the evening of the 15th. Here it was met with an enthusiastic reception, and escorted through the streets by the fire department to the Delavan House, where a bountiful supper was furnished by the Common Council, after which a fine torchlight procession, by the entire fire department of the city, was given in honor of its return.

The next day, again escorted by the fire department, the Twenty-eighth marched to the State House, and was received by the Governor. He addressed the men in a very complimentary manner, referring to their brilliant services in the army, and welcomed them back to the Capitol of the state. Colonel Brown responded, returning the thanks of the regiment. Three days were spent here before the final start for home was made. The time was employed

by the men in visiting the city, the barracks, Camp Morgan, even the Adams House, and other places familiar to them in the first days of their soldier life.

Many members, whose term of enlistment was not ended, having joined as recruits, subsequent to the muster of the regiment, had to be turned over to other organizations to serve the balance of their time. Nearly all of these chose to return to the battalion which had been formed from the men of the Tenth Maine regiment, who were also serving unexpired terms, after that fine organization had been mustered out. This battalion was assigned to General Slocum's headquarters as guard, and remained with the Twentieth corps during its eventful campaign to Atlanta, and the march to the sea. By this choice the men exhibited their attachment to the old brigade, and continued in this battalion the many pleasant associations they had formed in the old regiments.

May 19th, the Twenty-eighth left Albany for Lockport, where it arrived on the 20th, and was received with great rejoicings, shouts and cheers, from the thousands that thronged the streets. The pupils of the union school, from their grounds near the depot, sang a hymn of welcome, the chorus of which was:

"Welcome, welcome, gallant brothers,
High and low estate,
Join us in the cheerful welcome:
Gallant Twenty-eighth."

The procession to the Fair Ground was one of immense proportions, under command of Benjamin H. Fletcher, marshal of the day. It consisted of the Fire Departments from Lockport, Medina and Albion, the Masonic Order, Temperance Society, Home Guards, thirty-four young ladies in carriages, representing the States of the Union, the Board of Trustees, and the Twenty-eighth Regiment, numbering about three hundred and fifty men, under the command of Colonel Brown.

Arriving at the Fair Grounds, the returned Veterans, after passing in review, were formally welcomed by the President of the Board of Trustees, James Jackson, Jr., in an eloquent address. He was responded to by Colonel Brown with an admirable speech. The regiment then sat down and enjoyed an elaborate dinner, furnished and served by the ladies of Lockport.

After the dinner a poem, prepared for the occasion, was read by Mr. C. H. Squires. The first stanza will indicate its character:

"Welcome, gallant soldiers;
Heroes, true and tried,
Patriots, brave and fearless,
Old Niagara's pride."

Too late to participate in these rejoicings, the released prisoners of the regiment arrived by the evening train. They were in charge of Colonel Cook, and numbered about seventy men. The greetings of these paroled comrades were hearty indeed. All were furloughed to go to their homes until the day of the final discharge of the regiment, which was on June 2d, when all were mustered out of the United States service by Captain Sheldon Sturgeon.

Each man received his discharge on parchment, which certified that he was "Mustered out of service on the expiration of his term," and "no objection to his re-enlisting is known to exist."

This ended the history of the Twenty-eighth New York, but not the service in the army of the majority of its members. Very soon many of them again enlisted in the cause for which they had imperiled their lives during the past two years.

They re-enlisted in various organizations, and in all branches of the service. Honor was reflected on the old regiment by the men carrying to the new commands the fine experience as veterans they had gained in the Twenty-eighth New York. They always referred to their first service with especial pride and satisfaction.

To know the subsequent history of all the men mustered out at Lockport would be very interesting. How many in the new commands lost their lives in battle or in prison, and how many have since died, is not known. It is only known that two hundred and fifty-two were alive in 1896.

With the list of the dead increasing each year, soon the last survivor will have joined his comrades gone before, and the Twenty eighth New York will exist only in the memory of its friends, and in the archives of the government for which it fought, and did its humble part to maintain and defend.

SPECIAL ARTICLES

PREPARED FOR THE

History of the Twenty-eighth Regiment New York State Volunteers.

THE PEACE WE FOUGHT FOR.

CONTRIBUTED BY A COMRADE.

I CAN contribute nothing to the history of the Twenty-eighth New York Volunteers which, as history, will enlighten my surviving comrades or interest the general public. The regiment made its own history, and it is fresh yet in the memory of its still living members, although thirty-three years have passed. Its history was in no respect different from that of the majority of other regiments of our citizen soldiery. It marched and countermarched, advanced and retreated, won victories and suffered defeat, camped, and waited the word of command. Its soldiers suffered and enjoyed as soldiers always have and always will. They had their hours of relaxation, they had their hours of awful bitterness. There was sickness and death in camp, there was danger and death upon the battlefield. There were longings for home and loved ones that with some were never to be realized. Emotions of every sort swept over the soldiers, not only of the Twenty-eighth, but also over the soldiers of every regiment in the field. There were songs and tears and prayers and fears and hopes, and, underlying all, the stern, never shaken resolution to see our nation preserved unbroken: one united, liberty-loving people. When the two years' service for which the regiments of our period were called out had been rendered, and the men were free, some went back to home and duty, as it appeared to them, and others re-enlisted in other regiments for the remainder of the war; and when the war was over, they returned, "all that was left of them," to the quiet life out of which they had been called.

But though I can say nothing new or fresh as to the history of the regiment of which I was a part, the years have brought to me, as to us all, time for reflection as to the nature of the struggle through which we passed. It was a great struggle. No other such a war was ever fought. The history of the advance of mankind in civilization has been a history of war. But of all the wars of the world this one was unique. It was not the longest, it was not the most cruel, it was not the severest, but it was wholly and absolutely different from any other. Its object was different, that was, to maintain the perpetuity of the American Union; to answer to the world the question, can a voluntary compact between individual States be a bond of union so strong that once made it can never be broken? to answer the question to the world, can a government of the people, by the people and for the people stand strong and centralized against internal sedition and sectional differences? These questions this war answered. It said in thunder tones, Yes; this confederation of States is a nation, and not an aggregation. It said, practically, there is power enough in that portion of individual rights which each State that became a party to the compact surrendered to hold when consolidated into one general government, each State firmly, closely, indissolubly in one powerful union. That for which we fought was the doctrine of an indissoluble union; and that for which we fought we achieved. The armies of this war were different from any other armies which the world has ever seen. The soldiers were citizen soldiers. There were no hirelings. The men who made the armies at least in its early years were the best men of the nation. Young men out of every rank of life, from shop and store, and college, and seminary, from farm and field, from plow and pulpit, answered the calls for volunteers. Every family had its representative. The men of 1861 and

1862 were men who went at their country's call, because they loved their country. There has never been a sublimer example of pure patriotism than these men furnished. They were not forced into war by stern, hard military power. They were volunteers. They made of themselves a free-will offering There was no hope or thought of fame. They knew nothing of war and its promotions. But they did know they loved the flag of stars and stripes, and they made such a display of their love as this world had never seen made by any other people, for any other flag. It was patriotism pure and simple that made the soldiers of the armies of the Republic. I have read of the wonderful fidelity of the soldiers and officers of the Swiss guard who perished to a man at the palace of the Tuilleries in Paris on August 10, 1792, vainly trying to defend Louis XVI. against the mob of the city. Thorwaldsen has left as a monument to these heroic soldiers a thought embalmed in stone, in the colossal figure of the Lion of Lucerne, carved into the solid rock in the grotto back of the town. The dying lion is the Swiss soldiery; the lily of France lies under his protecting paw; not till he was dead did his power to defend it cease. It is a wonderful statute. The world admires it, and admires the valor it commemorates. But these soldiers were not patriots. Their stern fidelity to duty in no sense aided Switzerland. Native land was not the sentiment that actuated them. They were sold to war, and they died as soldiers die. But the soldiers of 1861 and 1862 were patriots. The most intelligent men of the world. Editors, teachers, printers, mechanics, lawyers, doctors, professors, preachers, farmers, merchants, laborers, and men of leisure, all alike put on the uniform of the private soldier, and marched to the dread front of battle, simply and only to maintain inviolate the integrity of the country which they called their own. The men who made the Twenty-eighth Regiment of New York Volunteers were of this character. Some of them died; some of them lived: some of them have died since the war closed; some of them still live. But all alike, living and dead, were actuated by the same great patriotic purpose.

There was never such another war. Its battles were the greatest battles that have ever been fought in the world. Think of Cedar Mountain and Antietam; think of the awful battles that marked Grant's movement toward Richmond; think of Chancellorsville: but, above all, think of Gettysburg! The writer of universal history says he can record no other such a single battle as that one of Gettysburg—greatest battle of all time. It was a battle not only in which vast forces were engaged on either side, but it was the battle of all the ages for valor. Such charges, such repulses, such onsets, such retreats; where has the eye of man ever seen such except at Gettysburg. It was a battle of the citizen soldiers of the North against the citizen soldiers of the South. The generals were there, major-generals and brigadiers, but it was the citizen soldier who was chiefly there. No general planned the conduct of Gettysburg. It planned itself. As Sheridan's soldiers went over Lookout Mountain because they could not be restrained, so the soldiers of the Republic won Gettysburg. It was the greatest battle of the world because the largest amount of intellectual force was there actively displayed that has ever been displayed in a battle, and that came from the character and intelligence of the individual soldier. And Gettysburg does not stand alone. It was a whole war after 1861 of great battles, great marches, great defeats, great victories. It developed a great nation, it plunged it into great debt, it created great measures of public policy and finance, it made great generals out of common soldiers, and saw great statesmen developed in our national congress at Washington. It was an era productive of greatness, and the world wonders at it still.

Its results also have been as wonderful as it was itself. Look at them from any standpoint, they were wonderful. We are perhaps now even yet too near the events to rightly estimate the greatness of these results. Who would have supposed that the outcome of such a war would have been to utterly extinguish the war spirit in the nation, and to make us in thirty-five years the champion among the nations of the world for the settlement of all variances by appeal, not to battle, but to fair adjudication after testimony in high courts of arbitration? But, that *that* is one result, and one most beneficient result, cannot be questioned. The peace for which we fought has become a doctrine of peace for all the world. Who for a moment thought that the tremendous debt into which, almost without warning, the nation was

plunged, and which appalled the men who stood at the front of affairs, was to be the means of creating financial policies which should carry our credit to the highest point credit ever attained among the nations, and unify our national monetary system to such an extent that National Bank bills should become the stable medium of exchange of a whole continent, and give the nation a better currency than it had known in all its history? Yet that this has been the result is beyond all question. There were doubtless some dreamers in the ranks of the Abolition and Free Soil element in the North who thought that the first gun fired on Fort Sumter was the first stroke of the bell sounding the death knell of slavery. But the rank and file of the men at the North did not think so. And when the act came that set the slave in the rebellious States free, it waked the hostility of so large a portion of our people as to make it seem to many a dangerous expedient. Who then for one instant entertained the hope that three decades would see the South itself foremost and heartiest in rejoicing over the death of the institution for which it sacrificed the choicest of its sons. Yet that is one happy result of this fearful struggle. Look at the Negro. Who would have dared in 1865 to prophesy the facts of 1896? What are they? In 1865 there were not fifty college bred negro preachers in America; to-day there are more than one thousand. In 1865 there were two negro attorneys; now there are two hundred and fifty. In 1865 there were three negro physicians; in 1895 there were regularly practicing seven hundred and forty-nine. There are two hundred and fifty black American students in the Universities of Europe. In 1865 you might as well have searched for hot ice as for an African school-teacher; now there are twenty thousand, and one hundred and fifty schools for advanced education, of which seven are colleges presided over by African presidents and faculties, and three of these college presidents were slaves. In 1861, when the war began, for a southern Negro to know how to read was a crime; now 2,250,000 have learned to read and write. Then they had not a single school; now they have 25,530 schools operating through some part of each year. Thirty years ago the entire taxable property of the negro was twelve thousand dollars; now it is $264,000,000. Who would have dared to prophesy part or all of this? And yet this is one direct result of that great fierce war. The settlement of the West, the building of our great trans-continental railroads, the development of the South, and the vast increase in wealth of the nation are all parts of the great outcome of the war. It was a peace worth fighting for: a peace which without the war could never have been. It settled forever the question of the power of self maintenance of Republican institutions. It ended the old struggle between cavalier and roundhead which had come down to us from our English ancestry; it settled the question as to the relative prowess of northerner and southern; it opened a door of escape for the poor whites of the middle East, and said to the world, here is a spot in deed and truth where every man of honest worth and honest purpose is the peer of every other man. To have had part in such a war is cause for self-congratulation. To be written in the roll of the patriots of 1861 to 1865 is glory and honor, and on that roll is written the name of each comrade of the Twenty-eighth Regiment of New York Volunteers.

IN MEMORY OF DEAR OLD

"PAP WILLIAMS."

By W. F. GOODHUE, Milwaukee, Wis.

Secretary Third Wisconsin Infantry Association.

IT IS with pleasure that I learn you are to publish a regimental history, and in it there is to appear a portrait and memoir of our brave old Division and Corps commander, Pap Williams of blessed memory. As the Hibernian said of his dead friend: "Peace to his soul and not to his ashes, for he hasn't gone where ashes are made." Although I haven't seen the old general for thirty-one years, yet with memory's eye I see him to-day as plainly as ever, and with the soughing and whispering of the wind amid these northern pines, I fancy myself back among the Virginia pines and the

pine savannahs of Georgia and the Carolinas, through which we followed for many a weary mile the devoted leader of the old Red Star Division.

His was a Cromwellian figure, sitting his horse like a centaur, sturdy, strong and imperturable under all the circumstances of bloody warfare: his strong, kindly face and grizzled beard indicated the stanch and rugged nature of the man, while beneath his black slouched hat gleamed in the southern sun the glasses he constantly wore, scintillating like the jewelled eyes of a war god when giving to the warriors of the nation the inspiration of battle and holding firmly in his teeth the never-lighted stub of a cigar.

When the rifles at the front began their crackling sound the horse he rode quickened its step and the advance of the division when it reached the front, found old Pap there too, and there he stayed until the field was won.

In all the four long years of that incessant warfare the brave old general was on hand and there was not a drum beat in the Red Star Division that he didn't hear and was the first to answer its call, no matter what the occasion — a review, a march or battle; he was there, and his boys had to get up very early in the morning, long before the roosters began to crow to beat him in punctuality and promptness, and it is doubtful if we ever *got there* ahead of him.

There were but two generals in the Union Army who acquired from the soldiers the affectionate soubriquet of "Pap" and there were Generals George H. Thomas, the beloved commander of the Army of the Cumberland, and our own division commander, Alpheus Starkey Williams of the Twelfth and Twentieth Army Corps, and it is a fact that both of these generals came from the old Red Star Division.

The commander of the Second Brigade, First Division, Banks' Corps, in August, 1861, was Colonel George H. Thomas, who was then promoted to brigadier-general and given a command in Kentucky: General Chas. S. Hamilton, the first colonel of the Third Wisconsin Infantry, succeeding him in the command of the brigade. This able officer was sent to McClellan's army, and the old Second Brigade fought under the direction of Gordon, Ruger and Hawley to the end of the war, respectively. That these two "Paps" were able soldiers goes without saying, and their worth as such is so recorded in history; but there was something else in their make-up — something more in their natures and character than the stern dominant qualities of militaryism, else they would not have acquired that soubriquet of endearment and respect which was spontaneously bestowed upon them by the overworked troops they so gallantly handled on many a hard fought field. "Pap" Thomas was educated at West Point; "Pap" Williams was educated in the Mexican war. The former was a regular army officer; the latter was a volunteer officer; but these differences count for naught when summarizing their characters; both were beloved by the troops they led through the war, and both were called "Pap" by the troops who knew them best.

That hard fighter and stern tyrant, Frederick the Great, used the term "my children" when he spoke of his troops, but his flinty old heart had no love for them, and his hypocritical term of affection, was one of sovereignty, and not of true affection, for he flogged, starved and slaughtered them remorselessly. History does not record an instance when his men called him "Pap" or anything akin to it. He held his army to its work by the sternest discipline, which his troops feared more than they did the enemy. The nobler instinct of patriotism, which gives a steadfast courage in battle and braces men to sustain the fatigues of warfare, was wanting in his army, because he degraded his men by punishment with the lash, and he also seems to have whipped patriotism pretty well out of his people, if Poultney Bigelow's articles on the "Struggle for German Liberty," now current in one of the magazines, are to be believed.

The American soldier had a personal dignity which such men as Thomas and Williams respected. These generals had duties to perform which, in their execution, placed exacting and onerous conditions upon their troops; but the men obeyed and respected such requirements with alacrity, even unto death, and each emulated the other in their service in the cause for the Union, which was an unquenchable faith common to all, and it is with feelings of pride and admiration that I now remember the abiding faith, the deep and hearty love and respect we then had and now have, I can safely say, for

the brave officer whom we loved to call "Pap" Williams, long since gone to his reward.

At the close of the War General Williams commanded the Temporary Division of the Fourteenth Army Corps, a division composed of the western troops of the Twentieth and Fourteenth Corps. This division was in camp on the old Crittenden place, near Louisville, Kentucky, held there by the government in expectation of going to Mexico and assist Juarez to drive the French troops from that country, who were then the main stay of Maximillian's throne. But "Napoleon the small" took the hint given him by Secretary Seward and withdrew Marshal Bazaine in due season, otherwise Pap Williams would have been engaged in a second Mexican war.

While in camp there the general would talk over, of an evening, the events of the civil war, and I remember one evening an officer present asked him what, in his experience, was the most critical hour he had seen during the civil war. "May 2d, the night before Chancellorsville," he promptly answered, and then he went on to say why he thought so. "My division had been divided and scattered by orders from headquarters. I didn't know exactly where all of it was; in that wooded, rugged region, brigades and regiments once separated were difficult to keep track of, and it couldn't be done with my limited staff of officers. Then at dusk Jackson broke the Eleventh Corps and came charging down upon our position and I was fairly at my wit's end to know what to do: my staff were looking after or trying to keep track of my absent regiments, and I had no one to help me gather together the remaining troops of the division, and all the time the cursed yelling and firing of the approaching rebels grew nearer and nearer. If Pleasanton had not posted his batteries on the ridge, along the little valley of Scott's Run, the rebel charging column would have gone straight through us, but the excellent work of those batteries saved us the day. For about an hour," the general went on to say, "I experienced a mental anguish which I never had before or afterwards during the whole war, and perhaps the reason why I never suffered so again was that never afterwards was my division so separated and scattered as it was that terrible night, and through no fault of mine." We all know how well the general brought up his division and posted it in the night on that fateful field, and how well he handled it that Sunday morning, when Jackson's corps charged us again and again, beaten every time, and our general took his division, he was so proud of, from the field with empty cartridge boxes, but not until relieved by fresh troops. Green shall be his memory in the hearts of us all as long as we remain on this earth, in this Republic he served so well.

ORGANIZATION AND MUSTER-IN OF THE TWENTY-EIGHTH.

COLONEL E. F. BROWN.

THE preliminary preparations for the organization of the Twenty-eighth Regiment, N. Y. Vols., has little of interest to the general public, but at the time was something that engaged the attention of the people of the country, especially those residing in Niagara, Orleans and Genesee counties, N. Y. Five companies — one half the Regiment — was the nucleus. Added to these were two from Orleans and one from Genesee. All of these were recruited almost simultaneously and in an incredible short time after the attack on Fort Sumpter, which occurred April 16, 1861. Colonel Donnelly, who had been for several years active in the Militia organizations of the State, and lieutenant-colonel of the Sixty-sixth Regiment, at once took an active part in organizing the companies, and to him is due the honor of perfecting and organizing the regiment. Familiar with every detail of preparation, he was enabled to give prompt advice and secure aid in supplying every need while the companies were being enlisted. The people were aroused, and the work of securing quarters, rations and general supplies was easy — indeed, only required the asking.

The seven companies mentioned were readily united in seeking a rendezvous at

the same point. It was the desire of State authorities that all the troops from the Central and Western counties should rendezvous at Elmira, where extensive preparations were making for a great military camp. A preference was expressed, and by a well-directed effort was successful, to have this regiment allowed to rendezvous at Albany. This was considered a favor, for which all were very grateful. As soon as the proper number of men were enlisted to form a company, orders were issued from the Adjutant-General's office for the transfer to Albany, and thus in a few days eight companies were ready for muster. Two companies were lacking, and it was the work of a few days and some fine diplomacy to secure the other two.

Captain FitzGerald, who was in Albany with a company from Ontario County, and Captain Waller, from Sullivan County, both unassigned, and both anxious to secure the best possible organization with which to unite the fortunes of their respective companies, were not long in reaching the conclusion that the Twenty-eighth was likely to perfect their organization first; and, although sought for by others, soon decided to join us, and thus the Twenty-eighth was ready to prepare for muster-in with ten full companies. While in Albany making these preliminary arrangements, the various companies were somewhat scattered, being quartered here and there in various vacant buildings — none of them too comfortable; but all better, as they subsequently learned, than tents, sheds, damp ground or swamps. Arrangements were made to feed all the men at the Adams House, and the food, while not served in the best style of first-class hotels on mahogany or maple extension tables, or served by skilled waiters, was, however, in the main satisfactory. The Delevan House, next door across the street, would have been a trifle more satisfactory, although the supplies for each were under the supervision of the celebrated caterer and hotel manager, Monsieur Roesselle, now proprietor of the Arlington Hotel at Washington. The men occasionally rebelled at the service, and scrimmages with the waiters were of frequent occurrence.

It was soon discovered that the center of a great city like Albany was not the best locality for organizing troops, and as soon as the muster rolls could be prepared the order for mustering-in the regiment was given, and we were numbered 28, although several earlier numbers were not mustered in until many days later.

The muster into the service of the United States for a specific time—say, "three months," or "two years," or "three years," or "during the war"—was at first somewhat misunderstood, and resulted later in serious disagreement between the Government and some of the New York troops, of which the Nineteenth N. Y. was a conspicuous example, although one of its field officers was a son of W. H. Seward, then Secretary of State of the United States.

The Twenty-eighth took no stock in this controversy. All, officers and men, were mustered in for two years or during the war, which was construed as meaning "during the war," provided the war continued less or no longer than two years.

As the day of muster-in to the United States service approached, it was perceptible that the enlisted men were discussing the question of what the "*muster*" meant, and also what the war meant, and they discussed it understandingly and reached proper conclusions.

On the 18th day of May the organization was completed and the field officers were elected by the votes of the company officers. Preparations were then made for immediate muster-in of the regiment, which great event took place on May 22, 1861.

A little episode which occurred between the 18th and 22d may not be wholly devoid of interest, although it is probably forgotten by most of the surviving members. A few of the men during their stay in Albany had discovered that a blanket on a hard floor and Adams House fare and the restraints of camp requiring a pass to leave for a few hours, and other little restrictions to their liberties, were not altogether to their tastes, and some of these not exceeding a half dozen in all, gave their company officers notice that they "wanted to go home." and some intimated that unless they could have leave they would go without leave. One captain having heard of this called his company in line, and after a few words of kindly advice to all to stand by the organization, made the inquiry: "How many of you have determined not to be mustered into the United States service. If there are any such let them step three paces to the front." With a halt and a limp and a hang-dog expression on their faces about a half dozen stepped out. He took

their names and after a good lecture directed them to return to their places in the ranks. On the following day he sent for them and kindly asked them if they had fully determined whether they would be mustered in or not. Five of the number decided to refuse the muster. The captain at once prepared to muster them out. For this extremely unpleasant duty he had secured the services of a barber and a drum and fife. Several brave men volunteered their aid and the men were placed in the barber's chair, their heads shaved on one side sufficient to mark them and then they were drummed out of camp to the tune of the Rogue's March. While there were unpleasant remarks about the barbe(a)rity of the proceeding, the question of refusal to muster was settled. The approval of the summary proceedings by the other members of the company was made apparent by the rousing cheers given for the captain.

It was not at all strange or singular that some boys who had left comfortable homes with pleasant surroundings, and who had never before been under other than mild parental restraint, should look upon it as a great deprivation to be placed under military discipline. The discouraging outlook of two years of camp life and the danger of battles to come, of hardships, of pleasures gone, all tended to homesickness, a disease termed nostalgia, which is often as fatal as other diseases and quite as painful and distressing. To the credit of those who were so summarily mustered out be it said that after their Albany experience and a visit to their mothers, most if not all again enlisted and served faithfully during their term of enlistment and were killed in battle or honorably mustered out at the expiration of their term of service.

The muster-in was a great occasion. It was so considered at the time, and has been held in remembrance as our great anniversary day from that time to the present. It has been and still continues to be the day of our annual reunion. No distinction is made —officers and men alike—regardless of rank or station in life, meet and join cordially in celebrating the great day of our muster-in. As our numbers decrease the interest of that day becomes more dear to those who remain. When we consider the fact that a thousand men stood in line and with uplifted hands took the oath in the most solemn and impressive manner to support the Constitution of the United States and defend the flag of our common country, it meant something in addition to the words of the oath to which we pledged our honor. It further said to each one of us, we must stand by each other as well as the government and the flag. Each man as he stepped to the front of the line for the purpose of identification by the mustering officer declared by this action that he was there for a purpose and wished the world to know it. Each and every man was deeply impressed with the responsibility he assumed. He saw that a base and wanton attempt was being made to destroy this great and powerful nation, to divide and distract the government under which we had lived and prospered for almost a century. And why should this be done? At this time the question of emancipation of the slaves was not thought of. The preservation of the Union and the defense of the flag, these were in danger, and whatever else might happen, these must be preserved. Patriotism pervaded the thoughts of the young volunteer, and danger did not deter him from standing up manfully and answering to his name promptly when called by the mustering officer. It was indeed a sight to remember, when, one by one, these noble young men stepped forward and declared to the world that, come what might, they were ready and willing for the sacrifice. From that hour the thousand men composing the Twenty-eighth Regiment became as one man ready to do battle for the Union and for each other, and for the flag that floats over us all.

Immediately after the organization was completed the work of discipline and training began. The number of officers who had received military training was limited to a few who had fortunately been serving in the State Militia. Those who had received the slightest military education were in great demand. It was several days before uniforms and equipments could be secured, and these were days of hard work and mental strain for the officers, who had many, yes, everything to learn, and that mostly by experience rather than by books. Requisitions were not in form, were taken to the wrong officer, had to be made over, and all for lack of early education. All had to be studied and there was little time to do it in. There were quartermaster and commissary stores, camp and garrison equipage, arms and ammunition, etc., etc.,—each in its turn had to be

obtained in the regular way — and all new to a New York volunteer officer. Before the lesson had been half learned, orders came for the Twenty-eighth to go into camp in the town of Bethlehem in Albany County, about three miles from the city. This was our first camp, named Camp Morgan, for our worthy Governor, Edwin D. Morgan. Here is where we received our first military instruction. Here we received our first education in the arts of war. Here our first effort at guard duty, and even at this day one smiles at the drills of the awkward squads and the still more awkward drill-master. Our outfit of arms was a feature and this was down at Camp Morgan. We had requested to be furnished with rifles, and as a mark of great confidence our request was gratified. We were supplied with a 44-caliber rifle with sword-bayonet and were greatly pleased thereat. While it must be admitted that the guns were at first very awkwardly handled, there was no lack of effort on the part of officers or men to perfect themselves in the manual of arms. Regular squad drills were organized and the enlisted men when off duty could be seen almost constantly engaged in private efforts to perfect themselves in the art of the soldier. This was an encouraging feature and relieved the officers of much anxiety. In fact, the majority of the officers required quite as much instruction as the enlisted men. Competition was active. The school of the officer was as important as the school of the soldier. Both felt the need of education and no time was lost by either in the effort to become efficient. Our first dress parade and several that followed will be recalled with a broad smile at the remembrance of the effort to conceal the gross ignorance of many of the officers and most of the men in the performance of that exercise at the close of the day. It was indeed a laughable farce as we now look at it in the light of subsequent drills and dress parades of the regiment. We proudly recall the fact that there was no lack of effort on the part of any officer or soldier to study and improve, and this was universal. After the muster in, came this short preparation in the art of war at Camp Morgan, and then we were ready for active service, indifferently so, it must be admitted at first, but by degrees and constant field duty from that on, improvement came readily, and finally the degree of perfection which enabled us to stand up before the cannon and musketry of the enemy and perform our duty without flinching.

THE BAND OF THE TWENTY-EIGHTH NEW YORK.

HOW ORGANIZED—ITS SERVICE AND DISCHARGE.

By Enos B. Whitmore, Rochester, N. Y.

WHEN, on the 22d of May, 1861, the Twenty-eighth New York State Volunteer Regiment was sworn into the United States service, at Albany, and received its number, it had no band. There were with the regiment some company musicians, and the nucleus of a fife and drum corps; and, besides, within its ranks were other musicians of ability and experience in band practice; but these, aside from the musicians first referred to, were all members of some of the various companies of the regiment, and regularly enlisted as privates to carry the knapsack and shoulder the gun.

But away from Albany, in the southern part of the State, and unknown to the members of the regiment, circumstances were soon to transpire which were destined at no distant day to provide for the regiment the substantial beginning of a good and acceptable brass band. At the time of the breaking out of the War there was at the village of Friendship, in Allegany county, a flourishing musical academy conducted by Professor James Baxter In the summer of 1861, and after many regiments had gone into the field, Major Roy Stone, of the Pennsylvania "Bucktail Regiment" (the first Pennsylvania rifles), came to Friendship and perfected an arrangement with Professor Baxter to organize and equip a band for his regiment, then at the front and in camp in Maryland.

In carrying out this agreement with Major Stone, and for the purpose of getting material from which to organize the contemplated band, Baxter issued invitations for local bands, and musicians generally, to meet at the Friendship Academy at an early day, the object being stated in

his call. This call met with a hearty response and brought a host of musicians and bands, the latter numbering one each from the villages of Angelica, Belfast, Cuba and Bolivar.

The result of this meeting was that about 26 men agreed to form a band under the lead of Prof. Baxter and join the Pennsylvania regiment. These men left Friendship on the 23d day of August, Baxter having the order for their transportation. After leaving Elmira Baxter either gave up or lost his order for transportation, as a result of which, when the men reached Harrisburg on their way South, they were practically stranded. At this place four of them returned home and the rest, paying their own fares, went on to Baltimore, "bound to go to war or bust."

From Baltimore the determined men got transportation in freight cars to Frederick City, Md., where they spent the night, this being August 25th, and in the morning struck out on foot for Hyattstown, near which place the "Bucktails" were encamped.

When arriving at camp, on August 26th, they were a forlorn looking lot of men — "a tough looking mob," as one of their number expressed it. Instead of being an organized band in uniform, they were really aggregated fragments of several bands, dressed in a haphazard manner, appearing more like musical tramps than volunteers for the United States service. Thus clad, and from their general appearance, they did not compare favorably with the well-uniformed bands of the Twelfth Massachusetts, the Fifth Connecticut, and bands of other regiments there in camp, and in consequence did not meet with a favorable reception from Colonel Bidwell and other officers of the Pennsylvania regiment. These officers, upon scanning the new comers and applicants for place at right of column, concluded they were not just then in search of a band.

Thus being rejected by the Pennsylvania regiment, which they expected would receive them as soon as they arrived, the musicians were greatly disappointed and disheartened. There was nothing now for them to do but to start back for their homes, which they reluctantly did that afternoon, "with," as one of their number expressed it, "satchels and horns in hand, no money, spirits below zero, and band stock away below par," taking the road leading to Frederick City which they had traveled in the morning with such high hopes and expectations.

But a brighter future lay before these disconsolate men. Their pilgrimage and weary search for a situation, and their trying failures and disappointments were destined to quite suddenly come to an end. After traveling two or three miles along the road they spied approaching them from the direction of Frederick City some federal officers. When they met the officers eyed them suspiciously, thinking, from their appearance, they might perhaps be some dissatisfied recruits "skipping out." (It is not recorded that the officers demanded the pass-word of the musicians, for likely they were without it themselves, having just "skipped over to Frederick City," you know, on a hurried visit to get some milk shake or soda water. And in case of an attempted arrest it might have been an even question which party should do the arresting.)

At all events the officers asked the musicians who they were, where they were going, and what this all meant. Their story was soon told, whereupon the officers, who proved to belong to the Twenty-eighth Regiment, Captain William Bush being one of the number, urged them to return with them to camp, promising to endeavor to get them a place in the regiment, failing which they would see the musicians safely to the railroad on their way home the next morning.

This proposition was briefly considered by the musicians and quickly decided, the men dividing and taking opposite sides of the road, those in favor of returning to camp with the officers taking one side and those opposed taking the other side. The result was that fourteen men, namely:

H. E. Dickinson,	Henry Buckley,
S. P. Lapham,	R. H. Grady,
C. E. Le Suer,	W. H. Withey,
James Baxter,	W. M. Daniels,
Rodolphus Talcott,	Joseph Crawford,
Lot Parshall,	John Quinton,
Orson A. Baldwin,	"Wick" Rigdon,

(with only seven instruments all told) decided to accompany Captain Bush and comrades to the camp of the Twenty-eighth Regiment, it being "Camp Church," near Hyattstown, Md., the rest of the men continuing homeward.

After a brief consultation of the officers of the regiment after the arrival of the musicians, it was decided to receive them

into the regiment as a band, the arrangement for their acceptance being completed August 28, 1861.

Now, and for the first time, the Twenty-eighth Regiment had a band of its own. Stephen P. Lapham, an accomplished musician, was its leader, Prof. Baxter having in the meantime decided not to remain, who, with Rigdon and Baldwin, left camp on the following day.

The muster roll of the band was made out October 31st, the members receiving their first pay November 6th, at camp near Muddy Branch.

Soon after the band became attached to and a part of the regiment, Colonel Donnelly wrote W. A. Thomas, an experienced band leader at Lockport, that the regiment had a band, but as yet he had not appointed a leader, and if he would enlist and join the regiment he (the colonel) would appoint him to the place. Thomas responded and soon joined the regiment, at camp near Darnestown, bringing with him from Lockport Benjamin Kaiser, another band musician of experience.

Upon his arrival, Thomas was duly installed as leader and reorganized the band. W. H. and J. S. Chambers and J. M. Ford were detailed from Company A to do service in the band; also Joel S. Davison from Company C and John Ferary from the drum corps.

On November 8th, E. B Whitmore and George Winter joined the band, from Lockport, and on the 20th of the month Lot Parshall and John Quinton were discharged.

This left the band as finally constituted, and organized as follows: W. A. Thomas, Lockport, leader; S. P. Lapham, Belfast, solo E♭ cornet; W. H. Chambers, Lockport, solo B♭ cornet; George Winter, Lockport, first B♭ cornet; R. Talcott, Cuba, second B♭ cornet; C. E. Le Suer, Bolivar, solo E♭ alto; E. B. Whitmore, Lockport, first E♭ alto; Henry Buckley, Bolivar, second E♭ alto; J. Crawford, Belfast, third E♭ alto; R. H. Grady, Cuba, first B♭ tenor; W. H. Withey, Bolivar, second B♭ tenor; Benjamin Kaiser, Lockport, B♭ baritone; H. E. Dickinson, Portville, B♭ bass; W. M. Daniels, Belfast, E♭ bass; J. S. Chambers, Lockport, E♭ bass; J. M. Ford, Lockport, bass drum; John Ferary, New York, snare drum; J. S. Davison, Lockport, cymbals; which organization remained without change until the band was discharged, save that in the spring of 1862, at camp near Edinburg, Va., J. S. Davison was returned to his company, and W. W. Eastman of Conneaut, Ohio, company musician, was detailed from Company D to take Davison's place and play the cymbals.

After the final organization of the band, under Thomas' lead, and during the time the regiment remained in Maryland before crossing into Virginia, in the spring of 1862, nothing specially occurred in the history worthy to relate. It performed the regular duties of a regimental band, played daily at guard mount and dress parade, and also on marches as the regiment moved from place to place. It also occasionally took part in serenading some official and played funeral dirges at burials; and, at times, on marches, made life miserable for the members of the regiment by the singing of songs and boisterous shouting.

For a cook the band had for a time a colored man from Baltimore, Md., named "George." Subsequently, while the regiment was moving up the Shenandoah Valley another "lamb of God in the fourth degree" presented himself for hire as a mess hand. He was a stout, sixteen-year-old slave, named "Harve," who had just bid adieu to his master near whose residence the regiment camped for the night. Harve's services were accepted for a stipulated compensation, and he remained with the band until its discharge, separating therefrom at Washington, D. C.

Harve proved to be a well-disposed boy, and many members of the band, notably W. M. Daniels, took great interest in his welfare. He was inclined to be studious and thirsted for knowledge, and had learned some of the letters of the alphabet during stealthy interviews, as he said, with the children of his master, whom he would sometimes induce to leave with him over night their books when returning from school. Soon after his connection with the band he asked for a book from which to learn to read, and one was procured for him at Harrisonburg, Va., by a member of the band. The stationer of whom the book was purchased grinned sardonically when informed of the use to which the book was to be put. It was then a violation of the law of the State of Virginia to teach a slave to read.

The band being composed of men from different places and from different organizations, each providing his own instrument, the latter were, as a consequence, of

many different makes and styles; and, although numbering some good pieces, the instruments were, as a whole, odds and ends of different kinds and material, and necessarily seriously lacking in uniformity of quality of tone. With such instruments the band could do justice neither to itself nor the regiment, a fact soon made apparent to the members of the regiment, particularly the officers. On account of this, soon after the final organization of the band under Thomas, the matter of obtaining a new and better set of instruments for the men was occasionally discussed among the officers and other members of the regiment who took an interest in its appearance and standing among other regiments with which it was associated. Finally, on the evening of May 19, 1862, at camp "Round Hill," near Strasburg, Va., at a meeting of the officers of the regiment, it was decided to make an effort to procure a new and better set of instruments.

To raise the necessary means for making the purchase the members of the regiment were assembled the next day and a proposition discussed and agreed to by vote that each private should subscribe 50 cents toward a fund for the purpose, the commissioned officers agreeing to subscribe liberally toward making up the necessary amount. The members of the band were assessed according to their pay, the assessment amounting to about $160.

This action of the regiment resulted successfully, and funds were at once guaranteed for a set of new instruments, which Leader Thomas ordered at once of a house in Boston, Mass., this being on May 20th.

But when this action by the regiment was taken its members little realized how soon and suddenly the wisdom of its action would be demonstrated. From Camp Round Hill the regiment moved toward Winchester, reaching that city late at night of May 24th. The next morning—Sunday—when the battle of that date promised to become interesting, Surgeon Helmer ordered the members of the band to put their instruments in a place of safety and report to him for further duty. The first part of this order the men obeyed with alacrity, but they did not generally report to the surgeon, this being rendered impossible on account of the movements of the contending forces and Banks' retreat. One result of this conflict was that, with the exception of four pieces, the old band instruments were lost and never recovered.

The new instruments, ordered on May 20th, were long coming, their delay causing a great deal of impatience to the members of the band as well as to the other members of the regiment who had liberally subscribed for their purchase. They finally arrived at the end of 40 days, reaching the regiment on June 29th at camp at Front Royal. The instruments were the "Allen" make, German silver, and cost about $900, and were vastly superior to the ones lost at Winchester. With the new instruments the members of the band were greatly pleased, and they were enabled to render much more acceptable service to the regiment.

Aside from the fact that some of its members carried private revolvers, the band was not armed. At one time a move was made to arm the band, which resulted in the members being supplied with artillerymen's sabres—broad, short, heavy, straight "stabbers," with sheaths and belts—but the boys did not take kindly to them on account of their weight and clumsiness.

But the regiment, after having subscribed liberally for the set of fine new instruments, was soon destined to be deprived of its band. By the fore part of the year 1862 the volunteer army of the Federal service had become large, and the bands of the volunteer regiments, taken together, would have made, as to numbers, a respectable division by themselves. However they may have been regarded by the various regiments, these bands were looked upon by men at the head of affairs to be unnecessary and expensive luxuries; and, as a result, on March 1st of that year, a bill was introduced into Congress by Mr. McPherson, providing for the discharge of such bands. This bill was referred to the Committee on Military Affairs, with the final result that an act for discharging bands was passed July 8, 1862, which received the President's signature on July 17th, the provision being that bands of volunteer regiments were to be mustered out of the service within thirty days of the date upon which the act became a law, *i. e.*, on or before August 16, 1862.

However, no haste was made in discharging many of the bands in accordance with this act, including the band of the Twenty-eighth Regiment. August 14th, when we were in camp at Culpeper Court House, an order came to discharge bands,

and on the 16th or 17th a leisurely, delinquent official made his appearance at camp (at Culpeper Court House) and gathered sufficient energy with which to muster out two bands, one at 11 o'clock in the forenoon and the other about 3.30 P. M. That evening the order to move came, and in the morning, August 18th, the regiment filed into the highway, headed northward, and no further opportunity was presented for making out discharge papers for the band until the regiment went into camp near Rockville, Maryland, a few days preceding the battle of Antietam.

At this camp, on September 6, 1862, Leader Thomas got an order for the discharge of the band, the discharge papers being made out and signed the next day. The clerk who filled out the blank discharges sat in one of the regimental covered wagons, the filled blanks being dated "At Camp near Rockville, Maryland, the 7th day of September, 1862," and signed by W. H. Mapes, "Captain Commanding Regiment."

The men here discharged were those of the band, who had enlisted as musicians, and who had not previously belonged to any of the companies or to the drum corps. They were:

W. A. Thomas,	H. E. Dickinson,
R. H. Grady,	George Winter,
R. Talcott,	C. E. Le Suer,
W. M. Daniels,	H. Buckley,
Benj. Kaiser,	E. B. Whitmore.

S. P. Lapham and J. Crawford were in hospital, and W. H. Withey was a prisoner. Withey had remained at Culpeper Court House to care for Lieutenant-Colonel Brown, when Pope's army moved northward after the battle of Cedar Mountain, the colonel being too feeble to be moved, both falling into the hands of the enemy.

S. P. Lapham's health failed him when the army commenced its retrograde movement from Culpeper Court House. Transportation was provided him, and he did not again do service in the band. He was in hospital at Washington a few days, then sent to Philadelphia, where he was in hospital when the band was discharged. His discharge paper, and that of Crawford, was made out at the same time the others were made out, and Crawford, soon appearing, received both, Lapham's being forwarded to him at Philadelphia.

Crawford having continual poor health, did little or no service as a musician while a member of the regimental band, and was in hospital much of the time.

Armed with the discharge papers from the regiment, the elated band boys started for Washington to receive their pay and mileage preparatory to returning home, meeting on their way a large part of McClellan's army hastening up the Potomac to meet Lee, who was then moving northward.

But puny man knoweth not what is before—what trials, sorrows and grievous disappointments. The boys walked nimbly to Georgetown, where they stopped for the night, and in the morning, with high hopes and cheerful countenances, pushed on to the War Office to have the final acts of their discharge completed. But when presenting themselves before the august officials of that institution, they were confronted with the astounding information that there was no such band in the Federal service. The officials told the astonished men that they could do nothing for them; but, by way of consolation, told them that the department had no claim on them, and they were at liberty to go home, but they could pay them no money. They didn't tell the men at the same time that the walking was good, but the disheartened men always believed the officials thought it if they didn't say so.

When told they could have no money, the crestfallen musicians instinctively felt in their pockets for money that wasn't there, there being, probably, not enough money among them all to pay one fare home. What to do under the circumstances suddenly became a question of great moment among the disheartened men. To be told that they could have no money was bad enough; but after the long months of service they had performed as a band, the long weary marches and skedaddles they had made, the wear and tear to which they had subjected the Maryland and Virginia turnpike roads, and the tons of hardtack they had faithfully helped to keep from spoiling, to be told they were never in the service was like adding insult to injury.

But ups in life sometimes come as suddenly and unexpectedly as downs; and so with the now thoroughly disheartened men. A way up out of their trouble and affliction came to them as unexpectedly as they were plunged into it. As good

fortune would have it, General Banks—the ever courteous, sympathetic, attentive and obliging General Banks—chanced to be in Washington, and was seen in and about the War Office.

The men cheered up when they saw him, for they now knew that, at least, they had a friend at hand. Their case was soon laid before the affable general, and he, having repeatedly seen the band in his command, and having on one or two occasions brought the nose of his fiery steed near the base drum when the band was practicing at camp to help get it accustomed to the racket of military life, differed in opinion with the war officials on the question of the band being in the service. He at once interceded for the helpless men, and his influence with the officials at the War Office was sufficient to have a peremptory order issued to "muster that band into the service (under the proper date) and muster it out."

As a result of this order the men were mustered into the service and out again as fast as the different sets of papers could be written out, it being all done in one day.

It appears that by some inadvertence or neglect on the part of the officer, whose duty it was to attend to the matter, the muster roll of the band had never been filed with the secretary of war and there was, in consequence, no record in the war office showing that the Twenty-eighth regiment ever had a band. Hence the sudden turn with which the men were fetched up by the officials of the war department on presenting themselves for final discharge.

After receiving their final discharge from the service and vouchers for pay and mileage due, the boys were not long in getting their money, which they received just after noon on the 18th day of September, 1862. And now everything was lovely with them and they were as happy as a lot of women with new bonnets. Their faces, which an hour before measured ten inches up and down and five inches horizontally, now measured ten inches on the level and five inches high.

Talcott, Grady and Kaiser found employment at Washington at their respective trades after being discharged from the regiment, but the rest of the men lost no time in getting to the Baltimore & Ohio depot to take a north-bound train, most of them returning home by way of New York.

Harve, the faithful young cook who had remained constantly with the band after coming into the regiment, was left at Washington, as there was an order in force that no transportation be given colored people northward on railroads leading out of Washington without a special permit from some one in authority.

When the men were discharged from the regiment, at camp near Rockville, as stated, W. H. and J. S. Chambers, J. M. Ford, W. W. Eastman and John Ferry returned to their respective companies. W. H. Withey, who was for some time a prisoner, was finally exchanged and received his discharge from the regiment in due time.

Thus, imperfectly recounted, began, continued and ended, the band of the Twenty-eighth New York Volunteers.

Some of the members of the band to whom I have addressed communications for facts have not responded.

I have not been able to trace Withey's movements after his capture at Culpeper, nor Crawford's after he left the band the last time.

I have an inkling that a man by the name of Stebbins once, nominally at least, belonged to the band, but died. I have been able to get no particulars as to the matter. I remember that a man by that name died at camp sometime in November or December, 1861, but was under the impression that he belonged to one of the companies.*

In conclusion I wish to express hearty thanks to old band comrades C. E. Le Suer, H. E. Dickinson, S. P. Lapham, R. H. Grady and W. W. Eastman, and comrade C. W. Boyce, for valuable assistance rendered in the matter of making up this history of the band.

---

* Henry K. Stebbins, Co. D, died June 22, 1862, at Front Royal, Va. There is no record of his connection with the band.—C. W. B.

THE FIFE AND DRUM CORPS.

By W. W. EASTMAN, Fifer, Company D.

THE Fife and Drum Corps of our regiment was originally supposed to be made up of two musicians from each company.

The organization was completed at Industrial School barracks in Albany, after we had sworn in as a regiment, and Mathew G. Tieranney was given the position of Drum Major; and, being a fine musician in both branches, Major Tieranney had full charge of both fifers and drummers.

The roster of musicians was made up as follows:

Company A.—Frank Repass, fifer; William Baker, drummer. Company B.—Joseph W. Chandler, fifer; Wright Bodger, drummer. Company C.—Daniel Olmstead, fifer; John Ferary, drummer. Company D.—William W. Eastman, fifer; John O. Swan, drummer. Company E.—Lorenzo A. Sabine, fifer; Mark J. Blakely, drummer. Company F.—W. H. Brady, fifer; John Brost, drummer. Company G.—Merritt Raymond, bass drummer; Origin Richardson, snare drummer. Company H.—Joseph Taylor, fifer; John Minor, Geo. Egner, Joseph Morris, drummers. Company I.—Horace L. Drake, fifer; Homer Fields, drummer. Company K.—Edmond Stony, fifer; Byron C. Anderson, drummer.

Major Tieranney was a tireless worker and a good-natured, popular instructor, and at once demonstrated himself to be master of the situation, and perfectly qualified to lead the drum corps to the front rank of martial bands in the service, and, with that end in view, he inaugurated a system of drills which accomplished the desired end, and the old Twenty-eighth will remember the unearthly racket we used to make while drilling in the woods and fields adjacent to camp. Major Tieranney, if he is living, will not forget how he used to rouse us out to play reveille at sunrise, and the companies used to dread the end as we struck "Three Camps," closing the eight parts of our regulation reveille, for that meant every man "turn out," "fall in for roll call," or be marked "absent without leave."

The Fife and Drum Corps was a disturber of the peace and quiet of the soldier's reverie, and he was not, as a consequence, very friendly to that branch of the service, and when Adjutant Sprout would call for Major Tieranney to bring out his corps for dress parade or guard mount, the boys would cuss and discuss the merits and demerits of the Drum Corps, and particularly the latter.

In camp near Stafford Court House, Virginia, it was currently reported the regiment was going to be ordered to Baltimore to finish our term of enlistment doing guard duty in the Fort, and the very idea filled our souls with unspeakable joy; but we were all able to say there was more "pleasure in anticipation" than in "participation," for one evening on dress parade, Colonel Cook addressed the regiment in a few words upon the subject of going to Baltimore, and finally said, "Soldiers, our going to Baltimore has played out," and then earnestly expressed the desire that we quit ourselves like noble, brave soldiers, and when our time expired we would return to our homes bearing bright laurels of victory with "our drums beating" and "our flags flying." But the boys saw it in a different light, and they all said, "We will go home indeed, but with our '*flags* beating' and the '*drums* flying.'"

At this time Major Tieranney was not with us. He suddenly and mysteriously disappeared on our march from Harper's Ferry, after the Antietam battle, and we never heard of him after that day. It was with profound regret that we lost him, and, if he is now in the land of the living, we would be delighted to be put in communication with him. We never knew why or how he left us, but the small remnant of the old Fife and Drum Corps would rejoice to extend fraternal greeting to our old leader after all these years of separation, while we

"Let the dead past bury its dead
With heart within and God o'er head."

While the musicians did not carry the musket they filled another prominent place in camp and on the battlefield, rendering invaluable service with the ambulance corps and surgeons, caring for the wounded on the field, and nursing the sick in the

hospitals — constantly under fire from the shells of the enemy while engaged on the field of battle, or exposed to the diseases of the hospital. Some of our casualties I might mention.

John O. Swan, the drummer of Co. D, was taken prisoner at the battle of Chancellorsville, but was paroled in time to be mustered out with the regiment. He died several years ago, after having studied medicine and practiced his profession a few years.

Merritt Raymond of Co. G, our bass drummer, was wounded and taken prisoner at Cedar Mountain fight, August 9, 1862. He was again captured at Chancellorsville. Merritt Raymond was born in Johnsburg, Warren County, N. Y., March 9, 1840, and died in Albion, N. Y., August 23, 1889. He was a brave and faithful soldier and left an untarnished record, the choicest monument the world ever beheld.

Origin Richardson, drummer of Co. G, we never hear from, but he is reported living somewhere in the State of Vermont.

John Minor, drummer of Co. H, was captured in our Winchester fight in the spring of 1862, under General Banks, but he used some cunning strategem with the Johnnies, and at Mt. Jackson he concealed himself under the floor of their quarters during the night, and when the rebels left in the morning Johnnie Minor crawled from his hiding place and returned to the regiment. He never reports, but is supposed to be alive and residing in Duchess County, N. Y.

Byron C. Anderson, the tall, rosy cheek drummer of Co. K, is a farmer in South Dakota, where in the past few years, together with the writer of this, we have often met and played the same old airs we used to play in our Southern camps, and many times have enlivened the old soldiers' gatherings with the martial music of war times. Last 4th of July the citizens of Huron, S. D., paid our transportation and entertainment to play for a three days' G. A. R. encampment and 4th of July celebration in that city.

But the ranks of our Twenty-eighth Drum Corps are thinning, and very soon the dead march will be played for the last one, and then the martial strains of our beloved band will be forever stilled.

From all sources I am able to account for only the following members:

Company D.—William W. Eastman, fifer. Company G.— Origin Richardson, drummer. Company H. — Joseph Taylor, fifer; John Minor, drummer. Company I. — Homer Fields, drummer. Company K.— Edmond Stony, fifer; Byron C. Anderson, drummer.

From the above it transpires that less than one half of our old Drum Corps are still "present or accounted for." The balance of our members are now sleeping on "fame's eternal camping ground," or if living are numbered among the missing.

We bow our heads in sorrow when we remember those who are gone forever from us, and we long for the day to come when we can grasp the hand of the small remnant left, before the final muster out of our old Twenty-eighth Fife and Drum Corps.

SURGERY IN THE TWENTY-EIGHTH REGIMENT.

THOMAS CUSHING, M. D.

THERE was nothing peculiar in the surgery of this regiment to distinguish it from that of others. Although the number of regiments in the field during the Civil War was immense, the general features of the surgery in each were very much like those of all others, varied only by different circumstances in the midst of which different regiments found themselves.

Many aspersions have been cast on the character of medical officers in the volunteer regiments, and although these severe criticisms were in many instances warranted by the facts, yet the proportion of unworthy medical men in the service was probably not much if any greater than in civil life. It is true that in the service there is not the same kind of personal responsibility that confronts practitioners in civil life; and those who were disposed to be indolent could indulge their laziness with a degress of impunity. Recklessness and empiricism were more prevalent among young army surgeons than the same physicians would have ventured to indulge or practice among

their patients in private life; but aside from these, the attention which sick soldiers received was as careful and unremitting as under similar circumstance would have been bestowed on them in civil life.

Army practice brought medical men many useful lessons. At home their patients are surrounded by all the cares and attentions — many of them worse than useless — that anxious mothers and sisters can bestow. They are kept out of "drafts," deprived of the share of fresh air which is more necessary for them when they are in bed than at any other time, almost smothered in bed coverings, and crammed with delicacies which their appetites do not crave and which they often loathed. In the field they are surrounded by quite different circumstances. If in camp, they are sheltered by airy tents, or perhaps canvas covers to keep off the rain, and they are often fortunate if they have even straw to lie on; and on the march they are jolted along in ambulances. After a battle the wounded are sheltered by barns, stables, outhouses, corn cribs and even pig pens, or shielded from the sun's rays by temporary shelter of straw; yet they are found to make more rapid and better recoveries than those who are surrounded with more comforts and less fresh air.

After the battle of Antietam three wounded men at the Twelfth Corps hospital were quartered in a house, but two windows and a door to the apartment where they lay were kept open. Even then they were not making as good progress as those that lay out of doors. They were taken out and placed on a height in a tent, the sides of which were raised so as to allow the wind to sweep freely over them; and from that time a marked improvement was visible.

At the hospital — or depot for the wounded — twenty-two amputations were made, and twenty recovered; but at another, a mile distant, according to the report of an inspector, there were seventy cases of amputation, nineteen of which were already dead and the twentieth was about to die. The operations appeared to have been skilfully performed and the patients well cared for, but something in the sanitary conditions of the place led to their great mortality. The hospital was a large stone farmhouse, and probably the patients were quartered in it.

It was found that when troops were on the march the health of the men was much better than when they were in camp. This was especially true with regard to the bowel complaints that were prevalent during operations in Virginia; and the medical officers always expected the health of the men to improve when camp was broken and a march commenced. This was largely due to the fresh air which the men inhaled as they marched through the country and temporarily bivouacked or encamped at night and in part to the absence of microbes which rapidly accumulate in camp, notwithstanding the measures adopted to prevent such accumulation.

The medical officers of the Twenty-eighth were Dr. Helmer, surgeon; and Dr. R. S. Paine, assistant surgeon. The author of this article was appointed an additional assistant surgeon in the summer of 1862, and some time after the resignation of Dr. Helmer, Dr. West, of Michigan, was appointed surgeon. The active surgical duties devolved mostly on the assistant surgeons.

Dr. Paine was always faithful and efficient in the discharge of these duties, and his native good heartedness led him to kind acts toward the sick that greatly assuaged the sufferings of many a poor fellow who was languishing on his straw and thinking of home, where mother, sister or wife would minister to him.

Of the other assistant surgeon modesty forbids that anything should now be said.

In the Twenty-eighth, as in all the regiments in the service, there were many scamps. Some of these were adroit and cunning in feigning illness to avoid duty, but their lack of knowledge as to what symptoms indicated the conditions which they assumed, or the disease with which they pretended to be affected usually betrayed them sooner or later.

The surgeons were more willing to be imposed on than to send a sick man to duty; but when it became evident that a dead beat was seeking to shirk his duties, they sought to make him appear ridiculous in the eyes of his comrades rather than to inflict severe punishments.

One soldier for several days practiced ligaturing his leg for a time before surgeons' call and because of the swollen and congested condition of the limb he was excused from duty. After the case had continued for some days without improving or becoming worse, the doctor "smelt a rat," and insisted on examining the leg

nearer his body. When his trousers had been pulled far enough up the string was discovered, and the doctor cut it in the presence of the fellow's jeering and laughing comrades.

The same man once came to surgeons' call reeling and staggering and with one eye closed, declaring that he could not walk straight, and that if he opened both eyes he saw double. He was told that his symptoms portended speedy death, but that while life lasted he might as well make himself useful by going on duty instead of straying six miles from camp, as he had done on the previous day.

Another, a recruit that had been picked up in Dixie land, had an ingrowing toe nail. He had cut away the part of his shoe that covered it, so that it did not lame him, but he insisted on being excused from the fatigue duty in which the regiment was then engaged. One morning the doctors were called to his quarters, where they found him feigning lockjaw. So firmly was his mouth closed that his lips could not be parted to enable him to speak. The doctors pronounced it a bad case, and in his presence decided that men should be detailed to bring water from a stream near by (it was winter) and pour it on his head from a height of four feet, during a half hour, and then, if necessary, for half an hour longer; and if that did not succeed, the nape of his neck was to be cauterized with a red-hot iron. They concluded, however, before entering on this heroic treatment to try a certain medicine. Accordingly, they sent him a tumbler partly filled with water and directed that a teaspoonful should be given once in fifteen minutes. After sucking the second dose through his lips the titanic spasm suddenly relaxed, and he exclaimed, "I'm all right now." His comrades bored him about his lockjaw until he finally deserted.

Surgical operations in regiments were generally limited to accidents or to wounds received in minor actions. After general engagements the wounded were collected in corps or division hospitals or depots, whence the slightly wounded were soon sent to general hospitals, and those who had received serious injuries were operated on and treated at these depots, and as soon as practicable sent to nearby field hospitals prepared for their reception.

Regimental surgeons and assistant surgeons were detailed for service at these depots, and thence, as soon as practicable, were sent to join their regiments and resume their duties there. To this rule the medical staff of the Twenty-eighth was not an exception.

THE SIGNAL SERVICE.

By Captain W. W. Rowley, Milwaukee, Wis.

AT EACH succeeding reunion of the Twenty-eighth New York my wish grows stronger to be present, but there is something always to intervene to prevent my doing so, and this year is no exception to the others. At your request I send a short sketch of the Signal Corps as connected with the gallant Twenty-eighth.

Early in September, 1861, an order came to the regiment detailing two officers and four men, ordering them to report to the school of instruction for Signal duty at Darnestown, Md. Our regiment had just gone into camp near that place. Lieutenant Frank Wicker and myself were selected as the officers, and we, together with four as fine men as the regiment could furnish, reported to Captain L. F. Hepburn, who was to instruct us in the art of sending messages by flag and torch from one point to another. There were assembled at this school of instruction about twelve or fifteen officers with their respective complement of men. The men had been selected with great care for their physical, as well as mental ability, and it would be difficult to find a body of men of equal number more able or better equipped than they were. In fact they were so very clever that before a week had elapsed they all were ordered back to their regiments, for the reason they had learned the code of signals and could transmit and receive a message as well as any of the officers. This code was designed to be kept a profound secret confined to the officers only. So we on the start lost the flower of our corps, their places being filled by men not as competent.

Colonel Donnelly told me he would pick out four men and pour lead in their ears so that they could not rival the officers

I now see the mistake of sending the men back to the regiments, for no man of any intelligence could be associated with an officer without picking up the code of signals, and as these men were just as trusty and reliable as any of the officers, they could have been retained with entire safety. This camp of instruction, made up of bright young officers and men, remains in my memory one of the few bright spots of the War. After a few weeks of instruction a line of signal stations was established from Darnestown to Maryland Heights (Harper's Ferry). The intermediate stations being Poolsville and Point of Rocks. Two officers with four men being assigned to each station. Many of the Twenty-eighth will remember the "Chestnut-tree Station" on the McGruder farm near Darnestown, it was picturesque. The upper limbs sustained a platform for the man to wave his flag, while just underneath was the platform for the officer, who, with his glass, kept watch of the communicating station. These platforms were some forty or fifty feet above the ground, and were reached by rustic ladders.

This was the first line of signal stations established on the Potomac. Each station had a telescope trained upon the communicating station, and a man sat at the glass constantly, night and day, so that when the station called by waving its flag the man on watch would notify the officer who would receive the message. At night a torch was used in place of the flag.

The engagement at "Ball's Bluff" furnished the first messages of battle transmitted over this line.

When the army was on the march, each signal officer, with his two men, carried a complete equipment of glasses, flags and torch, so that at any point he could set up a station and open communication at once. At the battle of Kearnstown, near Winchester, Va., fought in the spring of 1862, this corps received its "first baptism of fire," and covered itself with glory, so as to receive commendation by a special order from General Shields, commanding.

You all remember how, on marching to and fro through the Shenandoah Valley, the signal squad could be seen way towards the front, frequently in advance, with its little flag flying.

At first it was a mystery to you all, but you soon learned to look upon it as a sign of security feeling that it was the "eye" of the army, keeping watch of the enemy. It is impossible, without spinning this paper out to tediousness, to enter into details and incidents. Suffice it to say, this particular corps was with you back and forth through the Snenandoah, over the ridge to Culpeper, Cedar Mountain, across the Rappahannock to Bull Run No. 2, across the Potomac to South Mountain and Antietam, with faithful devotion and untiring activity. Of the two officers from the Twenty-eighth the writer was sent with the "Banks'-expedition" to the Department of the Gulf, where he remained until his term of service expired.

The other, Lieutenant Wicker, followed to the same department, in connection with the Field Telegraph. Afterwards he went to Alaska in the interest of the Overland Telegraph to Russia. At the beginning of the War the signal corps was an innovation on army methods. It was an experiment; but it made itself so useful that before its close it became a regular organized department of the army of the United States.

THE POSTAL SERVICE IN THE ARMY.

By C. W. Boyce, Postmaster, Twenty-eighth N. Y.

THE mail service in the army was ably managed by the Post-office Department at Washington, and the soldiers were well supplied with mail facilities,—considering the fact that the regiments so often changed positions.

Early in the war the Government arranged that all mail for the Army of the Potomac should be addressed "Washington, D. C.," the Post-office Department there being constantly advised of the location of the several commands. The mail was assorted into pouches and forwarded direct to the several corps headquarters wherever they were stationed.

Each corps had a postmaster, whose duties were to distribute the mail to the several divisions and brigades. These

distributed it to the organizations in their commands. In special cases regiments or batteries, which had a man detailed for this work were allowed to send direct to the corps, thereby saving delay. In many regiments the Chaplain had charge of the mails, when an orderly would be sent to the brigade headquarters for it.

The Twenty-eighth New York had a regularly appointed postmaster. While at Albany a lad from Company D was appointed to this position. Whether he performed his duties satisfactorily or not is not for the present writer to say. The officers and men of the regiment always seemed satisfied, and he retained the position during the entire term. He was allowed a horse to ride; was exempted from that very irksome part of a soldier's life — guard duty; had much more freedom and a better knowledge of the general situation of military affairs than was enjoyed by other members of the regiment. Besides, this boy postmaster was like most nineteen year old boys, fond of excitement; and the rides about the country in the performance of his duties were often exciting and very interesting. Not infrequently he found that a good square meal at some farmhouse helped wonderfully well to appease a boy's hearty appetite that "hard tack" did not *entirely* satisfy. His office did not excuse him from active service as a soldier, and he participated in every action in which the regiment was engaged, either in the ranks with his company, or when mounted, acting as orderly to Colonels Donnelly and Brown. This was the case at Cedar Mountain, where he was the only one at with Colonel Donnelly when he received his death wound, and assisted him off that fatal field, his Orderly, Oscar Draper, having had his horse shot early in the action.

The duties of the postmaster required active and often very hard service. At other times, when the Corps' Headquarters were near, it was very light. The time of receiving the mail and going with it, varied according to the distance to be traveled. The postmaster's tent was usually situated at the head of Company D street; the receptacle for the mail was a large tin box, which hung from some convenient tree. At a given hour, which had been previously announced in each company street, the contents of this box were put in saddle bags and thrown over the faithful horse "Dolly" that carried the mail for so long a time. With a last call of "Letters! Letters!" for the benefit of someone who was sure to be late, the departure for the headquarters of the corps would be made. There it would be exchanged for the newly arrived mail from Washington, and the return ride made with all despatch. The arrival in camp was always greeted with welcome shouts, and the men crowded about the Post-office tent to see if they had been remembered by loved ones at home. The Orderly Sergeants came for the mail for their several companies and distributed it to the men. The quantity of mail the regiment received daily, varied. Usually about a bushel of letters and papers were received. Often, however, when the army was moving, and the mail could not be delivered daily, an accumulation of several days brought the bulk up to several times this amount. In cases of this kind the ambulance would be called into use to bring it to the camp.

At times the Corps' Headquarters were so far from camp that the return trip had to be made the succeeding day. This was the case at Culpeper Court House. The ride had to be made in a July sun to Little Washington, a distance of nearly thirty miles, returning each alternate day. The intervening country was not occupied by the army, and the enemy's cavalry and "guerrillas" were often on the road, but were always successfully eluded. If the boy had been intercepted, it would have been a race or capture, perhaps both. The adventure best remembered on this route was in being "called down" by General Pope for fast riding. It was an extremely hot day, and Dolly was sweating profusely, when the General appeared, occupying his *usual* "Headquarters," riding at the head of an immense calvacade of Staff and body guard, when he encountered this solitary post boy. All were compelled to halt while this trembling youth was interviewed as to his destination, business, passes, etc. These being answered to the satisfaction of the general, the following parting admonition was given the boy, as he was allowed to ride on: "If I ever catch you riding a horse like this again, I'll tie you down to his tail." The dignity of the important personage, who then filled the office of commander of the Army of Virginia, was not increased in the estimation of one of his subordinates, at least, by the interview.

The experiences were sometimes hazardous as well as comical. An incident of

this nature occurred when the regiment was in camp at Muddy Branch in the fall of 1861. The route to the headquarters was over a ford of the branch, usually about three feet deep. But it had been swelled by heavy rains for two days, and had overflowed its banks to double its usual depth. Weighed down with a heavy mail and a heavier overcoat which was wet through, the crossing was attempted at the usual fording place. The horse was instantly carried off her feet, and with mail and mail-bag, swiftly carried down to what seemed a watery grave. Heavy trees and floodwood were lodged against some obstructions found in the torrent of waters, just below the usual fording place, and the current carried the horse and rider against this with such force that the boy was knocked off his horse, and both went together under the swaying mass for a long distance, coming out below, the horse, freed from his load, swimming to one bank and some soldiers on the opposite side, near by, rescued his rider, nearly drowned.

Nothing more serious resulted than the wetting of the mail, which was laying strewn about Colonel Brown's tent for the next two days to be dried out before it could be again started. If any one at home thought there was delay in the receipt of letters from the regiment at that time, and never knew the cause, they have now the explanation.

When the regiment was at Front Royal in June, 1862, the ride had to be made back to Middletown; and, as the mail did not arrive there till dark, the distance to Front Royal of some twelve miles had to be made in the night, arriving at camp about midnight. Sentinels on the way would suddenly challenge from the darkness,—"Who goes there!" and to say that this boy was often simply "scared" at real and imaginary foe, would be to tell only *half* the truth. If his hair could have been seen in the pitchy darkness of that lonely road,—through woods a large part of the way,—it is believed it would have been discovered lifting his cap bodily from his head.

The old mail-box was allowed to ride in the headquarters wagon on marches, and its weight was often observed. But many a comrade's knapsack was lightened by having some of the heavier things carried on long marches in this box, unknown to the driver, for the box was marked "U. S. Mail," and the boy had the key.

The last service the postmaster of the Twenty-eighth New York ever did in his official line was to get the mail at Stafford Court-House and distribute it to the members present. Several companies were on detached service whose mail could not be delivered. He was compelled to carry it, expecting to reach them soon. Colonel Cook was riding "Dolly" and the boy was in the ranks carrying a gun. The companies were never again together at the front, as the four which were in the battle of Chancellorsville were taken prisoners, and when captured with his company, the post boy had the letters for the absent ones. These were carried safely to Libby Prison, then on around to Annapolis, and when Lockport was reached, were distributed to the men, thus closing an experience of two years' service that was full of hardships, deprivation and pleasure, but no regrets.

DETACHED SERVICE.

By J. BYRON LOVELL, Company C.

THIS subject, in connection with the historical record of the regiment, deserves brief mention. It seems to be an opinion among those ignorant of the facts, that a man on special duty, detached from his company and regiment, had a "soft snap," when, in fact, the reverse was the case. Any soldier, detailed from his command on any special duty in the Q. M., A. A. G., C. S. or P. O. departments, had to obey the orders given, and very often had duties to perform which properly belonged to those above him in rank. Many of these were arduous and repulsive: and, besides, this deprived him of the home-like life of his company. Unless by good fortune, he became attached to a mess composed of his unfortunate associates, he became an object of charity, depending upon surroundings for subsistence. With the exception of guard duty, he was subjected to all of the exposures in camp and field, and, as to dangers and suffering, he had his full share, being constantly at the front.

ISAAC SLY.

Private Company A, the First Man Killed by a Rebel Bullet in the Twenty-eighth Regiment.

By Geo F. Gould, Company C

THE Twenty-eighth Regiment New York Rifle Volunteers had been lying in camp for several days somewhere between Martinsburg and Winchester, Va., summer of 1861, and the ambitious heroes who composed that regiment were getting very tired of loafing. Nothing chafed the spirit of the boys — or we might call them troops — like a condition, however brief, of masterly inactivity. They refused to be comforted unless they were on the war path all the time. They disliked so much drilling and policing of camp, guard mounting and dress parades. Their ideal of a brave soldier life was to take a rebel battery every morning before breakfast, storm a line of breastworks to give them an appetite for dinner, and spend the afternoon charging with cold steel the serried columns of the foe, climbing over heaps of slain and wading around through seas of gore.

"Companies A and C have been detailed to help guard a forage train to-morrow," said Orderly Wadhams one evening. "We have got to light out early; so you want to be up 'n' dressed, with your cartridge boxes full 'n' a day's rations in your haversacks. Be sure your guns are in good order, for, likely as not, we'll have a skirmish before we get back." Members of the other companies watched the preparations with jealous eyes; envious because they were not detailed for the expedition instead of companies A and C.

"Say," said Sergeant Gould to his chums, Privates Woods and Holtzheimer, "had I not better write a letter home? Who knows but we will be dead as door nails by to-morrow night."

"The deuce," said Woods. "What's the use of having a funeral before there is any corpse? We have been through one skirmish and did not get hurt, and I have made up my mind there is no use getting into a stew over a thing that may happen and may not. Don't cross the river until you get to the bridge. If we are going to be killed we can't help it. So let us not fret our lives away." And Woods crammed a handful of hardtack and boiled beef into his haversack.

Woods' view of the matter was not without its effect upon Gould and Holzheimer. Indeed, it cannot be denied that there was a great deal of common sense in his homely philosophy. Sooner or later every soldier came gradually to adopt Woods' idea as the governing principle of his military career.

"I would not wonder if you are about right," said Gould as he sliced up some bacon to have it ready for an early breakfast. "You are better than medicine to keep a fellow from getting the blues."

In the morning Orderly-Sergeant Wadams came around and stirred the boys up an hour before reveille, as they were to start at daylight. The primary object of the expedition was forage for the animals, the supply of which had run short. Besides this, each man had a secondary purpose, and that was to gather in something on his own hook that would satisfy his longing for a change of diet. This was always the unwritten part of an order to "go foraging."

Daylight was just streaking over the camp when Company C, equipped in light marching order, leaving knapsacks behind, moved out to where the wagons were in line, ready for a start. Company A soon joined us there. The impatient mules were braying and flapping their ears, as if they understood that they were to be the chief beneficiaries of the raid. "Pile in boys," said the Orderly, and we clambered into the wagons.

The guards were permitted to ride until there were symptoms of danger.

Early in the war of the Rebellion the government furnished each regiment with wagon-master and drivers, experts in the business, but later on their places were filled by the soldiers; most of the wagons were dispensed with, and the soldiers carried on their back, tent, blanket and rations. Then the muleteers, bestriding the big "wheelers," cracked their long whips, addressed to the mules the usual words of exhortation, and the procession drew out upon the stony pike and took a brisk trot. Considerable foraging had already been done in the vicinity, and it

was expected the train would have to go out several miles in order to accomplish its object. The boys were in fine spirits and enjoyed the morning ride, albeit the jolting of the wagons gave them a thorough shaking up.

"I guess they forgot to put any springs in when they built these 'waggins,'" said Woods, as he shifted his position so that he might catch the bumps in a new place for awhile.

"Just thinking that way myself," replied Gould; "but all the same it beats traveling on the hoof all holler, and don't you forget it."

Three or four miles out from camp the train was halted while the officers in command made inquiries of a cadaverous native, who was sunning himself on the fence, and whose principal occupation seemed to be watching or guarding his property and chewing tobacco, and distributing the resultant liquid around in a promiscuous way.

"Good morning, stranger," said the quartermaster. "Have you any corn on your place?"

"Hain't got a dog-goned ear left," was the surly answer. "Some o' you-unses men wus out here yesterday 'n' tuk every bit I hed."

This may or may not have been true. Inquiries of this nature always developed the fact that it was a man's neighbors who had plenty of "corn;" he never had any himself.

"Thar's ole man Sanders," he continued; "he lives two looks and ye' right smack up from hyar. I'low ye'll git sum if ye go thar. He growed a power o' cawn this yeah. He sold a heap, but I reckon he's got a right smart lot left."

During this time Woods and Holzheimer, sent for that purpose, had been making a hasty examination of the outbuildings on the place. They reported that they could find nothing in the way of forage. If the man had any corn he had carefully concealed it.

The boys did not report that they had been in the garden and filled their haversacks with tender onions and a few radishes sandwiched between. Of course, the question was not asked them—consequently, "mum" was the word. Somewhat later the three chums could have made a report if required.

The train started on to pay a visit to "ole man Sanders."

"Say, Mr.," asked Lieutenant Warren, as we rode past; "is there any rebs around here?"

"There waz a few Confedrit critter men riden 'bout hyar this mawnin. Mebby ye'll run agin 'em afore night."

"How many of your boys are among them?"

"We-uns is all Union."

"Just as long as we are around, I suppose," said Warren.

About half mile further on those who were in the lead, rising to the crest of a hill, saw, or thought they saw, a few vagrant cavalrymen or guerrillas, probably the latter. The train was halted and dispositions were made to meet any emergency likely to arise. The main body was formed in advance; a line of skirmishers were deployed in front, and flankers were thrown out on either side. Thus protected, the mule drivers again cracked their whips and the column moved cautiously forward.

"Now keep your eyes skinned," said Sergeant Gould to Woods and Holtzheimer, as they trailed along through the woods and fields and over fences on one of the flanks. "If any of those rebs come dodging around here, let us try and have the first crack at them and get the start of the rest of the boys." Keenly alert, with rifles loaded and capped, they crept carefully along, poking their noses into every building. It was clear that there would not be anything in the nature of a surprise, if the whole line was as well taken care of as the particular point guarded by Gould, Woods and Holzheimer.

"It is some like huntin' squirrels, ain't it, George," says Crist., as they forced their way through a patch of briars. "Wall, yes," replied George: "but this appears to be more exciting. You know squirrels don't shoot back at a fellow."

In due time the Sanders plantation was reached. A thorough search showed that there was an abundance of corn on the place to load the wagons, and arrangements for a sudden transfer of the property were quickly made. A part of the force established a cordon of picket posts around the working party, covering all the avenues of approach with reserves at convenient points. Captain E. W. Cook of Company A, with a squad of men, among them private Isaac Sly, were stationed ahead on picket. The men were placed on each side of the road, behind the fence.

Distance from the reserve about quarter of a mile. Part of the reserve were allowed to rest at ease: while the other part stacked their arms, and entered briskly upon the work of confiscation. The part resting at ease were allowed to feast on some delicious cherries on trees to the left of the road. Lieutenant Warren was among the boys, and gave us permission, after consulting with the assistant-surgeon, who said: "Let them have all they want; the acid is just what they need." So Warren said: "Boys, climb up and help yourselves;" and the boys were not there many seconds before the cherry orchard looked as if captured by a flock of blackbirds, and Warren's orders were quickly obeyed. All done with but very little ceremony. The trees were loaded with fruit of the choicest kind. In about ten or fifteen minutes the boys were ordered down, to go and relieve those that were loading the corn, and allow them to fill up on cherries.

The first assault was made on a well filled corn house, one of a group of dilapidated outbuildings a short distance from the dwelling. Old man Sanders protested with profane vehemence, reinforced by the old woman and the entire family of children. The head of the family cursed and swore, and his wife and the big girls looked as if they wanted to do the same thing, as they wrung their hands, their eyes flashing fire, while the small fry stood around and sobbed with a vague idea that some dire calamity had befallen them.

The old Virginian declared that he was a Union man It was noticed that there were no young men around as there should be, according to the economy of nature, to preserve the balance of sex in so large a family. The officer in command asked him where all his sons were.

"Wall, I kaint tell yer zactly whar they is," was the reply. "They ain't to hum just now I low they've got a right to go away if they want ter."

The officer had been informed by some of the slaves that there were several representatives of the Sanders family in the rebel army.

The old man's avowal of loyalty was taken for what it was worth. That it was not rated at a high figure was well attested by the appearance of the plantation an hour later.

Meanwhile, the soldiers kept right along in the duty assigned them.

The corn was surrounded by wagons, and in scarcely more time than it takes to tell the story six or eight of the wagons were heaped with the contents.

The mules wagged their ears and brayed in anticipation of the supply of rations they would have when they got back to camp.

"Fo' de Lawd, boss," said an old darkey, who had been roosting on the fence watching the spoilers, "I nebber seed de crib empty so quick since I'se bawn. You-uns all is pow'rful smart, dat's shuah!"

All at once, crack! crack! crack! in quick succession, came the sound of Remington rifles, intermingled with sounds of lesser caliber, from the direction Captain Cook had taken a couple of hours before.

An attack had been made on our pickets about a quarter of a mile ahead of us. All was in commotion, the drums beat the long roll, and the bugle blew the assembly. "Fall in, Company C!" came the quick, low order from Orderly Wadams. It did not take but a few moments, and the reserve were in line of battle.

Then Gould, Woods and Holtzheimer were ordered to go forward and learn what the firing meant. They advanced cautiously, and soon found out that a squadron of cavalry or guerrillas had made a dash up the road, intending to surprise and capture the foragers, but were surprised themselves by running up against our pickets.

Captain Cook was on the alert, and opened a brisk fire upon them from both sides of the road, checking the rebels, who opened fire on our pickets.

The pickets kept up their fire and fell back toward the reserve, keeping well out on the flanks so as not to come direct toward the reserve.

Private Isaac Sly could be plainly seen out in a meadow, walking slowly back, loading his gun. Then he would kneel down on one knee and take deliberate aim and fire. He was in this act when a bullet struck him in the head. Poor Ike was the first man of the Twenty-eighth Regiment to be killed by a rebel bullet

The reserve coming up in sight, the rebels beat a hurried retreat Several of the rebels were hit, but managed to get away.

The killing of Sly cast a gloom over everybody connected with the raid. The boys carried him to where the wagons were. Many tears were shed for our comrade.

He was placed in the wagon or ambulance, and the column marched silently back to camp, arriving after dark. That night our camp, generally very lively, was still as death out of respect for our dead comrade. The Lockport boys, comrades to Sly, could be seen in squads talking about the good qualities of Ike as a brave soldier.

Next day was a day of mourning for our lost comrade. He was laid to rest in his everlasting sleeping abode. Not to be troubled with roll call, tattoo or reveille until Gabriel blows his horn for the "recall of all."

He was buried with military honors. After these were paid, the escort returned to camp with very sad hearts, each one wondering who would be the next. "A sad farewell and we left him alone in his glory." Poor Ike did his whole duty as a soldier and gave his life that his country might live. He believed in one country and one flag, and that "Old Glory."

OUR FIRST INVASION.

By Capt. John Waller, Company H.

THIRTY-FIVE years is a long time to look backward for vivid recollections on a life well advanced in its rounds of daily ups and downs, and yet there are portions of every life that was ever lived that will remain in niches of the memory as long as things hold together.

Of this class of events was the stupendous Civil War of 1861–5, that tried the stability of free government and the Union of States as never before, and put to the test of endurance a people, such as has rarely if ever been equaled in modern times.

The boys will all remember what a whirl of army equipments and warlike preparations greeted the Twenty-eighth Regiment New York Volunteers when it encamped in Washington in June, 1861, and how generally uncomfortable were all the surroundings. Mud, mules, army wagons were in the ascendant. When the order came to move to the front no one was sorry. All must remember the long detour by rail from the Capital to Hagerstown, and the march thence to Williamsport. We reached there at night. Other regiments were before us. Camp fires were burning in all directions.

Next day, July 7th, we were in line as soon as coffee and hard tack had been disposed of and headed for the Potomac. No bridge, no boats; water high, morning cool! Ah! it causes the cold chills to run down my back to think of it, even at this late day. We were not compelled to buffet the waves with sinewy arms as Cæsar did the Tiber, but waded across knee-deep or more, and thus invaded the "sacred soil" of "Old Virginia," marched thence to Martinsburg, an important station on the B. & O. Railroad, where we found something of the dreadful destruction of war in the wrecks of thirty or forty locomotives, etc.

July 15th, Bunker Hill was reached. The rebels had been in possession here, but fell back as the Union army advanced, after a slight skirmish, in which but little damage was sustained on either side. On the 17th proceeded to Charlestown, twelve miles distant, remaining there till the 21st, when orders came to go to Harper's Ferry, a point of great importance. Encamped there on high ground. Here, also, were very marked evidences of what war means. The large government armory buildings had been utterly ruined. This place possessed much interest for Union soldiers as the scene of the John Brown tragedy; and there were not many points about it not interviewed by them during the seven days we remained there. Indeed, if there were any places inaccessible to Union soldiers about the time referred to, they were never heard of.

From Harper's Ferry we went to Knoxville, again fording the Potomac; thence to Berlin, Md., where we were without tents—our wagons having been detained.

On August 2d, an incursion was made into Virginia for the purpose of capturing a squad of rebel cavalry, but they got away. In crossing the river one of the boats was swamped, leaving several men up to their waists in water. Half dozen or so found temporary refuge on a big rock, and demanded of those wading ashore to "advance and give the countersign!"

For several weeks the Twenty-eighth Regiment did valuable service on picket duty on the Potomac, where constant effort was being made to keep up communications between Washington and Maryland by men who had taken refuge in Virginia or lived there, and were fully in sympathy with the secession movement, with those less pronounced, but fully identified with the movement, remaining within the Union lines. Efforts were unceasingly and persistently made to obtain information as to measures the government would probably adopt, as well as keep posted in regard to the anti-war feeling in Baltimore and elsewhere. It therefore required constant alertness and untiring vigilance to successfully guard the many points of communication; and the Twenty-eighth was selected for this very responsible duty until the advance up the Shenandoah Valley.

Above are a few recollections of earlier events that may be interesting to the old "boys."

CAPTURE AT POINT OF ROCKS, VA.

From the Diary of Sergeant W. L. HICKS, Company F.

Contributed by C. B. GILLAM, Sergeant-Major.

JULY 17, 1861, left Bunker Hill before daylight; passed through Smithfield, which was deserted by all able-bodied men; lay in ambush in a piece of wood till near 4 P. M.; again formed line; continued our march to Charlestown, and went into camp about three-quarters of a mile south from the spot where John Brown suffered the extreme penalty of Virginia law. Twelve miles from Bunker Hill to Charlestown.

July 21, 1861, at 5 o'clock A. M., struck tents, marched 7 miles and went into camp on Bolivar Hights. The rebels had mounted a battery of four guns, rifled 32's, but had spiked and left their guns. Captain Doubleday removed the spikes, and with very little trouble got them in working order. After we had been in camp only one day it was reported that immediately after leaving Charlestown, a body of rebel cavalry came and occupied the place. A detachment under the command of Colonel Donnelly was sent to ascertain their position and strength. This rumor proved untrue. The only trophy of the expedition was a rebel captain and four bottles of blackberry brandy. While encamped here, General N. P. Banks superseded General Patterson. The disastrous battle of Bull Run had been fought the day we marched to Bolivar Hights. The 25th our tents were struck, baggage packed and sent over the river. We were left on the Hights without covering and almost without food.

July 28th, left Bolivar Hights: marched through Harper's Ferry; forded the Potomac; marched through Sandy Hook, and went into camp near Weaverton.

July 29, 1861, in the afternoon struck tents and moved down the river a few miles, and went into camp near Berlin, on the Baltimore & Ohio Railroad.

While encamped here the regiment was mostly engaged in picket duty, being stationed by companies along the river for some 10 or 12 miles above and below Berlin and "Point of Rocks." About the 1st of August word was brought to the regiment that a small body of rebels was quartered at Lovettsville, a village across and about five miles from the river. A detachment of about 100 men, under command of Lieutenant-Colonel Brown, crossed the river in the night and marched in the vicinity of the town, and halted to await daylight. They halted near the bivouac of the rebels, but they had learned something of the expedition and had left. They had commenced preparations for breakfast, but left everything, even the feed for their horses behind them. Awhile after sunrise some women came loaded with provisions, that had been ordered the night before for a good breakfast. The ladies were much surprised when they found the change in parties, which they did not till they were in the midst of them. They manifested considerable delight at the change, and invited the whole party to the village. In the course of the forenoon the village was visited, and the men most hospitably entertained. Not a reb was to be found. The party returned to camp the next day.

Two companies, "A" and "E," were stationed at the "Point of Rocks." When the two companies above mentioned marched into the village a party of rebel cavalry left it, crossed the river and took up their quarters in a tollhouse and vicinity, and seemed inclined to watch the progress of affairs. August 9, 1861, Lieutenant-Colonel Brown, with a detachment consisting of Company "B," Captain Bush, and Company "F," Captain Fenn, crossed the river at Berlin in the evening, and during the night marched down the river on the Virginia side to opposite "Point of Rocks," for the purpose of surprising and capturing the party at the toll-house. The colonel had informed Captain Cook of his purpose, that Cook might render assistance if required. The first intimation Captain Cook had of the presence of Colonel Brown was a little after daylight, a volley of musketry, quickly succeeded by another, was heard from across the river, followed by a few scattering shots, and all was still. The surprise was complete, but owing to the dimness of the light and proximity to timber some of the rebels escaped. Ten were captured, one was killed. Twenty-one splendid horses and the arms and accoutrements fell into the hands of the party as trophies. Captain FitzGerald, Company "E," was sent across the river to demolish and burn the stables and huts that the rebels had erected.

August 19th, the pickets along the river were all called in and the regiment was once more together.

CAPTURE OF A COMPANY OF ASHBY'S CAVALRY AT HUDSON'S CORNERS, NEAR COLUMBIA FURNACE, VA.

By Major T. FitzGerald.

In making up the history of the war of the rebellion many incidents were lost sight of, which, while not of importance in determining the final result, and which, owing to the number of such, necessarily received but casual mention, or no mention at all, yet illustrate that go-ahead-and-do-something spirit—that spirit of adventure which pervaded the rank and file of our armies, and which became manifest whenever an opportunity presented itself, the parties engaged acting without orders, and "on their own hook," so to speak; and it was this spirit which made our forces as a rule ever ready to endure with cheerfulness the heavier labors of a campaign: the long and toilsome marches by day and by night, through heat and cold; ever ready to meet the enemy in skirmish or battle, ever ready for whatever the exigences of the service seemed to demand, only so that something might be accomplished or seem to be in the way of accomplishment, and which brought about the final downfall of as courageous, energetic and determined a foe as the annals of warfare, ancient or modern, can show.

A detailed account of such minor and outside affairs naturally pertains to the records of individuals, companies or regiments, and are of interest more especially to those, and to the friends of those, who were participants.

An account of the following little affair may very properly find a place in the records of the service of the Twenty-eighth New York, and the credit, whatever it may be, should of right go principally to that regiment.

As commanding officer of Company E, at that time, and as one of the participants, I will endeavor to give the facts and correct some errors that appear in connection with the accounts of this affair as they appear in the published records

It was on or about April 12, 1862, while the regiment was near Woodstock, Va., that I received orders to proceed with my company to Columbia Furnace for outpost duty.

Columbia Furnace was on Stony Creek some eight miles from the main pike through the Shenandoah Valley and on a general parallel line. It was the principal road by which a movement might be made around our right, and it was necessary to guard it to prevent or give notice of such action on the part of the enemy.

The furnace, the store, and, in fact, the principal part of this hamlet, was owned by a Mr. Wisler, a Canadian, who had bought the property several years before.

and who carried on quite an extensive business in mining and reducing the iron ore found in the neighboring mountain range.

He was not a citizen of the United States, and was not therefore liable to military duty, but he was known as a man of Union sentiments, and himself and family, especially his two sons, Frank and John, young men of about twenty and twenty-two years, were regarded by their rebellious neighbors with suspicion, and were under constant surveillance.

The family gave our men a kindly welcome, and the officers were invited to partake of the hospitalities of their home, which most of them did. The men were quartered in the lofts of the barns, while the horses of the cavalry occupied the furnace.

The various roads were picketed, and quiet reigned generally. The rebel cavalry were about, and occasional shots were exchanged between them and our pickets, but without especial results. Two men of Company E captured one of them, and that was about all we had to show for our work until the night of the 15th. On that day two men, who lived some miles up the valley, came in and gave information that a company of Ashby's cavalry were stationed at Hudson's Corners, or the cross-roads, as they called it, about eight miles up, and opposite to and some seven miles from Mount Jackson, where General Jackson had his headquarters. They told us they knew a mountain road leading to the corners, which was not picketed by Ashby's men, and that if we were agreeable, they would pilot us over that road, and that we could surprise and capture them.

Mr. Wisler assured us that our proposed guides were entirely trustworthy; that they knew the roads well, and that we might implicitly rely upon their integrity and their capacity to fulfill their promises.

This was a tempting opportunity for an adventure, but there were obstacles. We were there for a specific purpose, and that purpose was to guard our right, and not to go off on a night hunt for Ashby's men whom we might or might not find.

If all went well, all would be well, probably, but if mishap befel us or those we left behind from any unexpected movement on the part of the enemy, the prospects of a court martial were extremely flattering and not especially inviting.

A consultation was held by the officers, some favoring and some opposing, and I think I can truthfully say that but for the earnest and persistent arguments and appeals of Lieutenant Padelford and myself no action would have been taken.

However, it was finally decided that the attempt be made, all acquiescing with the exception of Captain Eisenbisen of the Forty-sixth Pennsylvania, who said he would be — something — if he took his men out on such a — something — wild goose chase, or words to that effect.

Our force then consisted of Company E, Twenty-eighth New York, Companies E and F of the Fifth Connecticut, Captain Eisenbisen's Company of the Forty-sixth Pennsylvania, and a squadron of the Washton and Ringold cavalry, commanded by Captain A. J. Greenfield.

Nothing was said to the men, and at the usual hour taps were sounded and all was still. About eleven o'clock such of the men as we selected were quietly aroused and formed in line. Those left in charge at the furnace were cautioned to be extremely vigilant, and we started out. After going a short distance, we took a road to the right, which soon brought us on to the mountain road leading to the corners.

The night was dark, the roads not very passable and the band didn't play. We had a ten-mile march ahead of us, and a prospect of a scrimmage at the end of it. On the whole it was somewhat interesting.

Silently we proceeded on our way. It was a quiet night, and scarce a sound was heard except the occasional barking of a dog.

After proceeding several miles a halt was made, and I took Lieutenant Padelford and a squad of selected men and went ahead with one of the guides, thinking we might the more quietly surprise and capture the picket if any had been posted on this road. We were to halt at a certain point in the woods about half a mile from the corners, and await the coming of the rest of the force.

Our aim was to make the dash about or a little before sunrise, and before the men were fully astir. We were anxious to make the capture complete, for the reason that Jackson's army was but seven miles away and, more than that, nearer our main force than we were.

The dawn was breaking when I halted at the point indicated, and we congratulated ourselves upon the good time we had made and expected to be soon joined by

those behind. In this we were disappointed. After waiting until it was fully light, I determined to ride back (I was mounted for this trip) to meet and hurry them along. After riding a short distance I met a native making his way through the wood in the direction of the corners. He seemed somewhat surprised at meeting a blue coat in that place and at that time in the morning. However, we exchanged salutations, and at my request he accompanied me back to the squad, where he remained for the time being. I then turned again, and shortly after met our men coming up. It seems that through some mistake of the guide they had got off the right road and had lost considerable time.

It was now sunrise, and Captain Greenfield suggested that we forego the attack and return. I demurred strongly and insisted that we proceed. This was finally agreed to, and we moved forward as rapidly as possible. When we finally came to a halt at the edge of the timber we found ourselves at the top of a slight rise of ground, probably 150 yards from the churches, standing on opposite corners, in which the rebs were quartered. Some were still in quarters; others were moving about attending to their horses, etc., etc., little thinking that they were so soon to make a forced march down the valley.

The halt was but for a moment. A quiet command of attention, ready, and then, forward, charge! and down the grade the boys went, howling like a legion of Comanches. If that Company of Virginia cavalry didn't think a brigade, at least, of Banks' army were down upon them that sunny spring morning it was because they had little conception of sound.

In a few brief moments it was over and done with. A rattle of musketry; a skurrying of some to the fields and brush, and their pursuit and capture; the quiet surrender of others; the hurried assembling of the men and the prisoners; the formation into line, and we were ready for our return trip.

The first to enter the nearest church were little Pat Sennett, of Company E, and myself, Pat calling at the top of his voice on those in the church to surrender. The lieutenant commanding came forward and, handing me his sword, asked by what road we came. When I informed him, he said he had told the captain that if he didn't picket that road we would be over there some morning, and, further, that he would be entirely satisfied if he, the captain, was only there then. His diction was to a considerable degree more forcible and direct than I have given it, but its general tenor was the same.

The surprise was complete, and the entire company, with possibly one exception, were captured, and this without the loss of a man. We secured about 60 men, including three officers, and about the same number of horses, and the arms and equipment mostly.

The company wagon, with its contents, we failed to bring in. We could not determine what horses they had used, and those we attached to the wagon became unmanageable and plunged off the road into the field, where the wagon sunk halfway to the hubs in the soft ground.

There we were compelled to leave it, after piling in what combustibles we could find and firing it. The company were mostly native Virginians, who furnished their own horses and arms. They were well uniformed, and armed with sabers, Colt's revolvers, Sharp's and Enfield rifles.

The return march was made in good time, and we reached the "Furnace" tired, but well satisfied with the success of the tramp.

There was some little surprise when we learned from the newspapers a few days afterward that Captain Eisenbisen with his company of the Forty-sixth Pennsylvania had made this capture. His company had been detailed to escort the prisoners to headquarters and the captain was probably too modest to refuse to accept the credit.

The Reb. Rec., vol. 12, pt. 1, page 427, in the record of events of the Cavalry Brigade says: "On the 15th inst. this squadron (First Squadron Pennsylvania Cavalry) under command of Junior Captain Greenfield, assisted by detachments from the Fourteenth Indiana, Fifth Connecticut, Twenty-eighth New York and Forty-sixth Pennsylvania made a dash upon a company of the enemy's cavalry, quartered in a church near Columbia Furnace, and succeeded in capturing the entire force of three officers and about fifty men, with all their horses, arms and baggage." It will be noted that there were no Fourteenth Indiana, or Forty-sixth Pennsylvania men present, nor was it very near Columbia Furnace.

General Banks' report reads:

WOODSTOCK, April 16, 1862, 7 P. M.

An entire company, more than 60 men, and horses were captured this morning at Columbia Furnace, about seven miles from Mount Jackson, by our cavalry and infantry. The capture includes all the officers but the captain. They will be sent to Baltimore to-morrow.

N. P. BANKS,
Major-General Commanding.

HON. E. M. STANTON,
Secretary of War.

More nearly correct is the report in Allan's "Jackson's Valley Campaign," page 61. This is Confederate authority, and is as follows: "A company of Ashby's cavalry on outpost duty between Mount Jackson and Columbia Furnace was surprised by the advance and captured This was Captain Harper's company of cavalry. They were captured by four companies of Donnelly's Brigade in conjunction with the Ringold and Washington cavalry.

OUR FLAG AT CEDAR MOUNTAIN.

By WM. LEWIS, Color Bearer, Twenty-eighth N. Y. Volunteers, Oklahoma City, Ok. Ter.

I have thought each and every year since our discharge at Lockport, now when the next reunion time comes round I will be present; but the distance is too great for me, more than 1,000 miles separates me from my old stamping ground and the place where the reunion is held. However, though great the distance you can rest assured my heart is with you. Physically, I am not the same man I was at the time when I used to step three paces in front of the line with the old flag. I am now 60 years old and broken in health, and still were I one of your number am inclined to think you might rely on me as "one of the boys" again. We, Western people, when we want to do something extraordinary, talk about "painting the town red," and if I were there you might count on my assistance. During our campaigns in the Valley of Virginia, when we were under the command of Major-General John Pope, headquarters in the saddle, it became my lot to be color-bearer of the regiment, a very pleasant position on dress parade or in camp, but when on the battlefield it was a horse of another color. For instance, when those bullets began to fly past your ears, like so many lightning bugs on a summer's evening, or when those "comets" (or shells) came flying over our heads — rather lively screaming, "Whar is yeh? Whar is yeh?" and one occasionally dropping among us, singing, here "I find you!" Well, I have seen things more pleasing! I could fill a volume referring to army episodes and incidents, but time and space forbid. I will refer to one very important event that occurred in the history of the Twenty-eighth New York at the Battle of Cedar Mountain, near Culpeper Court-House. We had been lying in the woods all night, and in the morning of the 9th of August, 1862, first we were covering a battery, then we were ordered out in the field to form line of battle. Those shells were singing their same old song over head and dropping around us, when I heard the clear, ringing voice of Col. Brown command — forward! I stepped three paces in front, to my place, standing nearly in front of Company D, when I heard a familiar voice calling my name. It was Pat Geary, addressing me (as brave a boy as ever wore a soldier's uniform), saying, "Serg't, and how wud yez loike to be back to Medina, instid of out here wid those colors now?" But I had no time to reply, and Medina was the last place I was thinking of at that time. Things were looking rather squally about then, rather indicating that somebody was liable to be hurt. We pushed on through the field, and a piece of timber — to the edge of a large wheatfield, wheat having been cut and standing in shocks (where were the shocks when we got through?) The enemy were in force on the other side of the field, we were satisfied, but as we gazed over the quietude of that wheatfield, not a thing could be seen stirring. What mind could think or conjecture at this time that that quiet field should be the scene of such strife and struggle as was enacted during that sultry afternoon, the mercury ranging at that time from 100° to 109° in the shade. After waiting a short time we were ordered to charge the enemy in the

woods on the other side of the field. We hardly struck the first edge of the wheat-field till we were made aware that the enemy were there in full force. Oh, how the bullets flew around and about us, but our boys pushed on at a double-quick across the field. Now, you will excuse an old soldier, who has a spark of fun in his make up, if he stops here and tells a joke. Ordinarily people would say this was no place for fun. Comrades falling all around us, both dead and wounded; but even under such circumstances funny things occur, which remain in memory, causing laughter years afterwards. We had a fellow in our company named Ziba Roberts, six feet tall, and broad according. A soldier that could stand behind him was pretty safe from rebel bullets. As we were charging across that field under an extremely heavy fire from the enemy, all standing as close to the ground as possible, I must confess, Ziba calls out, "By gorry, boys, I feel too tall to-day." But Ziba was an excellent soldier, and never known to shirk his duty. We went on, drove the rebels from their hiding place and through the woods. We re-formed and went back through them again, and then our trouble began; the rebs had swung around in our rear, and it seemed next to the impossible to recross that field. At this time I had two out of the eight corporals that were detailed to guard my left. Oscar Bayne was one, the other, I can't recall his name, he was from Company H. I learned afterwards he died at the hospital from wounds received at Cedar Mountain, and I understand that Comrade Bayne has heard his last roll-call and gone to a better land to join comrades gone on before.

Well, I succeeded in getting two-thirds of the way back across that field when I was compelled to drop from the wounds I had received some time before. I could struggle on no further. I turned the colors over to that corporal of Company H, and the last I saw of him he was within a few yards of the woods that we left when we made our first charge. But some thing came between myself and him, and I could not say whether he reached the woods or not That is the last I saw of our flag. I laid there on that field two nights and one day before I could get off and was gone from my regiment three months before my leg could travel. Now, comrades, I have already made this letter too long, and I have only one parting injunction to give you, always revere the old flag. Other emblems has our nation, but none of them have waded through the seas of blood the flag has. Educate your children to love and revere it. Tell them of the dear comrades we have buried on many a battlefield, who gave their lives in defense of it. Teach them in the words of the venerable John A. Dix, who gave the order, "If any man attempt to pull down the American Flag shoot him on the spot." Teach them to love this great country of ours that you gave the best years of your life to defend and save.

Long may it wave
"Over the land of the free
And the home of the brave."

CEDAR MOUNTAIN REVISITED IN 1892.

Sweet grasses clothe the valley where they fell;
Of that dark time Nature has naught to tell;
The tender flowers nod where breathed their last
A thousand soldiers in the bloody past.

You would not dream that once this tranquil spot
Had felt the burning hail of rifle shot;
Or heard the screaming of the deadly shell,
Or the wild triumph of the Rebel yell.

Hark! Is not that the marshalling of men?
Does not a war-like bugle wake the glen?
Is not the trampling of ten thousand feet
Heard, keeping rhythm to the drummer's beat?

No; not an infant in its mother's arms
Breathes freer than this scene from war alarms;
The record of that awful day is writ
In human hearts. Here is no trace of it.

It should be haunted. Phantom host should rise
And cloud with battle-smoke the smiling skies;
The clash of meeting bayonets we should hear;
And booming cannon shock the listening ear.

We stand in awe and list with bated breath
To catch some echo of their tragic death.
It does not seem that time could banish quite
The pain, the horror, or the dread affright.

But earth is not in sympathy with war;
How speedily she covers every scar!
Is not the screen she waves o'er graves forgot
A mute denial of the battle fought?

BATTLE FLAG OF THE TWENTY-EIGHTH NEW YORK.

THE STORY OF OUR FLAG.

HOW IT WAS RESTORED TO THE REGIMENT AFTER A SCORE OF YEARS.

By C. W. Boyce.

THE torn and tattered flag, pictured at the head of this page, is the idol of the surviving veterans of the Twenty-eighth Regiment New York Volunteers. It has such a remarkable record, and stands so unique as the bond of union between hundreds of Virginians from the lovely Shenandoah Valley, and citizens as well as veterans of Western New York, that a sketch of it is given here, as no history of the Twenty-eighth Regiment would be complete without it. Would it could speak for itself, and tell of its years of absence from the regiment, and the strange manner of its return, and tell of the many hearts which it was the means of drawing together in a beautiful bond of friendship that only death can sever.

It is not the purpose of this sketch to give the history of this flag previous to Cedar Mountain, as it was carried at the head of the regiment during the many marches the first year of the War. On drills, reviews, parades, skirmishes, and in the smoke of battle the men followed it, guarding it with great care, learning to love it as the emblem of that Union for which they fought. But not until the eventful 9th of August, at Cedar Mountain, when they saw its silken folds for the last time for many years, did they really appreciate how dear the old flag was.

The regiment, occupying its position in the First Brigade of the First Division of the Twelfth Corps, moved forward out of the woods at "double quick," across the

wheatfield, on its immortal charge, proudly following this flag borne by Color-Sergeant William Lewis of Company D, surrounded by the corporals composing the color guard.

As stated in the history, the little brigade was overpowered by thrice its force, and under fire from front, flank, and rear, "melted away like snow placed in a July sun." Sergeant Lewis was wounded and fell on the field, giving the flag to one of the color guard, who grasped it, with the hope of carrying it back into the Union lines; but he, too, fell, with scarcely a dozen men unharmed around him. Other members of the color guard tried to save the flag, but in vain. All were either prisoners, or went down in that awful fire of death that Stonewall Jackson's brigade delivered as they swung around the flank and captured the few who remained.

The last member of the color guard was wounded, and, cut off from all hope of escape, tore the flag from the staff which had been twice shot in two, and tried to conceal it under his coat, in his manly effort to save it, but it was discovered and taken from him by a member of the Fifth Virginia Regiment — some of their members say by Sergeant Peter Bell; others give to J. M. McManoway, of Augusta county, Va., the credit of first capturing the flag.

The night after the battle, as the prisoners were being taken to the rear, while waiting at Orange Court-House for the cars to carry them to Richmond, the Twenty-eighth flag was discovered among other trophies of the battle. One of the men of the regiment secretly cut out a small piece and carried it with him during all the months of his imprisonment in Libby Prison. His motive was simply to secure a memento of the old flag, little thinking that this missing piece would be the means of identifying it many years after the War was ended. But such proved to be the case.

On his return, having been paroled and exchanged, he gave the relic to Colonel Brown. For twenty years the colonel treasured it as all that was left to us of our colors which had been "lost but not disgraced" at Cedar Mountain. In 1882, while visiting the flag-room in the War Department, at Washington, D. C., where the flags were stored, in a collection of recaptured Union colors, which had been found in Richmond when the city was taken in 1865, he discovered one that looked singularly familiar to him. Upon investigation he found it to be indeed the old flag, lost so long but found at last, and identified beyond a doubt by the piece which he had kept all these years

He at once wrote to the Secretary of War in behalf of the surviving members, asking that the flag be restored to the regiment. The request was granted, and by order of Adjutant-General Drum it was turned over to Colonel Brown.

A special meeting of the members of the regiment was called to make arrangements for the formal return of the flag in a manner fitting the interesting event. It was learned that Stonewall Jackson's brigade were the Confederate forces opposed to us at Cedar Mountain, and the Fifth Virginia, of that brigade, was the regiment that came in on the flank and rear and captured the colors. It was thought that the Virginians might be induced to unite with the regiment in the ceremonies of the return of the flag, and to be the guests of the Twenty-eighth for the occasion, to meet as brothers and friends, when they had only met before as enemies in battle. Nothing of the kind had ever been attempted. A correspondence was opened, and it was found that they heartily reciprocated the sentiment and the invitation was accepted in the same good faith in which it was given.

On May 21, 1883, at Niagara Falls, 153 Virginians, from the Shenandoah Valley, responded to the invitation; eighty-three of the number being veterans of the Fifth Virginia. They were all noble types of the Confederate soldier, true gentlemen in every respect. They were quartered as the guests of the regiment at the International Hotel, and despite of the severe rain which continued during their visit, all seemed to enjoy the occasion.

Nothing more impressive can be imagined than the exercises attendant on the return of the flag, which were held on May 22d, in the pavilion at Prospect Park.

Major J. W. Newton, of Staunton, Virginia, dressed in the full uniform of an officer of the late Confederate Army, on behalf of his regiment, returned the flag with cordial words, saying:

"In the name of the Fifth Virginia Infantry, I now present this flag to its honored and worthy owners, and as an eye-witness at the time of its capture, in justice to you I delight to say that, losing it under the circumstances you did, reflects no discredit on you. * * * Take it, my valiant friends, and treasure

it as the emblem of a reunited country, signifying the return of the affections and good-will of brave men who met in strife on the field of battle."

Colonel Brown received the flag on behalf of the Association.

At the sight of the flag which Colonel Brown and Major Newton then held up to view, the entire audience arose to their feet amid deafening shouts and cheers. Many veterans shed tears of joy at the sight of the torn and shredded remnants of their once beautiful banner

Colonel Bowen, at the time of the battle of Cedar Mountain captain of Company D, who led his company in this charge and was taken prisoner, at this juncture could not restrain the impulses of his earnest nature, and, stepping forward with an apology for interrupting the exercises, asked, as the representative of Company D — the color company — that he be allowed to kiss the flag, which he did with great feeling. This touching incident was received with renewed cheers.

It was not many months before an invitation was received from the Virginians for a return visit to the lovely Shenandoah Valley.

The invitation was accepted, and the visit was made on the return of the anniversary of the Twenty-eighth's reunion, May 22, 1884. One hundred comrades, with as many more, consisting of their wives and friends, made the journey by way of Baltimore, Harper's Ferry, and Winchester to Staunton. From Baltimore on, the route was one that long ago was familiar to the Twenty-eighth veterans. At Harper's Ferry they were met by the booming of cannon, this time, however, in friendly greeting, instead of hostile defiance. At Woodstock and Harrisonburg addresses of welcome were made and responses given by members of the party. Staunton, the objective point, was reached on the evening of the 21st, the citizens exhibiting their kind feelings by acts of open-handed hospitality, for which they are justly famed. Not only their hearts, but their homes were thrown open to the Northern visitors, and with such a warmth of feeling that all were welcomed as old friends.

On the 22d the public exercises were held in the large opera house at Staunton, after a march through the streets, which were profusely decorated with flags and bunting. Everywhere was displayed the sign:

"Welcome, Twenty-eighth, to our hearts and homes."

The meeting was one of intense interest to all participants. Speeches of hearty welcome were made, and responses given, that were full of patriotic eloquence and fervor, and could not fail to bring the citizens of Virginia and New York into a more cordial feeling of friendship and good will.

The visitors, accompanied by many of their hosts, then journeyed to Lexington, where the tomb of General Lee was decorated with flowers by Colonel Brown in behalf of the Twenty-eighth New York Regiment.

AN EPISODE FROM THE BATTLEFIELD OF CEDAR MOUNTAIN, AND THE NIGHT SUBSEQUENT TO THE BATTLE.

By F. A. Camann, Company K.

OVER that wheat-field we sped in double quick pace upon the enemy lying in ambush behind the rail fence on the edge of the opposite woods. The missiles that were sent upon us did us but little harm, as but now and then a comrade from our closed column sank wounded to the ground. The arms of the enemy either did not carry far enough or their aim was taken too low. Whizzing, the bullets turned up the ground before our feet and excited the dust.

Our first tendered volley acted devastatingly upon the enemy, and what was spared by the bullet had to feel cold steel. Getting over the rail fence the fleeing remainder was pursued through the woods. Here a joint moving forward came to an end, as the woods prevented such a pursuit, and most of the combatants had to be guided in their action by their own judgment.

The majority of our comrades charged forward without having reloaded their rifles, but the writer of this sketch considered it advisable to have his arms ready for further use. While loading I noticed a

little to my left the fence being torn down and shifted toward there in order to reach the woods. Trying to reobtain the direction of the charging comrades of my company, I turned now to the right, and, advancing in right oblique tendency, I observed an approaching column moving along the edge of the woods and coming from our right flank, which at first sight I considered to be reinforcements for us. But at second thought this could hardly be possible, when my attention was called to several differently-shaped flags, which convinced me that the enemy had moved a column in our rear and we were cut off from our reserves. This column's point of view, though, were apparently more the grounds over which we had made our charges than the dismembered combatants in the woods, for I did not observe that we were molested in our rear.

I failed to meet my company, but struck the regimental colors, carried by the color-bearer, and accompanied by two or three non-commissioned officers, as color-guards. Isolated members of our regiment at my right and left were pressing forward. In charging forward the color bearer turned his face backward and summoned for a more speedy pushing forward, hence I concluded that comrades of my regiment were still advancing in my rear. As my company's position in the line of battle was left of the regimental colors, I supposed I had moved too far to the right and turned more to the left while the colors moved on toward the right. That was the last I saw of our regimental flag.

Without meeting much hinderance, covering myself where possible and necessary, I moved on. The woods in front of me were thinned, there being more shrubs than trees, while right and left large trees were predominating. Reaching the other edge of the woods, and trying to enter the excavated road, I was compelled to jump over the slain, so thickly were they lying there. On the other side of the road I mounted the bank and stood not far from the declivity of a hill, at the foot of which a valley dilated. In front of me, at about the distance of a gunshot, the fleeing enemy could be observed. It seemed to be the remainder of a regiment, and may have numbered about seventy-five men. If I am not mistaken, there was an officer mounted on horseback and a few officers on foot, in vain trying to bring the body to a halt. Once more I made use of my rifle, and, as I put it down to reload, heard behind me across the road a familiar voice (I think it was that of comrade Pecktill of my company) saying that orders had been given to fall back, as we had been cut off by the enemy, which, of course, I knew since I entered the woods.

After loading my rifle I turned about, but saw nobody; am therefore not able to tell who called me. In the woods there were but few of our men who tried to cut their way through, and of our opponents there were also but few. One I met. We both made ready to fire at the same time, but my opponent let down his gun, making an attempt to get out of my reach. Remembering that my rifle was not capped, I tried to do so now, but could not succeed quick enough, as my cap-box was deranged. My opponent seeing my lingering, raised his gun, aimed at me and fired. It was a skip for dear life I made, and the bullet struck behind me against a shrub. Without meeting another adventure I got through the woods into the open wheatfield. But I was exhausted My chest panted, and my breath threatened to give out. So I dragged myself up to a stack of sheaves, behind which I dropped down.

After but a short while someone stepped up and demanded my surrender. Getting up, I found that I was not his only prisoner. This fatality I had to share with four others. One was a first lieutenant from the Fifth Connecticut, who had one of his shoulder-straps (I think it was the left) shot off. Another was from the Second Massachusetts; the third from the Forty-ninth Pennsylvania; but from what regiment the fourth was I am unable to say. Our captor could not manage to get us in front of him, so we all went side by side towards the line of the enemy, while there was firing from the front and the rear. I did not like the situation at all, and considered means to escape. When we reached the brook that flowed through the field not a great distance from the woods, I managed to be a little in the rear, and let myself fall lengthways among the high grasses into the water, my head turned toward the right flank of our column of attack. Here I had found a safe place of concealment in the watery element. Should the field remain in our possession, I had escaped from imprisonment. At the other hand, there might be

a chance to get off during the dark of the night. As I remained unmolested, I laid me deep in the water as comfortably as possible, my head resting dry on a grass hillock, my body almost covered with water. Whoever momentarily passed by had to take me for one stretched out in everlasting slumber.

The billows of battle waved over me. To repulse the enemy, three charges were made over me, but were repelled as many times. With every repulse and repel the bullets struck right and left in the banks of the brook, but I lay low enough to be out of danger. After the enemy had repelled the last repulse, it became quiet. Soon after evening set in.

But with the fading of the day the disk of the moon scattered lustering light over the field, sowed with killed and wounded. The rattling of musketry ceased entirely, only the roaring of artillery continued till about midnight. Instead of the repetition of musketry, voices became audible — voices of the wounded, languishing for a drink of water. The longing and calling for it grew louder, more vehemently, and increased almost to distraction. Heart-rending was the lamenting, moaning and groaning of the wounded and dying. Merciful Samaritans came and brought the refreshing draught. Among those crying for water one was very urging. Maybe it came from one being wounded very seriously. When the water carrier came near him, he cried, "I am Lieutenant Y. from Company X of the Fifth Connecticut. Give me a drink of water." The reply was, "Whether lieutenant or not, it makes here no difference. Others must quench their thirst too." Many a dying soldier received ease in his death struggle by the refreshing draught.

The shrieks of pain and lamentation faded gradually. With the mother's name on the lips the moaning of many a young dying soldier ceased. Many an older soldier, leaving wife and children behind him, died lisping the names of the loved ones. Some struggled hard with death; others seemed to pass over quiet and content. At about midnight it was quiet; only now and then a sighing or a low moaning was heard.

A little after sunset my attention was called to some noise, sounding like the gathering of persons, at not a great distance to my right. What I conceived after a while was a reporting of a number of men present in companies of regiments. It seemed some brigade general had put up his temporal headquarters there. Of the regiments reporting were three at least, if not, all from Virginia. The number of present or accounted for were: Of one company five, of another eight, some twelve, seven, nine, fifteen, etc. If I remember right, the highest number was eighteen. The number of men from these regiments seemed to be according to these reports hardly more than seventy. In figuring up I found that from the whole brigade there were scarcely more than about 300 men reported for duty. As disconsolate as was the roll call of these regiments must have been that of ours after this battle.

At hearing distance my hiding place was the rendezvous of all that were getting water to refresh the languishing wounded. The water seemed to be more plentiful here than all round about. At first they came single in silent diligence. After a while two met, and conversation developed. Near by I heard the following dialogue:

"See, there lies one in the deep water."

"Yes, it must be one of ours."

"No, it is one of theirs."

"But he has a stripe on his pants"

"Some of them have stripes too."

"Let us search his pockets."

"Oh, no, do not; let him alone."

How I felt at such a conversation? Well, it was not at all a matter of indifference to me, and it made my blood run hot.

The terror which surrounded me lessened gradually, and I commenced to consider how it might be possible to get away there. The only possibility was in the dark of the night. But with such a bright moonshine like this every attempt was excluded. The position of the moon convinced me that her light would be obscured only by the break of the new day.

My moist lair had been my comfort after the heat of the battle. It was a soft and pleasant place of concealment; but when it became clear to me that there was no escape it grew wet. I began to feel cold, crept out the water and sat down on one of the dry hillocks of grass. I felt chilly and commenced to shiver, and at daybreak I called a passing soldier, asking him to bring me to my captured comrades.

WHY SHOULD WE MOURN?

Geo. H. Maxwell, Company B.

IN THE entire army of the Rebellion, both Federal and Confederate, there could not be found a braver lot of men than the officers of the Twenty-eighth Regiment New York Volunteers. They proved their loyalty, bravery and military knowledge on many a well-fought battlefield. Whether in victory or defeat, in the advance or retreat, the military discipline inculcated in the rank and file of that gallant regiment by their officers made the Twenty-eighth Regiment one of the best in the entire service.

The officers had good material to work with, for the Twenty-eighth was one of the first to respond to the call of our beloved country to save it from an ignominious end. It was made up from the very best of our young men of that day, who left their homes and those who were so dear to them, lucrative positions, to fight for the country that gave them birth — not for bounty, therefore it's no wonder that with such officers and men the Twenty-eighth won the praise and love of all who had their country at heart.

To this day the living cherish the memory of the dead, many mourn the loss of their dear ones who fell in battle. Why should we mourn the loss of our beloved Colonel Dudley Donnelly, or that true type of a soldier, Adjutant Charles P. Sprout? Both of these brave officers fell early in that terrible conflict; gave up their lives that their country might live; fighting desperately for the flag that they loved — for many a brave Confederate — fighting for what they thought was right — lay dead near where poor Sprout was found, as an evidence of the desperate defense he made for his life and the Union. I often heard Adjutant Sprout say he would never surrender. "Death before surrender," he would say, and he kept his word. When I heard of his death I wept like a child. Some say it's unmanly to weep, but tears shed over such heroes are honest tears and come from the well of truth. But we should not mourn the loss of these brave men or many others of that gallant regiment who fell in those dark days of our country. My limited vocabulary will not admit of bridging over the grief of those who were more closely related to those dead heroes, but why should any mourn or fear that which will eventually come to us all. Is not death a greater blessing than life? Death is not the end. We will know and love again the dear ones whom we loved here. We are all children of the same Father, and the same fate, Death, awaits us all. Then do not mourn their loss. I sometimes think the child who dies before he can lisp the name of mother is better off. Who knows what misery he may have escaped. This life is but one continual struggle for both rich and poor. Absolute contentment is a stranger here. This world is but a dark planet. We hope and believe there is a brighter one awaiting us all, and it is by Death's door we reach it. Then, are not they who have gone before far more blessed than we poor mortals who are left to continue the battle of life? I believe so! Therefore, let us be Christians. Help the living, cherish in our hearts the dead, but not mourn their loss.

"FOR TWO YEARS UNLESS SOONER DISCHARGED."

AN INCIDENT IN OUR HISTORY.

By Geo. W. Mayhe, Company H.

DURING the late summer or early autumn of 1861, while the Twenty-eighth Regiment was in camp at Berlin, a discussion arose as to the time limit of enlistment of the members, and this was brought about by the fact that some regiments of three months' men had been discharged and had returned to their homes. Many of the members of the Twenty-eighth had enlisted under the call for three months' men, but, as it afterwards proved, before the regiment was duly organized and mustered

into service at Albany, the quota of three months' men had been filled, and it was decided to muster the Twenty-eighth in as two-year men, and the men were so mustered into service. This was not known to most of the rank and file, and at the time of which I speak nearly all of the novelty of soldiering had worn off and the desire to return home was strong with very many members of the different companies, and the murmurings and mutterings grew stronger as the days, weeks, and even months rolled by, and no word of muster out came to the ears of the boys. At last threats of shooting the officers, and with arms in hand of marching to the capital and demanding a muster-out, or if discharged, where we were, and each man going home, reached the ears of Colonel Donnelly, and one afternoon, while on dress parade, he spoke about the matter, telling the men plainly that they had been mustered in for two years, and explaining how it came to be so done, and then referring to the threats to shoot the officers, he said in substance, while standing facing the entire regiment, drawn up in line, with guns in their hands, "Here I am," and placing his hand over his heart, "here is the vital part; if you want to shoot me, take good aim and fire to kill." The silence was oppressive for a moment, when three hearty cheers broke forth for the colonel, and the best of good feelings entered the breast of every man, and the colonel could have led these men into any place. The boys then settled down to business, and, as we all know, completed their term of enlistment (so many as lived and had ability physically to do so), and returned to their homes, although many of the members of Company H re-enlisted in the Second Mounted Rifles and again faced the enemy; but, wherever they are at this date, I think the incident above referred to, will recur to them. That incident, and the carrying of the colors in a wagon when we marched from Charleston to Harper's Ferry, by the order of the colonel, he saying that "he would never carry his colors in a retreat," are two incidents in the early history of the regiment that made very deep impressions on my mind, and each will be among my very latest recollections.

A FEW INCIDENTS IN THE EARLY HISTORY OF THE TWENTY-EIGHTH NEW YORK.

By Frank N. Wicker, New Orleans, La.

BUT few incidents worthy of note not heretofore recorded came under my observation or within my recollection during the brief period of my active service with the Twenty-eighth.

In looking back, however, through the long vista of time since the regiment was mustered in at Albany, May 22, 1861, I recall with pride the magnificent appearance of that splendid organization as it marched through the city of Baltimore, Md. — a city at that time, 1861, permeated with more disloyalty and hatred for the starry banner than the famed fire-eating denizens of Charleston, S. C.

It was well known to the rank and file that the Sixth Massachusetts Regiment, which passed through the Monumental City a short time before, had been fired on from the windows and housetops along the line of march, and indications pointed to a similar reception by the Twenty-eighth. The regiment was brought to a halt on the outskirts of the city where Colonel Donnelly, in his characteristic cool, deliberate, yet inspiring manner, directed that the rifles be loaded and that the men maintain a stolid indifference to any taunts or threats on the part of the civilians, many of whom were assembled in groups here and there at the various street corners, but who were soon afterwards very much in evidence in places of safety. Whatever the cause, whether through a sudden feeling of admiration for the old flag, or intuitive respect for a body of well-drilled, well-equipped, determined-looking men, with their short rifles and long, gleaming sword bayonets, no insults were offered or acts of disloyalty manifested by the inhabitants during the march through their city. The writer, several months afterwards, in Maryland, picked up a belt on the inside of which was inscribed, "Battle of Baltimore, April 19, 1861," evidently referring to the attack on the Sixth Massachusetts Regiment, before referred to.

Soon after crossing the river at Williamsport the regiment witnessed, in the terrible destruction of railroad property, torn-up tracks, ditched engines, broken machinery, burned cars, depots, roundhouses, etc., etc., the first real evidence that a state of war existed. The boys surveyed the scene, but indulged in few comments. Their thoughts quickly reverted to the peaceful homes and loved ones from whom, in many instances, they would forever be separated.

The first engagement in which a detachment of the Twenty-eighth took part was on a foraging expedition. The expedition having arrived at a point which promised a goodly supply of forage of all kinds for both man and beast, broke ranks, the members of the detachment scattering in different directions according to their individual inclinations. Some sought repose on the inviting grass in the fence corners, others visited neighboring farmhouses, where fresh milk could be obtained, while another small party strolled into an adjacent cornfield. Although in the enemy's country, no organized troops were known to be in the vicinity, hence the ordinary precautions to prevent or guard against surprises were omitted. Thus, while resting in fancied security, a handful of Confederate cavalry (Home Guards) made a sudden dash, firing a volley into the cornfield party, and instantly killing Isaac Sly. The rattle of musketry brought the foraging detachment quickly into line, but too late to capture the enemy or avenge the death of poor Sly, whose lifeless remains were tenderly placed in one of the forage wagons, and the expedition returned to camp. Sly being the first member of the Twenty-eighth Regiment to fall at the hands of the enemy, his death created a profound sensation, not only among his late comrades, but throughout the entire section of Western New York, from which the regiment was recruited. This was war.

The Twenty-eighth and other commands under Major-General Patterson having advanced to the Valley of the Shenandoah, it was understood that General Patterson received instructions to harass and annoy the Confederate General Johnson's flank, in order to prevent the latter from forming a junction with General Beauregard at Manassas. Instead, however, Patterson's division remained inactive and finally executed a retrograde movement, the Twenty-eighth bringing up at Harper's Ferry and going into camp on Bolivar Hights. It was on this march that Colonel Donnelly ordered the colors of the regiment furled and placed in the baggage wagon, remarking at the time that the colors of the Twenty-eighth should not be carried at the head of the regiment during a retreat. This was the first intimation that the regiment was not actually advancing on the enemy.

While in camp at Bolivar Hights word was brought in that a Confederate officer was visiting at a place about six miles distant. A midnight raid was ordered, the raiders taking passage in army wagons, the mules being driven to their full capacity of speed. Arriving at the place the house was surrounded and the Confederate officer duly arrested and honored with a cart ride into camp. He proved to be a full-fledged major, a dapper little fellow in a new uniform. He was merely on a visit to his best girl, and, being a good fellow, was, to the best of my recollection, allowed to escape.

A few weeks later the Twenty-eighth recrossed the Potomac, going into camp near Sandy Hook, and doing guard duty along the line of the river between that place and Point of Rocks.

TEMPERANCE WORK CONNECTED WITH THE TWENTY-EIGHTH NEW YORK.

By W. H. Crampton, Company A.

THIS article will necessarily be imperfect and incomplete in many respects. I am away from home and without any records whatever to refresh my memory as to circumstances, dates, names, etc., therefore much will be omitted that properly belongs to this branch of our history.

On the arrival of our regiment at Albany, N. Y., in May, 1861, realizing the special temptation and danger to which our boys would be subjected from strong drink,

I drew up and circulated a temperance pledge in which the signers agreed not to drink any intoxicating beverage during their absence from home in the army. This pledge was signed by about one hundred and fifty members of the regiment. There is no doubt but what its influence was most healthy and timely in that it was the means of preventing the formation of drinking habits on the part of many.

There were in the regiment active members of the order of the Sons of Temperance from Lockport, Medina and Akron. On consultation it was decided best to establish a division of the order in the regiment. In accord with this decision I wrote Wilson Hoag, the Grand Scribe of Western New York Grand Division Sons of Temperance, and a charter with supplies was immediately forwarded to us with full authority to organize, and "Federal Division No. 2, S. of T." was duly instituted.

The following officers were elected: W. H. Crampton, Worthy Patriarch; Almon M. Graham, Deputy; George W. Tucker, Worthy Associate; Samuel Williams, Chaplain; James Atwood, Recording Scribe; James F. Dunham, Treasurer; Enos Whitmore, Conductor; William Fox, Guard; Hugh Dunham, Sentinel.

This division had a varied experience. When in camp it met usually in some dwelling which had been deserted by the rebs on the advance of the Union Army. On account of constant change in location it was impossible to hold meetings with the regularity found under other circumstances, but we managed to keep alive an active temperance organization, holding meetings every week when not on the march.

At the battle of Cedar Mountain this society lost many of its most active members as well as its charter, books, etc. Almon M. Graham, who was at this time the Worthy Patriarch, ordered a new set of supplies and the work of the division was continued until the regiment was mustered out.

There is no estimating the amount of good done or the value of the work of this temperance organization. It is certain, however, that a goodly number of young men through its influence were saved from the formation of drinking habits and returned to their homes and have grown to manhood unstained and unfettered by intemperance.

When it is remembered that in those early days of the War whisky was dealt out by the Government as one of our regular rations (thought to be necessary), some idea of the firmness required to maintain a pledge of total abstinence may be conceived. The members of this temperance organization received their allowance of whisky with their other rations, but as they could not, in keeping with their principles, use it or give it others to use, it was thrown upon the ground where it could do no harm.

This action caused a deep sigh of regret upon the part of some who disliked to see the precious liquid wasted. But the Sons of Temperance were firm and this action was repeated as often as rations were issued.

There are many pleasant incidents connected with the meetings held in deserted rebel mansions, again in barns and at times in the open field; but space will not permit me to particularize. I will only refer to one amusing incident. While the regiment was encamped near Frederick, Maryland, a large number of the members obtained passes to visit a division of the Sons at Frederick. These passes were readily granted by the commanding officer, knowing that the members of this organization would not bring whisky into camp (this was the chief thing to guard against), but on the return of the members to the regiment at midnight, they were subjected to as rigid a search for whisky bottles as though they had been old soakers: but not any of the "critter" was found and the members all reached their quarters sober and in their right minds, having had a pleasant social time, notwithstanding the delay caused by the enforcement of the general order to the guards not to allow any whisky to be brought into camp.

I need not add that the members of this society always upheld the impartial enforcement of this prohibition whisky order.

THE ARMY MULE.

By J. Byron Lovell, Company C.

AFTER a great amount of historical research we cannot find that this noble animal has been written up as is eminently proper should be done. Every soldier who served with the mule in the Army will concede the fact that he was patient, faithful, thankful for favors, particularly those derived through the quartermaster. That within his hairy hide was wrapped up all that is great and noble in animal creation. He was endowed with great endurance, perversity, stubbornness, trickery, fraud, hypocrisy and more pure cussedness than any other animal in creation. When you fondle or pet him, and try to be his friend he was liable to remind you with a kick, either with fore or hind foot — both of which were quickly utilized for this purpose — that your friendship was not desirable. But, noble beast, with all your faults we loved you well. When on the march did you not, through hot and cold, wet and mud, bring us succor in our time of need. You seldom failed. Then, on the masterly retreats of Banks, Pope, Hooker, etc., did you not, by your perseverance and arduous activity, save for the Government thousands of dollars of property which, but for you, would have fallen into the hands of our enemies, thereby adding to our discomfiture and disgrace. For all that you did we thank you. We close by saying, "Long live the mule."

"OLD CHARLEY."

From the Lockport Journal, February 11, 1886.

A VETERAN of the late War passed away last week in Hartland. A good warrior he was, one who has marched under Southern summer skies and bivouacked in the mud of Virginia winters. He was with the Twenty-eighth New York at Cedar Mountain and braved the leaden storm of Antietam. He never wore shoulder straps and bore no official rank or title. This hero remained to the last just "Old Charley."

Charley fairly served his time, for he was eight years old when he went with Col. E. F. Brown to the war in 1861. Shortly after he became the property of Captain C. L. Skeels, who rode him through the streets when the town of Lockport turned out to welcome its returning soldiers in 1863. Charley went to Hartland with two Virginia comrades of lesser degree, "Pedro," a Spanish donkey, and "Dash," a Beaufort pointer. For years Charley was the children's pet, but of late he has lived a retired life, appearing only on state occasions such as the parade of C. L. Skeels Post G. A. R., when he carried himself as proudly as in old military days He now lies where reveille will not arouse him or the sunset gun startle him. It is to be hoped that in an equine hereafter, when he appears on dress parade, his beautiful cream uniform will bear at least a colonel's epaulets!

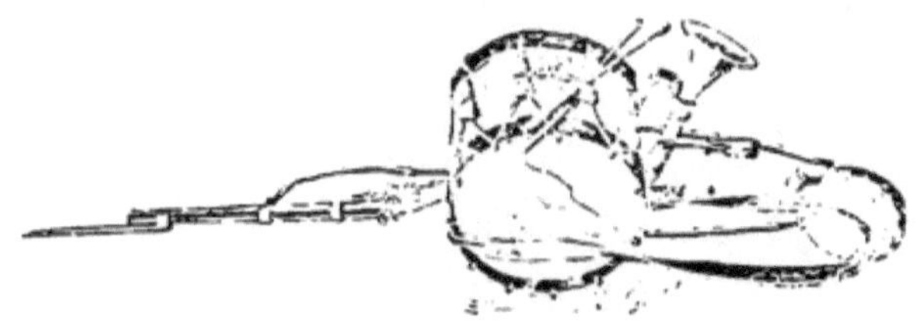

PROCEEDINGS

OF THE

THIRTY-FIFTH ANNUAL REUNION,

Twenty-eighth Regiment New York State Volunteers,

ALBION, N. Y., MAY 22, 1896.

OFFICERS FOR 1896 AND '97.

President, ...	GEO. IRISH, 105 Pearl Street, Buffalo, N. Y.
Vice-President, ...	JOSEPH PHILLIPS, 58 Genesee Street, Buffalo, N. Y.
Secretary and Treasurer, . .	C. W. BOYCE, 930 Main Street, Buffalo, N. Y.
Color Bearer, ...	JOHN T. GAILOR, Lockport, N. Y.

THE thirty-fifth annual reunion of the Twenty-eighth Regiment New York Volunteers was held at Albion, N. Y., May 22 1896. The day was a most delightful one; nature seemed to welcome the survivors of the organization with her brightest smiles. The comrades arrived early in the morning, and were met at the depot by the Vice-President of the society, Mr. William Collins, upon whom had fallen the entire charge of the arrangements for the meeting, owing to the death of the President, Captain David Hardie. Sergeant Collins was untiring in his efforts to make the reunion a success in every particular. The comrades and their friends received every attention possible at his hands.

The members were escorted to the Orleans House, which was finely decorated for the occasion, where they were received by General Benjamin Flagler, who stood in the doorway to welcome them, having come on from New York especially to meet his comrades and keep his record good of attending every one of the thirty-five reunions which the regiment has held since its organization. An hour was very pleasantly passed in social greetings. Some of the comrades had not met before since their discharge from the service, and the many pleasant and sad memories springing from their associations as brothers in arms were recalled. Every one referred to the admirable qualities of Captain Hardie, whose presence was so sadly missed. The reunion this year had been appointed at Albion on his invitation and request, and all knew how much he would have enjoyed greeting his old comrades could he have been present.

At ten o'clock the members assembled in the G. A. R. Hall, which had been kindly tendered for the use of the society.

The absence of Colonel Brown was regretted by all, as he had been expected; but no word had been received from him, and it was feared he would not be present; but soon after the organization of the meeting his familiar form was seen at the door, and he was received with the clapping of hands, and three hearty cheers by the men he had led during the War, and between whom and himself there still exists such a close bond of attachment. By making an extra effort he had reached the reunion, and his firm step and strong hand-grasp, indicated that his seventy-three years had not materially lessened his vital forces. He seemed as strong and vigorous as when he made his farewell address to the "boys" thirty-three years ago.

The colonel is still Inspector-General of the United States Homes for Disabled Volunteer Soldiers, which are under the able management of General W. B. Franklin, President of the Board. Colonel Brown had for several weeks been at the headquarters at Hartford, Conn; but was on his way to the Pacific States, making his usual tour of inspection.

The meeting was called to order by Sergeant William Collins, Vice-President. The Secretary, C. W. Boyce, called the roll, and the following comrades answered to their names:

Col. E. F. Brown, ... Dayton, O.
Sergt.-Maj. C. B. Gillam, ... Byron, N. Y.

BAND.

S. P. Lanham, ... Hornellsville, N. Y.
E. B. Whitmore, ... Rochester, N. Y.

COMPANY A.

Gen. Benjamin Flagler, ... Niagara Falls, N. Y.
J. W. Little, ... Lockport, N. Y.
John S. Chambers, ... Lockport, N. Y.
John T. Gailor, ... Lockport, N. Y.

COMPANY B.

James Goggin, ... Lockport, N. Y.
Michael Finnegan, ... Lockport, N. Y.
Robert Irving, ... Lockport, N. Y.

COMPANY C.

N. E. G. Wadhams, . . . Suspension Bridge, N. Y.
H. A. Collins, ... Pekin, N. Y.
Amos K. Welsher, ... Hartland, N. Y.
W. H. Gaskill, ... Wilson, N. Y.
J. Byron Lovell, ... Lockport, N. Y.
William Lutt, ... Northridge, N. Y.
Joseph Lee, ... Burlington, N. J.
Albert Richardson, ... Lockport, N. Y.
William E. Minard, ... Marathon, N. Y.
George B. Swick, ... Pekin, N. Y.

COMPANY D.

F. B. Seeley,	Lockport, N. Y.
C. W. Boyce,	Buffalo, N. Y.
J. Cornwell,	Lyndonville, N. Y.
John Kugler,	Lockport, N. Y.
Ziba Roberts,	E. Shelby, N. Y.
John A. Smith,	Shelby Centre, N. Y.
Robert Mortimer,	Rochester, N. Y.

COMPANY F.

James F. Bennett,	Alexander, N. Y.
Erastus Peck,	Brockport, N. Y.

COMPANY G.

W. M. Kenyon,	Rochester, N. Y.
William Collins,	Albion, N. Y.
Jacob Young,	Niagara Falls, N. Y.
E. C. Gould,	Hindsburgh, N. Y.
Benjamin Barker,	Fair Haven, N. Y.

COMPANY I.

George Irish,	Buffalo, N. Y.

COMPANY K.

Norman O. Allen,	Lockport, N. Y.
H. A. Jameson,	North Tonawanda, N. Y.
Frank O. McKinney,	Lockport, N. Y.
Joseph Phillips,	Buffalo, N. Y.

The visiting ladies, comrades and citizens present were:

Mrs. F. B. Seeley,	Lockport, N. Y.
Mrs. George B. Swick,	Pekin, N. Y.
Mrs. H. Colton,	Pendleton Centre, N. Y.
Mrs. C. W. Boyce,	Buffalo, N. Y.
Mrs. H. H. Boyce,	Buffalo, N. Y.
Mrs. W. M. Kenyon,	Rochester, N. Y.
Miss Ada Whitmore,	Rochester, N. Y.
Mrs S. P. Lapham,	Hornellsville, N. Y.
Mrs. E. C. Gould,	Hinosburgh, N. Y.
Mrs. J. R. Young,	Niagara Falls, N. Y.
Miss Clara Young,	Niagara Falls, N. Y.
Mrs. V. C. June,	Albion, N. Y.
Miss A. C. King,	Albion, N. Y.
Mrs. J. A. Smith,	Shelby Centre, N. Y.
Mrs. J. F. Bennett,	Alexander, N. Y.
Mrs. H. S. Perkins,	Byron, N. Y.
Mrs. C. H. Gillam,	Byron, N. Y.
Mrs. R. Mortimer,	Rochester, N. Y.
Maj. Thomas Bell, 8th N. Y. Cavalry,	Brooklyn, N. Y.
William Cobb, 151st N. Y.,	Medina, N. Y.
Col. H. Bowen, 151st N. Y.,	Medina, N. Y.
H. H. Bowen, 8th N. Y. H. A.	Medina, N. Y.
Luke Tower, 8th N. Y. H. A.	Youngstown, N. Y.
Sergt. F. Ellicott, Cothran's Battery,	Eagle Harbor, N. Y.
Maj. E. M. Spaulding, 8th N. Y. H. A.,	Albion, N. Y.
O. H. Taylor, 8th N. Y. H. A.,	Albion, N. Y.
C. Phipany, 8th N. Y. H. A.,	Albion, N. Y.
E. W. Phillips, 8th N. Y. H. A.,	Yates, N. Y.
George S. Hutchinson,	Albion, N. Y.
Hon. Dean F. Currie,	Albion, N. Y.
Dr. J. G. Dolley,	Albion, N. Y.
Rev. Dr. Fluhrer,	Albion, N. Y.
Rev. L. A. Stevens,	Albion, N. Y.
H. A. Osborne, Editor *Herald*,	Albion, N. Y.
H. F. Cady,	Albion, N. Y.
Oliver Clark,	Waterport, N. Y.
W. J. Brown,	Jeddo, N. Y.
H. H. Boyce,	Buffalo, N. Y.
T. O. Castle,	Wellsville, N. Y.

On motion, it was decided that the question of selecting a place for holding our next reunion be left to the comrades instead of referring it to a committee. The Secretary was instructed to call the roll and each be requested to signify the place of his choice, which result gave Buffalo twenty votes, Rochester four, and Niagara Falls two. Buffalo was then made the unanimous choice of the society.

The following officers were elected to serve for the ensuing year:

President,	George Irish, Buffalo, N. Y.
Vice-President,	Joseph Phillips, Buffalo, N. Y.
Sec'y and Treas'r,	C. W. Boyce, Buffalo, N. Y.
Color Bearer,	J. T. Gailor, Lockport, N. Y.

It was decided by vote that the Secretary should have the care of the album. The following persons, residing at the several localities mentioned, were elected, whose duty it shall be on hearing of the death of any member of our organization to cause notices to be published in the papers of said places, that surviving members may attend the funeral of any deceased comrade, and whose duty it shall also be to notify the Secretary of said death, sending any facts that may be used in the preparation of obituary notices:

N. E. G. Wadhams,	Niagara Falls.
J. H. Boyd,	Lewiston.
William Collins,	Albion.
H. Padelford,	Canandaigua.
J. B. Lovell,	Lockport.
John Bacon,	Medina.
J. F. Bennett,	Batavia.
J. Waller,	Monticello.

The Secretary's and Treasurer's reports were then called for, which, on motion, were accepted and ordered printed in the minutes. They were as follows:

SECRETARY'S REPORT
FOR 1895 AND '96.

Names on Roster at last report,	244
Added last year,	2
Added since—(the following, whose addresses were not previously known),	15
CAPT. H. H. MAPES, Co. C, Emporia, Kan.	
HENRY HADEN, Co. C, Corrunna, Mich.	
JOSEPH LEE, Co. C, Burlington, N. J.	
HENRY PETERS, Co. C, Gothenburg, Neb.	
ALBERT RICHARDSON, Co. C, Lockport, N. Y.	
CHAS. A. SMITH, Co. C, Togus, Me.	
JOHN CLARK, Co. D, Olympus, Iowa.	
ROBERT MORTIMER, Co. D, Rochester, N. Y.	
MARTIN MALONEY, Co. D, Chicago, Ill.	
S. P. QUICK, Co. E., Rochester, N. Y.	
PORTER L. HOWARD, Co. F, Kansas City, Mo.	
BENJ. BARKER, Co. G, Fair Haven, N. Y.	
CHARLES FERDUN, Co. G, Allegan, Mich.	
E. C. GOULD, Co. G, Hindsburg, N. Y.	
W. A. LOVETT, Co. H, Newark, Ohio.	
H. LOUNSBURY, Co. H, Fort Bennett, S. D.	
MARTIN LANE, Co. H, Shelton, Neb.	
KEARON BROPHY, Co. K, Easton, Mich.	
Total,	2[illegible]4
Lost, by death (as per obituary report), . 10	
Dropped, 2—	12
PALMER COLTON, Co. B, Buckland, O.,	
JACOB P. FAUROT, Co. E, Rising City, Neb. (whose letters have been returned marked "unclaimed.")	
Present number on Roster,	2[illegible]2

It will be seen by the above that, notwithstanding the large number who have died the past year, there are now on the Secretary's books six more names than were reported last year. It is very gratifying that the new addresses of these comrades have been found; and the Secretary urges the co-operation of all members to send the address of any survivor they may know, whose name is not published on our list. This is our only source

from which to recruit our rapidly depleting ranks; and these "absent and unaccounted for" comrades, should be looked up, and invited to join our association.

It is the earnest wish of the Secretary that the publication of the History, Pictures, Roster, etc., will tend to keep alive the friendships and memories of the past, and help in some small degree to maintain the true spirit of our organization — which is one of "mutual sympathy and good will."

Sincerely your comrade,

C. W. BOYCE,
Secretary.

TREASURER'S REPORT FOR 1895 AND '96.

Paid for Printing Invitations,	$ 4 00
" " " Badges,	6 00
" " " Report of Proceedings,	56 43
" " Postage,	12.00
" " Electrotypes,	6 00
" Balance from last year,	14 63
Total Expenses,	$99 06
Cash received from Comrades and Friends, by mail and at Reunion, as per itemized list,	$94 24
Balance,	$ 4 82
Paid subsequently by a Comrade,	4 82

C. W. BOYCE,
Treasurer.

The Obituary Committee reported the following memorial resolutions on deceased comrades for the year, which was, on motion, adopted and ordered printed.

REPORT OF THE OBITUARY COMMITTEE.

The year that has passed since our last reunion, has been a sad one to our regimental association. More members have died than in any previous year since the War.

Nine comrades, with whom we have yearly met, or, from whom we have received words of greeting, have been summoned by the hand of death; and with their immediate relatives, and many friends, we to-day, mourn their loss, and pay our tribute of deep respect to their memory:

Corporal, PETER GUELPH, Company G. Died at Brockport, N. Y., July 4, 1895.

EDWIN A. BOWEN, Company D. Died at Joliet, Ill., August 18, 1895.

A. B. MERVILLE, Company A. Died near New Cumberland, W. Va., October 24, 1895.

Quarter-Master Sergeant, GEO. E. SWAN. Died at Newburgh, N. Y., November 5, 1895.

CHAS. O. INGALLS, Company I. Died at Niagara Falls, N. Y., December 14, 1895.

HAMILTON T. HOLDEN, Company C. Died at Lockport, N. Y., December 19, 1895.

SYLVESTER C. TRIPP, Co. D. Died at Coleman, Mo., February 22, 1896.

Captain, DAVID HARDIE, Company G. Died at Albion, N. Y., March 20, 1896.

Lieutenant, JEREMIAH LONG, Company A. Died at Los Angelos, Col., April 3, 1896.

Surgeon, A. M. HELMER. Died at Milwaukee, Wis., April 20, 1896.

CORPORAL PETER GUELPH was an honored member of our regiment. He was wounded in the battle of Antietam, and taken prisoner at Chancellorsville. He re-enlisted in Company C First New York Veteran Cavalry, and was promoted to Sergeant, serving in that capacity in all the battles, in which this regiment participated with credit to himself and satisfaction to the officers and men of that command. Companions in arms from each of these regiments bore him to his grave, and fired the usual salute over his remains. His home had been at Brockport since the War, where he was a well-known and respected citizen.

EDWIN A. BOWEN, as soldier or citizen, was loved by all who knew him. No braver soldier, nor kinder friend, belonged to the regiment. He was taken prisoner at Cedar Mountain, when desperately fighting in the hand-to-hand conflict in the woods. He re-enlisted subsequent to his service in the Twenty-eighth in the Second New York Mounted Rifles, in which regiment he served until the close of the War. His comrades in that organization also attest to his fine soldierly qualities. His business, at his home, in Joliet, Ill., was that of a civil engineer. He was known as one of the best in the city, and esteemed by a wide circle of friends.

A. B. MERVILLE's death was extremely sad and very sudden. He was burned to death in his office in the gas and oil district of Western Virginia. He was an industrious, hardworking man, a good citizen, and loved by all. As a soldier in the Twenty-eighth his record was the very best; always performing his duties faithfully and well.

QUARTERMASTER-SERGEANT GEO. E. SWAN was originally a member of Company H, but later was detailed in the quartermaster's department, and finally made quartermaster-sergeant of the regiment on December 1, 1862. He was a good soldier, a faithful officer, discharging his duties with zeal and ability. Since the war he resided at Newburgh, N. Y., where he was an officer and a great favorite of the S. W. Fullerton Post, G. A. R., No. 58, Department of New York.

C. O. INGALLS had for many years been blind, and yet he often attended the reunions of this regiment and was interested in all the proceedings. His record in the army was that of a good soldier. He joined the regiment at its organization, and served with Company I till mustered out at the expiration of its term of enlistment. He was always ready for duty, and never feared to face the enemy.

HAMILTON T. HOLDEN enlisted November 19, 1861, in Company C, and served with the regiment until mustered out June 2, 1863. He was taken prisoner at Winchester, Va., May 25, 1862, and paroled June 9, 1862. His home since the war was at Lockport, N. Y., where he has been in the employ of the Holly Manufacturing Company until seven years ago, when his health failed. As a brave soldier, he was faithful in the discharge of his duties; and, as a citizen, industrious and respected by his neighbors and friends.

COMRADE TRIPP was one of the youngest members of the regiment, having enlisted in December, 1861, when less than 17 years of age.

He was universally known as "Buck" Tripp, and was a great favorite with his comrades. Many

an older soldier was cheered by the lively disposition and ready wit of this boy in years, who performed his full share of the duties of army life.

Genial and kind as a comrade in camp, he proved brave and fearless as a soldier in battle.

Subsequent to his service in the Twenty-eighth he re-enlisted in Co. A, Eighth New York Heavy Artillery on December 10, 1863. He was wounded at Reames Station, Va., August 24, 1864. And finally discharged, June 30, 1865. He has resided since the war at Coleman, Cass County, Mo., where he was engaged in farming until his health failed.

CAPTAIN DAVID HARDIE, our President, is dead. No other vacant chair in this society would be more conspicuous than his to-day, for no other member of our organization was more genial or more highly respected than he. His kindly disposition, his sympathy with his comrades, his frankness and uniform good nature, made him one of the most popular men in the regiment. As an officer, he always used his authority with a mild hand. He did not feel above the men he commanded, and it was on his motion that the question of rank was ignored in this society.

Gifted with humor himself and appreciating it in others he was always welcomed to any circle. He enjoyed to a very large degree the strong, personal attachment and love of his comrades, and the unlimited confidence and respect of his friends and neighbors, which is the best attestation that can be given to a man's character.

LIEUTENANT JEREMIAH LONG was a brave soldier and a kind and efficient officer. His record is one of the best in the regiment. Either as sergeant, lieutenant or commander of a company he filled every position with ability and satisfaction. A genial and kind nature was united with all the characteristics of a courteous gentleman, and no truer or better friend than "Jerry Long" ever wore the blue.

ALBERT M. HELMER, the eminent and efficient surgeon of the Twenty-eighth regiment, has also "passed over the river and rests in the shade." His abilities were so generally recognized in the army that he was made acting brigade surgeon for many months, and ranked as one of the best in the corps. He was always kind, considerate and conscientious as a professional man; while as a comrade and friend he was ever genial and obliging — one of nature's noblemen.

The hearts of all surviving comrades are especially saddened to-day that this roll of honor, including so many of our dearest friends, is the largest in our experience.

We lay our wreaths tenderly on their graves, and pay this tribute to their memory with sorrowful hearts.

GEO. IRISH,
ZIBA ROBERTS, } *Committee.*
C. W. BOYCE,

The secretary made his report on publishing the history of the regiment; giving a detailed account of the work, and the estimated expense, showing there would be a large deficiency, unless the comrades contributed more liberally than had as yet been done. It was decided after a full interchange of the views of the members to call the roll, and invite those present to designate the number of books they would subscribe for at $1.25 each, which was the cost of printing each book in cloth covers. All subscribed liberally, and by consultation after adjournment it was decided to make an appeal to the absent comrades to assist in raising the necessary funds to pay the expense of publishing the history.

The time for the dinner having arrived, all marched to the Orleans House, where they were seated in the dining room, which had been decorated for the occasion with bunting and flowers. Seventy-five comrades, with their ladies and invited guests, sat down and enjoyed an excellent dinner, well served.

Colonel Brown acted as toastmaster, and expressed great pleasure in once more meeting with his comrades. He referred, with much feeling, to the death of Captain Hardie, and to the fact that in all probability he would not be privileged to attend many more reunions himself, but assured his companions that they all had a warm place in his heart, and that he would try to meet with them as long as life should last. He called on the following persons, who made addresses: some of which were eloquent tributes to the memory of Captain Hardie, and all were inspiring, and received with applause: Hon. Dean F. Currie, Dr. Flubrer, Major Thomas Bell, O. H. Taylor, Lieut. W. M. Kenyon, Rev. L. A. Stevens, Lieut. F. B. Seeley, and Col. H. Bowen.

We regret that space forbids any sketch of the remarks, as a more interesting occasion has never been held by the organization. More eloquent or patriotic speeches have never been made at our banquets, and Colonel Brown heartily thanked the speakers for their encouraging words.

This closed the exercises for the day, and the veterans separated to their respective homes, having enjoyed another reunion, that will be remembered with great pleasure, by all present. The meetings seem to grow in interest as the years go by, and tend to keep alive the friendships, and pleasant memories of soldier days. All pledged to meet again next year, if spared to do so, at Buffalo, where, it is hoped, a large number will be present.

Letters and Telegrams from Absent Comrades and Friends.

LOWELL, MASS., April 30, 1896.

My dear Sir,—The circular inviting me to attend the thirty-fifth annual reunion of the survivors of the Twenty-eighth New York Regiment, on the 22d of May, is received.

As a survivor of the Second Massachusetts Regiment, which was part of the First Division of the Twelfth Corps, who fought with you in the war, I recognize the kindly feeling which prompts you to extend to members of other regiments the opportunity to attend this fraternal gathering, and to renew old friendships.

The generous and neighborly spirit towards other regiments, which was so evident during the War, appears again in the association of the survivors of your regiment.

I remember, with great pleasure, Colonel Donnelly, Captain Bush and other gentlemen of your regiment, and I remember your splendid record in the various campaigns and battles when in the Shenandoah Valley in 1862, and with the Army of the Potomac in same and following year.

I must ask to be excused from attending the reunion this year on account of the long distance and inability to spare the time, but I trust sometime to find a chance to shake hands all round and to renew the memories of the War.

Thanking you for your kindness, and with great respect, I remain,

Very truly yours,
JAMES FRANCIS,
Major Second Mass. Reg't.

MINNEHAHA, MINN., April 24, 1896.

Dear Comrade,—I have the honor to acknowledge the receipt of your invitation to the thirty-fifth annual reunion of the Twenty-eighth N. Y. Vol. Inf. It recalled many recollections—some pleasant and some sad—particularly that of Cedar Mountain, August 9, 1862.

I remember Colonel Donnelly and Adjutant Sprout, and all the circumstances of their noble deaths, for at that time I was adjutant of my own regiment. Among my personal friends I count Lieutenant James Smith, now residing in Minneapolis. I have also recently met Colonel Brown and Major Rowley of Milwaukee. Old times and old associations resume their full considerations, and our old battles are fought over again, at least to our satisfaction

I may be able to recall myself to your recollection. At the hanging of Laneham, of the Forty-sixth Pennsylvania, for the murder of the major of that regiment, I was the officer on the scaffold who read the findings of the court martial and sentence of death, and gave the signal to pull the trap as I left the scaffold. Time, I think, has dealt kindly with me since those eventful days, and after four years and three months' service, I still enjoy life and am able to wish all the comrades of the brave Twenty-eighth New York many happy reunions, although I am not able to be present.

I am a full-fledged New Yorker, of the Holland-Dutch persuasion—born and grew to manhood at Schenectady.

Very truly yours,
RALPH VAN BRUNT,
Late Captain A Company, Third Wis.

ORANGE, N. J., May 8, 1896.

My dear Comrade,—Your kind invitation and circular to attend the reunion of the Twenty-eighth N. Y. was duly received. I am compelled to say again that it will be impossible for me to be present and join with you in reviving the memories of your heroic days, when you fought so well to restore the Union you loved. A recent visit to Richmond, Va., enabled me to go over some of the ground we had tramped over and fought over from the Potomac to the James, and on one occasion, at least, in the rotunda of "The Jefferson," at Richmond, fight Gettysburg once again, in the hearing of a number, some of whom were Confederate officers of rank. I am glad to note that none enjoyed it more than they did, as viewed from a Yankee standpoint.

A visit to the Confederate Soldiers' Home, known as that of Robert E. Lee Camp, was also to me very full of interest, and it may revive interest to state that General Benjamin F. Butler, when the Home needed aid, was the first man from the North to send a check of $50 in aid of his old foes.

I heartily wish I could be with you, but you must take my good will for my only excuse not to respond to your annual invitation to join your reunion. I greatly appreciate the honor you do me, and some day will answer, I believe, in person your kind invitation.

Yours in F., C. and L.,
A. M. MATTHEWS,
Late Captain 13th New Jersey.

ROCHESTER, May 22, 1896.

SECRETARY TWENTY-EIGHTH N. Y.

Dear Sir,—Your letter, inviting me to be present at the thirty-fifth annual reunion of the Twenty-eighth Regiment, is received. I am grateful for your yearly remembrance, although the sad associations of such a meeting has prevented my accepting the invitations. My husband loved the Twenty-eighth and "dear old Company D," and in my own heart there is a warm place for its members, and I am glad to know, although he can no longer meet with you, I am not forgotten by his comrades.

With every return of this day, memory recalls scenes and incidents in a past so distant they seem almost like dreams.

Shall I repeat one circumstance which now comes vividly to my mind? In the winter of '61, you will remember, the regiment—I always say *us* regiment—was camped near Frederick City, Md. There, myself and baby daughter joined my husband, and spent several delightful weeks. From our large front room in the farmhouse where we

were boarding I could look up the road a quarter of a mile, across a field, to the hill where the camp was located.

I can still see the rows of white tents, outlined against the horizon, and in fancy hear the beat of the drum, calling the soldiers out to drill or on parade. I can hear the sweet notes of the bugle as they rose and fell on the still air at morning reveille or evening tattoo. I think it was on a Sabbath day. I remember the air grew colder and toward evening snow commenced falling.

A little past midnight we heard a call under our window

Throwing up the sash, we saw the camp all astir! Lights were flashing, drums beating, mules braying and teamsters shouting, confirming the words of the messenger, sent to summon my husband, that "marching orders" had been received. Just as the day was breaking I leaned from the window alone, listening to the tramp! tramp! of the regiment as it marched up and over the hill to the tune of "Dixie," splendidly played by the regimental band. My husband told me afterward, of your tedious march of twenty-five miles, in the slush of the melting snow, before you halted and, tired and footsore, lay down to rest in a church at Hagerstown. A few hours and you were again on the march to the little town of Hancock, which the "boys in gray," across the river, were threatening with their batteries. He gave me a humorous account of the irate mistress of the house which he occupied as headquarters of Company D during your stay in Hancock.

He said anger and disgust shone in her face as she entered her home, unannounced, to find furniture and carpets gone, and soldiers, with feet elevated to the level of their heads, lounging and smoking in her parlors.

Her thanks were expressed, however, when she was taken to a room, where, under lock and key, her house furnishings were stored until her unwelcome guests had departed.

I waited a week in Frederick City, when, by the kindness of beloved Colonel Donnelly, I was given a seat in his carriage with his wife and Mrs. Skeels.

With them I rode to Hagerstown, where Mr. Bowen joined me for a day before we parted—baby and I to go to our lonely home; my husband to the hardships of the summer's campaign.

I am glad to hear a history of the regiment has been written. One by one, and all too quickly, its members are passing the confines of time. Their children and their children's children will love to read the story of their journeyings, the privations they endured, the battles they fought, as well as the bright side they found in army life. The regiment owe you a debt of gratitude they will not be slow to acknowledge. While I know it has been with you a "labor of love," it is hardly possible for one to appreciate the sacrifice of time, as well as the expense incurred, in bringing this history to a successful completion.

For myself and children I wish personally to thank you. Hoping yourself and comrades may pass a very pleasant day,

I am, sincerely,
MRS. E. A. BOWEN.

39 HUDSON ST., ITHACA, N. Y., May 9, 1896.

Dear Sir,—I regret that illness will prevent my accepting the kind invitation to the reunion of the Twenty-eighth Regiment this year.

I visited my father, Quartermaster Skeels, when the regiment was at Sandy Hook, Md., in September, 1862. It was camped on Maryland Heights, and I remember the group of tents we occupied, father's clerk, A. S. Richmond; Frank McClenathan, Oscar Draper and Porter Howard, who cooked such good things for us. I can close my eyes and see it all, and a little way off the camp, where the wagon trains were; the big pile of grain bags, which father's bay horse, "Jim," used to steal whenever he could get loose

It seems each year an impossibility for me to attend the reunions, and it is a great disappointment I assure you

Very sincerely,
LAURA H. S. DOM.

702½ MARSHALL ST.,
MILWAUKEE, WIS., May 13th.

Dear Sir,—As it is not possible for me to attend the reunion I send my greetings and regrets. I hope you will have a large number in attendance, and that the day will be a happy one for all. I wish I could be with you on the 22d. Remember me kindly to all friends. Yours sincerely,
JULIE DONNELLY STETSON.

ANTIETAM AND THE VALLEY REVISITED.

PHILADELPHIA, May 18, 1896.

Nothing seems more certain than that I shall not be able to be present at our annual reunion. I am exceedingly sorry that I am again compelled to be absent. There are so few reunions in the future for us all in this life that I feel that in each recurring meeting I have missed something never to be regained.

My business is one of the most exacting in the world. A lawyer can frequently let a case go over, but a newspaper man is always supposed to be on tap. I do not suppose I will be particularly missed by any one except by a few comrades of my old company, E. Nevertheless, I feel it my duty to be present. I look forward to every reunion, and pledge myself that I will make ample preparations beforehand, but when the time comes to get ready to go something intervenes.

I had intended to write something to the "boys" about some of the Virginia and Maryland battlefields, which I visit every little while simply because they are near at hand. Even this labor of love I am compelled to forego. I may add this much here, however. The west and east woods, which flanked the dreadful cornfield at Antietam, have been cut down within the past two years. The men of the Twenty-eighth will recall to mind that the old Dunker Church stood near the southern end of the west woods That still stands and looks the same as when the battle raged around the sacred and venerable edifice. With "ghoulish glee," as President Cleveland would say, I may state, that in cutting up the trees into railroad ties, the syndicate purchasing them ruined several hundred dollars' worth of saws, for every little while a saw would strike a bullet or piece of shell The work of establishing the lines of the two armies engaged is going on slowly, owing to a lack of appropriations. With the woods gone the field no longer looks natural. The farmhouses on the field still stand, and look quite natural. The spot where Mansfield fell is now a peach orchard. The cornfield is in wheat. The huge boulders near the center of our

right in the cornfield still remain, and so do the trees that were there amid the boulders on the day of battle.

I was up the Valley not long since, and it looked gorgeous. Indeed, it looked the same as it did when we marched up it, in 1862. I took dinner at Strasburg, and visited that blessed old fort we toiled to erect on the little hill near the town. Woodstock, Newmarket, Mount Jackson and Harrisonburg have had a few fences whitewashed, but that was the only change noticed, except that Harrisonburg no longer relies on the old spring near the Court-House for its water supply. The water is now drawn from an immense spring on a high hill near the town, and it is great water, I assure you. Nevertheless, I presume to the old "boys" it would not quench their thirst as quick nor taste as good as the water from the old spring did.

But I must close. I hope this reunion will be among the happiest of the series. Those who have gone before will be fittingly remembered, and while their vacant seats may tinge the meeting with sadness, it is well with them, no doubt. They served their generation well. Peace to their ashes.

Yours truly,

L. D. SALE.

Com. Sergt.

17 CENTRE ST.,

NEWARK, NEW JERSEY, May 18, 1896.

DEAR COMRADES:

I find as the time approaches for our annual reunion that it will not be feasible for me to answer to roll-call this year, as I had wished. My thoughts, however, will be with you on the 22d. I can but think of the sadness that will be cast over your gathering by the absence of the brave and generous Captain Hardie. He will ever be held in kindly remembrance by all the members of the Twenty-eighth New York Volunteers.

With kind regards to all comrades, both present and absent, I remain cordially yours.

W. H. CRAMPTON, Co. A.

RENFREW, PA., May 12, 1896.

DEAR COMRADES:

I thought a year ago that I should certainly be with you to-day, but am very sorry that I am compelled to be absent from your ranks. I am very much pleased, however, by the thought that though absent, I shall still have the pleasure of seeing the faces of the surviving members of old Twenty-eighth published in the proceedings of the reunion. Hoping that you may all have a high old time, without getting high yourselves, and that I may be able to meet with you next year, with love to all, I remain, comrades,

Yours truly,

P. B. KELCHNER,

Company B.

WAUPACA, WIS., May 1, 1896.

DEAR COMRADES:

Your kind invitation for me to be present at the thirty-fifth annual reunion of the Twenty-eighth N. Y. Vols. at hand.

Another year has rolled by and the number of the surviving members of the Twenty-eighth is lessened by nine; all dearly loved by me. It will not be long before death will claim us all.

I know it is the duty of all who can afford it to be at each yearly reunion, for as each year rolls by it lessens our number, and by remaining away we lose the chance of grasping the hands of those we love, who touched elbows with us during those dark days of our country. My position is such, and has been for the past ten years, that I could not leave it to others, and it has deprived me of meeting with you; but I am positive that this will be my last year "on the road;" also the last time I will be obliged to send regrets that I am unable to attend the reunions on account of business. Sickness only will prevent. My whole heart will be with you on the 22d day of May.

With a hope our lives may be spared, that many years may roll by before the last reunion of the surviving members of our gallant Twenty-eighth is the fervent prayer of

Yours very sincerely,

GEO. H. MAXWELL,

Company B.

MATTOON, ILL., May 7, 1896.

DEAR COMRADES:

Your cordial invitation to be present at the thirty-fifth annual reunion of the Twenty-eighth Regiment is before me.

It would give me great pleasure to be present and answer to my name at "roll call," also to touch elbows once again with my old chums and comrades; stand in line, and have Orderly N. E. G. Wadhams give the command: "Right dress," "front," "attention," to "roll call:" Sergeant J. D. Woods, "here;" Sergeant Wm. H. Adriance, "here;" Sergeant A. M. Graham, "here:" Corporal Charles Baker, "here;" Corporal Flynn, "here;" Corporal Sims, "here;" Corporal G. F. Gould, "here;" Private, etc., etc. How familiar would be the sound.

But circumstances are such that I cannot be there in person. However, my thoughts will be with you on that memorial occasion.

My health is not good — have retired from business on account of disability.

With kind regards and best wishes to all members of the old Twenty-eighth Regiment, and hoping that you will have a grand, good time at the reunion,

I remain, yours in F., C. and L.,

GEORGE F. GOULD,

Company C.

NATIONAL MILITARY HOME,

TOGUS, ME., May 20, 1896.

DEAR COMRADES:

By the courtesy of our beloved colonel, who has kindly given me your address, it affords me the greatest of pleasure to forward to you these few lines.

I have been a member of this home since February 17, 1892, and have always been contented with the home. A man is used well here if he behaves himself. I was appointed head keeper of the deer park May 1, 1892. We have 40 head of deer, 2 ring-tailed monkeys, that I have taught to perform on rope ladders, rings and trapeze; 3 performing black bears, 10 trick dogs, 2 squirrels on the revolving wheel, and 1 ocelot, an inhabitant of South America, beautifully spotted, like the leopard. We had a wild bull moose, which I succeeded in breaking to harness, and he was driven around the hospital for the convalescents to see and admire. He was a natural trotter and very speedy.

This and many other amusements are for the pleasure of the old volunteers.

This Home contains more than 1,700 acres, part of which is laid out in beautiful walks and driveways, with a grand display of flowers.

It has been conceded that we have the finest herd of imported Holstein cows in the State of Maine.

There are borne upon the rolls 2,600 members, with about 400 on furlough.

We have a fine opera house and a chapel for religious instruction. Clergymen of different denominations officiate alternate Sundays during the year.

Our much beloved colonel was here in his official capacity last year, and the same this year, having bid us goodbye to-day (Tuesday) to attend the thirty-fifth reunion at Albion, on the 22d. I had not seen him since we were mustered out of the service June 2, 1863.

I have the first furlough signed by the late Colonel Donnelly from Darnestown, Md., to Washington City. Colonel Brown can tell you all about it.

Dear comrades, I hope the thirty-fifth reunion will be most enjoyable to you all. I regret very much that business will not permit me to reunite with you.

With best wishes to you all, and hoping that your last days will be your pleasantest,

I remain, yours, etc.,

CHAS. A. SMITH,
Company C.

BANGOR, WIS., May 1, 1896.

COMRADES:

Your invitation to attend the thirty-fifth annual reunion is received. I regret exceedingly that I cannot meet with the old Vets as I expected, but it seems impossible this time, being unable physically and financially, for which I am sorry, as I would enjoy very much to look the members of the old Twenty-eighth in the face, and feel the friendly grasp of men who some thirty odd years ago stood shoulder to shoulder on the old camp ground. Although absent in person my heart will be with you. Each year our ranks will be thinned by that reaper called death, until the Twenty-eighth New York will be known only in history and its noble deeds of valor repeated by children and grandchildren around the hearthstone we left to defend the country and flag we loved so well. Comrades, I wish you all a pleasant, happy time, and commend you to the care of Him who doth not let even a sparrow fall unnoticed. May God bless you one and all is the prayer of yours,

In F., C. and L.,

JOHN YONKEY,
Company C.

CLARKS, NEB., May 5, 1896.

DEAR COMRADES OF THE TWENTY-EIGHTH:

The invitation to the thirty-fifth reunion of the old regiment is received, and I regret to say I cannot be with you, but I will answer here, at a distance. Be assured my spirit will be with you. We have been requested to furnish some incident in the history of the regiment. I will contribute a short account of the retreat after the battle of Chancellorsville. Soon after sunrise on May 5, 1863, we left Chancellorsville and started northward. After crossing the Rappahannock River we were halted and ordered to protect the engineers while they took up the pontoons.

The ford was covered by artillery and sharpshooters on the heights. We were posted near the water to protect the engineers. We remained until the last man had crossed the river and the last pontoon placed on the wagons, and drawn up by the infantry with drag ropes. The roads were like mortar and horses could not be used.

After this we were marched upon the heights, and I saw no forces but the men of the Twenty-eighth New York. They were the last to cover that retreat, which I esteem an honor to any troops.

When ordered to our camps on Stafford Heights, it commenced to rain, and poured down just as it knows how to in old Virginia.

This march will long be remembered by those who participated in it. The streams were so swollen that they became raging torrents. I thought I should be carried away while crossing. This was an experience that tried men's hearts. It is seldom men made such a march, in so short a time, under as trying circumstances.

Company C, under Lieutenant N. E. G. Wadhams, was division provost guard at General Williams' headquarters during the battle of Chancellorsville, and was subject to orders from headquarters at all times.

I send my best regards to all old comrades, and wish you a happy reunion.

Your comrade,

WILLIAM SIMS.

SUNDANCE, WYOMING, May 15, 1896.

DEAR COMRADES:

Sorry it is impossible for me to be with you this year in person, to spend a few happy hours in grasping the hands of the old comrades, and in talking over old times. The events of those old times crowd in on my memory as I plod behind the breaking plow, turning the virgin soil of these beautiful prairies, obliterating the trails and wallows, the last traces of the buffalo, which once roamed here as free and happy as was the hearts of us young soldiers when the order sounded to strike tents and get ready to march. I send greeting to the surviving members who will be present at the coming reunion.

Yours,

A. A. FOX, Co. D.

OMAHA, NEB., May 18, 1896.

COMRADES OF THE TWENTY-EIGHTH:

I am again reminded of the return of our annual gathering, by the invitation to "roll-call" from our worthy secretary, and how I wish I could be with you next Friday, but I am again doomed to be disappointed. I am too far away, and times are too hard. I am waiting anxiously to see the publication that will contain so many of your faces and reports from you all.

Wishing you a pleasant meeting and trusting we may meet some time — it may be in the great hereafter — I am your comrade and brother,

WM. W. EASTMAN, Co. D.

1114 HANCOCK ST.,
BROOKLYN, N. Y., May 18, 1896.

DEAR COMRADE:

As I expected, and as I believe it will continue on to the end, I shall not be able to meet my old comrades of the Twenty-eighth at their next annual reunion, on the 22d inst. I anticipate great pleasure

in looking through the "picture gallery" that I hope you will succeed in being able to give us in the history of the regiment, and I hope to be able by a careful scrutiny to recall the features of old companions in arms that I have not seen for thirty odd years. I hope you may have a large and joyous gathering and a good time generally, and I would like through you to give them all a kindly greeting and best wishes for their health, happiness and prosperity.

Very truly yours,
G. A. BAKER, Co. D.

ALBION, MICH., April 27, 1896.

DEAR COMRADES:

I do not think I shall be able to come to the reunion of the old Twenty-eighth, but will be there in spirit. When the secretary lived in Albion we used to go and get a dish of ice cream and have a good smoke and talk over old times on the day the boys were together. Now there is no one here, but we always have an extra dinner on that day. If I was there I could "swap lies" with the boys, but putting it down on paper is another thing. I wonder if the boys of C and D remember the Saturday night in '62 that we went out to Hall Town? I think it was to try and catch some rebel officers. We were gone all night, but got nothing but some honey.

I wish to be remembered to all the comrades present.

Yours in F., C. and L.,
O. G. HUBBARD,
Company D.

NORTHVILLE, May 2, 1896.

DEAR COMRADES:

Another year has fled, and with it all hopes of meeting my old comrades this year, but still the hope clings to me that I will see you all next year. The ranks are getting thin, comrades, soon there will be none to respond, either by letter or person; but as one by one they step in the great beyond to answer to roll call, may those left grasp each other's hand, with a loyalty firmer and truer than before.

Comrades, when you are meeting those by whose side you stood when the bullets were falling like hail, remember there is one in Northville, who deeply regrets not being able to be present with you.

Yours in F. C. L.,
LOREN HAYNER,
Company D.

PLATTE CENTER, May 1, 1896.

COMRADES OF THE TWENTY-EIGHTH:

Once more I acknowledge the invitation to our annual reunion, and have to say that it will be impossible for me to be with you. I would like to meet the comrades again, but my health is poor, so that I cannot travel far, and shall have to be content to read the letters and look at the pictured faces of the comrades.

Eighteen hundred and ninety-six finds our ranks growing smaller, as we receive the notice often that some comrade has passed over to the summer land. Accept my best wishes, and if we are not permitted to meet again here, may we all meet on the eternal camping ground on high, and hear the welcome words; well done, faithful soldier, enter into rest.

Yours in F., C. and L.,
JOHN KEELER,
Company D.

ELYSIAN, MINN., May 19, 1896.

DEAR COMRADES:

I often wish I could be with you all on such a day as this will be to you. * * * As you are all well aware, the next national assembling of all old soldiers will take place at St. Paul, Minn., next September. Now, you all come to this great gathering of heroes. And here I wish to say, a room will be provided for a reunion of the Twenty-eighth New York, and the boys who have remained among the scenes of their early life can again meet with those who, after the War, came to the then wild wilderness and helped to make it the seat of a mighty Northwestern Empire, yet welded by a band of blood to the great east and south. Come out and see what the west is.

Should any of the Twenty-eighth New York boys come I wish they would write me in advance so I can have arrangements made by which we will all be sure to meet each other.

Ever yours in friendship and comradeship,
WALLACE M. STERLING.

VICTORIA, ILL., May 4, 1896.

Dear Old Comrades:

I had made all the arrangements last summer to attend this reunion of the Old Twenty eighth, but a circumstance has happened that causes me to give up the great pleasure, said circumstance being a little daughter, who, six weeks ago to-day drove in the pickets, charged the camp, and captured the entire outfit, and is now in supreme command.

Just think of it, a war-scarred (and often scared), grizzled, bald-headed, old veteran, of 52 years, who has withstood the shock of thousands (when he couldn't get away), to be utterly routed, and finally captured by a little nine pound girl, yea, verily, I am undone, but I stand the captivity remarkably well. Have been married over twelve years, and this is my first circumstance. My wife has always managed to have bread on hand, and I have skirmished around and furnished water, and now I will have to skirmish for milk and baby carriages and nursing bottles. Such is life.

I have never attended a reunion, and should like to be with you very much, and next year, if possible, I shall be on hand. I look forward with pleasure to the perusal of our Twenty-eighth history. I think that a grand thing, and hope every surviving member of the old regiment will get one.

I often think of our first march toward the enemy, from Hagerstown to Williamsport, that hot, Sunday afternoon, our hearts swelled with patriotism, and our knapsacks with boiled shirts, combs, brushes, etc., and that night, and next morning how many of such things were traded off for those hardshell Maryland pies, and how we expected to clean out the rebs in a short time, little realizing the long and bloody struggle which it proved to be, but thanks to the God of battles and our righteous cause, we won at last, but at what a cost of lives, of bright and noble men, on both sides! Think how many fell in our one regiment, from our loved colonel down, and many regiments lost more than we did.

Hoping you will have a goodly number, and knowing you will have a glorious time, for it will be a glorious time, if only to meet and greet each other, aside from all the other enjoyments attendant.

Hoping we may all live to join in many more reunions, I remain yours fraternally,

C. A. SAYRE,
Company E.

NUNDA, N. Y., May 20, 1896.

COMRADES:

Your notice of reunion received. I should like to be present on the occasion but find it impossible to do so. I hope you will have a good attendance and that the comrades will all enjoy themselves and live to enjoy many more reunions of the old regiment. Give my respects to all visiting comrades, and my regrets at not being able to be present. I would like to ask all comrades of the Twenty-eighth, who served in the Tenth Maine Battalion, to send their address to Major John M. Gould, First, Tenth, and Twenty-ninth Maine Regimental Association, Portland, Me.

Very respectfully yours in F., C. and L.,

WM. H. BRADY,
Company F.

NEW YORK, May 16, 1896.

DEAR COMRADES:

It pains me to be obliged every year to send regrets instead of giving my presence at the annual reunion of the Twenty-eighth, for I well know what I miss, having been present on two such occasions.

The meeting with old comrades in Rochester, N. Y., in 1877, and again in Staunton, Va., 1884, has been, and always will be, a pleasant memory, and I sincerely hope it may again be my privilege to be with the few survivors at some future reunion. Yours in F., C. and L.,

C. H. LISCOM,
Company F.

KANSAS CITY, MO., April 26, 1896.

DEAR COMRADES:

Once more our reunion is at hand, and as it is impossible to meet with you, I send you greeting. It would give me great pleasure to meet you all once more. But as it will be impossible this year, I hope you all will have a happy time, and remember, we will all be thinking of you. Hoping to be able to attend some future reunion, I am, as ever, one of the old Twenty eighth.

Respectfully yours,

PORTER HOWARD,
Company F.

GRANT, NEB., May 9, 1896.

DEAR COMRADES:

As our secretary suggests that we write a little history in our letters of regret, I suppose we will have to obey orders, as we did thirty-four years ago the latter part of this month, when the Twenty-eighth broke camp about five miles west of Strasburg, Va., and started toward Winchester and the Potomac, for the purpose of saving our scalps, as well as sundry wagons that had been left in our care, from the clutches of the noted Stonewall Jackson, whom report said was then well on the road to Winchester by another route. We moved along rapidly till we had crossed Cedar Creek, when we found that some of his men had got in ahead and attacked our train. We unslung knapsacks and moved to the front, and soon came to where a good many of our wagons were parked in a field close by the road. We halted a few minutes, and right there I had my first and last experience of seeing negroes whipped. Our mule drivers at that time were negroes, and at the first alarm they had cut loose their mules and skipped, but soon after we halted they began to return. The wagonmaster was standing on horseback by the roadside with a big mule whip, when one of the drivers came along on his mules he would dash out, and riding alongside, belabour them severely over the head and shoulders. They did not seem to mind it, but ducked their heads, whipped up their mules and got out of the way as quick as possible. The rebs were gone and we moved on through Middletown, and about 2 o'clock had reached the vicinity of Newtown, when we were faced about and marched back some four or five miles to where the rebs and our rear were having a dispute about the right of way. The rebs had a battery in position, and so had we, and the shells were flying quite lively. I remember well the first shell that came near us. Every man in the regiment from the colonel down, ducked their heads. Our company (G) was at once ordered out as skirmishers. We were marched out to the rear, and the right of our battery then deployed and moved about 400 yards to the front, bringing us between our guns and those of the enemy immediately in our front. I remember well noticing Captain Hardie as he was in front of the skirmish line in the advance. After being under two fires for about an hour we were ordered back. The old captain formed us in company and marched us by the flank across the rear of our battery, the rebel shell dropping around at the rate of three or four a minute, but for some reason they did not explode. I remember one coming so close that Jack Welch made a jump and fell, the shell striking not more than ten feet away. I started to pick it up out of curiosity, when there came another and hit right by it. I made up my mind that I did not want one, and we soon got out of range, and, it getting late, we started again for Winchester. When we were a mile or two away we could look back and see the rifles of our rear guard flash in the dark as the rebs would crowd up too closely. I was detailed with Sergeant Gaskill and a few more to scout along the right of the pike, some 400 yards from our main column. I did not think it real pleasant to go across lots in the dark in a strange country. We had not gone more than a half mile when we heard someone say, halt, who comes there? It proved to be some of Company I, who were out on the same business. We went on together. In crossing a creek on a small log I fell off and got quite a wetting. We finally got to Winchester about 12 o'clock, tired and hungry, found the regiment and laid down without any supper. If I had the space I might tell how we fought and run the next day. How the long-legged fellows in front went so fast that I could not keep up. How I, with a good many more, took the railroad to Harper's Ferry. When we arrived about sundown we were all used up. How the Eighth New York Cavalry treated us like brothers. How by canal boat and walking we finally joined the regiment at Williamsport, Md., where we were warmly welcomed by them. Yours truly,

W. W. HUNT,
Company G.

ADALASKA, MICH., May 3, 1896.

COMRADES:

With much pleasure I answer your letter, but sorry to say I can't be with you at the reunion. I have been sick nearly three months in the winter,

and am now laid up with a bone broken in one of my ankles. I had intended to meet with you this spring, but you see I can't do as I should like to. Tell my comrades when the roll is called I will answer to my name fit for duty, nothing would do me more good than to meet with you. Please tell Company G to plant a flower on the grave of Capt. Hardie for me. Give my love to all of the regiment. I will try and be with you next year if I am alive. Good-by.

WARREN H. CREGO,
Company G.

FORT BENNETT, S. D., May 11, 1896.

COMRADES OF THE TWENTY-EIGHTH:

I had hoped to attend the reunion this year, but as on other occasions, the fates seem against me. Mrs. Lounsbury has recently lost her eyesight by cataracts, and we are in hopes, through surgical operation, to get her sight restored, and I want to say that such a result is the only thing which would give me more real joy than meeting you, dear comrades, in your reunion and in memory going over the old "camp, tramp and jayhawk" times. Yes, as I write I can almost hear our band strike up the old tune they used when we broke camp, "Ain't you mighty glad you're getting out the wilderness" and how we all joined the song when we broke camp for home?

I met Comrade W. W. Eastman out here and he told of Byron Anderson. Eastman has his old fife he carried through the service. "By" was a drummer, of the old Twenty-eighth Regiment. I would be glad to get a list of the survivors, with their residence. And now, comrades, let us each strive to smooth the path of our comrades as they descend the plain toward the final muster, and may the Twenty-eighth reunions long continue, is the wish of your friend and comrade.

My pet name in the company was "Yankee."

HERBERT LOUNSBURY,
Company H.

NYACK, N. Y., April 30, 1896.

DEAR SECRETARY:

I have just received the invitation to be present at the thirty-fifth annual reunion. I am very sorry I will not be able to attend this year, as business calls me to other parts, and the distance will be too far to come. I send greetings to all the boys, and on the 22d day of May I will think of the boys of the Twenty-eighth and the good times they are having at Albion, with but one regret, that I shall not be with you this year, but will try to be with you the next reunion — 1897.

I send the following sketch, that I trust will be of interest to the boys.

In 1861, when the news came that Fort Sumter was fired on and our flag insulted, I was with a company of players in Philadelphia, Pa. Our manager, John E. McDonough, stood on the stage with the dispatch in his hand. Never have I heard before or since such an appeal for the Union as I did on that night. He bade the women and children go home and the men stay. It did not take us long to turn the theater into a drill room. With swords of Lear, and muskets of Richard the 3d, and spears of all descriptions, we drilled from 9 P. M. to 12 30 A. M., when in a body we marched to Broad and Prince streets, the P., W. & B. R. R. depot, to take train for Washington. We made coffee at the cooper-shop, which afterwards became known from Maine to California. We took cars for Baltimore about 3 45. When we arrived there we were attacked by a mob. We had nothing with which to defend ourselves. It was a free fight all around. I was hit in the head with a blunt missile, and it stunned me. I wandered about in a half-dazed condition until I saw the Twenty-eighth N. Y. Vols. coming through when I joined them, as I wanted revenge, and the ball did not open any too quick for me. I enlisted in Company I on the 25th of June in the city of Washington, D. C. I followed the ups and downs of the regiment until it was mustered out. I was wounded at Cedar Mountain August 9, 1862, in the leg. Captain Bush bound up my leg. He was not in command of his company at the time. He had a club of wood instead of a sword, and was in the thickest of the fight. It was he that saved me from being taken prisoner, and I never can forget brave Captain Bush. I was also wounded at a skirmish at Winchester, Va., with a spent ball, in the arm. Was not mustered out with the regiment, but was left in Albany, to be sent back to serve out my full time. * * *

I have never forgotten the boys of the Twenty-eighth. I remain, your comrade,

JOSEPH H. KAMP,
Company I.

NEW ORLEANS, LA., May 19, 1896.

DEAR SIR:

My husband, H. H. Paige, is ill and not able to write, but he wishes me to say that he is very sorry to learn of the death of Captain Hardie. We are all traveling the same way. He hopes that you may have a pleasant reunion, and regrets that he is not able to meet with you once again.

I regret much not being able to send his picture, but he is not well enough to sit for one.

Yours sincerely,
MRS. HELEN M. PAIGE.

RICHMOND, IND., May 22, 1896.

SECRETARY REUNION TWENTY-EIGHTH NEW YORK REGIMENT, Albion, N. Y.

I am with you in heart and spirit and the same loyalty as of yore. My love to the boys.

S. S. MARVIN,
Company K.

CRIPPLE CREEK, COLO., May 16, 1896.

DEAR COMRADES OF THE TWENTY-EIGHTH REGIMENT, Albion, N. Y.

I sincerely regret that I cannot be with you the 22d to revive the memories of our glorious regiment, but here in the mountains of Colorado I will observe the day and be with you in spirit.

With kindest regards to all, I remain most truly yours,

J. N. PHILLIPS,
Company K.

WESSINGTON, S. D., May 1, 1896.

COMRADES OF THE TWENTY-EIGHTH REGIMENT, ALBION, N. Y.

Again our worthy secretary has notified me to attend the thirty-fifth anniversary of the old Twenty-eighth. How I regret that I cannot be present, but my heart is with you. I will decorate my house with flags on the 22d. I sincerely hope you will have a good attendance and have a regular love feast. I hope I may meet some of you in St. Paul at the national encampment. I shall be there, if alive.

Comrade Eastman, of Company D, visited me last July, and we had a regular good old visit with fife and drum accompaniment. Your reunion this year will have a solemnity connected with it, which you, no doubt, will feel in the loss of Captain Hardie. Our ranks are getting thin from year to year. I wish I could grasp the hands of those that still remain. Accept my best wishes is the prayer of your old comrade and brother.

B. C. ANDERSON,
Company K.

ST. JOHNS, MICH., April 27, 1896.

DEAR COMRADES:

Please say to those present, and to those who, like me, are not present, but would like to be, that nothing in the whole world would give me so much pleasure as to meet with them. It has been my dearest hope as each anniversary has come that perhaps I might be able to attend the next reunion. But each year comes and goes and the possibility seems farther away than ever. Though absent in person, in spirit and in all well wishing and kindly feeling I am with them, with my whole heart.

My thoughts have been on the return trip from Richmond. How well I remember that ride on the transports from Aikens Landing to Washington, after being paroled from a five weeks' sojourn on Belle Isle. It was a glorious night, bright moonlight, and not a breath of wind—all was as calm and lovely as though the demon War was not raging in all its fury a few miles away.

I wonder how many who were on that boat are now living and remember the panic that occurred during the night. The upper cabin was full of men, sleeping on the floor, on tables, in chairs, wherever they could sit or lie down; I was sick and unable to sleep, and saw or heard what caused the excitement. Suddenly a man gave a screech in a dream. This awoke others, who being startled, began excitedly asking, What is the matter? What is the matter? This in turn woke others, and, presently, some one raised the cry of "fire!" and then pandemonium reigned for a time. Three or four hundred men yelling and screaming. Fire! fire! Help! help! The boat is sinking! and all imaginable calls. The men wildly gesticulating and hurrying about. There was danger that some might jump overboard, so panic-stricken were a large number

I, having been awake, knew the causelessness of the fright, and as soon as I could make myself heard and, with the help of some cool-headed men, could explain that a man dreaming has caused the alarm, quiet was restored, the whole excitement lasting but a few minutes. It was my intention to tell of our arrival in Washington, and being marched the whole length of the city, and what a forlorn crowd we were, almost naked, our hair long and uncombed, black with dirt, scrawny, wild-eyed, and hideous with suffering, truly we were a pitiable crowd! After marching us through the city, we were taken to Annapolis, Md., and I could write pages of experiences while there but this is getting too long. After a week in Annapolis we were removed to Parole Camp, at Alexandria. Of our experience while there, of our attempts to obtain clothing and blankets and so on, I will not write. But it would be incomplete if I did not tell of our rejoining the regiment, which we did some time in November. What there was left, a mere handful, was encamped on Maryland Heights. Some companies were without a commissioned officer, Company K being commanded by H. A. Jamison, Orderly Sergeant. After a month in the hospital I resumed duty, and from that time until the regiment came home I took my rations with the others.

With respect,
NEHEMIAH PECKTIL.

The following comrades send greetings and regrets that they cannot be with us, and hope all present will have an enjoyable time. Space will not allow us to publish their letters in full.

COMPANY A.

W. H. Merville, ... Centerview, O.
E. A. Eaton, ... Portis, Kans.
John F. Taylor, ... Youngstown, N. Y.
D. R. Whitcher, ... Lockport, N. Y.
Frank Church, ... Matfield Green, Kans.

COMPANY C.

Captain W. P. Warren, ... Saginaw, Mich.
William H. Adriance, ... Paw Paw, Mich.
W. T. Gillingham, ... Solon, O.
S. P. Hayes, ... Adalaska, Mich.
Frank Haner, ... Pullman, Ill.
George H. Hunt, ... Kalamazoo, Mich.
Joel Davison, ... Smith's Crossing, Mich.
A. M. Graham, ... Lockport, N. Y.

COMPANY D.

William Canham, ... Bellwood, Neb.
Daniel Stockwell, ... Adrian, Mich.
William McDonald, ... Saltvale, N. Y.

COMPANY E.

Henry S. Gulick, ... Newark, N. J.
Hiram M. Moore, ... San Luis, Abispo.

COMPANY F.

Riley Thayer, ... Alabama, N. Y.
Captain W. W. Rowley, ... Saginaw, Mich.

COMPANY G.

L. D. C. Gaskill, ... Fraser, Col.
Charles Ferdun, ... Allegan, Mich.

COMPANY H.

N. B. Bradley, ... Ithaca, Mich.
S. H. Beach, ... Jersey City, N. J.
Oliver J. Moffett, ... Fairmount, Neb.
Michael Wasim, ... New York City.
Levi Kimball, ... Wakefield, Neb.
G. W. Maybe, ... Narrowsburg, N. Y.

COMPANY I.

J. D. Woods, ... Lockport, N. Y.
R. W. Bell, ... Cleveland, O.

COMPANY K.

J. H. Smith, ... Aurora, Ill.

BAND.

Lot Parshall, ... Atlanta, Ga.

5TH VA.

G. E. McEndree, ... Cumberland, O.

A LIST OF THE

REUNIONS AND OFFICERS

OF THE

Twenty-eighth Regiment New York Volunteers.

VETERAN ASSOCIATION.

Date.	Place.	President.	Vice-President.	Secretary.
May 22, 1861.	Organized at Albany.	....	....	....
" 1862.	Strasburg, Va.	....	....	....
" 1863.	....	....	....	....
" 1864.	....	....	....	....
" 1865.	Medina.	Col. E. F. Brown.	....	....
" 1866.	Lockport.	Col. E. W. Cook.	Major T. FitzGerald.	Capt. J. D. Ames.
" 1867.	Lockport.	Col. E. F. Brown.	Col. E. W. Cook.	Capt. J. D. Ames.
" 1868.	Canandaigua.	C. L. Skeels.	Major T. FitzGerald.	J. B. Lovell.
" 1869.	Niagara Falls.	Capt. B. Flagler.	C. L. Skeels.	J. Byron Lovell.
" 1870.	Batavia	Lieut. L. R. Bailey.	Capt. W. P. Warren	J. Byron Lovell.
" 1871.	Albion.	No Record.	....	....
" 1872.	Lockport.	Capt. W. H. H. Mapes.	....	J. Byron Lovell.
" 1873.	Medina.	Col. E. A. Bowen.	....	Sergt. L. B. Swift.
" 1874.	Niagara Falls.	Dr. R. T. Paine.	George Davy.	Capt. B. Flagler.
" 1875.	Albion.	Capt. D. Hardie.	C. L. Skeels.	J. Byron Lovell.
" 1876.	Lockport.	Capt. W. W. Bush.	Capt. W. H. H. Mapes.	J. Byron Lovell.
" 1877.	Rochester.	Capt. H. Padelford.	Lieut. L. R. Bailey.	J. Byron Lovell.
" 1878.	Dayton, Ohio.	Col. E. F. Brown.	....	J. Byron Lovell.
" 1879.	Niagara Falls.	Capt. B. Flagler.	C. W. Boyce.	J. B. Lovell.
" 1880.	Medina.	Col. E. F. Brown.	Capt. D. Hardie.	J. B. Lovell.
" 1881.	Batavia.	Major J. R. Mitchell.	....	Lieut. L. R. Bailey.
" 1882.	Lockport.	Capt. W. W. Bush.	T. Boodger.	J. Byron Lovell.
" 1883.	Niagara Falls.	Capt. B. Flagler.	Lieut. J. J. Sullivan.	J. Byron Lovell.
" 1884.	Staunton, Va.	Capt. D. Hardie.	Capt. E. A. Bowen.	J. Byron Lovell.
" 1885.	Canandaigua.	Capt. H. Padelford.	M. L. Parkhurst	J. B. Lovell.
" 1886.	Lockport.	Lieut. F. N. Wicker.	Corp. J. W. Little.	J. Byron Lovell.
" 1887.	Albion.	Capt. D. Hardie.	Lieut. W. M. Kenyon.	J. Byron Lovell.
" 1888.	Medina.	John Bacon.	Ziba Roberts.	J. Byron Lovell.
" 1889.	Niagara Falls.	Capt. B. Flagler.	James H. Boyd.	J. Byron Lovell.
" 1890.	Lockport	Corp. J. W. Little.	Lieut. N. O. Allen.	J. Byron Lovell.
" 1891.	Niagara Falls.	Capt. B. Flagler.	Lieut. J. J. Sullivan.	J. Byron Lovell.
" 1892.	Medina.	Ziba Roberts.	John Bacon.	C. W. Boyce.
" 1893.	Niagara Falls.	Capt. B. Flagler.	Corp. J. W. Little.	C. W. Boyce.
" 1894.	Lockport.	Capt. B. Flagler.	Lyman Field.	C. W. Boyce.
" 1895.	Niagara Falls.	Capt. B. Flagler.	William H. Crampton.	C. W. Boyce.
" 1896.	Albion.	Capt. D. Hardie.	William Collins.	C. W. Boyce.
" 1897.	Buffalo.	Sergt. Geo. Irish	Joseph Phillips.	C. W. Boyce.

OUR COLORS.

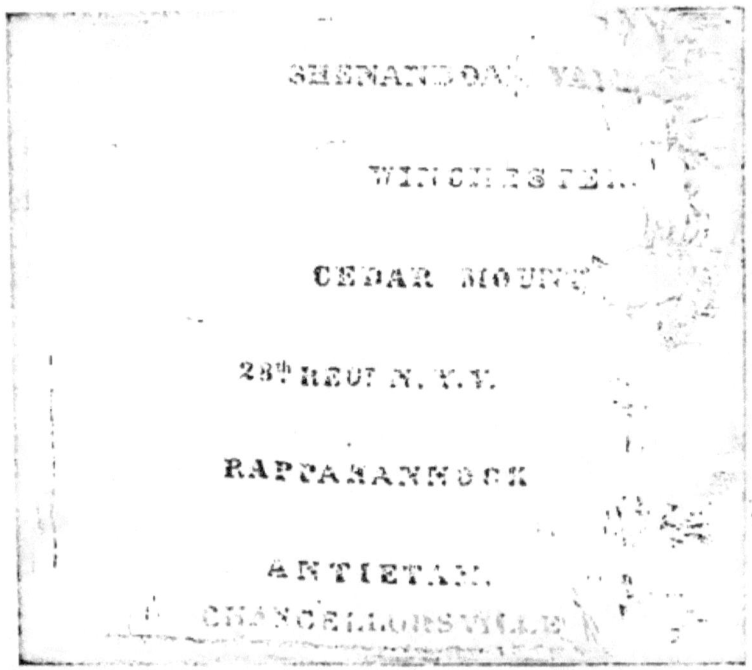

REGIMENTAL FLAG.

Twenty-eighth Regiment New York State Volunteers,

FIRST BRIGADE, FIRST DIVISION,

TWELFTH CORPS.

MUSTER-OUT ROLL

OF THE

Twenty-eighth Regiment New York State Volunteers,

COMPILED FROM THE RECORDS IN THE ADJUTANT-GENERAL'S OFFICE, ALBANY, N. Y.,

With the Present Residence of all Known Survivors.

FIELD AND STAFF.

Name and Present Residence, Where Known.	Remarks.
Colonels.	
Dudley Donnelly	Mustered in, May 22, '61, Colonel. Commanding 1st Brigade, 1st Division, 5th Corps, from March 20, '62, to June 15, '62; also commanded 1st Brigade, 1st Division, 2d Corps, Army of Virginia, July 31, '62. Wounded in action at Cedar Mountain, Va., Aug. 9, '62. Died of wounds, at Culpeper, Va., Aug. 15, '62.
Edwin F. Brown, Dayton, Ohio.	Mustered in, May 22, '61, Lieut. Col. Wounded in action at Cedar Mountain, Va., Aug. 9, '62. Left arm amputated. Left at Culpeper, Va., Aug. 19, '62, and captured. Paroled at Aikens Landing, Va., Oct. 6, '62. Rejoined, Feb. 9, '63. Promoted, Col., Nov. 1, '62. Mustered out, June 2, '63.
Elliott W. Cook	Mustered in, Sept. 14, '61, Major. Promoted from Capt. Co. A. Promoted, Lieut. Col., Nov. 2, '62. Captured at Cedar Mountain, Va., Aug. 9, '62. Exchanged, Nov. 11, '62. Captured at Chancellorsville, Va., May 2, '63. Paroled at City Point, Va., May, 11, '63. Mustered out, June 2, '63. Died in California in 1877.
Majors.	
James R. Mitchell	Mustered in, May 22, '61, Major. Resigned, Sept. 13, '61. Died in 1886.
Theophilus FitzGerald, 213 1st St. N. W., Washington, D. C.	Mustered in, Nov. 2, '62, Major. Promoted from Captain, Co. E. Mustered out, June 2, '63.
Adjutants.	
Charles P. Sprout	Mustered in, May 22, '61, Adjutant. Detached on recruiting service, Feb. 1, '62. Rejoined, May, '62. Killed in action at Cedar Mountain, Va., Aug. 9, '62.
George Davis	Mustered in, Sept. 5, '62, Adjutant. Promoted from 1st Lieut. Co. D. Mustered out, June 2, '63.
Quartermasters.	
Christopher L. Skeels	Mustered in, May 22, '61, Quartermaster. Acting Quartermaster 1st Brigade, 1st Division, 5th Army Corps, March 20, '62, to Oct. 16, '62. On duty in Chief Quartermaster's Dept., Oct. 16, '62, to Feb. 7, '63. Promoted Capt. Co. A, Oct. 21, '62. Died in 18[illegible].
Edwin A. Swan	Mustered in, May 22, '61, Quartermaster Sergt. Promoted Quartermaster, Dec. 1, '62. Mustered out, June 2, '63.
Surgeons.	
Albert M. Helmer	Mustered in, May 22, '61, Surgeon. Acting Brigade Surgeon, 1st Brigade, 1st Division, 5th Corps, from March 20, '62, to Oct. 22, '62. Resigned, Nov. 10, '62. Died, April 20, '96, in Milwaukee, Wis.
Joseph E. West	Mustered in, Nov. 18, '62, Surgeon. Promoted from Asst. Surgeon, 11 N. Y. Vols., on detached service at Sharpsburg and Frederick, Md., from Nov. 18, '62, to Feb. 14, '63. Mustered out, June 2, '63.
Mathew F. Reagan	Mustered in, May 22, '61, 1st Asst. Surgeon. Discharged for disability, Dec. 5, '61.
Robert T. Paine	Mustered in, Dec. 28, '61, 1st Asst. Surgeon. Mustered out, June 2, '63. Died in 1886.
Thomas Cushing, Barre Center, N. Y.	Mustered in, Aug. 25, '62, 2d Asst. Surgeon. Resigned, March 12, '63.
Chaplain.	
Charles N. Platt	Mustered in, May 22, '61, Chaplain. Resigned, Sept. 12, '62. Died in 1869.

NON-COMMISSIONED STAFF AND BAND.

Name and Present Residence, Where Known.	Remarks.
NON-COMMISSIONED STAFF.	
Sergeant Majors.	
Chandler B. Gillam, Byron, N. Y.	Transferred from Sergt. Co. F, Oct. 1, '62. Mustered out, June 2, '63.
Edwin A. Newberry	Transferred from Co. B, July 6, '61. Discharged, July 17, '62.
William F. Williams	Transferred from Co. K, March, 23, '62. Captured at Cedar Mountain, Va., Aug. 9, '62. Paroled at Aikens Landing, Va., Sept. 13, '62. Discharged, Sept. 16, '62, for promotion to 2d Lieut. Co. K.
Charles B. Wright	Mustered in, May 22, '61. Borne only on roll for May and June, '62, as discharged. No further information on register.
Quartermaster Sergeant.	
George E. Swan	Transferred from Co. H, Dec. 1, '62. Mustered out, June 2, '63. Died, Nov. 8, 1895, in Newburg, N. Y.
Commissary Sergeant.	
Leonard D. Sale, Philadelphia "Press," Philadelphia, Pa.	Transferred from Co. E, Oct. 1, '62. Mustered out, June 2, '63.
Hospital Stewards.	
Thomas Bentley	Mustered in, May 22, '61, Hospital Steward. "Discharged, but what for, when, or by whose authority, not recorded." Hospital steward from July 1, '61, to Aug. 11, '61. No further information on register.
Albert U. Angevine	Transferred from Co. D, Aug. 11, '61. Left in charge of wounded at Culpeper, Va., Aug. 20, '62, and captured. Exchanged, Nov. 19, '62. Rejoined, Jan. 13, '63. Mustered out, June 2, '63.
Drum Majors.	
John Minor	Mustered in, May 22, '61. Transferred to Co. H, July 29, '61, as private.
Mathew G. Tieranncy	Transferred from Co. I, July 1, '61. Deserted, April 20, '62, at Strasburg, Va.
Fife Majors.	
William H. Chambers, 182 Tremont St., Boston, Mass.	Transferred from Co. A, Oct. 12, '61. Transferred to Co. A, Aug. 17, '62.
Alonzo J. McMaster	Mustered in, May 22, '61. Discharged for disability, at Darnestown, Md., Sept. 21, '61.
Benjamin Repasz	Transferred from Co. A, Dec. 25, '61. Transferred to Co. A, Oct. 1, '62, as musician.
BAND.	
Leader of Band.	
W. A. Thomas	Mustered in, Oct. 1, '61. Mustered out, Aug. 16, '62, at Washington, D. C., per act of July 8, '62.
1st Class Musicians.	
William Daniells	Mustered in, Sept. 1, '61. Mustered out, Aug. 16, '62, at Washington, D. C., per act of July 8, '62.
Benjamin Kelzer	Mustered in, Oct. 1, '61. Mustered out, Aug. 16, '62, at Washington, D. C., per act of July 8, '62.
Stephen P. Lapham, Hornellsville, N. Y.	Mustered in, Sept. 1, '61. Discharged, Sept. 29, '62.
Cyrus E. LeSuer, Bolivar, N. Y.	Mustered in, Sept. 1, '61. Mustered out, Aug. 16, '62, at Washington, D. C., per act of July 8, '62.
George Winter	Mustered in, Nov. 1, '61. Mustered out, Aug. 16, '62, at Washington, D. C., per act of July 8, '62.
2d Class Musicians.	
Hebron E. Dickenson, 721 Main St., Buffalo, N. Y.	Mustered in, Sept. 1, '61. Mustered out, Aug. 16, '62, at Washington, D. C., per act of July 8, '62.
Royal H. Grady, Cuba, N. Y.	Mustered in, Sept. 1, '61. Mustered out, Aug. 16, '62, at Washington, D. C., per act of July 8, '62.
Rodolphus Talcott	Mustered in, Sept. 1, '61. Mustered out, Aug. 16, '62, at Washington, D. C., per act of July 8, '62.
Enos B. Whitmore, Rochester, N. Y.	Mustered in Nov. 1, '61. Mustered out, Aug. 16, '61, at Washington, D. C., per act of July 8, '62.
William Withey, Sioux Falls, S. D.	Mustered in, Sept. 1, '61, Washington, D. C. Left behind as nurse at Culpeper, Va., Aug. 20, '62, and captured. Paroled at Aikens Landing, Va., Oct. 6, '62. Mustered out, Oct. 8, '62.
3d Class Musicians.	
Henry Buckley, West Salamanca, N. Y.	Mustered in, Sept. 1, '61. Mustered out, Aug. 16, '62, at Washington, D. C., per act of July 8, '62.
Orson A. Baldwin	Mustered in, Sept. 1, '61. Discharged for disability, Nov. 21, '61.
John Chambers, Lockport, N. Y.	Transferred from Co. A, Oct. 12, '61. Transferred to Co. A, Aug. 17, '62.
Joseph B. Crawford	Mustered in, Sept. 1, '61. Mustered out, Aug. 16, '62, at Washington, D. C., per act of July 8, '62. Died in 1892.
Joel S. Davison, Smith's Crossing, Midland Co., Mich.	Transferred from Co. C, Oct. 14, '61. Transferred to Co. C as musician, March 21, '62.
William W. Eastman, 1114 N. 25th St., Omaha, Neb.	Transferred from Co. D, April 10, '62. Transferred to Co. D as musician, Aug. 17, '62.
John Ferary	Transferred from Co. C, Oct. 14, '61. Transferred to Co. C, Aug. 17, '62, as musician.
James W. Ford, Lockport, N. Y.	Transferred from Co. A, Oct. 12, '61. Transferred to Co. A, Aug. 17, '62, as musician.
Lot Parshall, 81½ Grand St., Atlanta, Ga.	Mustered in, Sept. 1, '61. Discharged for disability, Nov. 24, '62.
John Quinton, Belfast, N. Y.	Mustered in, Sept. 1, '61. Discharged for disability, Nov. 20 '61.
Lorenzo A. Sabine	Transferred from Co. E, Nov. 5, '61. Transferred to Co. E, Dec. 20, '61, as private. Died Feb. 1892.

COMPANY A.

Name and Present Residence, Where Known.	Remarks.
Captains.	
Elliott W. Cook	Mustered in, May 22, '61, Capt. Discharged, Sept. 13, '61, for promotion to Major. Died in California in 1875.
Benjamin Flagler, Niagara Falls, N. Y.	Mustered in, Oct. 21, '61, Capt. Assumed command, Nov. 4, '61. Acting Assistant Adjutant-General 1st Brigade, 1st Division, Dept. Shenandoah, March 30, '62, till June, '62. Resigned, Oct. 21, '62.
Christopher L. Skeels	Mustered in, Oct. 21, '62. Promoted from Quartermaster. Mustered out, June 2, '63. Died in 1879.
Lieutenants.	
Daniel R. Whitcher, Lockport, N. Y.	Mustered in, May, 22, '61, 1st Lieut. Resigned, Jan. 21, '62.
Frank N. Wicker, 618 Common St., New Orleans, La.	Mustered in, March 14, '62, 1st Lieut. Promoted from 2d Lieut., Co. C. Detailed on signal service, Aug. 25, '61, to Dec. 1, '62. Transferred to Co. C, Dec. 1, '62.
John Repasz	Mustered in, May 22, '61, as 2d Lieut. Promoted, 1st Lieut., Jan. 30, '62. Resigned, Feb. 12, '62. Died, June 19, 1892.
Jeremiah Long	Mustered in, May 22, '61, 1st Sergt. Promoted, Jan. 30, '62, 2d Lieut.; July 21, '62, 1st Lieut. Transferred to Co. C, July 21, '62. Retransferred to Co. A, Dec. 1, '62. Captured at Cedar Mountain, Va., Aug. 9, '62. Paroled at Aikens Landing, Va., Sept. 24, '62. Mustered out, June 2, '63. Died in Santa Monica, Cal., April 3, 1886.
Lewis D. C. Gaskill, Fraser, Col.	Mustered in, Oct. 9, '62, 2d Lieut., promoted from Sergt. Co. G. Detailed to command Co. C, from Jan. 18, '63, to March 16, '63. Mustered out, June 2, '63.
Sergeants.	
Riley P. Butrick	Mustered in, May 22, '61, Corp. Promoted, Sergt., Nov. 20, '62. Captured at Cedar Mountain, Va., Aug. 9, '62. Paroled at Aikens Landing, Va., Sept. 13, '62. Mustered out, June 2, '63.
Michael Casey	Mustered in, May 22, '61, private. Promoted, Corp., Aug. 6, '61; Sergt., Feb. 1, '62; 1st Sergt., Dec. 30, '62. Captured at Cedar Mountain, Va., Aug. 9, '62. Paroled, Aikens Landing, Va., Sept. 13, '62. Mustered out, June 2, '63.
Henry Foster	Mustered in, May 22, '61, Corp. Discharged, Sergt., Feb. 15, '62, for disability, at Baltimore, Md. Died in 1883.
James Lewis	Mustered in, May 22, '61, Corp. Promoted, Sergt., Jan. 20, '62; 1st Sergt., March or April, '62. Discharged, Oct. 24, '62, for disability, at Maryland Heights, Md. Died in 1890.
Henry Repasz, Lockport, N. Y.	Mustered in, May 22, '61. Promoted, Ordnance Sergt., Aug. 13, '61; 1st Sergt., Feb. 1, '62. Captured at Winchester, Va., May 25, '62. Paroled at Aikens Landing, Va., Sept. 13, '62. Mustered out, June, 2, '63.
Charles Sowter, Lockport, N. Y.	Mustered in, May 22, '61, private. Promoted, Corp., July 27, '62; Sergt., Feb. 3, '63. Captured at Cedar Mountain, Va., Aug. 9, '62. Paroled at Aikens Landing, Va., Sept. 13, '62. Mustered out, June 2, '63.
William Winthrop, Lockport, N. Y.	Mustered in, May 22, '61, private. Promoted, Corp., July 28, '61; Sergt., Feb. 15, '62. Mustered out, June 2, '63.
Sergeants.—Continued.	
Thomas Herbert	Mustered in, May 22, '61. Discharged, Aug. 6, '61, for disability, at Berlin, Md.
George W. Tucker	Mustered in, May 22, '61, private. Promoted, Corp., Feb. 1, '62; Sergt., July 27, '62. Killed in action at Cedar Mountain, Va., Aug. 9, '62.
Nathan J. Wright	Mustered in, May 22, '61, private. Promoted, Sergt., March 1, '62. Wounded in action, at Cedar Mountain, Va., Aug. 9, '62. Left at Culpeper, Va., Aug. 18, '62; taken prisoner and paroled. Detached on recruiting service, Feb., March and April, '62. Discharged, Nov. 17, '62, for disability, at Annapolis, Md.
Corporals.	
Alonzo Greenman	Mustered in, May 22, '61, private. Promoted, Corp., Feb. 3, '63. Captured at Cedar Mountain, Va., Aug. 9, '62. Paroled at Aikens Landing, Va., Sept. 13, '62. Mustered out, June 2, '63.
Joseph W. Little, Lockport, N. Y.	Mustered in, May 22, '61, private. Promoted, Corp., Nov., '62. Mustered out, June 2, '63.
Wesley G. Ray	Mustered in, May 22, '61. Discharged, July 17, '61, for disability, at Washington, D. C.
James L. Atwood	Mustered in, May 22, '61, private. Promoted, Corp., Feb. 28, '62. Wounded in action at Cedar Mountain, Va., Aug. 9, '62. In hospital, Oct. '62, to Dec. 30, '62. Detached as clerk at Camp Distribution, Alexandria, Va., Dec. 30, '62, to April 30, '63. Mustered out, June 2, '63.
William H. Crampton, Lockport, N. Y.	Mustered in, May 22, '61, private. Promoted, Corp., March or April, '62. Wounded in action at Cedar Mountain, Va., Aug. 9, '62. Discharged for disability at General Hospital, Alexandria, Va., Sept. 21, '62. Right arm amputated.
Musicians.	
William Baker	Mustered in, May 22, '61. Mustered out, June 2, '63.
Benjamin F. Repasz	Mustered in, May 22, '61. Transferred, Dec. 25, '61, to Fife Major. Mustered out, June 2, '63. Died in 1880.
Privates.	
Jacob M. Armstrong	Mustered in, May 22, '61. Wounded in action at Cedar Mountain, Va., Aug. 9, '62. Discharged at Harper's Ferry, Va., Dec. 3, '62, for disability from wounds received at Cedar Mountain.
Jeremiah Babcock	Mustered in, May 22, '61. Wounded and taken prisoner at Winchester, Va., May 25, '62, and released on parole. Discharged for disability, July 11, '62, at Circle Hospital, Washington, D. C.
Chester Barry	Mustered in, May 22, '61. Discharged for disability, Aug. 6, '61, at Berlin, Md.
Thomas Boodger, Hart, Mich.	Mustered in, May 22, '61; Ambulance Driver Aug. 27, '62 to March 31, '63. Mustered out, June 2, '63.
Joseph B. Boyce	Transferred from Co. C, Dec. 22, '62. Transferred to depot at Albany, May 10, '63. Subsequently transferred to Veteran Reserve Corps. Died in 1880.

COMPANY A.—Continued.

NAME AND PRESENT RESIDENCE, WHERE KNOWN.	REMARKS.
Privates.—Continued.	
Benjamin B. Brown ... Cooperstown, Griggs Co., N. Dak.	Mustered in, May 22, '61. Wounded in action at Cedar Mountain, Va., Aug. 9, '62. Discharged for disability, Baltimore, Md., Dec. 20, '62.
Luther L. Bosserman ...	Mustered in, May 22, '61. Wounded at Cedar Mountain, Va., Aug. 9, '62. Mustered out, June 2, '63.
Augustus W. Caman ... La Cygne, Kan.	Mustered in, Aug. 26, '62. Transferred to Depot at Albany, N. Y., May 19, '63, and joined the 10th Maine Battalion.
Patrick Carroll ...	Mustered in, May 22, '61. Deserted, Nov. 26, '61, at Muddy Branch, Md. Subsequently enlisted in Co. F, 7th Pa. Cavalry, Sept. 15, '62, under name of William Smith.
Anson Carson ...	Mustered in, May 22, '61. Captured at Manassas, Va., Aug. 21, '62. Paroled at Falls Church, Va., Aug. 28, '62. Mustered out, June 2, '63.
John S. Chambers ... Lockport, N. Y.	Mustered in, May 22, '61. Transferred to Regimental Band, Oct. 12, '61. Transferred from band, Aug. 17, '62. Mustered out, June 2, '63.
William B. Chambers ... 94 Tremont St., Boston, Mass.	Mustered in, May 22, '61. Transferred to Regimental Band, Oct. 12, '61. Transferred from band, Aug. 17, '62. Mustered out, June 2, '63.
Francis H. Church ... Mansfield Green, Kan.	Mustered in, May 22, '61. Mustered out, June 2, '63.
John Clark ...	Mustered in, May 22, '61. Deserted, Sept. 3, '62, etc., Darnestown, Md.
Charles G. Davis ...	Mustered in, May 22, '61. Deserted, Nov. 26, '61, at Muddy Branch, Md.
Martin W. Demerest ...	Mustered in, May 22, '61. Deserted, Nov. 26, '61, at Muddy Branch, Md.
Orlando E. Dickerson ...	Mustered in, May 22, '61. Captured at Winchester, Va., May 25, '62; released on parole. Rejoined Regt., Nov. 26, '62. Mustered out, June 2, '63.
Alva A. Eaton ... Portis, Kan.	Mustered in, May 22, '61. Discharged for disability, July 21, '61, at Washington, D. C.
George Elenze ...	Mustered in, Aug. 26, '62. Transferred to Depot at Albany, May 19, '63.
Bernard Englert ...	Mustered in, May 22, '61. Wounded in action at Cedar Mountain, Va., Aug. 9, '62. Discharged for disability at Alexandria, Va., Nov. 1, '62. Died, June 20, '91.
Edgar A. Enus ...	Mustered in, Dec. 25, '61. Mustered out, June 2, '63.
Samuel Farr ...	Mustered in, May 22, '61. Killed in action at Cedar Mountain, Va., Aug. 9, '62.
Lyman Field ... Lockport, N. Y.	Mustered in, May 22, '61. Detached on recruiting service by order General Banks, Oct. 14, '61, to Jan., '62. Detailed as nurse at Culpeper, Va., Aug. 10, '62, and remained there by order of A. M. Helmer, Surgeon. Paroled at Aikens Landing, Va., Sept. 21, '62. Mustered out, June 2, '63.
William P. Field ...	Mustered in, Aug. 22, '62. Discharged, March 13, '63, at Stafford C. H., Va., by order of Secretary of War. Died, Jan., 1880.
James M. Ford ... Lockport, N. Y.	Mustered in, May 22, '61. Transferred to Regimental Band, Oct. 12, '61. Transferred from band, Aug. 17, '62. Mustered out, June 2, '63.
William D. Fox ...	Mustered in, May 22, '61. Discharged for disability at Central Park Hospital, New York, April 21, '63.
Privates.—Continued.	
Michael Gaffney ...	Mustered in, May 22, '61. Deserted Aug. 15, '62. Surrendered at Convalescent Camp, Va., March, '63, under President's proclamation. Mustered out, June 2, '63.
John T. Guilor ... Lockport, N. Y.	Mustered in, May 22, '61. Discharged for disability at Front Royal, Va., June 22, '62.
George W. Good ...	Mustered in, May 22, '61. Killed in action at Cedar Mountain, Va., August 9, '62.
Augustus Hankey ...	Mustered in, Oct. 23, '61. Killed in action at Cedar Mountain, Va., Aug. 9, '62.
Ezra H. Harwood ...	Mustered in, Nov. 11, '61. Discharged for disability at New Market, Va., May 8, '62.
John Henning ...	Mustered in, May 22, '61. Mustered out, June 2, '63.
William H. Holland ...	Enlisted, March 13, '63. "Substitute for William P. Field, Discharged by order of Secretary of War." Transferred to Depot at Albany, N. Y., May 19, '63.
John Kinardt, Sr. ...	Mustered in, Oct. 26, '61. Mustered out, June 2, '63.
John Kinardt, Jr. ...	Mustered in, May 22, '61. Discharged for disability, Feb. 21, '63, at Elmira, N. Y.
Amos E. Kniffen ...	Mustered in, May 22, '61. Deserted, Dec. 22, '61, at Frederick, Md.
William H. Langdon ... 273 Union St., Lockport, N. Y.	Mustered in, May 22, '61. Mustered out, June 2, '63.
Jeremiah Lasher ...	Mustered in, Nov. 11, '61. Deserted, Dec. 26, '61, at Frederick, Md.
Noah B. Lincoln ... Pipestone, Minn.	Mustered in, May 22, '61. Mustered out, June 2, '63.
Henry W. Logan ... Ransomville, N. Y.	Mustered in, May 22, '61. Admitted to Hospital, Baltimore, Md., May 10, '62, with fever. Transferred to Philadelphia, May 21, '62. Discharged May 21, '62.
Charles Lureman ... Wendleville, N. Y.	Mustered in, May 22, '61. Captured at Cedar Mountain, Va., Aug. 9, '62. Paroled at Aikens Landing, Va., Sept. 13, '62. Mustered out, June 2, '63.
John McLeland ...	Mustered in, May 22, '61. Mustered out, June 2, '63.
Philo. A. Matson ...	Mustered in, May 22, '61. Deserted, June 9, '61, at Albany.
Alexander Mehwaldt ... 101 Plymouth Ave., Buffalo, N. Y.	Mustered in, May 22, '61. Mustered out, June 2, '63.
Adam B. Merville ...	Mustered in, May 22, '61. Mustered out, June 2, '63. Detailed to take boats to Harper's Ferry, Feb., '62. Died, Oct. 21, 1895.
William H. Merville ... Center View, Ohio.	Mustered in, May 22, '61. Discharged for disability, Aug. 6, '61, at Berlin, Md.
Phillip Moyer ...	Mustered in, May 22, '61. Detailed to take boats to Harper's Ferry, Va., Jan. and Feb., '62. Detailed for duty at Brigade Headquarters, Feb. 4, '63, to April '63. Mustered out, June 2, '63. Died in 1888.
Augustus Nearst ...	Mustered in, April 2, '62. Transferred to Depot at Albany, N. Y., May 19, '63, later joined 10th Maine Battalion.
Daniel A. Nuaker ...	Transferred from Co. D., Jan. 1, '62. Mustered out, June 2, '63.

COMPANY A.—Continued.

NAME AND PRESENT RESIDENCE, WHERE KNOWN.	REMARKS.
Privates—Continued.	
Aaron G. Oakley	Mustered in, May 22, '61. Regimental Wagon Boss, July 21, '62, to Jan. 18, '63. Corps teamster, Jan. 18, '63, to May 10, '63. Mustered out June 2, '63. Died in 1890.
Thomas Pasco, 36 Victoria St., Montreal, Que.	Mustered in, May 22, '61. Captured at Cedar Mountain, Va., Aug. 9, '62. Discharged, Jan. 14, '63, for disability, at Fort Delaware, Del.
Ambrose Peacock	Mustered in, May 22, '61. Deserted, Dec. 22, '61. Returned under President's Proclamation, April 1, '63. Mustered out, June 2, '63.
Nathan Z. Peterson	Mustered in, May 22, '61. Discharged for disability, July 21, '61, at Washington, D. C.
William E. Reed, 180 N. Y. St., Aurora, Ills.	Mustered in, Aug. 12, '62. Transferred to Depot at Albany, N. Y., May 19, '63.
Levi Reed	Mustered in, Aug. 23, '62. Transferred to Depot at Albany, N. Y., May 19, '63.
Elias Reid	Mustered in, May 22, '61. Discharged for disability at Berlin, Md., Aug. 6, '61.
William Robinson	Mustered in, Dec. 7, '61. Absent, sick at Baltimore, Md., since March 1, '62. No further information on register.
Isaac W. Sly	Mustered in, May 22, '61. Killed, July 11, '61, in skirmish, near Martinsburg, Va.
Robert Southard	Mustered in May 22, '61. Detached for signal service, Oct. 1, '61, to April 22, '62. Mustered out, June 2, '63.
George Squires	Mustered in, May 22, '61. Mustered out June 2, '63.
John H. Stahl, Niagara Falls, N. Y.	Mustered in, May 22, '61. On extra duty as teamster, Aug. 6, '61, to Jan., '62; Regt. teamster, May, '62, to Nov., '62. Mustered out, June 2, '63.
Henry V. Sterling	Mustered in, May 22, '61. Captured at Cedar Mountain, Va., Aug. 9, '62. Paroled at Aikens Landing, Va., Sept. 13, '62. Mustered out, June 2, '63.
Lyman A. Stickles, 491 South Division St., Grand Rapids, Mich.	Mustered in, May 22, '61. Discharged for disability, Sept. 22, '62, at Sandy Hook, Md.
Lucius E. Stickney, Alabama, N. Y.	Mustered in, Nov. 22, '61. Discharged for disability, May 26, '62, at New Market, Va.
Charles B. Sullivan	Mustered in, May 22, '61. Wounded at Cedar Mountain, Va., Aug. 9, '62, taken prisoner and paroled at Culpeper, Va. Mustered out, June 2, '63.
John F. Taylor, Youngstown, N. Y.	Mustered in, May 24, '61. Discharged for disability, Nov. 8, '62, at Albany.
Malcomb G. Taylor	Mustered in, May 22, '61. Killed in action at Cedar Mountain, Va., Aug. 9, '62.
William Taylor	Mustered in, May 22, '61. Discharged for disability, July 21, '61, at Washington, D. C.
Harrison Thomas, 86 Franklin St., Auburn, N. Y.	Mustered in, May 22, '61. Ambulance driver, July and Aug., '62. Mustered out, June 2, '63.
Bergen F. Tyler	Mustered in, May 22, '61. Deserted, Aug. 23, '61, at Hyattstown, Md.
Edward J. Williams	Mustered in, Sept. 5, '62. Transferred, May 19, '63, to Depot at Albany.
John R. Wright	Mustered in, May 22, '61. Ambulance driver, July 25, '62, to May, '63. Mustered out, June 2, '63.
John L. Wright, Lockport, N. Y.	Mustered in, May 22, '61. Discharged, July 12, '61, for disability, at Berlin, Md.

COMPANY B.

NAME AND PRESENT RESIDENCE, WHERE KNOWN.	REMARKS.
Captain.	
Wm. W. Bush	Mustered in, May 22, '61, Capt. Captured at Cedar Mountain, Va., Aug. 9, '62. Paroled at Aikens Landing, Va., Sept. 21, '62. Detached on transportation service via Chesapeake & Ohio Canal, Feb., '62. Dismissed, court martial, March 23, '63. Recommissioned, May 6, '63, to date March 23, '63. Mustered out, June 2, '63. Died, April 19, 1886.
Lieutenants.	
Alfred B. Judd, 729 Sycamore St., Milwaukee, Wis.	Mustered in, May 22, '61, Lieut. Mustered out, June 1, '62, for promotion to Captain Co. G.
John D. Woods	Mustered in, June 1, '62, 2d Lieut. Commanded company, Dec. 23, '62, to Jan. 26, '63. Promoted, 1st Lieut. Co. I, Feb. 20, '63.
George Maxwell, Royal Oak, Mich.	Mustered in, May 22, '61, 1st Sergt. Promoted, Jan. 30, '62, 2d Lieut. Transferred to Co. I, March 1, '62.
John C. Walsh	Mustered in, May 22, '61, 2d Lieut. Promoted, June 1, '62, 1st Lieut. Dismissed, March 16, '63.
Lieutenants—Continued.	
Peter B. Kelchner, Renfrew, Pa.	Mustered in, May 22, '61, Sergt. Promoted, 1st Sergt., March 13, '62; 2d Lieut. May 6, '63. Seriously wounded at Antietam, Sept. 17, '62. Mustered out, June 2, '63.
Sergeants.	
John M. Lacy	Mustered in, May 22, '61, private. Promoted, Sergt., March 13, '62; 1st Sergt., May 11, '63. Captured at Winchester, Va., May 25, '62. Paroled at Aikens Landing, Va., Sept. 13, '62. Mustered out, June 2, '63.
William White	Mustered in, May 22, '61. Discharged for disability, Feb. 4, '63, at Philadelphia, Pa.
George Southard	Mustered in, May 22, '61, private. Promoted, Corp., Nov. 10, '62; Sergt., Feb. 4, '63. Mustered out, June 2, '63.
Shuler T. Smedley	Mustered in, May 22, '61, Corp. Promoted, Sergt., March 13, '62. Detailed to take charge of wounded at Culpeper, Aug. 10, '62. Captured at Culpeper, Va., Aug. 19, '62. Paroled at Aikens Landing, Va., Oct. 6, '62. Detached on recruiting service at Lockport, N. Y., Feb. 1, '63, to May, '63. Mustered out, June 2, '63.

COMPANY B.—Continued.

Name and Present Residence, Where Known.	Remarks.
Sergeants.—Continued.	
James F. Bush	Mustered in, May 22, '61. Reduced to private, Jan. 24, '63. Mustered out, June 2, '63.
William Smith	Mustered in, May 22, '61, private. Promoted Corp., July 1, '61. Wounded in action, Cedar Mountain, Va., Aug. 9, '62. Promoted Sergt., Jan. 24, '63. Mustered out, June 2, '63. Died in 1890.
Corporals.	
Thomas P. Bateman	Mustered in, May 22, '61, as Corp. Discharged for disability at Maryland Heights, Md., Oct. 21, '62.
Wright Boodger, Lockport, N. Y.	Mustered in, May 22, '61, as musician. Promoted, Corp., Nov. 10, '62. Captured and paroled at Culpeper, Va., Aug. 18, '62. Mustered out, June 2, '63.
Stephen Clark	Mustered in, May 22, '61, private. Promoted, Corp., Feb. 1, '63. Captured at Winchester, Va., May 25, '62. Paroled at Aikens Landing, Va., Sept. 13, '62. Mustered out, June 2, '63.
James Goggin, Lockport, N. Y.	Mustered in, May 22, '61, private. Promoted Corp., Jan. 21, '63. Captured at Culpeper and paroled, Aug. 18, '62. Mustered out, June 2, '63.
James McMullen	Mustered in, May 22, '61, Corp. Mustered out, private, June 2, '64.
Phillip H. Murphy	Mustered in, May 22, '61. Discharged from hospital, Alexandria, Va., Nov. 3, '62, for wounds received in action at Cedar Mountain, Va., Aug. 9, '62.
Musician.	
Joseph W. Chandler	Mustered in, May 22, '61. Discharged for disability, Dec. 13, '62, from Convalescent Camp, Va.
Privates.	
John Balantine	Mustered in, May 22, '61. Wounded in action at Cedar Mountain, Va., Aug. 9, '62. Mustered out, June 2, '63.
Joseph Baker	Mustered in, May 22, '61. Deserted, Aug. 23, '61, at Hyattstown, Va. Died in 1870.
Joseph Bayard	Mustered in, May 22, '61. Discharged for disability at Washington, D. C., July 24, '61.
William F. Behan	Mustered in, May 22, '61. Deserted, Sept. 21, '61. Returned at Stafford C. H., April 12, '63, under President's proclamation of March 10, '63. Mustered out, June 2, '63.
Alfred Bell	Mustered in, May 22, '61. Discharged for disability, Aug. 12, '61, at Berlin, Md.
William Blackwell	Mustered in, May 22, '61. Discharged for disability, July 1, '62, Douglass Hospital, Washington, D. C.
Henry Bollon	Mustered in, May 22, '61. Discharged for disability, July 24, '61, at Washington, D. C.
Sylvester Bowen	Mustered in, Aug. 21, '62. Transferred to depot at Albany, N. Y., May 19, '63.
Amos M. Brown	Mustered in, May 22, '61. Captured at Cedar Mountain, Va., Aug. 9, '62. Paroled at Aikens Landing, Va., Sept. 13, '62. Mustered out, June 2, '63.
Dewett C. Bulmen	Mustered in, May 22, '61. Killed in action at Cedar Mountain, Va., Aug. 9, '62.

Name and Present Residence, Where Known.	Remarks.
Privates.—Continued.	
Henry Burk	Mustered in, May 22, '61. Mustered out, June 2, '63.
John Burk	Mustered in, May 22, '61. In charge of wounded at Frederick, Md., Sept. 18, '62, to Oct., '62. Mustered out, June 2, '63.
James Colle	Mustered in, May 22, '61. Captured at Manassas, Va., Aug. 29, '62. Paroled, Sept. 3, '62. Sick in hospital at Alexandria, Va., March 21, '63. No further information on Register.
John Calbeck	Mustered in, May 22, '61. Discharged for disability at Berlin, Md., Aug. 3, '61.
James Campbell	Mustered in, May 22, '61. Mustered out, June 2, '63.
Stephen H. Chandler	Mustered in, May 22, '61. Mustered out, June 2, '63.
Henry Colton	Mustered in, May 22, '61. Mustered out, June 2, '63. Died at Pendleton Center, March 12, '95.
Palmer Colton	Mustered in, May 22, '61. Discharged for disability, Aug. 8, '61, at Berlin, Md.
William Conner	Mustered in, May 22, '61. Killed in action at Cedar Mountain, Va., Aug. 9, '62.
George M. Cook	Mustered in, May 22, '61. Wounded in action at Cedar Mountain, Va., Aug. 9, '62. Died in hospital, Culpeper, Va., Aug. 29, '62. Amputation of thigh.
Patrick Cooney	Mustered in, May 22, '61. Captured at Cedar Mountain, Va., Aug. 9, '62. Paroled, Aikens Landing, Va., Sept. 13, '62. Mustered out, June 2, '63.
James Coville	Mustered in, May 22, '61. Mustered out, June 2, '63. Died, Aug. 23, 1893.
William H. Crampton	Mustered in, May 22, '61. Died, March 17, '62, of disease, in hospital, at Winchester, Va.
Thomas Dalton	Mustered in, May 22, '61. Captured at Cedar Mountain, Va., Aug. 9, '62. Paroled at Aikens Landing, Va., Sept. 13, '62. Mustered out, June 2, '63.
Frederick Dohring	Mustered in, May 22, '61. Wounded at Cedar Mountain, Va., Aug. 9, '62. Mustered out, June 2, '63.
George Eolinger	Mustered in, May 22, '61. Mustered out, June 2, '63.
Michael Finnegan, Lockport, N. Y.	Mustered in, May 22, '61. Mustered out, June 2, '63.
John Finn	Mustered in, May 22, '61. Driving supply train, Dec., '61, to May, '63. Mustered out, June 2, '63.
James Garnum	Mustered in, May 22, '61. Deserted, Nov. 11, '61, at Muddy Branch, Md.
William Geer, Clintonville, Wis.	Mustered in, May 22, '61. Discharged for disability at Washington, D. C., Dec. 15, '62.
Alanson A. Hall	Mustered in, Sept. 12, '62. Transferred to depot at Albany, N. Y., May 19, '63; later, assigned to 10th Maine Battalion.
Robert Hamilton	Mustered in, May 22, '61. Mustered out, June 2, '63. Died in 1887.
Patrick Hanley	Mustered in, May 22, '61. Captured at Cedar Mountain, Va., Aug. 9, '62. Paroled at Aikens Landing, Va., Sept. 13, '62. Mustered out, June 2, '63.
William Hans	Mustered in, May 22, '61. Deserted, Sept. 10, '61, at Darnestown, Md.
James Hatch	"Enlisted to fill vacancy, July 21, '61." Deserted, Aug. 28, '61, at Hyattstown, Md.

COMPANY B.—Continued.

Name and Present Residence, Where Known.	Remarks.
Privates.—Continued.	
Martin Hooner	Mustered in, May 22, '61. Deserted on march, near Sandy Hook, Md., Oct. 4, '62.
Robert A. Hyne	Enlisted in Lockport, N. Y., date not given. Died of disease, May 17, '62 at Strasburg, Va.
Robert Irving, Lockport, N. Y.	Mustered in, Feb. 22, '62. Transferred to depot at Albany, N. Y., May 19, '64; later, joined 10th Maine Battalion.
John Jacobus	Mustered in, May 22, '61. Mustered out, June 2, '63.
John Johnston	Mustered in, May 22, '61. Wounded in action at Cedar Mountain, Va., Aug. 9, '62. Died in hospital, Culpeper, Va., Sept. 10, '62, after amputation.
John Johnston	Mustered in, May 22, '61. Captured at Cedar Mountain, Va., Aug. 9, '62. Paroled at Aikens Landing, Va., Sept. 13, '62. Discharged for disability at Fort Schuyler Hospital, N. Y., Jan. 13, '63.
Thomas Leonard	Mustered in, May 22, '61. Captured at Winchester, Va., May 25, '62. Paroled at Aikens Landing, Va., Sept. 13, '62. Mustered out, June 2, '64.
Joel A. Lindsley	Mustered in, Feb. 22, '62. Discharged for disability at Convalescent Camp, Va., Feb. 6, '63.
Franklin McClanathan, Vienna, N. Y.	Mustered in, May 22, '61. Ambulance driver from July 1, '61, to July, '62. In Brigade Quartermaster's Dept., Aug., '62. Mustered out, June 2, '63.
John R. Mabee, Jackson, Mich.	Mustered in, May 22, '61. Detached on signal service, Oct., '61, to May, '63. Mustered out, June 2, '63.
Peter Mangin	Mustered in, May 22, '61. Deserted at Muddy Branch, Md., Nov. 11, '61.
John Miller	Mustered in, May 22, '61. Mustered out, June 2, '63.
Henry Milger	Mustered in, May 22, '61. Wounded in action, Aug. 9, '62, at Cedar Mountain. Mustered out, June 2, '63.
Burnett Murphey	Mustered in, May 22, '61. Detailed with ambulance corps, Oct. 25, '62, to May, '63. Mustered out, June 2, '63.
Edward S. Newman	Mustered in, May 22, '61. Captured at Cedar Mountain, Va., Aug. 9, '62. Paroled at Aikens Landing, Sept. 21, '62. Mustered out, June 2, '63.
Oscar H. Palmer	Mustered in, Sept. 29, '62. Transferred to depot at Albany, N. Y., May 19, '63.
William D. Parker	Mustered in, May 22, '61. Discharged for disability, at Berlin, Md., Aug. 5, '61.
Commodore O. Perry, Gordon Avenue, Niagara Falls, N. Y.	Mustered in, May 22, '61. Mustered out, June 2, '63.
William Reeder	Mustered in, Aug. 30, '62. Transferred to depot at Albany, N. Y., May 19, '63.
William Robinson	Mustered in, May 22, '61. Discharged for disability, Washington, D. C., July 21, '61.
William Roche	Mustered in, Feb. 17, '62. Transferred to depot at Albany, N. Y., May 19, '64. Assigned to 10th Maine Battalion. Died in 1879.
Peter Rollon	Mustered in, May 22, '61. Mustered out, June 2, '64.
Luther A. Russell, Eaton Rapids, Mich.	Mustered in, May 22, '61. Mustered out, June 2, '63.
William Rutz	Mustered in, May 22, '61. Killed in action, at Cedar Mountain, Va., Aug. 9, '62.
James Scott	Mustered in, May 22, '61. Captured at Winchester, Va., May 25, '62. Paroled Aikens Landing, Va., Sept. 13, '62. Mustered out, June 2, '63.
William Silk	Mustered in, May 22, '61. Discharged, Jan. 15, '63, for disability, at Fairfax Station, Va.
John Skinner	Mustered in, May 22, '61. Deserted, Nov. 6, '61, at Muddy Branch, Md.
William Skinner	Mustered in, May 22, '61. Deserted, Nov. 6, '61, at Muddy Branch, Md.
Alexander Smith	Mustered in, May 22, '61. Deserted, June 20, '62, at Front Royal, Va.
George Sutton	Mustered in, Feb. 18, '62. Brigade butcher, Sept. '62, to Feb. 28, '63. Transferred to depot at Albany, N. Y., May 19, '63.
John Sutton	Mustered in, Nov. 22, '61. Mustered out, June 2, '63.
Nelson J. Tubbs	Mustered in, May 22, '61. Detailed to 4th U. S. Artillery, Aug., '62, to Oct., '62. Mustered out, June 2, '63.
James Turner	Mustered in, May 22, '61. Died at regimental hospital, Sandy Hook, Md., Nov. 17, '62.
John Turner	Mustered in, May 22, '61. Died from sunstroke in hospital at Baltimore, Md., July 8, '62.
Henry Walter	Mustered in, Aug. 30, '62. Transferred to depot at Albany, N. Y., May 19, '63.
Edward White	Mustered in, Oct. 31, '61. Captured at Cedar Mountain, Va., Aug. 9, '62. Paroled at Aikens Landing, Va., Sept. 13, '62. Mustered out, June 2, '63.
Arthur Woods	Mustered in, May 22, '61. Deserted at Darnestown, Md., Sept. 22, '61.

COMPANY C.

Name and Present Residence, Where Known.	Remarks.
Captains.	
William H. H. Mapes Emporia, Kan.	Mustered in, May 22, '61, Capt. Commanding Pioneer Corps from April 5, '62, to June 1, '62. Commanding Regt., Sept. 4, '62, to Nov. 1, '62. Resigned, Nov. 6, '62.
William P. Warren Saginaw, E. S., Mich.	Mustered in, May 22, '61, as Lieut. On recruiting service at Lockport, N. Y., from Oct. 11, '61, to Jan., '62. Acting Adjutant, Feb. 1, '62, to May, '62. Seriously wounded in action at Cedar Mountain, Va., Aug. 9, '62. Left at Culpeper, Va., Aug. 19, '62. Promoted, Captain, May 23, '63. Mustered out, June 2, '63.
Lieutenants.	
Norman E. G. Wadhams Niagara Falls, N. Y.	Mustered in, May 22, '61, 1st Sergt. Promoted, May 20, '62, 2d Lieut.; May 5, '63, 1st Lieut. Commanding Co., April 2, '62, to May, '62, and from Aug. 9, '62, to Sept. 10, '62, and March 15, '63, to April 10, '63. Mustered out, June 2, '63.
Frank N. Wicker 648 Common St., New Orleans, La.	Mustered in, May 22, '61, 2d Lieut. Promoted, 1st Lieut., March 10, '62, and transferred to Co. A, Feb. 25, '63.
Charles S. Baker	Mustered in, May 22, '61, Corp. Promoted, Sergt., March 10, '62; 1st Sergt., June 30, '62. Captured at Cedar Mountain, Va., Aug. 9, '62. Paroled at Aikens Landing, Va., Sept. 13, '62. Promoted, 2d Lieut., May 5, '63. Mustered out, June 2, '63. Died in 1881.
Sergeants.	
Almon M. Graham Lockport, N. Y.	Mustered in, May 22, '61, as private. Promoted, Corp., March 19, '62; Sergt., June 30, '62; 1st Sergt., May 5, '63. Mustered out, June 2, '63.
John D. Woods	Mustered in, May 22, '61, Sergt. Promoted, 1st Sergt., March 17, '62. Promoted, 2d Lieut., Co. H, June 26, '62.
William H. Adriance Paw Paw, Mich.	Mustered in, May 22, '61, Sergt. Captured, on retreat from Winchester, Va., May 25, '62. Paroled at Aikens Landing, Va., Sept. 13, '62. Mustered out, June 2, '63.
Aaron F. Balliet	Mustered in, May 22, '61, private. Promoted, Corp., June 30, '62; Sergt., May 5, '63. Captured at Cedar Mountain, Va., Aug. 9, '62. Paroled at Aikens Landing, Va., Sept. 13, '62. Mustered out, June 2, '63. Died in Lockport, March 1, 1883.
George Brown, Jr.	Mustered in, May 22, '61. Reduced, June 19, '62. Discharged for disability, Tenleytown, Sept. 5, '62.
Francis Flynn	Mustered in, May 22, '61, private. Promoted, Corp., March 15, '62; Sergt., March 1, '63. Detached with Pioneer Corps, April 7, '62, to Sept. 26, '62. Mustered out, June 2, '63. Died at Belleville, Ontario, March 6, '95.
George F. Gould Mattoon, Ill.	Mustered in, May 22, '61, private. Promoted, Sergt., March 19, '62. Discharged for disability, Dec. 8, '62, at New York.
Joseph Lee Burlington, N. J.	Mustered in, May 22, '61, private. Promoted, Corp., March 15, '62; Sergt., Dec. 10, '62. Detached to Ambulance Corps, Oct. 16, '62, to May 31, '63. Mustered out, June 2, '63.
Sergeants.—Continued.	
James T. Wright	Mustered in, May 22, '61, private. Promoted, Sergt., March 15, '62. Detached on signal service, July 26, '61, to Aug., '61. In command of Company, Sept. 5, '62, to Oct. 10, '62. Died, Feb. 27, '63, of disease at Regt. hospital, Stafford C. H., Va.
Corporals.	
Robert H. Carlisle	Mustered in, May 22, '61, private. Promoted, Corp., June 19, '62. Captured at Manassas, Va., Aug. 28, '62. Paroled, same place, Sept. 3, '62. Mustered out, June 2, '63.
Henry Clark	Mustered in, May 22, '61. Died of disease in hospital at Winchester, Va., March 31, '62.
Homer A. Collins Pekin, N. Y.	Mustered in, May 22, '61, private. Promoted, Corp., March 19, '62. Discharged for disability at Sandy Hook, Md., Dec. 3, '62.
Christ'r F. Holzheimer	Mustered in, May 22, '61, private. Promoted, Corp., May 5, '63. Mustered out, June 2, '63. Died, June 20, '91.
George Poyfair	Mustered in, May 22, '61, private. Promoted, Corp., Aug. 11, '61. Discharged for disability, Dec. 3, '62, at Sandy Hook, Md.
William Sims Clarks, Neb.	Mustered in, May 22, '61, private. Promoted, Corp., June 30, '62. Mustered out, June 2, '63.
Amos K. Welsher Hartland, N. Y.	Mustered in, May 22, '61, private. Promoted, Corp., Aug. 19, '62. Left as nurse to the wounded at Culpeper, Va., Aug. 19, '62, and captured. Paroled at Aikens Landing, Va., Oct. 6, '62. Mustered out, June 2, '63.
Musicians.	
John Ferory	Mustered in, June 21, '61. Transferred to band, Oct. 14, '61. Transferred from band, Aug. 17, '62. Mustered out, June 2, '63.
Daniel Olmstead	Mustered in, May 22, '61. Mustered out, June 2, '63. Died, 1881.
William Pearson	Mustered in, May 22, '61. Deserted at Hyattstown, Md., Aug. 24, '61.
Privates.	
James S. Baldwin	Mustered in, May 22, '61. Wounded in action at Cedar Mountain, Va., Aug. 9, '62. Mustered out, June 2, '63.
Alfred W. Barrett	Enlisted, Sept. 5, '62. Deserted from hospital, Washington, D. C., March 7, '63.
Baldwin S. Beach	Mustered in, May 22, '61. Captured on retreat from Winchester, Va., May 25, '62. Paroled at Aikens Landing, Va., Sept. 13, '62. Mustered out, June 2, '63.
Joseph B. Boyce	Joined Co., Oct. 20, '62. Transferred to Co. A, Dec. 22, '62. Died in 1889.
John Bredell	Mustered in, May 22, '61. Captured on retreat from Winchester, Va., May 25, '62. Paroled at Aikens Landing, Va., Sept. 13, '62. Mustered out, June 2, '63. Died in 1889.
John Brauer St. Johnsburgh, Niagara Co., N. Y.	Mustered in, May 22, '61. Mustered out, June 2, '63.

COMPANY C.—Continued.

Name and Present Residence, Where Known.	Remarks.
Privates — Continued.	
George Brown	Mustered in, Dec. 4, '61. Wounded in action at Cedar Mountain, Va., Aug. 9, '62. Discharged for disability from wounds, Alexandria, Va., Nov. 4, '62.
Henry Cole	Mustered in, May 22, '61. Detached with Ambulance Corps, Oct. 29, '62, to April 30, '63. Mustered out, June 2, '63.
Henry T. Daggett	Mustered in, Nov. 4, '61. Captured at Winchester, Va., May 25, '62. Discharged, June 18, '62, for disability at Washington, D. C. Died in 1889.
Samuel Davis Edgerton, Mich.	Mustered in, May 22, '61. Left as nurse with wounded at Culpeper, Va., Aug. 19, '62, and captured. Paroled at Aikens Landing, Va., Oct. 6, '62. Mustered out, June 2, '63.
Joel S. Davison Smith's Crossing, Midland Co., Mich.	Mustered in, May 22, '61. Transferred to band, Oct. 14, '61. Transferred from band, March 31, '62. Captured on retreat from Winchester, Va., May 25, '62. Paroled at Aikens Landing, Va., Sept. 13, '62. Mustered out, June 2, '63.
Oscar B. Draper	Mustered in, May 22, '61. Colonel's orderly, May to Oct., '62. Detached to Ambulance Corps, Oct. 29, '62, to April, '63. Mustered out June 2, '63.
Theron D. Fellows Bronson, Mich.	Mustered in, Nov. 12, '61. Regimental and Division teamster, March and April, 1863. Mustered out, June 2, '63.
Stephen Folger	Mustered in, May 22, '61. Mustered out, June 2, '63. Died in 1890.
James Force	Mustered in, May 22, '61. Wounded and captured at Cedar Mountain, Va., Aug. 9, '62. Paroled at Aikens Landing, Va., Sept. 7, '62. Mustered out, June 2, '63.
George Frazer	Mustered in, Nov. 12, '61. Captured on retreat from Winchester, Va., May 25, '62. Paroled at Aikens Landing, Va., Sept. 13, '62. Mustered out June 2, '63.
William H. Gaskill Wilson, N. Y.	Mustered in, May 22, '61. Mustered out, June 2, '63.
John Gilbert	Mustered in, May 22, '61. Killed in action at Cedar Mountain, Aug. 9, '62.
William T. Gillingham Salem, O.	Mustered in, May 22, '61. Captured at Winchester, Va., May 25, '62. Mustered out, June 2, '63.
Thomas J. F. Granville 130 Jackson St., Lockport, N. Y.	Mustered in, May 22, '61. Discharged for disability, Aug. 8, '61, at Berlin, Md.
Edward Green	Mustered in, May 22, '61. Discharged for disability, July 26, '61, at Camp Harris, D. C.
Henry Haden Corunna, Mich.	Mustered in, Dec. 10, '61. Mustered out, June 2, '63.
John G. Haden	Mustered in, May 22, '61. Mustered out, June 2, '63.
Francis Hauer Pullman, Ill.	Mustered in, May 22, '61. Regt. teamster, Sept. '62, to April 10, '63. Mustered out, June 2, '63.
Solander Hayes Adalaska, Presque Isle Co., Mich.	Mustered in, May 22, '61. Detached with Corps supply train, Jan. 1, '63, to April, '63. Mustered out, June 2, '63.
Henry J. Higgins	Mustered in, May 22, '61. Discharged for disability, Aug. 8, '61, at Berlin, Md.
Privates — Continued.	
John M. Hill Maple Grove, Jasper Co., Mo.	Mustered in, May 22, '61. Discharged for disability, July 21, '61, at Washington, D. C. Re-enlisted, Nov. 1, '61. Captured at Front Royal, Va., May 23, '62. Paroled at Aikens Landing, Va., Sept. 13, '62. Detached in Pioneer Corps, April 7, '62, to May 24, '62. Mustered out, June 2, '63.
Thomas Hill	Mustered in, Oct. 29, '61. Wounded in action at Cedar Mountain, Va., Aug. 9, '62. Died of wounds, Aug. 17, '62, at Alexandria, Va.
Jedediah Hoag	Mustered in, May 22, '61. Wounded in action at Cedar Mountain, Va., Aug. 9, '62. Discharged for disability from wounds, Nov. 4, '62, at Baltimore, Md.
Hamilton T. Holden	Mustered in, Nov. 28, '61. Captured at Winchester, Va., May 25, '62. Paroled, same place, June 9, '62. Mustered out, June 2, '63. Died in 1866.
Edward Houghton	Mustered in, May 22, '61. Killed in action at Cedar Mountain, Va., Aug. 9, '62.
George H. Hunt Kalamazoo, Mich.	Mustered in, May 22, '61. Discharged for disability, Oct. 13, '62, at Georgetown, D. C.
Nathaniel Hyatt Lockport, N. Y.	Mustered in, May 22, '61. Discharged for disability, July 21, '61, at Washington, D. C.
John Jackson	Mustered in, Nov. 1, '61. Captured on retreat from Winchester, Va., May 25, '62. Paroled at Aikens Landing, Va., Sept. 13, '62. Mustered out June 2, '63.
John Kempter Saginaw E. S., Mich.	Mustered in, May 22, '61. Mustered out, June 2, '63.
Sidney B. King	Mustered in, May 22, '61. Detailed as teamster, May to Oct., '62. Detached in Corps supply train, Jan. 25, '63. Mustered out, June 2, '63. Died, April 5, 1891.
Warren G. Kniffin Maywood, Cook Co., Ill	Mustered in, Dec. 23, '61. Detached to Co. F, 4th U. S. Artillery, Aug. 11, '62, to Sept. 30, '62. Mustered out, June 2, '63.
Joseph J. Lecount	Mustered in, May 22, '61. Detailed as ambulance driver, Oct. 31, '62. Mustered out, June 2, '63. Died in 1893.
C. R. Leinbaugh	Mustered in, May 22, '61. Discharged, July 30, '61.
James Littis	Mustered in, May 22, '61. Died, Oct. 1, '61, of disease at Darnestown, Md.
J. Byron Lovell Lockport, N. Y.	Mustered in, May 22, '61. Adjutant's clerk, May 22, '61, to Feb., '62. Clerk at Brigade headquarters, March 20, '62, to May, '63. Mustered out, June 2, '63.
William Luff North Ridge, N. Y.	Mustered in, May 22, '61. Detached in Ambulance Corps, Oct. 29, '62, to Dec. 31, '62. Mustered out, June 2, '63.
Hiram Luke	Mustered in, Dec. 16, '61. Killed in action at Cedar Mountain, Aug. 9, '62.
Samuel McDonald	Enlisted, Dec. 5, '61. Captured at Winchester, Va., May 25, '62. Again captured at Manassas, Va., Aug. 29, '62. Paroled at Bull Run, Va. Discharged for disability, Jan. 15, '63, at Fairfax Station, Va. Died, May 8, '92.
William McGill	Mustered in, Dec. 5, '61. Killed in action at Cedar Mountain, Va., Aug. 9, '62.
John Manning	Mustered in, May 22, '61. Deserted, Nov. 7, '61, at Muddy Branch, Md.
William H. Mason	Enlisted, Nov. 5, '61. Captured at Winchester, Va., May 25, '62, and paroled. Deserted from Camp Parole, Md.

COMPANY C.—Continued.

Name and Present Residence, Where Known.	Remarks.
Privates—Continued.	
William Mathews	Mustered in, May 22, '61. Mustered out, June 2, '63.
Edwin F. Mead	Mustered in, May 22, '61. On recruiting service, Feb. 1, '62, to April, '62. Mustered out, June 2, '63.
Benjamin Mills	Mustered in, May 22, '61. Killed in action at Cedar Mountain, Va., Aug. 9, '62.
William E. Minard, Marathon, N. Y.	Mustered in, Dec. 25, '61. Mustered out, June 2, '63.
Edward Morrow	Mustered in, May 22, '61. Discharged for disability, Aug. 8, '61, at Berlin, Md. Died in 1890.
Frank W. Morse, Plainfield, N. J. P. O. Garwood, N. J.	Mustered in, May 22, '61. Captured at Winchester, Va., May 25, '62. Paroled at Aikens Landing, Va., Sept. 13, '62. Mustered out, June 2, '63.
James A. Nellist	Mustered in, May 22, '61. Captured at Winchester, Va., May 25, '62. Paroled at Aikens Landing, Va., Sept. 13, '62. Mustered out, June 2, '63.
Charles C. Papworth	Enlisted, Aug. 11, '62. Joined Co. Oct. 30, '62. Discharged, Dec. 18, '62, for disability at Philadelphia, Pa.
Charles Peters	Enlisted, Dec. 16, '61. Deserted from hospital at Hagerstown, Md., April 9, '63.
Henry Peters, Gothenburg, Neb.	Mustered in, May 22, '61. Detached on Signal duty, Sept. 1, '61, to May, '63. Mustered out, June 2, '63.
Thomas Pickwell, Lockport, N. Y.	Mustered in, May 22, '61. Discharged, June 24, '61, for disability.
Lafayette Randall	Mustered in Dec. 25, '61. Mustered out, June 2, '63.
George Reiber	Mustered in, May 22, '61. Assistant in hospital, at Baltimore, Md., Oct. 1, '61, to Feb., '62. Mustered out, June, 2, '63.
Albert Richardson, Odd Fellows Home, Lockport, N. Y.	Mustered in, May 22, '61. Mustered out, June 2, '63.
Charles Robillard, Lewiston, N. Y.	Mustered in, May 22, '61. Captured at Cedar Mountain, Va., Aug. 9, '62. Paroled at Aikens Landing, Va., Sept. 13, '62. Mustered out, June 2, '63.
Edward Rumery	Mustered in, May 22, '61. Mustered out, June 2, '63.
Orin Salsbury	Mustered in, May 22, '61. Mustered out, June 2, '63.
William H. Salsbury	Mustered in, May 22, '61. Mustered out, June 2, '63. Died, in 1885.
Charles A. Smith, Soldiers' Home, Togus, Me.	Mustered in, May 22, '61. Mustered out, June 2, '63.
Daniel A. Stahl	Mustered in, May 22, '61. Regiment teamster, Feb. 21, '62, to May '63. Mustered out, June 2, '63. Died in 1879.
George B. Swick, Pekin, N. Y.	Mustered in, May 22, '61. Mustered out, June 2, '63.
James Taylor, Vassar, Mich.	Mustered in, May 22, '61. Wounded in action at Cedar Mountain, Va., Aug. 9, '62. Discharged for disability from wounds, Nov. 10, '62, at Alexandria, Va.
William Taylor	Enlisted, Nov. 5, '61. Deserted, June 1, '62, at Williamsport, Md.
Milton Thrawl	Mustered in, Nov. 5, '61. Died of disease, Feb. 16, '62, at Hancock, Md.
Alexander F. Wallace	Mustered in, Aug. 14, '62. Joined Co., Oct. 30, '62. Transferred to Depot at Albany, N. Y., May 19, '63.
Robert J. Wallace, Lockport, N. Y.	Enlisted, Aug. 14, '62. Entered Lincoln Hospital, Washington, D. C., Jan. 18, '63, with chronic rheumatism.
Isaac W. Wheeler	Mustered in, May 22, '61. Died, Aug. 19, '62, at Alexandria, Va., of wounds received at Cedar Mountain, Va., Aug. 9, '62.
John W. Wilkenson	Mustered in, Nov. 12, '61. Captured at Manassas, Va., Aug. 27, '62. Paroled, Aug. 29, '62. Mustered out, June 2, '63.
John Williams	Mustered in, May 22, '61. Deserted at Muddy Branch, Md., Nov. 9, '61.
George Woods, Lewiston, N. Y.	Mustered in, May 22, '61. Mustered out, June 2, '63.
John Youkey, Bangor, Wis.	Mustered in, May 22, '61. Mustered out, June 2, '63.

COMPANY D.

Name and Present Residence, Where Known.	Remarks.
Captains.	
Erwin A. Bowen	Mustered in, May 22, '61, as Captain. Captured at Cedar Mountain, Va., Aug. 9, '62. Paroled at Aikens Landing, Va., Sept. 13, '62. Mustered out, Oct. 31, '62, for promotion to Lieut. Colonel 151st N. Y. V. Died in Medina, Jan 22, 1889.
Lafayette Chaffee	Mustered in, May 22 '61, 2d Lieut. Promoted 1st Lieut. Co. I, Feb. 12, '62. Commanded Co. I from July 1, '62, to Aug. 9, '62. Promoted to Capt. and transferred to Co. D, Dec. 23, '62. Mustered out, June 2, '63. Died in Ypsilanti, Mich., about 1881.
Lieutenants.	
George Davis	Mustered in, May 22, '61 Lieut. Promoted to Adjt., Sept. 5, '62.
Orson Southworth, 5 Jackson Ave., Jersey City, N. J.	Mustered in, May 22, '61, Sergt. Promoted 2d Lieut., Feb. 18, '62. Promoted 1st Lieut. Feb. 20, '62. Commanding Co. D, Nov. 21, '62, to Dec. 19, '62. Captured at Cedar Mountain, Va., Aug. 9, '62. Rejoined, Oct., '62. Mustered out, June 2, '63.
Lieutenants.—Continu'd.	
Frank B. Seeley, Lockport, N. Y.	Mustered in, May 22, '61. 1st Sergt. Captured at Cedar Mountain, Va., Aug. 9, '62. Paroled at Aikens Landing, Va., Sept. 13 '62. Promoted, 2d Lieut., Feb. 10, '63. Mustered out, June 2, '63.
Sergeants.	
William Lewis, 402 Noble St., Oklahoma, O. T.	Mustered in, May 22, '61, Sergt. Wounded in action at Cedar Mountain, Aug. 9, '62. Promoted 1st Sergt., Feb. 19, '63. Mustered out, June 2, '63.
George W. Palmer	Mustered in, May 22, '61, Sergt. Died of disease in hospital Pleasant Valley, Md., Nov. 10, '62.
Gustavus A. Baker, 1114 Hancock St., Brooklyn, N. Y.	Mustered in, May 22, '61, private. Promoted to Corp., June 21, '61; Sergt., March 1, '62. Captured at Cedar Mountain, Va., Aug. 9, '62. Paroled at Aikens Landing, Sept. 13, '62. Mustered out, June 2, '63.

COMPANY D.—Continued.

Name and Present Residence, Where Known.	Remarks.
Sergeants.—Continued.	
Oscar Bayne	Mustered in, May 22, '61, private. Promoted, Corp., March 1, '62; Sergt., Feb. 9, '63. Captured at Cedar Mountain, Aug. 9, '62. Paroled at Aikens Landing, Sept. 13, '62; again captured at Chancellorsville, May 2, '63. Paroled at City Point, Va., May 15, '63. Mustered out, June 2, '63. Died in Medina, Oct. 5, 1892.
Lucius B. Swift, Hubbard Block, Indianapolis, Ind. (Known as Burrie Swift.)	Mustered in, Sept. 14, '61, private. Promoted, Corp., March 1, '62; Sergt., Nov. 25, '62. Captured on Banks' retreat, at Bunker Hill, Va., May 25, '62. Paroled at Aikens Landing, Sept. 13, '62. Captured at Chancellorsville, Va., May 2, '63. Paroled at City Point, May 14, '63. Mustered out, June 2, '63.
William H. Lusk	Mustered in, May 22, '61, Corp. Promoted, Sergt., March 1, '62. Mustered out, June 2, '63.
Corporals.	
Adelbert A. Fox, Sundance, Wy.	Mustered in, May 22, '61, Corp. Mustered out, June 2, '63.
Andrew M. Hood	Mustered in, May 22 '61, Corp. Deserted June 21, '61, at Albany.
David Sanderson	Mustered in, May 22 '61, private. Promoted, Corp., July 6, '61. Killed in action at Cedar Mountain, Va., Aug. 9, '62.
David Bennett	Mustered in, May 22, '61, private. Promoted, Corp. March, '62. Killed in action at Antietam, Md., Sept. 17, '62.
Bartley Salmon, Lead City, S. D.	Mustered in, May 22, '61, private. Promoted, Corp., March 1, '62. Wounded in action, Cedar Mountain, Va., Aug. 9, '62. Mustered out, June 2, '63.
Frank Sanderson	Mustered in, May 22, '61, private. Promoted, Corp., Nov. 25, '62. Mustered out, June 2, '63.
Thomas Smalley	Mustered in, May 22, '61, private. Promoted, Corp., Oct. 8, '62. Mustered out, June 2 '63. Died, near Muskegon, Mich., 1879.
Elias S. Taylor, Lowell, Mich.	Mustered in, May 22, '61, private. Promoted, Corp., March 1, '62. Captured at Cedar Mountain, Va., Aug. 9, '62. Paroled at Aikens Landing, Sept. 13, '62. Mustered out, June 2, '63.
Musicians.	
William W. Eastman, 1113 N. 25th St., Omaha, Neb.	Mustered in, May 22, '61. Transferred to regimental band, April 10, '62. Transferred from band, Aug. 17, '62. Mustered out, June 2, '63.
John O. Swan	Mustered in, May 22, '61. Leg injured, and home on furlough, March 1, '62, to Oct., '62. Mustered out, June 2, '63.
Privates.	
Henry Allen	Mustered in, Dec. 10, '61. Killed in action, Cedar Mountain, Va., Aug. 9, '62.
John Anderson	Mustered in, Nov. 28, '61. Discharged, May 20, '63, for disability, at Buffalo.
Albert U. Angevine	Mustered in, May 22, '61. Transferred to Hospital Steward, Aug. 11, '61.
Daniel W. Ainsworth, Ware, Mass.	Mustered in, Oct. 20, '61. Mustered out, June 2, '63.
Privates.—Continued.	
John Bacon, Medina, N. Y.	Mustered in, May 22, '61. Captured at Cedar Mountain, Va., Aug. 9, '62. Paroled at Aikens Landing, Sept. 13, '62. Mustered out, June 2, '63.
Sheldon S. Baker, Blackstone, Va.	Mustered in, May 22, '61. Discharged for disability, July 17, '61, at Camp Harris, D. C.
William H. H. Bartram	Mustered in, May 22, '61. Wounded seriously in abdomen in action at Cedar Mountain, Va., Aug. 9, '62. Acting Hospital steward from Oct. 14, '62, to Jan., '63, by order of Captain Mapes commanding Regt. Mustered out, June 2, '63. Died in Lockport, in 1889.
Enos Bathrick, Hartland, N. Y.	Mustered in, May 22, '61. Discharged for disability, July 17, '61, at Camp Harris, D. C.
William H. Bayne	Mustered in, Nov. 18, '61. Discharged for disability, May 22, '62, at Winchester, Va.
George Bigford	Mustered in, May 22, '61. Discharged for disability, July 17, '61, at Washington, D. C.
Dennison Bowdoin	Mustered in, May 22, '61. Captured at Winchester, May 25, '62. Paroled at Aikens Landing, Sept. 13, '62. Mustered out, June 2, '63.
Edwin A. Bowen	Mustered in, May 22, '61. Captured at Cedar Mountain, Va., Aug. 9, '62. Paroled at Aikens Landing, Sept. 13, '62. Mustered out, June 2, '63. Died, Aug. 20, '95, at Joliet, Ills.
Charles W. Boyce, 930 Main St., Buffalo, N. Y.	Mustered in, May 22, '61. Captured at Chancellorsville, Va., May 2, '63. Paroled at City Point, Va., May 14, '63. Mustered out, June 2, '63.
James M. Brannen	Mustered in, Oct. 10, '61. Transferred to Co. H, Dec. 31, '61.
Francis S. Brown	Mustered in, Jan. 6, '62. Mustered out, June 2, '63.
Charles Bruce, 8 Harpers Court, South Bend, Ind.	Mustered in, May 22, '61. Mustered out, June 2, '63.
George Bull	Mustered in, Oct. 25, '61. Wounded in action at Cedar Mountain, Va., Aug. 9, '62. Mustered out, June 2, '63.
James Burrell	Mustered in May 22 '61. Mustered out, June 2, '63.
Michael Burns	Mustered in, May 22, '61. Captured at Cedar Mountain, Va., Aug. 9, '62. Paroled at Aikens Landing, Va., Sept. 13, '62. Mustered out, June 2, '63.
Clinton Butler	Mustered in, Nov. 11, '61. Killed in action at Cedar Mountain, Va., Aug. 9, '62.
Frank O. Butterfield	Mustered in, May 22, '61. Captured at Cedar Mountain, Va., Aug. 9 '62. Paroled at Aikens Landing, Va., Sept. 13, '62. Mustered out, June 2, '63.
Morris Butts	Mustered in, May 22, '61. Captured on Banks' retreat near Bunker Hill, Va., May 25, '62. Paroled at Aikens Landing, Va., Sept. 13, '62. Mustered out, June 2, '63.
N. Ward Cady, 32 Liberty St., New York City.	Mustered in, May 22, '61. On recruiting service. By order of General Banks, Oct. 12, '61, to Jan., '62. Mustered out, June 2, '63.
William Canhan, Bellwood, Butler Co., Neb.	Mustered in, May 22, '61. Mustered out, June 2, '63.
John J. Cornwell, Lyndonville, N. Y.	Mustered in, Jan. 6, '62. Mustered out, June 2, '63.

COMPANY D.—Continued.

Name and Present Residence, Where Known.	Remarks.
Privates.—Continued.	
William Carn	Mustered in, May 22, '61. Died of disease, March 7, '62, at Hagerstown, Md.
Thomas J. Chapman	Mustered in, Dec. 10, '61. Died, Oct. 4, '62, in Hospital at Philadelphia, Pa., of wounds received at Antietam, Md., Sept. 17, '62.
Albert W. Chichester, Albion, N. Y.	Mustered in, Nov. 28, '61. Discharged for disability at Fairfax, Va., Jan. 15, '63.
Charles H. Clark	Mustered in, May 22, '61. Mustered out, June 2, '63.
John Clark, Olympus, Iowa.	Mustered in, Nov. 11, '61. Captured May 25, '62, in Hospital at Winchester, Va., and paroled. Discharged, June 13, '62.
John B. Clayton	Mustered in, Oct. 9, '61. Transferred to Co. H, Jan. 1, '62.
James Cook	Mustered in, May 22, '61. Captured at Culpeper, Va., Aug. 13, '62. Paroled at Aikens Landing, Va., Oct. 6, '62. Wounded in action, May 1, '63, at Chancellorsville, Va. Mustered out, June 2, '63.
Henry A. Cox	Mustered in, May 22, '61. Discharged for disability, July 24, '61, at Washington, D. C.
Samuel Densmon	Mustered in, Nov. 28, '61. Discharged for disability, May 22, '62, at Winchester, Va.
James L. Dunham	Mustered in, Oct. 25, '61. Wounded in action at Cedar Mountain, Va., Aug. 9, '62. Mustered out, June 2, '63. Died in Lockport, in May, 1890.
Luke Dunham	Mustered in, Oct. 25, '61. Captured at Frederick, Md., Sept. 6, '62. Paroled at same place, Sept. 16, '62. Detailed in Pioneer corps, May to Aug., '62. Discharged for disability, at Annapolis, Md., Jan. 19, '63. Died in 1880.
Ephriam Fish	Mustered in, May 22, '61. Discharged at Berlin, Md., Aug. 5, '61.
Elmer Gage	Mustered in, May 22, '61. Discharged for disability, July 17, '61, at Washington.
Patrick Garry	Mustered in, May 22, '61. Mustered out, June 2, '63.
Martin C. Gilbert, Yates, N. Y.	Mustered in, Dec. 25, '61. Wounded in action at Cedar Mountain, Va., Aug. 9, '62. Discharged for disability from General Hospital at Alexandria, Oct. 23, '62, from wounds received at Cedar Mountain, Va.
Perry Gilbert	Mustered in, May 22, '61. Killed in action at Cedar Mountain, Va., Aug. 9, '62.
Thomas Gilliam	Mustered in, May 22, '61. Discharged, June 10, '61, at Albany, N. Y.
Mathias Guisen	Mustered in, May 22, '61. Mustered out, June 2, '63.
George Hamilton	Mustered in, Jan. 6, '62. Deserted, Aug. 5, '62, at Culpeper, Va.
Henry J. Harrington	Mustered in, May 22, '61. Discharged for disability, July 17, '61, at Washington, D. C.
Loren Hayner, Northville, Mich.	Mustered in, Nov. 11, '61. Wounded in action, May 1, '63, at Chancellorsville, Va. Mustered out, June 2, '63.
Luther Hayner	Mustered in, May 22, '61. Mustered out, June 2, '63.
Willis S. Havens	Mustered in, May 22, '61. On special secret service duty since July 25, '62, by order of General Banks. Probably hung as a spy. No further information on regt. rec.
Phillip Hickey	Mustered in, May 22, '61. Deserted, Aug. 5, '62, at Culpeper, Va.
Asa C. Hill	Mustered in, Nov. 28, '61. Discharged, Jan. 14, '63, for disability, Central Park Hospital, New York. Died in 1881.
Oscar G. Hubbard, Albion, Mich.	Mustered in, Nov. 28, '61. Mustered out, June 2, '63.
James Hughes	Mustered in, May 22, '61. Wounded in action at Cedar Mountain, Va., Aug. 9, '62. Mustered out, June 2, '63.
George Johnson	Mustered in, Jan. 6, '62. Captured at Cedar Mountain, Va., Aug. 9, '62. Paroled Aikens Landing, Va., Sept. 13, '62. Mustered out, June 2, '63.
Clinton D. Keeler	Mustered in, Nov. 28, '61. Mustered out, June 2, '63. Died in New York in 1873.
John Keeler, Box 114, Platte Center, Platte Co., Neb.	Mustered in, Nov. 28, '61. Wounded in action at Winchester, Va., May 25, '62. Discharged for disability at Convalescent Hospital, Va., Oct. 18, '62.
Leroy Kenyon	Mustered in, May 22, '61. Wounded in action at Cedar Mountain, Va., Aug. 9, '62. Discharged for disability, Nov. 17, '62, at Fort Monroe, Va.
Richard Kirk	Mustered in, Oct. 9, '61. Transferred to Co. H, Dec. 31, '61.
John Kugler, Lockport, N. Y.	Mustered in, Sept. 10, '61. Discharged for disability at Harper's Ferry, Va., March 23, '63.
Patrick Lavin	Mustered in, Jan. 6, '62. Mustered out, June 2, '63.
John Lawson	Mustered in, Oct. 9, '61. Transferred to Co. H, Dec. 31, '61.
Aaron Lewis	Mustered in, May 22, '61. Died of disease at Hagerstown, Md., March 4, '62.
Perry J. Lincoln	Mustered in, May 22, '61. Died of disease at Harrisonburg, Va., May 1, '62.
Frederick Lureman, Joliet, Ills.	Mustered in, Aug. 28, '62. Wounded in action, May 3, '63, at Chancellorsville, Va. Left at Aquia Creek, Va.
Charles Lozier	Mustered in, May 22, '61. Nurse in Hospital at Harper's Ferry, Dec. 10, '62, to Jan. 19, '63. Mustered out, June 2, '63.
Chauncy W. Lum	Mustered in, Dec. 25, '61. Captured at Cedar Mountain, Va., Aug. 9, '62. Paroled, Aikens Landing, Va., Sept. 13, '62. Mustered out, June 2, '63.
William McCannon	Mustered in, May 22, '61. Dropped from rolls, Oct. 31, '61.
William McDonald, Saltvale, Wyoming Co., N. Y.	Mustered in, May 22, '61. Wounded in action at Antietam, Md., Sept. 17, '62. Mustered out, June 2, '63.
Samuel Male	Mustered in, May 22, '61. Died, Nov. 25, '61, in Regimental Hospital, at Muddy Branch, Md.
Byron Mason	Mustered in, Nov. 28, '61. Died of disease, March 7, '62, at Hagerstown, Md.
John Miller, Shelby Center, N. Y.	Mustered in, May 22, '61. Detailed in Battery F, 4th U. S. Artillery, June to Aug., '62. Detailed in Ambulance Corps service, March 1, '63, to April, '63. Mustered out, June 2, '63.
Martin Malony, 6903 Peoria St., Chicago, Ills.	Mustered in, May 22, '61. Mustered out, June 2, '63.
John A. Morgan (Known as Adelbert Morgan.)	Mustered in, May 22, '61. Wounded in action at Cedar Mountain, Va., Aug. 9, '62. Mustered out, June 2, '63. Died at Muir's Center, Mich., May [illegible]

COMPANY D.—Continued.

Name and Present Residence, Where Known.	Remarks.
Privates—Continued.	
Robert Mortimer Rochester, N. Y.	Mustered in, May 22, '61. Captured on Banks' retreat near Bunker Hill, Va., May 25, '62. Paroled at Aikens Landing, Va., Sept. 13, '62. Mustered out, June 2, '63.
George Nelson	Mustered in, Sept. 6, '62. Transferred, May 20, '63 to Depot at Albany.
Edwin A. Newberry	Mustered in, May 22, '61. Transferred, July 6, '61. Promoted to Sergt.-Major.
Daniel Noaker	Mustered in, Oct. 25, '61. Transferred, Jan. 1, '62, to Co. A.
Simeon Pratt	Mustered in, May 22, '61. Transferred Jan. 1, '62, to Co. H.
Charles C. Price	Mustered in, May 22, '61. Detailed with Ambulance Corps Oct. 29, '62, to April, '63. Mustered out, June 2, '63.
Thomas Purcell	Mustered in, May 22, '61. Wounded in head at Antietam, Md., Sept. 17, '62. Mustered out, June 2, '63.
John Read	Mustered in, Aug. 30, '62. Transferred to Depot at Albany, May 29, '63.
Nicholas Reinhart	Mustered in, Dec. 10, '61. Captured at Cedar Mountain, Va., Aug. 9, '62. Rejoined, Oct. 19, '62. Captured at Chancellorsville, Va., May 1, '63. Paroled at City Point, Va., July 19, '63. Mustered out, —
Ziba Roberts .... East Shelby, N. Y.	Mustered in, Nov. 11, '61. Captured on Banks' retreat, near Bunker Hill, Va., May 25, '62. Paroled at Aikens Landing, Va., Sept. 13, '62. Mustered out, June 2, '63.
Benjamin Sheppard	Mustered in, May 22, '61. Discharged for disability, July 17, '61, at Washington, D. C.
Eugene Sheppard ...... North Ridgeway, N. Y.	Mustered in, May 22, '61. Mustered out, June 2, '63.
Thomas Shorten	Mustered in, May 22, '61. Mustered out, June 2, '63.
John A. Smith ...... Shelby Center, N. Y.	Mustered in, May 22, '61. Detailed in Pioneer Corps, May to Aug., '62. Mustered out, June 2, '63.
Morris Smith	Mustered in, Nov. 11, '61. Mustered out, June 2, '63.
Ozial Southworth	Mustered in, Dec. 25, '61. Captured at Cedar Mountain, Va., Aug. 9, '62. Paroled at Aikens Landing, Va., Sept. 13, '62. Mustered out, June 2, '63.
Henry K. Stebbins	Mustered in, Nov. 28, '61. Died of disease, June 26, '62, near Front Royal, Va.
Wallace M. Sterling ... Elysian, Minn.	Mustered in, May 22, '61. Captured at Winchester, Va., May 25, '62. Paroled at same place. Mustered out, June 2, '63.
Caleb Stillwell	Mustered in, May 22, '61. "Left at Hagerstown, Md., March 1, '62, in arrest, then sent to Frederick, Md." "This soldier

Name and Present Residence, Where Known.	Remarks
Privates—Continued.	
	alleges he was in Co. D., 28th N. Y. V., from April, '61, to spring of '63, when, by reason of trouble with an officer, he lit out."
Daniel Stockwell .... Adrian, Mich.	Mustered in, Dec. 25, '61. Detailed as hospital nurse in Alexandria, Va., Aug. 15, '62, to March, '63. Mustered out, June 2, '63.
Myron Stockwell .... Sealy, Texas.	Mustered in, May 22, '61. Captured at Cedar Mountain, Va., Aug. 9, '62. Paroled at Aikens Landing, Va., Sept. 13, '62. Detailed in Ambulance Corps, Nov. 12, '62. Teamster, 12th Army Corps, April 10, '63. Mustered out, June 2, '63.
Almond C. Thomas	Mustered in, Nov. 11, '61. Discharged at Fairfax Station, Va., Jan. 15, '63, for disability.
William Thurston .	Mustered in, Nov. 28, '61. Teamster in brigade train, from Feb. 10, '63, to March, '63. Mustered out, June 2, '63.
Sylvester Tripp	Mustered in, Dec. 25, '61. Mustered out, June 2, '63. Died, February 22, '96.
John Tuckson .... Montevideo, Minn.	Mustered in, May 22, '61. Wounded in action at Cedar Mountain, Va., Aug. 9, '62. Mustered out, June 2, '63.
Eugene G. Van Arnum	Mustered in, Nov. 28, '61. Mustered out, June 2, '63.
Abram Vreeland	Mustered in, May 22, '61. Discharged Aug. 7, '61, at Berlin, Md., cause not stated.
William G. Wade ...... Monmouth, Maine.	Mustered in, Jan. 6, '62. Captured on Banks' retreat near Bunker Hill, Va., May 25, '62. Paroled at Aikens Landing, Va., Sept. 13, '62. Wounded in action May 2, '63, at Chancellorsville, Va. Mustered out, June 2, '63.
William West	Mustered in, May 22, '61. Teamster in brigade train, Dec. [illegible], '62, to April, '63. Mustered out, June 2, '63.
Newton White .... Chesaning, Mich.	Mustered in, May 22, '61. Captured at Cedar Mountain, Va., Aug. 9, '62. Paroled at Aikens Landing, Va., Sept. 13, '62. Mustered out, June 2, '63.
Royal White	Mustered in, May 22, '61. Killed in action at Cedar Mountain, Va., Aug. 9, '62.
George L. Worland	Mustered in, Dec. 25, '61. Discharged for disability May 30, '62, at Frederick, Md.
Henry C. Worland	Mustered in, Dec. 25, '61. Mustered out, June 2, '63.
Charles Yorrington	Mustered in, Dec. 25, '61. Detailed to Battery F, 4th U. S. Artillery, July, '62. Deserted Oct. 20, '62.
George Young	Mustered in, June 21, '61. Mustered out, June 2, '63.
James Zenner	Mustered in, Oct. 15, '61. Transferred to Co. H, Jan. 1, '62.

COMPANY E.

Name and Present Residence, Where Known.	Remarks
Captains.	
Theophilus Fitzgerald, 213 1st St., N. W., Washington, D. C.	Mustered in, May 22, '61. Mustered out, Nov. 2, '62, for promotion to Major.
William W. Rowley ..., Q. M. & C. S., Soldiers' Home, Milwaukee, Wis.	Mustered in, Aug. 15, '62. Promoted from 1st Lieut., Co. F. Detailed as Signal Officer, Sept. 1, '61. Mustered out, June 2, '63.
Lieutenants.	
Walter J. Brown	Mustered in, May 22, '61, as 1st Lieut. Resigned, June 7, '62.
Harry Padelford .... Padelford, N. Y.	Mustered in, May 22, '61, 2d Lieut. Promoted 1st Lieut., June 8, '62. Acting Capt. of Co. G, May 29, '62, to June 27, '62. Mustered out, June 2, '63.
Myron F. Warfield ..... Rushville, N. Y.	Mustered in, May 22, '61, 1st Sergt. Promoted, June 28, '62, 2d Lieut. Mustered out, May 5, '63, for promotion to 1st Lieut., Co. K. Acting Adjt., March 25, '63, to April, '63.

COMPANY E.—Continued.

Name and Present Residence, Where Known.	Remarks.
Lieutenants.—Continued.	
Henry S. Gulick, 121 2d Ave., Newark, N. J.	Mustered in, May 22, '61, Sergt. Promoted, July 4, '62, 1st Sergt.; May 5, '63, 2d Lieut. Mustered out, June 2, '63.
Sergeants.	
Oscar L. Teachout, 1002 Monroe St., Ft. Worth, Texas.	Mustered in, May 22, '61, private. Promoted Corp., Aug. 28, '61; Sergt., March 17, '62; 1st Sergt., May 11, '63. Mustered out, June 2, '63.
Sele P. Quick, 82 William St., Rochester, N. Y.	Mustered in, May 22, '61. Discharged, Aug. 7, '61, for disability at Berlin, Md.
Erastus H. Green, Canandaigua, N. Y.	Mustered in, May 22, '61. Discharged, May 7, '62, for disability at New Market, Va.
Charles P. Aiken	Mustered in, May 22, '61, private. Promoted, Corp., Dec. 2, '61; Sergt., July 4, '62. Mustered out, June 2, '63. Died in 1881.
Edwin E. Clark	Mustered in, May 22, '61, private. Promoted Corp., May 18, '62; Sergt., July 4, '62. Mustered out, June 2, '63.
Washington L. Hicks	Mustered in, May 22, '61, private. Promoted, Corp., March 17, '62; Sergt., May 18, '62. Mustered out, June 2, '63.
John Henry Stall	Mustered in, May 22, '61, Corp. Promoted, Sergt., Aug. 28, '61; Reduced, April 17, '63. Mustered out, June 2, '63.
Andrew J. Warner, Rushville, N. Y.	Mustered in, May 22, '61, private. Promoted, Corp., July 25, '62; Sergt., May 11, '63. Mustered out, June 2, '63.
Corporals.	
Merritt J. Belding	Mustered in, May 22, '61. Mustered out, June 2, '63.
Allen Burgess	Mustered in, May 22, '61, private. Promoted, Corp., July 25, '62. Mustered out, June 2, '63.
Patrick Lovell	Mustered in, May 22, '61, private. Promoted, Corp., April 17, '63. Captured at Bunker Hill, Va., May 25, '62. Paroled Aikens Landing, Va., Sept. 13, '62. Mustered out, June 2, '63.
James W. Moore, Victor, N. Y.	Mustered in, May 22, '61, private. Promoted, Corp., July 25, '62. Mustered out, June 2, '63.
Mathison L. Parkhurst, Canandaigua, N. Y.	Mustered in, May 22, '61, private. Promoted, Corp., May 11, '63. Mustered out, June 2, '63.
Thomas C. Townsend	Mustered in, May 22, '61. Detailed to remain with wounded at Culpeper, Va. Captured, Aug. 20, '62. Paroled at Aikens Landing, Va., Oct. 6, '62. Mustered out, June 2, '63.
Musicians.	
Mark J. Blakeley, 301 Beldon Ave., Syracuse, N. Y.	Mustered in, May 22, '61. Mustered out, June 2, '63.
Lorenzo A. Sabine	Mustered in, May 22, '61. In regimental band, Nov. 5, '61, to Dec. 20, '61. Mustered out, June 2, '63. Died, Feb., 1892.
Privates.	
Francis J. Anderson	Mustered in, May 22, '61. Mustered out, June 2, '63.
William Barnhart	Mustered in, May 22, '61. Deserted, Dec. '61, at Darnestown, Md.
George Benson	Mustered in, May 22, '61. Mustered out, June 2, '63.
Charles F. Biddlecom, Macedon, N. Y.	Mustered in, May 22, '61. Discharged for disability, Aug. 22, '61, at Berlin, Md.
Richard H. L. Brigham	Mustered in, May 22, '61. Discharged for disability, May 8, '62, at New Market, Va.
Privates.—Continued.	
William H. Brown, 93 West St., South, Hillsdale, Mich.	Mustered in, May 22, '61. Brigade Blacksmith, Jan. 15, '63, to May, '63. Mustered out, June 2, '63.
Peter Burgess	Mustered in, May 22, '61. On detached duty at Division Headquarters, March 20, '63, to May '63. Mustered out, June 2, '63.
James H. Chamberlain, Grand Ledge, Eaton Co., Mich.	Mustered in, May 22, '61. Mustered out, June 2, '63.
Allen B. Cooper, Telluride, San Miguel Co., Colorado.	Mustered in, May 22, '61. Mustered out, June 2, '63.
Michael Dalton, Hopewell Center, N. Y.	Mustered in, Dec. 25, '61. Mustered out, June 2, '63.
Leonard Darling	Mustered in, May 22, '61. Discharged, for disability, Aug. 22, '61, at Berlin, Md.
Joseph Davis	Mustered in, May 22, '61. Discharged for disability, Aug. 22, '61, at Berlin, Md.
Samuel Davy	Mustered in, May 22, '61. Mustered out, June 2, '63. Died in 1885.
Jacob P. Faurot	Mustered in, May 22, '61. Mustered out, June 2, '63.
Benjamin Frazer	Mustered in, May 22, '61. Died, Oct. 21, '61, of disease. Regt. Hospital.
Franklin Gage	Mustered in, May 22, '61. Captured at Manassas, Va., Aug. 29, '62. Paroled, same place, Sept. 3, '62. Captured at Chancellorsville, Va., May 2, '63. Paroled at City Point, Va., May 14, '63. Mustered out, June 2, '63.
James Gay	Mustered in, May 22, '61. Mustered out, June 2, '63.
Henry M. George	Mustered in, May 22, '61. Captured, May 25, '62, on Banks' retreat, near Bunker Hill, Va. Rejoined, Oct. 21, '62. Detached in Ambulance Corps, Nov. 17, '62 to April, '63. Mustered out, June 2, '63.
Frederick Gravlier	Mustered in, May 22, '61. Mustered out, June 2, '63.
John Gravlier	Mustered in, May 22, '61. Mustered out, June 2, '63.
Thomas Harris	Mustered in, May 22, '61. Deserted, June 30, '62, at Front Royal, Va.
Henry W. Herrick	Enlisted, May 18, '61. Deserted, Dec. 30, '61, from Hospital, Baltimore, Md.
Mortimer V. Hill, Rising City, Neb.	Mustered in, May 22, '61. Detailed to remain as Nurse, at Culpeper, Va., Aug. 12, '62, and captured, Aug. 20, '62. Paroled at Richmond, Va., Sept. 7, '62. Mustered out, June 2, '63.
John H. Hogle	Mustered in, May 22, '61. Regimental teamster, March and April, '62. Killed in skirmish at Chancellorsville, Va. May 1, '63.
Homer Hubbard	Mustered in, May 22, '61. Discharged for disability, Aug. 22, '61, at Berlin, Md.
Henry Hune	Mustered in, Nov. 1, '61. Captured at Manassas, Va., Aug. 29, '62. Paroled same place, Sept. 3, '62. Captured at Chancellorsville, Va., May 2, '63. Paroled at City Point, Va., May 14, '63. Mustered out, June 2, '63. Died Aug. 21, '91.
William H. Irwin	Mustered in, May 22, '61. Mustered out, June 2, '63.

COMPANY E.—Continued.

Name and Present Residence, Where Known	Remarks
Privates.—Continued.	
Leonard A. Knapp	Mustered in, May 22, '61. Died, Sept. 19, '62, of wounds received in action at Antietam, Md.
Lafayette Lee	Mustered in, May 22, '61. Detailed to remain with wounded at Culpeper, Va., Aug. 12, '62, and captured Aug. 20, '62. Paroled at Aikens Landing, Va., Sept. 14, '62. Mustered out, June 2, '63.
James McMynn	Mustered in, May 22, '61. Mustered out, June 2, '63.
Delevan Mathews	Mustered in, May 22, '61. Mustered out, June 2, '63.
Marcus M. Mallison	Mustered in, May 22, '61. Mustered out, June 2, '63.
George H. Miller	Mustered in, May 22, '61. Mustered out, June 2, '63.
Lewis M. Miller	Mustered in, May 22, '61. Regimental and Brigade teamster, Nov. '61 to May '63. Mustered out, June 2, '63.
Hiram M. Moore, San Luis, Obispo, California	Mustered in, May 22, '61. Discharged for disability, July 21, '61, at Washington, D. C.
James B. Moore	Mustered in, May 22, '61. Brigade saddler, Feb. 9, '63, to May '63. Mustered out, June 2, '63.
Amos H. Neatie	Mustered in, May 22, '61. Mustered out, June 2, '63.
Edward Payne	Mustered in, May 22, '61. Mustered out, June 2, '63.
George Rundall, Hudson, Wis.	Mustered in, May 22, '61. Mustered out, June 2, '63.
Daniel L. Reynolds, New Richmond, Mich.	Mustered in, May 22, '61. Detailed in Pioneer Corps, April 8, '62 to Sept. '62. Mustered out, June 2, '63.
Milton A. Reynolds	Mustered in, Dec. 25, '61. Discharged for disability, April 29, '62 at Harrisonburg, Va.
Leonard D. Sale, Philadelphia "Press," Philadelphia, Pa.	Mustered in, May 22, '61. Promoted to Com. Sergeant, Oct. 1, '62.
Thomas C. Sanders	Mustered in, Oct. 21, '61. Mustered out, June 2, '63.
Dwight Sanderson	Mustered in, May 22, '61. Discharged Feb. 4, '63, for disability, at Washington, D. C.
Charles A. Sayre, Victoria, Ills.	Mustered in, May 22, '61. Captured at Manassas, Va., Aug. 26, '62. Paroled same place, Sept. 3, '62. Mustered out, June 2, '63.
Michael Scanthing	Mustered in, May 22, '61. Mustered out, June 2, '63.
Patrick Sennett	Mustered in, May 22, '61. Mustered out, June 2, '63.
William Smith	Mustered in, Oct. 21, '61. Mustered out, June 2, '63.
Thomas Sodon	Mustered in, May 22, '61. Mustered out, June 2, '63.
Porter Stevens	Mustered in, May 22, '61. Mustered out, June 2, '63. Died in 1885.
Henry S. Strubble, Wilson, N. Y.	Mustered in, May 22, '61. Mustered out, June 2, '63.
James Taylor, 636 Ross Ave., Station O., Chicago, Ill.	Mustered in, May 22, '61. Captured on Banks' retreat, May 25, '62. Paroled at Aikens Landing, Va., Sept. 13, '62. Captured at Chancellorsville, Va., May 2, '63. Paroled at City Point, Va., May 14, '63. Mustered out, June 2, '63.
Ward M. Taylor	Mustered in, May 22, '61. Discharged for disability, Nov. 10, '62, at Albany.
Thomas Todd	Mustered in, May 22, '61. Died of disease, June 5, '61, at Albany.
Henry H. Tubbs	Mustered in, May 22, '61. Mustered out June 2, '63.
Henry M. Tuttle	Mustered in, Dec. 25, '61. Detailed to remain as nurse to wounded at Culpeper, Va., and captured Aug. 20, '62. Paroled at Aikens Landing, Va., Oct. 6, '62. Mustered out, June 2, '63. Died, Feb., 1891.
John A. Vanderhoof, Dansville, N. Y.	Mustered in, May 22, '61. Discharged, May 8, '62, for disability, at Frederick, Md.
George M. Walling	Mustered in, May 22, '61. Discharged, Aug. 22, '61, for disability, at Berlin, Md.
John Waters	Mustered in, May 22, '61. Teamster in Post train, Jan. to May, '63. Mustered out, June 2, '63.
Isaac S. Wilson, Baxter, Mich.	Mustered in, May 22, '61. Discharged, Sept. 3, '61, for disability, at Darnestown, Md.
Samuel D. Wood	Mustered in, Jan. 6, '62. Mustered out, June 2, '63.
Watson Wykoff	Mustered in, May 22, '61. Died, Nov. 12, '62, of disease at Baltimore, Md.
John A. Yeckley	Mustered in, May 22, '61. Brigade teamster, March to May, '63. Mustered out, June 2, '63.
John Youngs	Mustered in, May 22, '61. Mustered out, June 2, '63.

COMPANY F.

Captain.	
Charles H. Fenn	Mustered in, May 22, '61, Capt. Acting Brigade Inspector, 1st Brigade, 1st Div., 12th A. C., March 5, '63. Mustered out, June 2, '63. Died in Rochester, N. Y., in 1876.
Lieutenants.	
William W. Rowley, Quartermaster and C.S. Soldiers' Home, Milwaukee, Wis.	Mustered in, May 22, '61, 1st Lieut. Transferred, Dec. 1, '62, 1st Lieut., for promotion to Capt. Co. E.
George M. Elliott	Mustered in, May 22, '61, 2d Lieut. Promoted, 1st Lieut., Dec. 1, '62. Detailed as Commander of Ambulance Corps, Oct. 18, '62 to May, '63. Mustered out, June 2, '63.
Lieutenants.—Continu'd.	
Lucius R. Bailey	Mustered in, May 22, '61, 1st Sergt. Wounded in action at Cedar Mountain, Va., Aug. 9, '62. Promoted 2d Lieut., Jan. 14, '63. Mustered out, June 2, '63. Died, June 12, '85.
Sergeants.	
George W. Sherwood	Mustered in, May 22, '61, Sergt. Promoted 1st Sergt., Feb. 21, '63. Mustered out, June 2, '63. Subsequent service in Co. E., 15th N. Y. Cavalry. Died, Jan. 25, '92.
Darwin Fellows	Mustered in, May 22, '61, Corp. Promoted Sergt., Nov. 9, '62. On recruiting service, Oct. 15, '61, to Jan., '62. Mustered out, June 2, '63.

COMPANY F.—Continued.

Name and Present Residence, Where Known.	Remarks.
Sergeants.—Continued.	
Charles Gillam Byron, N. Y.	Mustered in, May 22, '61, Corp. Promoted to Sergt.-Major Oct. 1, '62
Cleveland Gillett	Mustered in, May 22, '61, private. Promoted Corp. Sept. 29, '61. Sergt., Feb. 1, '63. Mustered out, June 2, '63.
Charles C. Searls Grand Rapids, Mich.	Mustered in, May 22, '61, Sergt. Discharged, Sept. 29, '61, for disability, at Darnstown, Md.
Edmund Watts	Mustered in, May 22, '61, Sergt. Mustered out, June 2, '63.
Robert F. Whitney	Mustered in, May 22, '61, Corp. Promoted Sergt., Nov. 9, '62. Mustered out, June 2, '63. Died in 1890.
Corporals.	
James F. Bennett Alexander, N. Y.	Mustered in, May 22, '61, private. Wounded in action at Cedar Mountain, Va., Aug. 9, '62. Promoted Corp., Nov. 9, '62. Mustered out, June 2, '63.
Henry Close	Mustered in, May 22, '61, private. Promoted Corp. Nov. 9, '62. Mustered out June 2, '63.
George W. Hamilton 36 Buckley St., Grand Rapids, Mich	Mustered in, May 22, '61, private. Promoted Corp. March 6, '62. Captured at Cedar Mountain, Va., Aug. 9, '62. Paroled Aikens Landing, Va., Sept. 13, '62. Mail agent 12th Army Corps, by order Gen. Slocum, Feb. 25, '63 to May, '63. Mustered out, June 2, '63.
Leander Hamilton Fairport, N. Y.	Mustered in, May 22, '61. Accidentally wounded, July, '62. Detailed as wagon master, Jan., '62 to July, '62. Discharged, Sept. 24, '62, for disability, Washington, D. C.
Michael Ryan Mill Grove, N. Y.	Mustered in, May 22, '61, private. Captured at Cedar Mountain, Va., Aug. 9, '62. Paroled at Aikens Landing, Va., Sept. 13, '62. Promoted Corp., Feb. 25, '63. Mustered out, June 2, '63.
Musicians.	
William H. Brady Nunda, N. Y.	Mustered in, July 25, '62. Transferred, June 3, '63, to Co. D, 10th Maine Battalion.
John Brost	Mustered in, May 22, '61. Discharged, July 17, '61, for disability, at Washington, D. C.
Privates.	
William F. Albro	Mustered in, May 22, '61. Discharged, July 21, '61, for disability, at Washington, D. C.
George H. Allen	Mustered in, May 22, '61. Killed in action at Cedar Mountain, Va., Aug. 9, '62.
Calvin Annis	Mustered in, May 22, '61. Discharged, July 8, '61, for disability at Ft. Columbus, N. Y. Harbor.
Lafayette Baker	Mustered in, May 22, '61. Discharged, July 7, '61, for disability, at Washington, D. C.
Henry C. Baldwin	Mustered in, May 22, '61. Killed in action at Cedar Mountain, Va., Aug. 9, '62.
John Barber	Mustered in, May 22, '61. Discharged, June 5, '61, at Albany.
George Barnard	Mustered in, May 22, '61. Died of disease at Frederick, Md., May 28, '62.
Oscar Barnes	Mustered in, May 22, '61. Discharged, Dec. 3, '62, for disability at New York.
Philip Bettinger	Mustered in, May 22, '61. Discharged, Dec. 29, '62, for disability at Albany.

Name and Present Residence, Where Known.	Remarks.
Privates.—Continued.	
George Bolton	Mustered in, Dec. 10, '61. Detailed to Artillery, March 19, '63 to May, '63. Mustered out, June 2, '63.
Riley Blount	Mustered in, May 22, '61. Wounded in action at Cedar Mountain, Va., Aug. 9, '62. Died, Sept. 11, '62, of wounds at Alexandria, Va.
George H. Bolton	Mustered in, May 22, '61. Discharged, July 17, '62, for disability at Washington, D. C.
Edmund Bragden	Mustered in, May 22, '61. Mustered out, June 2, '63.
Silas Bragg	Mustered in, May 22, '61. Killed in action at Cedar Mountain, Va., Aug. 9, '62.
Byron Brinkerhoff	Mustered in, May 22, '61. Mustered out, June 2, '63.
Valentine B. Byron	Transferred from 13th N. Y. V., July 1, '61. Deserted, Nov. 19, '61, from Muddy Branch, Md.
Robert Chappell	Mustered in, May 22, '61. Mustered out, June 2, '63.
Roswell Coddington	Mustered in, May 22, '61. Died, March 5, '62, of disease, at Hagerstown, Md.
William H. Colburn	Mustered in, May 22, '61. Captured at Winchester, Va., May 25, '62. Paroled at Aikens Landing, Va., Sept. 13, '62. Mustered out, June 2, '63.
Alexander Comgue	Mustered in, May 22, '61. Killed in action at Cedar Mountain, Va., Aug. 9, '62.
Charles Crandall	Mustered in, May 22, '61. Died, April 17, '62, of disease at Woodstock, Va.
Joshua C. Davis	Mustered in, May 22, '61. Discharged, Dec. 3, '62, for disability at Sandy Hook, Md.
Melvin Dodge Horton, Mich.	Mustered in, May 22, '61. Mustered out, June 2, '63.
Decatur Doty	Mustered in, May 22, '61. Discharged, Jan. 17, '62, for disability at Baltimore, Md.
Henry Dykeman Enterprise, Pa.	Mustered in, May 22, '61. Discharged, Jan. 3, '62, for disability at Baltimore, Md.
Theodore Eldridge	Mustered in, May 22, '61. Killed in action at Cedar Mountain, Va., Aug. 9, '62.
Joseph Enos	Mustered in, May 22, '61. Captured at Winchester, Va., May 25, '62. Paroled, Aikens Landing, Va., Sept. 13, '62. Left arm amputated on account of accidental gunshot wound received while on duty, Jan. 16, '63. Discharged for disability at Stafford C. H., Va., April 17, '63.
Ervin H. Ewell St. Louis, Mich.	Mustered in, May 22, '61. Captured at Cedar Mountain, Va., Aug. 9, '62. Paroled, Aikens Landing, Va., Sept. 13, '62. Mustered out, June 2, '63.
Kirkland Ewell	Mustered in, May 22, '61. Detailed in Ambulance Corps as driver, Feb. 28, '62, to May, '63. Mustered out, June 2, '63.
James Fox	Mustered in, July 1, '61. Wounded in action at Cedar Mountain, Va., Aug. 9, '62. Discharged, Oct. 3, '62, for disability, Annapolis, Md.
Joseph Gibson	Mustered in, May 22, '61. Discharged, Sept. 13, '61, for disability, at Hyattstown, Md.
George Griffin	Mustered in, May 22, '61. Deserted, May 23, '61. Albany.
Israel Holt 99 Decker Ave., Cleveland, Ohio.	Mustered in, Aug. 12, '62. Transferred to Barracks at Albany, May 28, '63. Discharged for disability, Oct. 2, '63, at Albany.
Truman M. Hawley	Mustered in, May 22, '61. Mustered out, June 2, '63.

COMPANY F.—Continued

Name and Present Residence, Where Known.	Remarks.
Privates—Continued.	
Isaac Hotchkiss	Mustered in, May 22, '61. Detached service as messenger for Gen. Banks, Aug. 30, '61, to Aug. 28, '62. Captured at Manassas, Va., Aug. 28, '62. Paroled, same place, Sept. 3, '62. Mustered out, June 2, '63.
Porter L. Howard, 1628 Jefferson St., Kansas City, Mo.	Mustered in, May 22, '61. Wounded in shoulder at battle of Cedar Mountain, Va., Aug. 9, '62. Mustered out, June 2, '63.
Peter Howland	Mustered in, May 22, '61. Mustered out, June 2, '63.
William Howland	Mustered in, May 22, '61. Mustered out, June 2, '63.
James G. Lawton	Mustered in, May 22, '61. Discharged, July 17, '61, for disability, at Washington, D. C.
Charles H. Liscom, Amsterdam Ave. and 155th St., New York City.	Mustered in, May 22, '61. Detailed as nurse in Hospital, Hagerstown, Md., June 12, '62, to March, '63. Detailed in Hospital, York, Pa., as nurse, April, '63. Mustered out, June 2, '63.
Joseph Luce	Mustered in, May 22, '61. Discharged, June 5, '61, at Albany.
William McCracken	Mustered in, May 22, '61. Captured at Cedar Mountain, Va., Aug. 9, '62. Paroled, Aikens Landing, Va., Sept. 13, '62. Died of disease at Fairfax Seminary Hospital, Nov. 17, '62.
John McGrath	Mustered in, Dec. 10, '61. Captured at Winchester, Va., May 25, '62. Paroled at Aikens Landing, Va., Sept. 13, '62. Detailed to Ambulance Corps, Oct. 28, '62, to April, '63. Mustered out, June 2, '63.
Lyman B. Miner, Jamestown, N. D.	Mustered in, May 22, '61. Mustered out, June 2, '63.
James L. Moore	Mustered in, Aug. 13, '62. Transferred to Barracks at Albany, May 20, '63.
John Moran	Mustered in, May 22, '61. Mustered out, June 2, '63.
Barnard Murray	Mustered in, May 22, '61. Killed in action at Cedar Mountain, Va., Aug. 9, '62.
Richard Outhoudt, N. Adams, Mich.	Mustered in, May 22, '61. Mustered out June 2, '63.
Edward C. Peck, Batavia, N. Y.	Mustered in, May 22, '61. Clerk at Division Headquarters, July 25, '61, to May, '63. Mustered out, June 2, '63.
Erastus Peck, Brockport, N. Y.	Mustered in, May 22, '61. Discharged, July 24, '61, at Washington, D. C.
Franklin Peck	Mustered in, May 22, '61. Mustered out, June 2, '63.
Charles H. Perkins	Mustered in, May 22, '61. Wounded in action at Cedar Mountain, Va., Aug. 9, '62. Discharged Dec. 22, '62, of wounds, Alexandria, Va.

Name and Present Residence, Where Known.	Remarks.
Privates.—Continued	
Flavius Perkins	Mustered in, May 22, '61. Died, Nov. 14, '61, at Darnestown, Md.
Michael Quick	Mustered in, May 22, '61. Transferred, Sept. 27, '61, to Co. B., 3d N. Y. Cavalry, in place of Henry De St. Croix, transferred.
Charles B. H. Rapp	Mustered in, May 22, '61. Discharged, Oct. 31, '62, for disability, at Baltimore, Md.
John Rapp	Mustered in, Dec. 9, '61. Mustered out, June 2, '63.
Harlow M. Reynold	Mustered in, May 22, '61. Mustered out, June 2, '63.
Henry Scott	Mustered in, May 22, '61. Deserted, May 21 '61, at Albany.
William B. Simmons	Mustered in, May 22, '61. Captured at Cedar Mountain, Va., Aug. 9 '62. Paroled at Aikens Landing, Va., Sept. 13, '62. Mustered out, June 2, '63.
Howard M. Snell	Mustered in, May 22, '61. Killed in action at Cedar Mountain, Va., Aug. 9, '62.
Henry De St. Croix	Transferred from Co. B., 3d N. Y. Cavalry. Exchanged for Michael Quick. Mustered out, June 2, '63.
Albert Taylor	Mustered in, Oct. 31, '62. Discharged, March 23, '63, for disability at Harper's Ferry, Va.
Leonard B. Taylor	Mustered in, Sept. 2, '62. Transferred, May 20, '63, to Barracks at Albany. Later, assigned to 10th Maine Battalion.
Stephen Taylor	Mustered in, May 22, '61. Discharged, July 17, '61, for disability at Washington, D. C.
George W. Thayer, Pembroke, N. Y.	Mustered in, May 22, '61. Acting Hospital Steward at Harper's Ferry, Va., Dec. 10, '62, to March 31, '63. Mustered out, June 2, '63.
Milo L. Thayer	Mustered in July 14, '62. Transferred to Veteran Reserve Corps. Died of variolоid, Feb. 20, '64.
Riley Thayer, Basom, N. Y.	Mustered in, May 22, '61. Mustered out, June 2, '63.
Robert Thompson	Mustered in, May 22, '61. Mustered out, June 2, '63. Died in 1879.
Milton Tripp	Mustered in, May 22, '61. Discharged, May 8, '62, for disability, at Frederick, Md.
John Van Buren	Mustered in, May 22, '61. Detailed as ambulance driver, Dec. 10, '62, to April 10, '63. Mustered out, June 2, '63.
Francis M. Weatherson	Mustered in, May 22, '61. Mustered out, June 2 '63.
John Wells	Mustered in, Nov. 1, '61. Mustered out, June 2 '63.

COMPANY G.

Name and Present Residence, Where Known.	Remarks.
Captains.	
David Hardie	Mustered in, May 22, '61, Capt. Resigned, June 1, '62. Died, March 26, '96, at Albion, N. Y.
Alfred B. Judd, 729 Sycamore St., Milwaukee, Wis.	Promoted from 1st Lieut. Co. B, June 1, '62. Detailed as Acting Assistant Adjutant General at brigade headquarters, Dec. 3, '62, to May, '63. Mustered out, June 2, '63.
Lieutenants.	
James O. Nickerson, Hemlock Lake, N. Y.	Mustered in, May 22, '61, 1st Lieut. Resigned, Jan. 28, '62.
Lieutenants—Contin'd	
William M. Kenyon, 158 Caukey Ave., Rochester, N. Y.	Mustered in, May 22, '61. 2d Lieut. Promoted 1st Lieut., Jan. 30, '62. Captured at Cedar Mountain, Va., Aug. 9, '62. Rejoined, Dec. 5, '62. Commanded company, Dec. 5, '62, to May, '63. Mustered out, June 2, '63.
James Smith, 267 Masonic Temple, Minneapolis, Minn.	Mustered in, May 22, '61, Sergt. Promoted 1st Sergt., July, 18, '61. 2d Lieut., Feb. 20, '63. Mustered out, June 2, '63.

COMPANY G.—Continued.

Name and Present Residence, Where Known.	Remarks.
Sergeants.	
Burnum Slocum	Mustered in, May 22, '61, 1st Sergt. Discharged, July 18, '61, for disability, at Washington, D. C.
Henry V. Coleman	Mustered in, May 22, '61, Corp. Promoted Sergt., July 2, '61. 1st Sergt., Feb. 25, '63. Mustered out, June 2, '63.
William Collins, 2d, Albion, N. Y.	Mustered in, May 22, '61, private. Promoted Corp., Feb. 22, '62. Sergt., Dec. 7, '62. Captured at Cedar Mountain, Va., Aug. 9, '62. Paroled at Aikens Landing, Va., Sept. 13, '62. Captured at Chancellorsville, Va. May 2, '63. Paroled at City Point, Va., May 14, '63. Mustered out, June 2, '63.
John P. Curran	Mustered in, May 22, '61, private. Promoted Corp., Feb. 22, '62. Sergt., Dec. 7, '62. Captured at Cedar Mountain, Va., Aug. 9, '62. Paroled, City Point, Va., Sept. 11, '62. Mustered out, June 2, '63.
Charles S. Johnson	Mustered in, May 22, '61, Corp. Promoted Sergt., Feb. 22, '62. Mustered out, June 2, '63.
Willis Raymond	Mustered in, May 22, '61, Musician. Promoted Corp., Jan. 5, '62. Captured at Cedar Mountain, Va., Aug. 9, '62. Paroled, Aikens Landing, Va., Sept. 3, '62. Promoted Sergt., Feb. 28, '63. Mustered out, June 2, '63.
William Wylie	Mustered in, May 22, '61. Deserted June 21, '61, Albany.
Lewis D. C. Gaskill, Fraser, Colorado.	Mustered in, May 22, '61. Promoted 2d Lieut., Co. A, Oct. 9, '62.
Corporals.	
Joseph Brannan	Mustered in, May 22, '61, private. Promoted Corp., Dec. 7, '62. Mustered out, June 2, '63.
Thomas Brown	Mustered in, May 22, '61, private. Promoted Corp., Oct. 26, '62. Mustered out, June 2, '63.
Edward Cary	Mustered in, May 22, '61. Mustered out, June 2, '63.
Peter Guelph	Mustered in May 22, '61 private. Promoted Corp., Feb. 25, '62. Mustered out, June 2, '63. Joined 1st Veteran N. Y. Cavalry, July 9, '63, and served until close of War. Died, July 4, '95. Brockport, N. Y.
August Hawn	Mustered in, May 22, '61, private. Promoted, Corp., Dec. 7, '62. Mustered out, June 2, '63.
Alexander Hosberry	Mustered in, May 22, '61, private. Promoted Corp., Feb. 28, '62. Killed in action at Cedar Mountain, Va., Aug. 9, '62.
George M. Moore	Mustered in, May 22, '61. Mustered out, June 2, '63.
Musicians.	
Meritt Raymond	Mustered in, May 22, '61, musician. Discharged, July 17, '61, for disability at Camp Harris, D. C.
Origen A. Richardson	Mustered in, May 22, '61, private. Promoted, Musician, July 18, '61. Captured at Cedar Mountain, Va., Aug. 9, '62. Paroled at Aikens Landing, Va., Sept. 13, '62. Mustered out, June 2, '63.
Privates.	
Samuel Avery	Mustered in, May 22, '61. Captured near Winchester, Va., May 25, '62. Paroled, Aikens Landing, Va., Sept. 13, '62. Captured at Chancellorsville, Va., May 2, '63. Paroled at City Point, Va., May 14, '63. Mustered out, June 2, '63.
Privates.—Continued.	
Oscar Barber	Mustered in, Feb. 21, '62. Transferred to Albany, N. Y.
Benjamin Barker, Fair Haven, N. Y.	Mustered in, May 22, '61. Captured at Manassas, Va., Aug. 29, '62. Paroled at Bull Run, Va., Aug. 31, '62. Mustered out, June 2, '63.
George Barwick	Mustered in, March 20, '62. Captured, Aug. 9, '62, at Cedar Mountain, Va. Rejoined, Oct. 21, '62. Died, Dec. 5, '62, of disease, at Sandy Hook, Md.
Albert Bean	Mustered in, May 22, '61. Mustered out, June 2, '63.
Richard Bean	Mustered in, May 22, '61. Wounded in action at Cedar Mountain, Va., Aug. 9, '62. Mustered out, June 2, '63.
James Black	Mustered in, May 22, '61. Captured at Manassas, Va., Aug. 18, '62. Paroled at Lee Camp, Aug. 31, '62. Mustered out, June 2, '63.
Merrit Brocket	Mustered in, May 22, '61. Discharged, June 18, '61, for disbility, at Albany.
James Brown	Mustered in, May 22, '61. Mustered out, June 2, '63.
Richard Brown	Mustered in, May 22, '61. Wounded in action at Cedar Mountain, Va., Aug. 9, '62. Discharged, on account of wounds, at Alexandria, Va., Oct. 24, '62.
Edward Canfield	Mustered in, May 22, '61. Died of disease in Hospital, Baltimore, Md., Oct. 21, '61.
William H. Chapin	Mustered in, May 22, '61. Killed in action at Cedar Mountain, Va., Aug. 9, '62.
William Collins	Mustered in, May 22, '61. Captured at Winchester, Va., May 25, '62, and paroled. Wounded accidentally. Discharged, June 16, '62, from wounds, at Washington, D. C.
Daniel Conner	Mustered in, May 22, '61. Deserted, June 10, '61, Albany, N. Y.
William Craig	Mustered in, May 22, '61. Discharged, Aug. 13, '61, for disability, at Berlin, Md.
Warren H. Crego, Adalaska, Presque Isle Co., Mich.	Mustered in, May 22, '61. Discharged, June 11, '62, for disability, at Front Royal, Va.
Isaac J. Crittenden	Mustered in, May 22, '61. Discharged, Aug. 8, '62, for disability, Philadelphia, Pa.
Francis De Lacy	Transferred from Co. I. Mustered out, June 2, '63.
James Deppa	Mustered in, May 22, '61. Captured near Winchester, Va., May 25, '62. Paroled at Aikens Landing, Va., Sept. 13, '62. Captured at Chancellorsville, Va., May 2, '63. Paroled, May 10, '63, at City Point, Va. Mustered out, June 2, '63.
Edward R. Douglass	Mustered in, May 22, '61. Died, March 23, '62, of disease, at Winchester, Va.
John Duppey	Mustered in, May 22, '61. Wounded in action, Sept. 17, '62, at Antietam, Md. Mustered out, June 2, '63.
Charles Ferdun, Allegan, Mich.	Mustered in, May 22, '61. Wounded in action at Cedar Mountain, Va., Aug. 9, '62. Discharged at Washington, D. C., Sept. 29, '62, on account of wounds received at Cedar Mountain.
George E. Furdon	Mustered in, May 22, '61. Captured at Winchester, Va., May 25, '62. Died, July 10, '62, of disease, at Lynchburg, Va. Prisoner of War.
David Gulaman	Mustered in, May 22, '61. Accidentally wounded, and died of wounds at Harrisonburg, Va., May 3, '62.

COMPANY G.—Continued.

Name and Present Residence, Where Known.	Remarks.
Privates.—Continued.	
Peter Goodrich	Mustered in May 22, '61. Mustered out, June 2, '63.
Edward C. Gould	Mustered in, May 22, '61. Discharged, June 16, '61, for disability, at Albany.
John Houratty	Mustered in, May 22, '61. Captured at Cedar Mountain, Va., Aug. 9, '62. Paroled at Aikens Landing, Va., Sept. 13, '62. Mustered out, June 2, '63.
Jacob Herman	Mustered in, May 22, '61. Deserted, Jan. 6, '62, from hospital, Frederick, Md.
Elliot Hoagland	Mustered in, May 22, '61. Captured, Winchester, Va., May 25, '62. Paroled Aikens Landing, Va., Sept. 13, '62. Captured at Chancellorsville, Va., May 2, '63. Paroled, City Point, Va., May 14, '63. Mustered out, June 2, '63.
Joseph Houlmes	Enlisted August 15, '62. Never mustered. Deserted, March 1, '63, from hospital, Alexandria, Va. Later, enlisted 129th N. Y. Vol.
Lyman Howe	Mustered in, May 22, '61. Mustered out, June 2, '63.
Wallace W. Hunt Grand, Neb.	Mustered in, May 22, '61. Mustered out, June 2, '63.
George Ireland	Mustered in, May 22, '61. Discharged, Oct. 13, '62, for disability, at New York.
John James	Mustered in, May 22, '61. Captured May 25, '62, on Banks' retreat, near Winchester, Va. Paroled at Aikens Landing, Va., Sept. 13, '62. Mustered out, June 2, '63.
Nathaniel R. Jones	Mustered in, May 22, '61. Discharged, July 11, '61, for disability, at Washington, D. C.
Wheeler King	Mustered in, May 22, '61. Captured at Winchester, Va., May 25, '62. Paroled at Aikens Landing, Va., Sept. 13, '62. Mustered out, June 2, '63.
Frederick Kruss	Mustered in, May 22, '61. Killed in action at Cedar Mountain, Va., Aug. 9, '62.
William Lamb	Mustered in, May 22, '61. Captured at Cedar Mountain, Va., Aug. 9, '62. Paroled at Aikens Landing, Va., Sept. 13, '62. Captured at Chancellorsville, Va., May 2, '63. Paroled at City Point, Va., May 15, '63. Mustered out, June 2, '63.
Stephen Lane	Mustered in, May 22, '61. Mustered out, June 2, '63.
Edward Lankish	Mustered in, August 25, '62. Transferred, May 20, '63, to Barracks at Albany. Mustered out, at Hart Island, N. Y. H., May 27, '65, as of 28th N. Y.
Hugh Lavery	Mustered in, May 22, '61. Died, March 25, '62, of disease, at Winchester, Va.
John Lewis	Mustered in, May 22, '61. Discharged, Aug. 8, '61, for disability, at Berlin, Md.
Owen McAllister Clarendon, N. Y.	Mustered in, May 22, '61. Captured at Winchester, Va., May 25, '62. Paroled at Aikens Landing, Va., Sept. 13, '62. Captured at Chancellorsville, Va., May 3, '63. Paroled at City Point, Va., May 15, '63. Mustered out, June 2, '63.
Andrew J. McCord	Mustered in, May 22, '61. Deserted, June 10, '61, Albany.
Privates.—Continued.	
Patrick McDonald	Mustered in, May 22, '61. Discharged, June 18, '61, for disability, at Albany.
Arthur McKenney	Mustered in, May 22, '61. Discharged, June 28, '61, for disability, at Albany.
Joseph McMahon	Mustered in, May 22, '61. Captured at Cedar Mountain, Va., Aug. 9, '62. Paroled at Aikens Landing, Va., Sept. 13, '62. Captured at Chancellorsville, Va., May 2, '63. Paroled at City Point, Va., May 14, '63. Mustered out, June 2, '63.
Ernest M. C. Mansfield	Mustered in, May 22, '61. Mustered out, June 2, '63.
James McNiven 1101 Jackson Boulevard, Chicago, Ills.	Mustered in, May 22, '61. Division butcher, Nov. 1, '61, to April, '63. Mustered out, June 2, '63.
James McWeeney	Mustered in, May 22, '61. Captured at Winchester, Va., May 25, '62. Paroled at Aikens Landing, Va., Sept. 13, '62. Mustered out, June 2, '63.
Shepard R. Malone	Mustered in, May 22, '61. Killed in action at Cedar Mountain, Va., Aug. 9, '62.
Ora B. Mitchell	Mustered in, May 22, '61. Deserted, Aug. 10, '61, to the enemy, at Berlin, Md.
Thomas B. Moffat	Mustered in, May 22, '61. Died, July 10, '61, of disease at Williamsport, Md.
Francis Mooney	Mustered in, Sept. 8, '62. Transferred, May 20, '63, to barracks, Albany. Transferred, Feb. 8, '64, to Co. D, 60th N. Y. Vols. Died, March 2, '91.
Ranson S. Newton	Mustered in, May 22, '61. Discharged, Oct. 21, '62, for disability at Maryland Heights, Md.
James A. Orr	Mustered in, May 22, '61. Deserted, Sept. 30, '61, at Darnestown, Md.
Edgar Otis	Mustered in, March 20, '62. Died, June 26, '62, of disease, at Hagerstown, Md.
George W. Pier	Mustered in, May 22, '61. Captured at Culpeper, Va., Aug. 10, '62. Paroled at Aikens Landing, Va., Oct. 6, '62. Mustered out, June 2, '63.
Warren W. Putnam	Mustered in, March 8, '62. Captured at Winchester, Va., May 24, '62. Rejoined, Aug. 30, '62. Captured at Chancellorsville, Va., May 2, '63. Paroled at City Point, Va., May 11, '63.
Peter Schneider	Mustered in, May 22, '61. Captured at Winchester, Va., May 25, '62. Paroled at Aikens Landing, Va., Sept. 13, '62. Mustered out, June 2, '63.
Edward St. John	Mustered in, May 22, '61. Mustered out, June 2, '63.
John Welch	Mustered in, May 22, '61. Mustered out, June 2, '63.
William Wigley	Mustered in, May 22, '61. Mustered out, June 2, '63.
George D. W. Wilson	Mustered in, May 22, '61. Discharged, July 17, '61, for disability at Camp Harris, D. C.
Mark Woolster	Mustered in, May 22, '61. Mustered out, June 2, '63.
Jacob Young Niagara Falls, N. Y.	Enlisted, Aug. 21, '62. Discharged, Feb. 2, '63, for disability at Washington, D. C.

COMPANY H.

Name and Present Residence, Where Known.	Remarks.
Captains.	
John Waller, Monticello, N. Y.	Mustered in, May 22, '61, Capt. Detached on Recruiting Service, Aug. 26, '61, to Nov. 12, '61. Discharged, Dec. 30, '62, for promotion to Major 132d N. Y. Vols.
John C. Terry	Mustered in, May 22, '61, Lieut. Promoted, Capt., Dec. 30, '62. Acting Regt. Quartermaster, March 20, '62, to Dec. 1, '62. Commanding Co., Jan. 12, '63. Mustered out, June 2, '63.
Lieutenants.	
Lee M. Brown	Mustered in, May 22, '61, 2d Lieut. Discharged, Feb. 25, '62.
John H. Buckbee	Mustered in, May 22, '61, Sergt. Wounded in action at Cedar Mountain, Va., Aug. 9, '62. Promoted, 2d Lieut., Feb. 2, '63. Mustered out, June 2, '63.
William J. S. McAllister	Mustered in, May 22, '61, Sergt. Promoted, 2d Lieut., May 18, '62. Captured at Cedar Mountain, Va., Aug. 9, '62. Paroled at Aikens Landing, Va., Sept. 24, '62. Resigned, Nov., '62.
Sergeants.	
John P. Carpenter	Mustered in, May 22, '61, 1st Sergt. Killed in action at Cedar Mountain, Va., Aug. 9, '62.
Riasoon B. Cooper	Mustered in, May 22, '61, Corp. Captured at Cedar Mountain, Va., Aug. 9, '62. Paroled at Aikens Landing, Va., Sept. 13, '62. Promoted, Sergt., Nov. 1, '62. Mustered out, June 2, '63.
William B. Gillespie, Bethel, Sullivan Co., N. Y.	Mustered in, May 22, '61. Discharged, March 19, '63.
Levi Kimball, Wakefield, Neb.	Mustered in, May 22, '61, private. Promoted, Corp., Aug. 1, '61. Sergt., Feb. 1, '63. Mustered out, June 2, '63.
Graham Moffett, Parksville, N. Y.	Mustered in, May 22, '61, private. Promoted, Corp., Nov. 1, '62. Sergt., April 1, '63. Mustered out, June 2, '63.
Napoleon B. Bradley, Ithaca, Gratiot Co., Mich.	Mustered in, May 22, '61, private. Promoted, Corp., March 27, '62. Sergt., Nov. 1, '62. Detailed a scout, July 29, '62. Rejoined, Sept. 29, '62. Mustered out, June 2, '63.
Alfred R. Pierson	Mustered in, May 22, '61. Killed in action at Cedar Mountain, Va., Aug. 9, '62.
Leander M. Young, Jeffersonville, N. Y.	Mustered in, May 22, '61, corp. Promoted, Sergt., May 21, '62. 1st Sergt., Feb. 1, '63. Mustered out, June 2, '63.
Corporals.	
Richard Beebe, Monticello, N. Y.	Mustered in, May 22, '61, private. Promoted, Corp., Nov. 1, '62. Mustered out, June 2, '63.
Augustus Hinman	Mustered in, May 22, '61, private. Promoted, Corp., Nov. 1, '62. Detailed Clerk at Regt. Quartermaster's office, May 8, '62, to Aug. 3, '62. Detailed in Brigade Quartermaster's Dept., Dec. 9, '62, to May, '63. Mustered out, June 2, '63.
Matthew Linsen	Mustered in, May 22, '61, private. Promoted, Corp., May 21, '62. Wounded in action at Cedar Mountain, Va., Aug. 9, '62, and left at Culpeper, Va. Died, Sept. 1, '62, of wounds at Culpeper, Va.
William A. Lovett, Newark, Ohio	Mustered in, May 22, '61, private. Wounded in action at Cedar Mountain, Va., Aug. 9, '62. Mustered out, June 2, '63.
Corporals,—Continued.	
Gabriel W. Misner	Mustered in, May 22, '61, private. Promoted, Corp., May 21, '62. Mustered out, June 2, '63.
John C. Smith	Mustered in, May 22, '61. Discharged, July, '61, for disability, at Washington, D. C.
Lafayette Van Duzer	Mustered in, May 22, '61, private. Promoted, Corp., Feb. 1, '63. Mustered out, June 2, '63.
Musicians.	
George Egner	Mustered in, May 22, '61. Killed in action at Cedar Mountain, Va., Aug. 9, '62.
Joseph Morris	Mustered in, May 22, '61, private. Promoted, musician, Nov. 26, '62. Mustered out, June 2, '63.
Joseph Taylor, Parksville, N. Y.	Mustered in, May 22, '61. Mustered out, June 2, '63.
Privates.	
John Allen	Mustered in, May 22, '61. Mustered out, June 2, '63.
James Babcock	Mustered in, May 22, '61. Wounded in action at Cedar Mountain, Va., Aug. 9, '62. Mustered out, June 2, '63.
Joseph Babcock	Mustered in, May 22, '61. Discharged, Dec. 21, '62, for disability, at Philadelphia, Pa.
Edward Barker, Livingston Manor, N. Y.	Mustered in, May 22, '61. Mustered out, June 2, '63.
Amos O. Barnhart	Mustered in, May 22, '61. Deserted, August 21, '61, Darnestown, Md.
Silas H. Beach, 808 Montgomery St., Jersey City, N. J.	Mustered in, May 22, '61. Captured at Cedar Mountain, Va., Aug. 9, '62. Paroled at Aikens Landing, Va., Sept. 13, '62. Mustered out, June 2, '63.
Dewey J. Boyce	Mustered in, May 22, '61. Deserted, June 14, '62, Front Royal, Va.
James M. Brennen	Mustered in, Oct. 9, '61. Discharged, May 31, '62, for disability, at Frederick, Md.
Bernard Burns	Mustered in, May 22, '61. Wounded in action at Antietam, Md., Sept. 17, '62. Mustered out, June 2, '63.
Rowland J. Burr	Mustered in, May 22, '61. Mustered out, June 2, '63.
Harrison Chandler	Mustered in, Dec. 11, '61. Captured May 25, '62. Died, June 29, '62, of disease, in Academy, General Hospital, Winchester, Va.
John B. Clayton	Transferred from Co. D. Mustered out, June 2, '63.
Benjamin S. Coddington	Mustered in, Oct. 9, '61. Brigade Blacksmith, Dec. 8, '61, to May, '63. Mustered out, June 2, '63.
Charles Coddington	Mustered in, Oct. 9, '61. Died, February 25, '62, of disease at Hancock, Md.
Ebenezer Coddington, Edgerton, Mich.	Mustered in, May 22, '61. Captured at Cedar Mountain, Va., Aug. 9, '62. Paroled at Aikens Landing, Va., Sept. 13, '62. Mustered out, June 2, '63.
James Coddington, Wurtsboro, Sullivan Co., N. Y.	Mustered in, Oct. 9, '61. Discharged, Jan. 30, '63, for disability, at Philadelphia, Pa.
William H. Curry	Mustered in, May 22, '61. Captured in hospital, Winchester, Va., May 25, '62. Paroled at Aikens Landing, Va., Sept. 13, '62. Captured at Chancellorsville, Va., May 2, '63. Paroled at City Point, Va., May 14, '63. Mustered out, June 2, '63.

COMPANY H.—Continued.

Name and Present Residence, Where Known.	Remarks.
Privates.—Continued.	
Charles H. Comfort	Mustered in, May 22, '61. Deserted, June 26, '62, Front Royal, Va.
Adolphus Eichman	Mustered in, May 22, '61. Mustered out, June 2, '63.
Richard I. Fair	Mustered in, May, 22, '61. Mustered out, June 2, '63.
Vincent Ferguson	Mustered in, May 22, '61. Discharged, Feb. 29, '61, for disability from Convalescent Camp, Va.
John D. Fisher	Mustered in, May 22, '61. Wounded in action, at Cedar Mountain, Va., Aug. 9, '62. Mustered out, June 2, '63.
Alonzo Foster	Mustered in, Oct 16, '61. Captured at Cedar Mountain Va., Aug. 9, '62. Rejoined, Oct. 22, '62. Mustered out, June 2, '64.
John French	Mustered in, May 22, '61. Died, Oct. 11, '61, of disease, at Darnstown, Md.
Sanford N. Fuller	Mustered in, Nov. 28, '61. Mustered out, June 2, 63.
Henry E. Gillett	Mustered in, May 22, '61. Captured at Cedar Mountain, Va., Aug. 9, '62. Rejoined, Oct. 24, '62. Mustered out, June 2, '63.
William Gillett	Transferred from Co. F, 5th Heavy Artillery. Transferred, April 30, '63, to Co. F, 5th Heavy Artillery.
Nelson H. Grout	Mustered in, May 22, '61. Mustered out, June 2, '63.
William Hill	Mustered in, Nov. 7, '61. Mustered out, June 2, '63.
Philip Hinkle	Mustered in, Dec. 11, '61. Mustered out, June 2, '63.
William H. Hinton	Mustered in, May 22, '61. Mustered out, June 2, 63.
George W. Hoyt	Mustered in, May 22, '61. Detailed as nurse in Hospital at Hancock, Md., Jan., 11, '62 to Feb. 20, '62. Detailed as clerk in Quartermaster's Dept., April 1, '62. Discharged by order of President at Harrisonburg, Va., April, 26, '62.
Samuel Hunt	Mustered in, May 22, '61. Lost an arm in action at Cedar Mountain, Va., Aug. 9, '62. Left in Hospital at Culpeper, Va., and captured, Aug. 20, '62. Paroled, Richmond, Va., Sept. 7, '62. Mustered out, June 2, '64.
Russell H. Hurd	Mustered in May 22, '61. Mustered out, June 2, '63.
Michael Hutchinson	Mustered in, May 22, '61. Captured at Winchester, Va., May 25, '62. Paroled at Aikens Landing, Va., Sept. 21, '62. Mustered out, June 2, '63.
Charles F. Kent	Mustered in, May 22 '61. Mustered out, June 2, '63.
Alonzo Kinne	Mustered in, May 22 '61. Detailed in Pioneer Corps, June 1, '62, to Sept. 25, '62. Mustered out, June 2, '63.
Martin Lane Shelton, Neb.	Mustered in, May 22, '61. Wounded in action at Cedar Mountain, Va., Aug. 9, '62. Mustered out, June 2, '63.
John Lawson	Transferred from Co. D. Died, Feb. 19, '62, of disease at Hancock, Md.
David Lott	Mustered in, Dec. 11, '61. Detailed to drive ambulance, Jan. to Aug., '62. Discharged, Jan. 13, '64, for disability, at Central Park Hospital, New York.
Herbert Lounsbury Fort Bennett, S. D.	Mustered in, May 22, '61. Detailed as ambulance driver, Aug., '62, to April, '63. Mustered out, June 2, '63.
William McIntyre Mongaup Valley, Sullivan Co., N. Y.	Mustered in, May 22, '61. Mustered out, June 2, '63.
Samuel J. McWilliams	Mustered in, Oct. 9, '61. Mustered out, June 4, '63.
Samuel McWilliams	Mustered in, May 22, '61. Discharged, July 9, '62, for disability at Annsville, Va.
Robert Moffett	Mustered in, May 22, '61. Wounded in action at Cedar Mountain, Va., Aug. 9, '62. Discharged for disability from wounds, Sandy Hook, Md., Dec. 3, '62.
Riley Margison	Mustered in, Dec. 11, '61. Teamster in Corps Supply Train, Jan. 12, '63, to May 1, '63. Mustered out, June 2, '64.
Squire N. Marsh Bridgeville, N. Y.	Mustered in, May 22, '61. Captured at Cedar Mountain, Va., Aug. 9 '62. Paroled at Aikens Landing, Va., Sept. 13, '62. Driver in regimental brigade and Post wagon train, Nov., '61, to May, '63. Mustered out, June 2, '63.
George W. Mabee Narrowsburgh, N. Y.	Mustered in, May 22, '61. Discharged for disability, at Patterson Park Hospital Baltimore, Md., June, 1, '62.
Charles Meyers	Mustered in May 22, '61. Mustered out, June 2 '63.
James Milliken	Mustered in, May 22, '61. Mustered out, June 2, '63.
John Minor	Transferred from Non. Com. Staff. Captured at Chancellorsville, Va., May 2, '63. Paroled, City Point, Va., May 14, '63. Mustered out, June 2, 63.
Oliver J. Moffett Fairmount, Neb.	Mustered in, May 22, '61. Discharged, April 24 '63, for disability, at Washington D. C.
William J. Monroe	Mustered in, May 22, '61. Mustered out, June 2, '63.
Jacob Myers	Mustered in, May 22, '61. Detailed as hospital nurse at Hancock, Md., Jan. 11, '62, to Feb. 25, '62. Died, Aug. 16, '62, at Culpeper, Va., of wounds received in action at Cedar Mountain, Va., Aug. 9, '62.
Stephen D. Myers	Mustered in, May 22, '61. Regt. wagoner, March 4, '62, to May, '63. Mustered out, June 2, '63.
Abram Neer	Mustered in, Oct. 9, '61. Killed, Aug. 9, '62, in action, Cedar Mountain, Va.
Joseph Orr	Mustered in, May 22, '61. Discharged, June 1, '61, at Albany by civil authority.
James A. Palmer	Mustered in, Oct. 9, '61. Killed in action at Cedar Mountain, Va., Aug. 9, '62.
John W. Pinney	Mustered in, May 22, '61. Mustered out, June 2, '63.
Simon Pratt	Transferred from Co. D. Captured at Cedar Mountain, Va., Aug. 9, '62. Paroled at Aikens Landing, Va., Sept. 11, '62. Captured at Chancellorsville, Va., May 2, '63. Paroled at City Point, Va., May 14, '63. Mustered out, June 2, '63.
Joseph Robinson	Mustered in, May 22, '61. Brigade and regimental wagoner, Nov. '61, to May '62. Wounded in action at Cedar Mountian, Va., Aug. '62. Died Oct. 18, '62, of wounds at Alexandria, Va.
Allan S. Rose Rose City, Ogemaw Co., Mich.	Mustered in, May 22, '61. Discharged for disability, Aug. '61.
Henry Staibe	Mustered in, May 22, '61. Mustered out, June 2, '63. Died in 1879.
William Sutton	Mustered in, May 22, '61. Deserted, June 14, '62, Front Royal, Va.
George E. Swan	Mustered in, May 22, '61. Transferred, Dec. 1, '62, to Quartermaster Sergt. Detailed in Quartermaster Dept. from Dec., '61, to Dec., '62. Died, Nov. 8, '95.
John Van Aradall	Mustered in, May 22, '61. Regt. wagoner, April, '62. Detailed in Ambulance Corps, Oct. 29, '62, to May, '63. Mustered out, June 2, '63.

COMPANY H.—Continued.

NAME AND PRESENT RESIDENCE, WHERE KNOWN.	REMARKS.
Privates.—Continued.	
Abram Van Lone	Mustered in, May 22, '61. Deserted, June 14, '62, at Front Royal, Va.
Stephen Wakeman	Mustered in, May 22, '61. Wounded in action at Cedar Mountain, Va., Aug. 9, '62. Mustered out, June 2, '63.
Uriah Wakeman	Mustered in, Oct. 12, '61. Wounded at Cedar Mountain, Va., Aug. 9, '62. Discharged, Dec. 20, '62, at Ft. McHenry, Md., on account of wound in knee, at Cedar Mountain.
Michael Wasim, 17 Eighth Avenue, New York City	Mustered in, May 22, '61. Captured at Cedar Mountain, Va., Aug. 9, '62. Paroled at Aikens Landing, Va., Sept. 13, '62. Mustered out, June 2, '63.
John Williams	Mustered in, May 22, '61. Wounded in action at Cedar Mountain, Va., Aug. 9, '62. Mustered out June 2, '63.
George Young, Ellenville, N. Y.	Mustered in, May 22, '61. Discharged, Aug. 30, '6., at Darnestown, Md., by civil authority.
James G. Zenner	Transferred from Co. D. Mustered out June 2, '63

COMPANY I.

NAME AND PRESENT RESIDENCE, WHERE KNOWN.	REMARKS.
Captain.	
Theodore P. Gould	Mustered in, May 22, '61, Capt. Detached service, Nov. 1, '61, to Jan. 31, '62. Special duty, General Supt. Forage and Supplies, April 14, '62. Ordered on recruiting service, June 30, '62 Rejoined, Feb. 6, '63. Mustered out, June 2, '63. Died at Baltimore, Md., soon after the war.
Lieutenants.	
Justin C. Ware	Mustered in, May 22, '61, 1st Lieut. Commanding Co., Nov. 1, '61, to Dec. 31, '61. Resigned, Feb. 12, '62. Died, Dec. 21, '91.
Lafayette Chaffee	Mustered in, Feb. 12, '62, 1st Lieut. Promoted from 2d Lieut. Co. D. Captured at Cedar Mountain, Va., Aug. 9, '62. Paroled at Aikens Landing, Va., Sept. 24, '62. Mustered out, Dec. 20, '62, for promotion to Capt. Co. D. Died in Ypsilanti, Mich., about 1880.
George W. Cooley	Mustered in, Sept. 25, '62, 1st Lieut. Discharged, Jan. 24, '63.
John D. Woods, Lockport, N. Y.	Transferred from 2d Lieut. Co. B. Promoted, 1st Lieut., Feb. 20, '63. Commanding Co. March 21, '63, to May, '63. Mustered out, June 2, '63.
George A. Bingham	Mustered in, May 22, '61, 2d Lieut. Resigned, Jan. 30, '62.
George H. Maxwell, Royal Oak, Mich.	Promoted from 1st Sergt. Co. B, March 1, '62, 2d Lieut. Resigned, July 14, '62.
John J. Sullivan, Niagara Falls, N. Y.	Mustered in, May 22, '61, Sergt. Promoted, 1st Sergt., Aug. 28, '61. Captured at Cedar Mountain, Va., Aug. 9, '62. Paroled at Aikens Landing, Va., Sept. 11, '62. Promoted, 2d Lieut., Feb. 20, '63. Mustered out June 2, '63.
William P. Williams	Temporarily assigned to Co., Oct. 16, '62, 2d Lieut. Transferred, Nov. 2, '62, to Co. K.
Sergeants.	
Charles Brown	Mustered in, May 22, '61, 1st Sergt. Discharged, July 24, '61, for disability, at Washington, D. C.
Thomas J. Frarey	Mustered in, May 22, '61, private. Promoted, Corp., July 21, '61; Sergt., Aug. 23, '61; 1st Sergt., Feb. 10, '63. Mustered out, June 2, '63.
John L. Booth	Mustered in, May 22, '61, private. Promoted, Sergt., June 10, '61. Discharged for disability at Convalescent Camp, Va., Dec. 27, '62.
Sergeants.—Continued.	
Edward G. Brooks	Mustered in, May 22, '61, Sergt. Discharged, Feb. 19, '63, for disability, at Washington D. C. Died in 1890.
George Irish, 186 Pearl Street, Buffalo, N. Y.	Mustered in, May 22, '61, private. Promoted, Corp., March 19, '62; Sergt., Feb. 9, '63. Mustered out, June 2, '63.
Gatien A. Liger	Mustered in, May 22, '61, private. Promoted, Corp. Aug. 23, '61; Sergt., Jan. 1, '63. Captured at Cedar Mountain, Va., Aug. 9, '62. Paroled at Aikens Landing, Va., Sept. 13, '62. Mustered out, June 2 '63. Died in 1885.
Francis L. Shipman	Mustered in, May 22, '61, private. Promoted, Corp., Dec. 15, '61; Sergt., March 13, '62. Captured at Cedar Mountain, Va., Aug. 9, '62. Paroled at Aikens Landing, Va., Sept. 13, '62. Mustered out, June 2, '63.
Corporals.	
Louis Bapp	Mustered in, May 22, '61. Died, Jan. 7, '62, of disease, at Baltimore, Md.
Andrew Brennan	Mustered in, May 22, '61, private. Promoted Corp., Dec. 6, '62. Mustered out, June 2, '63.
George Davy	Mustered in, May 22, '61, private. Promoted Corp., Jan. 24, '63. Mustered out, June 2, '63. Died in 1885.
William H. Frank	Mustered in May 22, '61, private. Promoted Corp., March 17, '62. Wounded in action at Cedar Mountain, Va., Aug. 9, '62 Discharged, Dec. 3, '62, for wounds, at Sandy Hook, Md.
Charles R. Haight	Mustered in, May 22, '61, private. Promoted Corp., March 13, '62. Killed in action at Cedar Mountain, Va., Aug. 9, '62.
James Hany, Niagara Falls, N. Y.	Mustered in, May 22, '61, private. Promoted Corp., Jan. 24, '63. Mustered out, June 2, '63.
Francis Keimer	Mustered in, May 22, '61, Corp. Discharged, Aug. 7, '61, for disability, at Berlin, Md.
Martin McMahon	Mustered in, May 22, '61, Corp. Killed in action at Cedar Mountain, Va., Aug. 9, '62.
Lawrence Metzger, Niagara Falls, N. Y.	Mustered in, May 22, '61, private. Promoted, Corp., Dec. 8, '62. Mustered out, June 2, '63.
Musicians.	
Horace L. Drake	Mustered in, May 22, '61. Mustered out, June 2, '63.

COMPANY I.—Continued.

Name and Present Residence, Where Known.	Remarks.
Musicians.—Continued	
Homer H. Fields, 19 Emslie Street, Buffalo, N. Y.	Mustered in, May 22, '61. Mustered out, June 2, '63.
Privates.	
Henry Appelby	Mustered in, May 22, '61. Deserted, July 2, '61, Washington, D. C.
Mathew Barton	Mustered in, May 22, '61. Drummed out, June 16, '61, for theft, order of Col. Davis.
Richard W. Bell, 3 Shelburn Street, Cleveland, Ohio.	Mustered in, May 22, '61. Discharged, May 11, '62, at Georgetown, D. C., for wounds received accidently.
John Busch	Mustered in, May 22, '61. Captured at Cedar Mountain, Va., Aug. 9, '62. Paroled at Aikens Landing, Va., Sept. 13, '62. Mustered out, June 2, '63. Died, June 12, '93.
Charles Benton	Mustered in, May 22, '61. Ambulance driver, Sept. to Dec., '61. Killed in action at Cedar Mountain, Va., Aug. 9, '62.
George E. Bostwick	Mustered in, May 22, '61. Detailed as scout, July 28, '62, to Nov. '62. Clerk for Brigade Inspector, March 16, '63, to April 10, '63. Mustered out, June 2, '63.
George Bower	Mustered in, May 22, '61. Captured at Cedar Mountain, Va., Aug. 9, '62. Paroled at Aikens Landing, Va., Sept. 13, '62. Mustered out, June 2, '63.
James H. Boyd, Lewiston, N. Y.	Mustered in, May 22, '61. Discharged, Aug. 7, '61, for disability, at Berlin, Md.
Edward K. Bullock	Mustered in, May 22, '61. Deserted, June 27, '61, at Albany.
Parker Burknapp	Mustered in, May 22, '61. Deserted, June 1, '61, at Albany.
Alonzo W. Cline, Marletta, Mich.	Mustered in, May 22, '61. Teamster, Nov., '61, to Feb. 28, '63. Brigade blacksmith, April 14, '63, to May, '63. Mustered out, June 2, '63.
Lanty Conklin	Mustered in, May 22, '61. Captured at Cedar Mountain, Va., Aug. 9, '62. Paroled at Aikens Landing, Va., Sept. 13, '62. Mustered out, June 2, '63.
Thomas Cooper	Mustered in, May 22, '61. Deserted at Edward Ferry, Md., Oct. 22, '61. Returned, March 25, '63, under President's proclamation. Mustered out, June 2, '63.
Robert Deppo	Mustered in, May 22, '61. Mustered out, June 2, '63.
James Dougan	Mustered in, May 22, '61. Wounded in action at Cedar Mountain, Va., Aug. 9, '62. Mustered out, June 2, '63.
William Dunn	Mustered in, May 22, '61. Captured at Cedar Mountain, Va., Aug. 9, '62. Paroled at Aikens Landing, Va., Sept. 13, '62. Mustered out, June 2, '63.
Peter Ensfield	Mustered in, May 22, '61 Detailed in Hospital Dept., Sept., '61, to April, '63. Mustered out, June 2, '63.
David Evans	Mustered in, May 22, '61. Mustered out, June 2, '63.
James Fitzgibbons	Mustered in, May 22, '61. Deserted, Sept. 25, '61, at Darnestown, Md.
John Gaffney	Mustered in, Jan. 28, '63. Transferred, May 19, '63, to barracks at Albany. Later, assigned to 10th Maine Battalion.
William O. Garner	Mustered in, May 22, '61. Discharged, March 14, '62.
Austin Gould	Mustered in, May 22, '61. Mustered out, June 2, '63.
Jacob Hagerman	Mustered in, May 22, '61. Discharged, Aug. 7, '61, for disability, Berlin, Md.
Privates.—Continued.	
John Haney	Mustered in, May 22 '61. Mustered out, June 2, '63.
John H. Harrington, Hartland, N. Y.	Mustered in, Aug. 21, '62. Discharged, Dec. 3, '62, for disability, at Race St. Hospital, Philadelphia, Pa.
Oscar L. Harvey	Mustered in, May 22, '61. Captured at Winchester, Va., May 25, '62. Paroled at Aikens Landing, Va., Sept. 13, '62. Mustered out, June 2, '63.
Charles O. Ingalls	Mustered in, May 22, '61. Mustered out, June 2, '63. Died, Dec., 1895.
Joseph H. Kamp, Known as J. H. Camp, Box 328, Nyack, N. Y	Mustered in, June 28, '61. Detailed in Brigade Ambulance Corps, Nov. 1, '62, to May 10, '63. Transferred, May 19, '63, to barracks at Albany. Later, assigned to 10th Maine Battalion.
Peter Kearns	Mustered in, May 22, '61. Discharged, July 17, '61, for disability, at Washington, D. C.
James A. Kearnes	Mustered in, May 22, '61. Deserted, Aug. 17, '61, at Point of Rocks, Md.
Simon Keifer	Mustered in, May 22, '61. Discharged, March 20, '63, for disability, at Convalescent Camp, Va.
William Keller	Mustered in, May 22, '61. Deserted, June 21, '61, Albany.
Michael Kilberer	Mustered in, May 22, '61. Killed in action at Cedar Mountain, Va., Aug. 9, '62.
Francis De Lacy	Mustered in, May 22, '61. Transferred, Jan. 1, '62, to Co. G.
Edward H. Lampohler	Mustered in, May 22, '61. Died of disease at Baltimore, Md., Nov. 19, '61.
Philip Lasher	Mustered in, June 28, '61. Transferred to barracks at Albany, May 19, '63.
Stanley Lefferty	Mustered in, May 22, '61. Deserted, Aug. 5, '62, at Culpeper, Va.
John McCann	Mustered in, May 22, '61. Captured at Cedar Mountain, Va., Aug. 9, '62. Rejoined, Oct. 20, '62. Mustered out, June 2, '63.
James McCleary	Mustered in, May 22, '61. Deserted, July 4, '61, at Washington, D. C.
William McMullen	Mustered in, May 22, '61. Mustered out, June 2, '63.
Marcus A. Manderville, Newfane, N. Y.	Mustered in, Jan. 28, '63. Transferred, May 19, '63, to barracks at Albany. Later, assigned to 10th Maine Battalion.
Henry C. Miller, Niagara Falls, Ont.	Mustered in, May 22, '61. Captured at Cedar Mountain, Va., Aug. 9, '62. Paroled at Aikens Landing, Va., Sept. 13, '62. Mustered out, June 2, '63.
Edward Moody	Mustered in, May 22, '61. Mustered out, June 2, '63.
James Morrority	Mustered in, May 22, '61. Captured at Cedar Mountain, Va., Aug. 9, '62. Paroled at Aikens Landing, Va., Sept. 13, '62. Mustered out, June 2, '63.
John Myers	Mustered in, May 22, '61. Discharged, Sept. 4, '62, for disability at Fairfax Seminary General Hospital, Va.
George Nash	Mustered in, May 22, '61. Captured at Cedar Mountain, Va., Aug. 9, '62. Paroled at Aikens Landing, Va., Sept. 13, '62. Mustered out, June 2, '63.
John H. Polt	Mustered in, June 28, '61. Discharged, June 20, '63, Albany, expiration of term.
Albert Price	Mustered in, May 22, '61. Deserted, May 29, '61, at Albany.
Alfonso Pursall	Mustered in, May 22, '61. Deserted, Aug. 17, '61, at Point of Rocks, Md.

COMPANY I.—Continued.

Name and Present Residence, Where Known.	Remarks.
Privates.—Continued.	
John Rau	Mustered in, Sept 8, '62. Discharged Feb. 10, '63, for disability, at Harper's Ferry, Va.
Alvan S. Richmond	Mustered in, May 22, '61. Quartermaster's Clerk, Aug. 1, '61, to May, '63. Mustered out, June 2, '63.
George Robinson	Mustered in, May 22, '61. Mustered out, June 2, '63.
James Scaroon	Mustered in, May 22, '61. Deserted, Sept. 25, '61, at Darnestown, Md.
Alexander Simpson, Lewiston, N. Y.	Mustered in, May 22, '61. Captured at Cedar Mountain, Va., Aug. 9, '62. Paroled at Aikens Landing, Va., Sept. 13, '62. Mustered out, June 2, '63.
Charles Stevenson	Mustered in, May 22, '61. Mustered out, June 2, '63.
James W. Stewart	Mustered in, Jan. 28, '63. Transferred to barracks at Albany, May 19, '63.
Matthew G. Tierunney	Mustered in, May 22, '61. Promoted, July 1, '61, to drum major.
Charles Vice	Mustered in, May 22 '61. Mustered out, June 2, '63.
Francis M. Wadsworth, Toledo, Oregon.	Mustered in, May 22, '61. Wounded in action at Cedar Mountain, Va., Aug. 9, '62. Discharged, Nov. 4, '62, on account of wounds at Alexandria, Va.
Ernest Wagner	Mustered in, May 22, '61. Mustered out, June 2, '63.
John Walker	Mustered in, May 22, '61. Missing in action at Winchester, Va., May 25, '62. Rejoined, June 1, '62. Wounded in action at Cedar Mountain, Va., Aug. 9, '62. Mustered out, June 2, '63.
Thomas Walkins	Mustered in, May 22, '61. Deserted, Sept. 25, '61, at Darnestown, Md.
John Zurker	Mustered in, May 22, '61. Captured at Winchester, Va., May 25, '62. Paroled at Aikens Landing, Va., Sept. 7, '62. Discharged, Jan. 13, '63, for disability, at Annapolis, Md.

COMPANY K.

Name and Present Residence, Where Known.	Remarks.
Captains.	
Henry H. Paige, 555 Prytonia St., New Orleans, La	Mustered in, May 22, '61, Capt. Resigned, July 21, '62.
James D. Ames	Mustered in, May 22, '61, 2d Lieut. Promoted, 1st Lieut., June 16, '62; Capt., Jan. 7, '63. Detailed on recruiting service, Feb. 1, '62, to April 1, '62. Captured at Cedar Mountain, Va., Aug. 9, '62. Paroled at Aikens Landing, Va., Sept. 21, '62. Mustered out, June 2, '63. Died, April 10, '91.
Lieutenants.	
Volney Farley	Mustered in, May 22, '61, Lieut. On recruiting service, Oct. 12, '61, to Dec. 31, '61. Resigned, June 16, '62. Died in 1867.
Myron F. Warfield, Rushville, N. Y.	Promoted from 2d Lieut. Co. E. Mustered in, May 5, '63, 1st Lieut. Mustered out, June 2, '63.
Norman O. Allen, Lockport, N. Y.	Mustered in, May 22, '61, Corp. Wounded in action at Cedar Mountain, Va., Aug. 9, '62. Promoted, 2d Lieut., May 5, '63. Mustered out, June 2, '63.
William F. Williams	Mustered in, May 22, '61, Sergt. Transferred, temporarily, to I. Transferred, March 23, '62, to Sergt.-Major. Promoted, Sept. 16, '62, 2d Lieut. Resigned, Feb. 1, '63.
Sergeants.	
Hugh A. Jameson, N. Tonawanda, N. Y.	Mustered in, May 22, '61, 1st Sergt., on recruiting service, Oct., '61, to Nov. 18, '61. Mustered out, June 2, '63.
Henry F. King	Mustered in, May 22, '61, Sergt. Discharged, Jan. 17, '63, for enlistment as Hospital Steward, U. S. Army.
Wilbur F. Lawton, Petoskey, Mich	Mustered in, May 22, '61, Corp. Promoted, Sergt., May 4, '63. Mustered out, June 2, '63.
Sylvester S. Marvin, Pittsburg, Pa.	Mustered in, May 22, '61, private. Promoted, Corp., Aug. 12, '61; Sergt., July 30, '62. Wounded in action at Cedar Mountain, Va., Aug. 9, '62. Detailed in Commissary Dept at Harper's Ferry, Va., Feb. 11, '63, to April 10, '63. Mustered out, June 2, '63.
Sergeants.—Continued.	
John H. Moyses, Corunna, Mich.	Mustered in, May 22, '61, Sergt. Wounded and captured at Cedar Mountain, Va., Aug. 9, '62. Paroled at Aikens Landing, Sept. 13, '62. Mustered out, June 2, '63.
William H. Tenbrook, Olcott, N. Y.	Mustered in, May 22, '61, private. Promoted, Corp., March 13, '62; Sergt., Jan. 24, '63. Captured at Cedar Mountain, Va., Aug. 9, '62. Paroled at Aikens Landing, Va., Sept. 21, '62. Mustered out, June 2, '63.
Samuel Williams	Mustered in, May 22, '61. Killed in action at Cedar Mountain, Va., Aug. 9, '62.
Corporals.	
Frederick A. Camann, 304 19th St., Milwaukee, Wis.	Mustered in, May 22, '61, private. Promoted, Corp., July 30, '62. Captured at Cedar Mountain, Va., Aug. 9, '62. Paroled at Aikens Landing, Va., Sept. 13, '62. Mustered out, June 2, '63.
Samuel Lewis	Mustered in, May 22, '61. Discharged, July 19, '61, for disability, at Camp Harris, D. C.
James N. Phillips, Custom House, Omaha, Neb.	Mustered in, May 22, '61, private. Wounded in action at Cedar Mountain, Va., through left hand, Aug. 9, '62. Nurse in Hospital, Baltimore, Jan. 1, '62, to Feb. 2, '62. Promoted, Corp., Jan. 24, '63. Mustered out, June 2, '63.
Charles L. Pickard	Mustered in, May 22, '61, private. Promoted Corp., March 10, '62. Killed in action, Cedar Mountain, Va., Aug. 9, '62.
Joshua B. Smith	Mustered in, May 22, '61, private. Promoted, Corp., Sept. 21, '62. Mustered out, June 2, '63.
Thomas C. Tenbrook	Mustered in, May 22, '61, private. Promoted, Corp., April 24, '62. Mustered out, June 2, '63. Died in 1885.
Musicians.	
Byron C. Anderson, Wessington, S. Dak	Mustered in, May 22, '61. Mustered out, June 2, '63
Edmond Stoney	Mustered in, May 22, '61. Mustered out, June 2, '63.

COMPANY K.—Continued.

Name and Present Residence, Where Known.	Remarks.
Privates.	
Nathaniel Angevine	Mustered in, May 22, '61. Discharged for disability, July 17, '61, at Camp Harris, D. C.
Andrew Baker	Mustered in, Aug. 27, '62. Transferred to depot at Albany, May 19, '63.
Charles A. Beebe	Mustered in, May 22, '61. Hospital attendant, Nov., '62, to April 10, '63. Mustered out, June 2, '63.
Nelson H. Beebe, Big Rapids, Mich	Mustered in, May 22, '61. Captured in hospital at Winchester, Va., May 25, '62. Paroled, same place. Rejoined, Dec. 20, '62. Mustered out, June 2, '63.
Leman A. Brace, Eau Claire, Wis	Mustered in, Nov. 11, '61. Mustered out, June 2, '63.
Kearon Brophy, Easton, Mich	Mustered in, May 22, '61. Captured at Cedar Mountain, Va., Aug. 9, '62. Paroled at Aikens Landing, Va., Sept. 13, '62. Detailed in Ambulance Corps, Oct. 29, '62, to April 10, '63. Mustered out, June 2, '63.
Francis Burnell	Mustered in, Aug. 27, '62. Transferred to depot at Albany, May 19, '63, and assigned to 19th Maine Battalion.
John S. Bush	Mustered in, May 22, '61. Mustered out, June 2, '63.
William Bush	Mustered in, May 22, '61. Discharged, July 17, '61 for disability, at Washington, D. C.
Dexter F. Carpenter	Mustered in, May 22, '61. Deserted, June 22, '61, at Albany.
David Caton	Mustered in, May 22, '61. Captured at Cedar Mountain, Va., Aug. 9, '62. Paroled at Aikens Landing, Va., Sept. 13 '62. Mustered out, June 2, '63.
William H. Cleveland	Mustered in, May 22, '61. Deserted, June 22, '61, Albany.
Joseph Coty	Mustered in, May 22, '61. Captured at Winchester, Va., May 25, '62. Paroled, same place, June 26, '62. Captured at Manassas, Va., Aug. 29, '62. Paroled, same place, date not given. Mustered out, June 2, '63.
William Crowley	Mustered in, May 22, '61. Discharged, Aug. 16, '61, at Berlin, Md., for disability.
Daniel H. Davis	Mustered in, May 22, '61. Died, May 14, '62, of disease, at Strasburg, Va.
Ingraham D. Eaton	Mustered in, May 22, '61. Discharged, Aug. 4, '61, for disability, at Berlin, Md.
Franklin S. Eggart	Mustered in, May 22, '61. Captured and Paroled, at Winchester, Va., May 25, '62. Mustered out, June 2, '63.
William O. Engler	Mustered in, May 22, '61. Clerk, Brigade Headquarters, Quartermaster's Dept., Sept. '61, to Oct. '62. Discharged, April 28, '63 at Baltimore, Md., for disability and expiration of service.
Frank Erbacker	Mustered in, Aug. 20, '62. Transferred, May 19, '63, to Depot at Albany.
Stephen Flynn	Mustered in, May 22, '61. Mustered out, June 2, '63.
Henry Forman	Mustered in, Sept. 8, '62. Deserted Feb. 11, '63, from Lincoln Hospital, Washington, D. C.
Truman B. Goodenough, Randall Road, N. Y.	Mustered in May 22, '61. Mustered out, June 2, '63.
John Griffen	Mustered in May 22, '61. Killed in action, at Cedar Mountain, Va., Aug. 9, '62.
Eli S. Hamblin, Wilson, N. Y.	Mustered in Nov. 28, '61. Mustered out, June 2, '63.
Privates.—Continued.	
Isaiah Harrington	Mustered in, May 22, '61, wounded in action, at Cedar Mountain, Va., Aug. 9, '62. Mustered out, June 2, '63.
Charles Hartwig	Mustered in, May 22, '61. Teamster in brigade and in ammunition train, Nov. '61, to April 10, '63. Mustered out, June 2, '63.
Henry H. Helmes, Ransomville, N. Y.	Mustered in, May 22, '61. Mustered out, June 2, '63.
Emerson Hilton	Mustered in, Jan. 6, '62. Discharged, Sept. 8, '62, for disability, at Fairfax Seminary Hospital, Va.
Emory Hilton	Mustered in, May 22, '61. Mustered out, June 2, '63.
Charles E. Halstead	Mustered in, May 22, '61. Discharged, Aug. 8, '62, for disability, at Berlin, Md.
Michael Hutchinson	Mustered in, May 22, '61. Discharged, June 18, '61, for disability, at Albany.
William Kruske, Youngstown, N. Y.	Mustered in, May 22, '61. In Brigade Quartermaster's Dept., Feb. '62. Detailed in Battery K, 1st N. Y. Light Artillery, March 19, '63, to May 10, '63. Mustered out, June 2, '63.
Alexander W. Lowne	Mustered in, May 22, '61. Brigade saddler, in ammunition train, Dec. '61, to May '63. Mustered out, June 2, '63.
Patrick McCann	Mustered in, May 22, '61. Wounded in hip, at Cedar Mountain, Va., Aug. 9, '62. Mustered out, June 2, '63.
Schuyler McKenzie	Mustered in, May 22, '61. Discharged, July 12, '61, for disability, at Albany.
Franklin O. McKinney, 78 Lock St., Lockport, N. Y.	Mustered in, May 22, '61. Captured at Cedar Mountain, Va., Aug. 9, '62. Paroled at Richmond, Va., Sept. 7, '62. Mustered out, June 2, '63.
Terence Mahoney	Mustered in, Aug. 25, '62. Discharged, Jan. 15, '63, for disability at Fairfax Station, Va.
James Mason	Mustered in May 22, '61. Died, Oct. 3, '62, of disease at Baltimore, Md.
Gottfried Meirs	Mustered in, May 22, '61. Discharged Aug. 7, '61, for disability, at Berlin, Md.
Selinous A. Miner	Enlisted, March 5, '62. Killed in action at Cedar Mountain, Va., Aug. 9, '62.
John Moll	Mustered in, May 22, '61. Killed in action at Cedar Mountain, Va., Aug. 9, '62.
Peter C. More	Mustered in, May 22, '61. Discharged, Aug. 7, '61, for disability, at Berlin, Md.
Mathew Moyses	Mustered in, May 22, '61. Mustered out, June 2, '63.
Walter Mullet	Mustered in, May 22, '61. Mustered out, June 2, '63.
Joseph J. G. Nellist	Mustered in, May 22, '61. Captured at Cedar Mountain, Va., Aug. 9, '62. Paroled at Aikens Landing, Va., Sept. 13, '62. Mustered out, June 2, '63.
George A. Nye	Mustered in, May 22, '61. Captured at Winchester, Va., May 25, '62. Paroled at Aikens Landing, Va., Sept. 13, '62. Mustered out, June 2, '63.
William Parsons	Mustered in, May 22, '61. Captured at Cedar Mountain, Va., Aug. 9, '62. Paroled at Aikens Landing, Sept. 13, '62. Mustered out, June 2, '63.
Marcellus E. Patricks	Mustered in, Dec. 10, '61. Died, May 25, '62, of disease at Winchester, Va.

COMPANY K.—Continued.

Name and Present Residence, Where Known.	Remarks.
Privates.—Continued.	
Nehemiah Pecktil, St. Johns, Mich.	Mustered in, May 22, '61. Captured at Cedar Mountain, Va., Aug. 9, '62. Paroled at Aikens Landing, Va., Sept. 13, '62. Mustered out, June 2, '63.
Joseph Phillips, 58 Genesee St. Buffalo, N. Y.	Mustered in, May 22, '61. Mustered out, June 2, '63.
Perry Putnam	Mustered in, May 22, '61. Captured at Winchester, Va., May 6, '62. Paroled at Aikens Landing, Va., Sept. 13, '62. Detailed in Battery K, 1st N. Y. Light Artillery, March 17, '63, to June 2, '63. Mustered out, June 2, '63.
William E. Richardson	Mustered in, May 22, '61. Mustered out, June 2, '63.
Stephen C. Roberts	Mustered in, May 22, '61. Killed in action at Cedar Mountain, Va., Aug. 9, '62.
Albert Rogers	Mustered in, May 22, '61. Died of disease at Harrisonburg, Va., April 23, '62.
Charles Seger	Mustered in, May 22, '61. Mustered out, June 2, '63. Died, in 1873.
William H. Simonds, Mt. Pleasant, Mich.	Mustered in, May 22, '61. Captured at Cedar Mountain, Va., Aug. 9, '62. Paroled at Aikens Landing, Va., Sept. 21, '62. Mustered out, June 2, '63.
John H. Smith, 351 South Broadway, Aurora, Ill.	Mustered in, May 22, '61. Brigade blacksmith, Dec., '61, to May, '63. Mustered out, June 2, '63.
Privates.—Continued.	
Don C. Smith	Mustered in, May 22, '61. Discharged, Aug. 6, '61, for disability, at Berlin, Md.
August Strasburg, Sanborn, N. Y.	Mustered in, May 22, '61. Served in Quartermaster's Department, Feb., '62, to May, '63. Mustered out, June 2, '63.
Dennis Sullivan	Mustered in, May 22, '61. Killed in action at Cedar Mountain, Va., Aug. 9, '62.
Watson Swick	Mustered in, May 22, '61. Died, June 18, '62, at Williamsport, Md.
Charles Vogt	Mustered in, May 22, '61. Discharged, Feb. 3, '63, for disability, at Fairfax Seminary, General Hospital, Va.
William H. Ward	Mustered in, May 22, '61. Mustered out, June 2, '63.
Henry Webb	Mustered in, May 22, '61. Mustered out, June 2, '63.
Abram Wheeler	Mustered in, May 22, '61. Discharged, Aug. 8, '61, for disability, at Berlin, Md.
Willard White	Mustered in, May 22, '61. Died, Sept. 5, '62, of disease, at Baltimore, Md.
Hixon Woolever	Mustered in, May 22, '61. Killed in action at Cedar Mountain, Va., Aug. 9, '62.
Oliver B. Young	Mustered in, April 8, '62. Transferred, May 10, '63, to depot at Albany. Later, assigned to 10th Maine Battalion.
William D. Young	Mustered in, May 22, '61. Died, Sept. 1, '62, in hospital at Alexandria, Va., of wounds received in action at Cedar Mountain, Va., Aug. 9, '62.

UNASSIGNED RECRUITS.

There is no evidence that any of these men ever joined the regiment.

Unassigned Recruits.	
Henry C. Bowen	Mustered in, Jan. 6, '62.
Samuel Bowman	Enlisted, March 6, '62.
William Butlan	Dropped, Oct. 31, '61. No further information on register.
William H. Ennig	Enlisted, Sept. 30, '62.
William Erving	Enlisted, Oct. 25, '61. Deserted, Oct. 22, '61.
John Flattery	Enlisted, Oct. 12, '61. Deserted, Nov. 25, '61.
Eugene Nammond	Mustered in, Nov. 28, '61.
Jacob A. Morgan	Enlisted, Aug. 30, '62.
William G. Reynolds	Mustered in, Dec. 25, '61.
Peter Russel	Mustered in, Nov. 12, '61.
Carl Schisty	Enlisted, Feb. 26, '62.
Wasson D. Wicks	Enlisted, Dec. 8, '61. Deserted, Dec. 19, '61.
Henry Williams	Mustered in, Nov. 28, '61.

RECAPITULATION, TWENTY-EIGHTH NEW YORK REGIMENT.

	F. and S. and N. C. S.	Band.	Company A.	Company B.	Company C.	Company D.	Company E.	Company F.	Company G.	Company H.	Company I.	Company K.	Total.
Original Muster-in,	11	2	83	78	76	79	78	77	79	78	77	78	796
Recruits,	12	25	15	13	26	50	8	13	9	18	13	12	214
Total in Regiment,	23	27	98	91	102	129	86	90	88	96	90	90	1,010
Killed in battle and died from wounds,	2	0	6	5	7	7	2	8	4	8	4	9	62
Died of disease,	0	0	0	4	4	7	3	5	8	4	2	6	43
Discharged, from wounds and disability,	7	17	28	16	17	24	14	23	18	18	19	17	218
Transferred, missing, deserted and resigned,	2	10	22	23	13	20	7	11	14	8	25	10	165
Total lost from all causes,	11	27	56	48	41	58	26	47	44	38	50	42	488
Mustered out,	12	0	42	43	61	71	60	43	44	58	40	48	522
Total,	23	27	98	91	102	129	86	90	88	96	90	90	1,010
Served full term, two years,	10	0	39	40	50	52	55	37	43	46	40	45	457
Surviving in 1896,	5	9	31	11	39	30	23	19	14	22	15	25	282

COLONEL EDWIN F. BROWN,

TWENTY-EIGHTH NEW YORK VOLUNTEERS,

Inspector-General United States Soldiers' Homes.

Born in Ridgeway, Orleans Co., N. Y., April 23, 1823. Mustered into the U. S. service at Albany, N. Y., May 22, 1861, as Lieutenant-Colonel 28th N. Y. Vols. Wounded in action at Cedar Mountain, Va., August 9, 1862. Left arm amputated. Left at Culpeper August 19, 1862, and captured by the enemy. Paroled at Aikens Landing, Va., October 6, 1862. Promoted Colonel November 1, 1862. Mustered out, June 2, 1863.

Col. Brown, born in Ridgeway, has never lost his residence there. He remained on his father's farm until 1837. Attended Gaines Academy three years, and Canandaigua Academy one year, then taught one year in Gaines Academy. Returned to farming in 1843, and carried on a large grain and stock farm until 1856, part of the time, also, superintending the 12th section of the Erie Canal. Left the farm in 1856 and engaged in grain and produce business in Medina, N. Y. About 1860, Col. Brown engaged in a manufacturing enterprise in East Cambridge, Mass., which was abandoned on the breaking out of the war.

In April, 1861, he took an active part, with Col. Donnelly, in organizing the Twenty-eighth Regiment. Was elected Lieutenant-Colonel, and served continuously with the regiment until the battle of Cedar Mountain, where he lost his arm. After the death of Col. Donnelly he was promoted Colonel, which position he held until mustered out with the regiment.

Col. Brown was elected Clerk of Orleans County while still in command of the Twenty-eighth, but did not take possession of the office until the regiment was discharged. Later, he went South and engaged in mercantile business in Vicksburg. Was appointed Military Mayor of Vicksburg in 1866. He resigned two years later to accept the position of Governor of the Central Branch of the National Home for Disabled Volunteer Soldiers, at Dayton, Ohio, where he remained from January 1, 1869, to November 1, 1880, when he was appointed Inspector-General for all National Homes in the United States. He still occupies that office, traveling from Maine to California, having made the round trip six times, and supervising the building of the Home at Leavenworth, Kansas, the one at Santa Monica, Cal., also the one at Marion, Ind. His life is a busy one. He has a large farm in Central Ohio, where he goes occasionally for rest and recreation.

It was largely through the efforts of Col. Brown that the memorable meeting of the Twenty-eighth New York and the Fifth Virginia Regiments was held at Niagara Falls in May, 1883. This was the first time that Union and Confederate regiments had met together in fraternal greetings, and was an event of great interest.

DUDLEY DONNELLY,

LATE COLONEL 28TH REGIMENT, N. Y. S. VOLS.

Mustered into the U. S. service, May 22, 1861, at Albany, N. Y. In command of the 1st Brigade, 1st Division, 5th Corps, Army of Virginia (General Banks), from March 20, 1862, to June 15, 1862, also July 31, 1862. Mortally wounded at Cedar Mountain, Va., August 9, 1862. Died of wounds at Culpeper, Va., August 15, 1862. Buried at Lockport, N. Y., where the members of his regiment have erected a monument to his memory. His ability as commander of his regiment or brigade was always recognized and highly commended in official reports. His death ended a career that was a brilliant one, indeed. His death was a personal loss to every member of the regiment. Association with such a man was an honor, and the remembrance of him and his heroic services will ever be a loving and cherished memory.

GENERAL ALPHEUS S. WILLIAMS,

BRIGADE, DIVISION, AND CORPS, COMMANDER.

DIED IN DETROIT, MICH., IN 1863.

The members of the 28th New York "uncover" at the sight of this loved commander, and his name is an inspiration to any comrade of his old 1st Division—"First of the 12th Corps and second to none." It was the exceeding good fortune of the 28th N. Y. Regiment to serve under his command during most of its history. The men can never forget his fatherly kindness and care. He was universally known throughout the Division by the homely but loving title, "Old Pap Williams." As a brave and able General, he was fully equal to any position where the fortunes of war placed him.

Long after the war he wrote: "I remember warmly the 28th New York. It was my favorite regiment, and I shall remember it to the day of my death."

ELLIOTT W. COOK,

DIED IN CALIFORNIA, IN 1873.

Born in 1819. Mustered in, May 22, 1861, as Captain of Co. A. Promoted to Major, September 13, 1861. Captured at Cedar Mountain, Va., August 9, 1862. Exchanged, November 11, 1862. Promoted Lieut.-Colonel, November 2, 1862. Captured at Chancellorsville, Va., May 2, 1863. Paroled at City Point, Va., May 14, 1863. Mustered out, June 2, 1863.

As Captain, Major, or Lieut.-Colonel, E. W. Cook was always the reliable, capable officer, the kind, genial, courteous gentleman and friend.

THEOPHILUS FITZGERALD,

WASHINGTON, D. C.

Born in 1836. Mustered in, May 22, 1861, as Captain of Co. E. Promoted Major, November 2, 1862. Mustered out, June 2, 1863.

Mr. FitzGerald has for many years been in the Government Printing Office at Washington, D. C. Is a prominent and influential G. A. R. Comrade of the District of Columbia.

CHARLES P. SPROUT,

LATE ADJUTANT 28TH N. Y. VOLUNTEERS.

Born in Stafford, Genesee County, N. Y., August 26, 1828. Mustered into the U. S. service at Albany, N. Y., May 22, 1861, as Adjutant, 28th N. Y. Detailed on recruiting service, February, 1862, to May, 1862. Killed in action at Cedar Mountain, Va., August 9, 1862. Buried where he fell, "on the field of honor."

No name is mentioned in the long list of heroic dead of the 28th with feelings of deeper respect and admiration than that of Adjutant Sprout. He met a death of glory in the most advanced position of our forces in the charge at Cedar Mountain. The bravest of the brave, the model soldier, the Christian gentleman, the true friend. The heart-pulses beat quicker, the eyes of his comrades moisten, at the mention of this grand and noble man who offered his life at Cedar Mountain, on the altar of his country.

CHRISTOPHER L. SKEELS.

Born at Rutland, Vt., January 12, 1823. Died October 6, 1879. Mustered into service as Quartermaster May 22, 1861. Acting Quartermaster 1st Brigade, 1st Division, 5th Army Corps, March 20, 1862, to October 16, 1862. In Chief Quartermaster's Department, 1st Division, 12th Corps, October 16, 1862, to February 7, 1863. Promoted to Captain Co. A, October 21, 1862. Mustered out, June 2, 1863.

After the War, was traveling agent for the Commerce Insurance Company of Albany, N. Y. In 1865 removed to New York City, where he was manager of an extensive fire insurance agency until his death. Member of the New York Board of Underwriters, the Manhattan Club and the New England Society. His sword is in possession of C. L. Skeels Post, G. A. R., of Hartland, N. Y. Presented Decoration Day, [illegible]

ALBERT M HELMER,

DIED IN MILWAUKEE, APRIL 20, 1896.

Born at Oak Hill, Montgomery County, N. Y., March 10, 1832. Mustered in, May 22, 1862, as Surgeon, 28th N. Y. Volunteers. Acting Surgeon 1st Brigade, 1st Division, 5th Army Corps, (from March 20, 1862, to October 22, 1862, under General Banks.

Dr. Helmer remained in charge of the disabled soldiers taken at Culpeper Court House, Va., after the battle of Cedar Mountain, Va. Was taken prisoner and sent to Libby Prison. Subsequently he was exchanged and sent to Fortress Monroe. Resigned, November 10, 1862, on account of poor health

Dr. Helmer went to Milwaukee, soon after leaving the army, and did not resume the practice of medicine, but engaged in the brokerage business. His home has been in Milwauker since the war.

ROBERT T. PAINE,

DIED IN 1886.

Born in 1834. Mustered in, December 28, 1861, as Assistant Surgeon. Mustered out, June 2, 1863.

Dr. Paine was a skillful surgeon and a faithful officer of the 28th Regiment. He had hosts of friends and no enemies. A more genial or welcome addition to any circle could not be found.

Trusted alike by officers and men, careful, kind, and conscientious in the discharge of his duties, he was loved by the members of the regiment while living, and his memory will be ever cherished.

THOMAS CUSHING, M D.,

BARRE CENTER, N. Y

Mustered into the service of the United States, August 25, 1862, as Assistant Surgeon of the 28th N. Y. Volunteers. Resigned, March 12, 1863.

Subsequent to the war Dr. Cushing was a practicing physician of prominence and ability at Medina and other places in Orleans County, New York. Several years ago he retired from active practice and resides at Barre Center, where he devotes much of his time to study. Dr. Cushing is a naturalist, and a man of education and research; and has written many articles on his favorite subject.

CHANDLER B. GILLAM,

BYRON, N. Y.

Born in Byron, Genesee County, N. Y., July 19, 1833. Enlisted, April 27, 1861. Mustered in, May 22, 1861, as Corporal in Co. F. Promoted Sergeant-Major and transferred to Non-commissioned staff, October 1, 1862. Wounded by piece of a shell at Chancellorsville, Va., May 3, 1863. Mustered out, June 4, 1863.

Mr. Gillam is engaged in farming on the farm where he was born. Is a member of Fuller Post, No. 412, G. A. R., Department of New York, at Bergen, N. Y.

LEONARD DENNISON SALE,

PHILADELPHIA, PA.

Born in Victor, N. Y., January 24, 1842. Mustered in, May 22, 1861, as private in Co. K. Detailed to act as Commissary Sergeant early in August, 1862, and appointed to that office, October 1, 1862. Mustered out, June 2, 1863. In '66 he settled near Chesters Gap, Va., in the sheep grazing business. In '69 he purchased the "Adrian Weekly Journal," since which time he has been engaged in journalism, having occupied the following positions: In '70 was editor of the Detroit "Daily Union." Subsequently published the "Lapeer Democrat" and "Pontiac Journal." From '70 to '85 was connected with the daily press of Detroit. In '85 he represented the "Detroit Free Press" at Washington. From '85 to '89 was Librarian of the Patent Office. In February, 1896, joined the Editorial Staff of the "Philadelphia Press," which position he now occupies.

ERWIN A. BOWEN,

DIED IN MEDINA, N. Y., JANUARY 22, 1889.

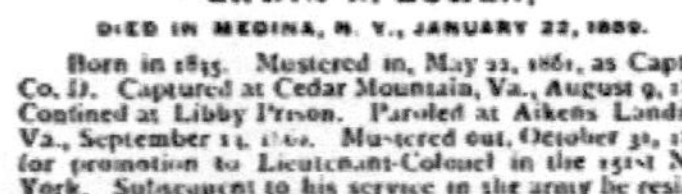

Born in 1835. Mustered in, May 22, 1861, as Captain Co. D. Captured at Cedar Mountain, Va., August 9, 1862. Confined at Libby Prison. Paroled at Aikens Landing, Va., September 13, 1862. Mustered out, October 31, 1862, for promotion to Lieutenant-Colonel in the 151st New York. Subsequent to his service in the army he resided at Medina, N. Y., engaged in manufacturing.

Captain Bowen was one of the best disciplinarians in the Twenty-eighth Regiment, and as a drill-master had few superiors in the army. He was a model soldier, a steadfast friend, a perfect gentleman. Uniformly courteous, he was beloved by all who knew him. No name is recalled in the long list of the Twenty-eighth Regiment with feelings of greater respect and admiration than Captain Bowen.

DAVID HARDIE,

DIED MARCH 28, 1896, AT ALBION, N. Y.

Born in Edinburgh, Scotland, September 16, 18[illegible]. Mustered in, May 22, 1861, Captain Co. G. Resigned June 1, 1862.

In 18[illegible] he entered the British army as a gunner in the Royal Artillery. He served in England and Ireland, and in 1846 was sent to Canada and stationed at Quebec. He soon after left the army and was employed in newspaper work in London and Hamilton. In 18[illegible] he moved to Albion and engaged in the newspaper and book trade. When the civil war broke out he raised a company in Orleans county, which became Co. G of the 28th Regiment.

After his return from the army he resumed the book and newspaper business and continued it until his death.

JEREMIAH LONG,

DIED APRIL 3, 1896.

Born at Lockport, N. Y., September 29, 1836. Enlisted at Lockport in April, 1861. Mustered in, May 22, 1861, as 1st Sergeant in Co. A. Promoted 2d Lieutenant, January 30, 1862, and 1st Lieutenant, July 21, 1862. Was captured at Cedar Mountain, Va., August 9, 1862. Was confined at Belle Island. Paroled at Aikens Landing, September 24, 1862. Mustered out, June 2, 1863. Was Acting Captain, commanding Co. A, when mustered out.

Mr. Long went to California soon after the war and was for a time conductor on the Southern Pacific Railroad.

Later he engaged in mining in California for several years. After which he occupied a position in the Soldiers' Home at Santa Monica, Cal. He died at Los Angeles, Cal., April 3, 18[illegible], and was buried at Lockport, N. Y., April 11, 18[illegible].

CAPTAIN W. W. BUSH,

DIED APRIL 19, 18[illegible].

Born in 1832. Mustered in, May 22, 1861, as Captain of Co. B. Detached on transportation service, via Chesapeake & Ohio Canal, in February, 1862. Captured at Cedar Mountain, Va., August 9, 1862, and confined at Staunton, Va. Taken to Richmond, Va., August 28, 1862. Paroled at Aikens Landing, Va., September 24, 1862. Mustered out, June 2, 1863.

Capt. Bush enjoyed the distinction of having been the "First Volunteer" for the War under President Lincoln's call for 75,000 troops.

He resided at Lockport, N. Y., subsequent to the War. Was prominent in G. A. R. circles, and was elected President of the 12th Army Corps and Vice President of the Society of the Army of the Potomac in 18[illegible].

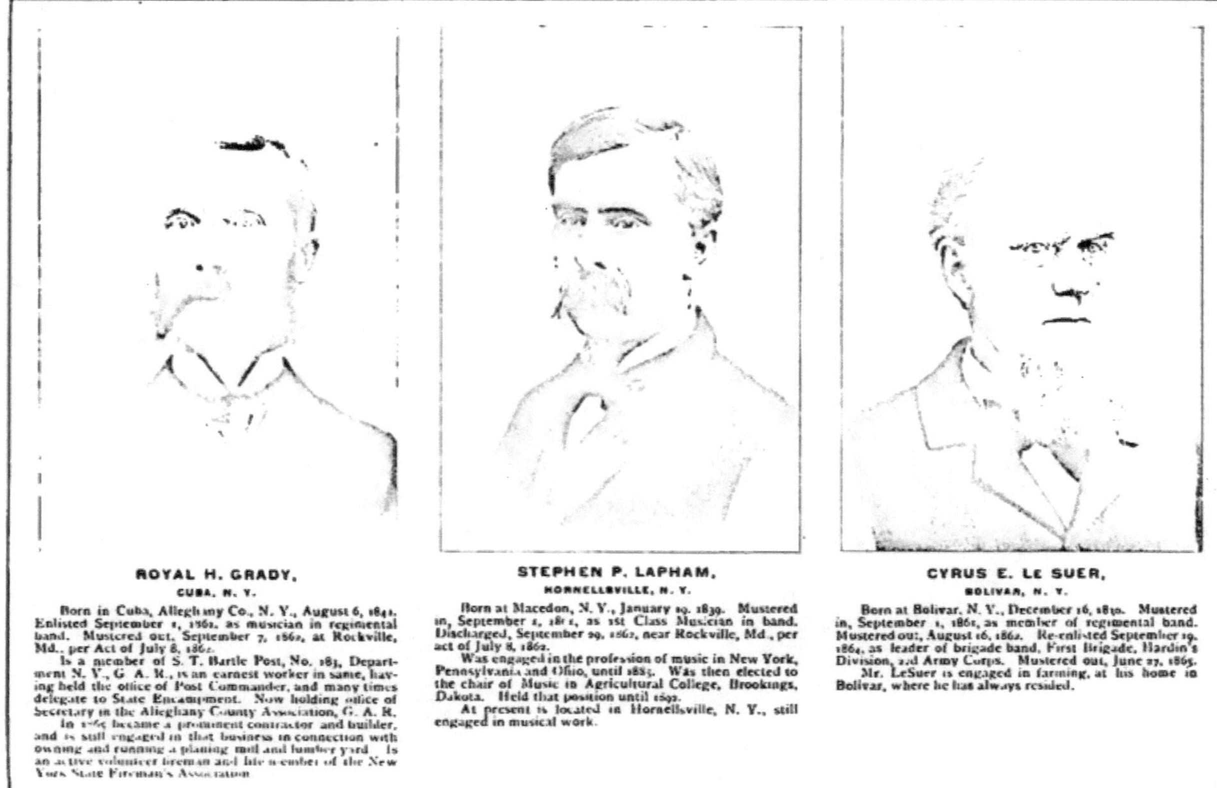

ROYAL H. GRADY,

CUBA, N. Y.

Born in Cuba, Alleghany Co., N. Y., August 6, 1841. Enlisted September 1, 1861, as musician in regimental band. Mustered out, September 7, 1862, at Rockville, Md., per Act of July 8, 1862.

Is a member of S. T. Bartle Post, No. 183, Department N. Y., G. A. R., is an earnest worker in same, having held the office of Post Commander, and many times delegate to State Encampment. Now holding office of Secretary in the Alleghany County Association, G. A. R.

In 1865 became a prominent contractor and builder, and is still engaged in that business in connection with owning and running a planing mill and lumber yard. Is an active volunteer fireman and life member of the New York State Fireman's Association.

STEPHEN P. LAPHAM,

HORNELLSVILLE, N. Y.

Born at Macedon, N. Y., January 19, 1839. Mustered in, September 1, 1861, as 1st Class Musician in band. Discharged, September 29, 1862, near Rockville, Md., per act of July 8, 1862.

Was engaged in the profession of music in New York, Pennsylvania and Ohio, until 1885. Was then elected to the chair of Music in Agricultural College, Brookings, Dakota. Held that position until 1892.

At present is located in Hornellsville, N. Y., still engaged in musical work.

CYRUS E. LE SUER,

BOLIVAR, N. Y.

Born at Bolivar, N. Y., December 16, 1840. Mustered in, September 1, 1861, as member of regimental band. Mustered out, August 16, 1862. Re-enlisted September 19, 1864, as leader of brigade band, First Brigade, Hardin's Division, 22d Army Corps. Mustered out, June 27, 1865.

Mr. LeSuer is engaged in farming, at his home in Bolivar, where he has always resided.

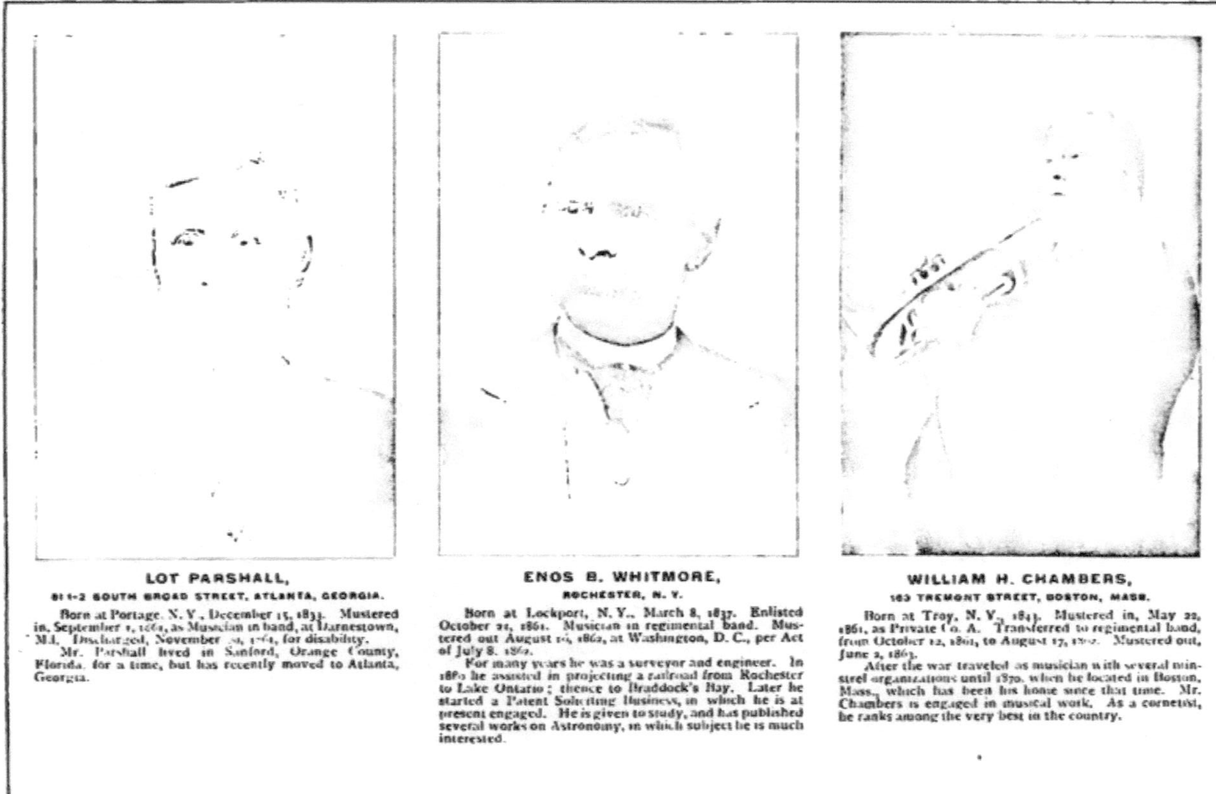

LOT PARSHALL,

811-2 SOUTH BROAD STREET, ATLANTA, GEORGIA.

Born at Portage, N. Y., December 15, 1833. Mustered in, September [illegible], 1861, as Musician in band, at Darnestown, Md. Discharged, November [illegible], 1861, for disability.

Mr. Parshall lived in Sanford, Orange County, Florida, for a time, but has recently moved to Atlanta, Georgia.

ENOS B. WHITMORE,

ROCHESTER, N. Y.

Born at Lockport, N. Y., March 8, 1837. Enlisted October 21, 1861. Musician in regimental band. Mustered out August 16, 1862, at Washington, D. C., per Act of July 8, 1862.

For many years he was a surveyor and engineer. In 1880 he assisted in projecting a railroad from Rochester to Lake Ontario; thence to Braddock's Bay. Later he started a Patent Soliciting Business, in which he is at present engaged. He is given to study, and has published several works on Astronomy, in which subject he is much interested.

WILLIAM H. CHAMBERS,

163 TREMONT STREET, BOSTON, MASS.

Born at Troy, N. Y., 1843. Mustered in, May 22, 1861, as Private Co. A. Transferred to regimental band, from October 12, 1861, to August 17, [illegible]. Mustered out, June 2, 1863.

After the war traveled as musician with several minstrel organizations until 1870, when he located in Boston, Mass., which has been his home since that time. Mr. Chambers is engaged in musical work. As a cornetist, he ranks among the very best in the country.

BENJAMIN FLAGLER,

NIAGARA FALLS, N. Y.

Born in Lockport, N. Y., December 10, 1833. Mustered in, October [illegible], as Captain of Co. A. Resigned, on account of disability, October 21, 1862.

He was one of four brothers who served in the War. Mr. Flagler was appointed Inspector of Customs in the District of Niagara in 18[illegible], and later Collector of Customs, which office he held until June 1, 1886. He has been a prominent citizen of Niagara Falls, and an active member of the Masonic fraternity; also a member of the G. A. R., and Commander of Dudley-Donnelly Post.

January 1, [illegible], he was appointed Chief of Ordnance on the staff of Governor Morton, with the rank of Brigadier General, and is also Acting Quartermaster-General and Acting Commissary-General of New York State.

General Flagler is one of the most faithful at the yearly [illegible]

DANIEL R. WHITCHER,

LOCKPORT, N. Y.

Born in Lockport, N. Y., December 7, 1830. Enlisted in the United States Army March 4, 1854. Joined the 9th Regiment, December, 1856, ordered to Oregon Territory. Promoted Quartermaster-Sergeant, and was present at the massacre of the Cascades under Philip H. Sheridan. Was honorably discharged at Fort Walla Walla, Oregon, March 4, 1859.

Enlisted, April [illegible], 1861. Mustered in, May 22, 1861, as 1st Lieutenant Co. A. Resigned, February 14, 1862, at Washington, D. C.

Re-enlisted in Battery B, 1st Michigan Light Artillery, September 14, 1863. Promoted Sergeant, November, [illegible], and detailed to Ordnance Department until mustered out, July 12, 1865.

Was appointed Brevet Captain Co. C, [illegible] Michigan Infantry. Wounded at the Battle of [illegible]

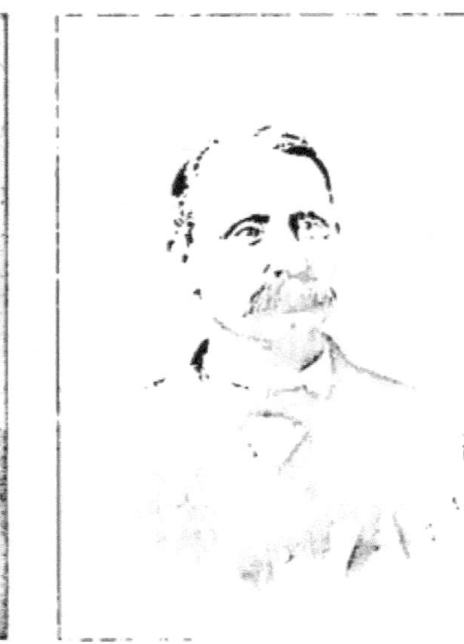

WILLIAM H. CRAMPTON,

LOCKPORT, N. Y.

Born in Orleans County, N. Y., December 17, 1840. Mustered in, May 22, 1861, Private Co. A. Promoted Corporal, March, 1862. Wounded in action at Cedar Mountain, Va., August 9, 1862. Right arm amputated. Discharged for disability from wounds, at General Hospital, Alexandria, Va., September 24, 1862.

He has always been an active temperance worker, has repeatedly represented temperance organizations in State and National Conventions. Last year he represented the Supreme Council as a Fraternal Delegate to the National Convention of the W. C. T. U. which met at Denver, Colorado, and was also one of the representatives to the World's Temperance Congress at Chicago.

He has for many years been successfully engaged in organizing and instituting councils of the "Royal Templars of Temperance."

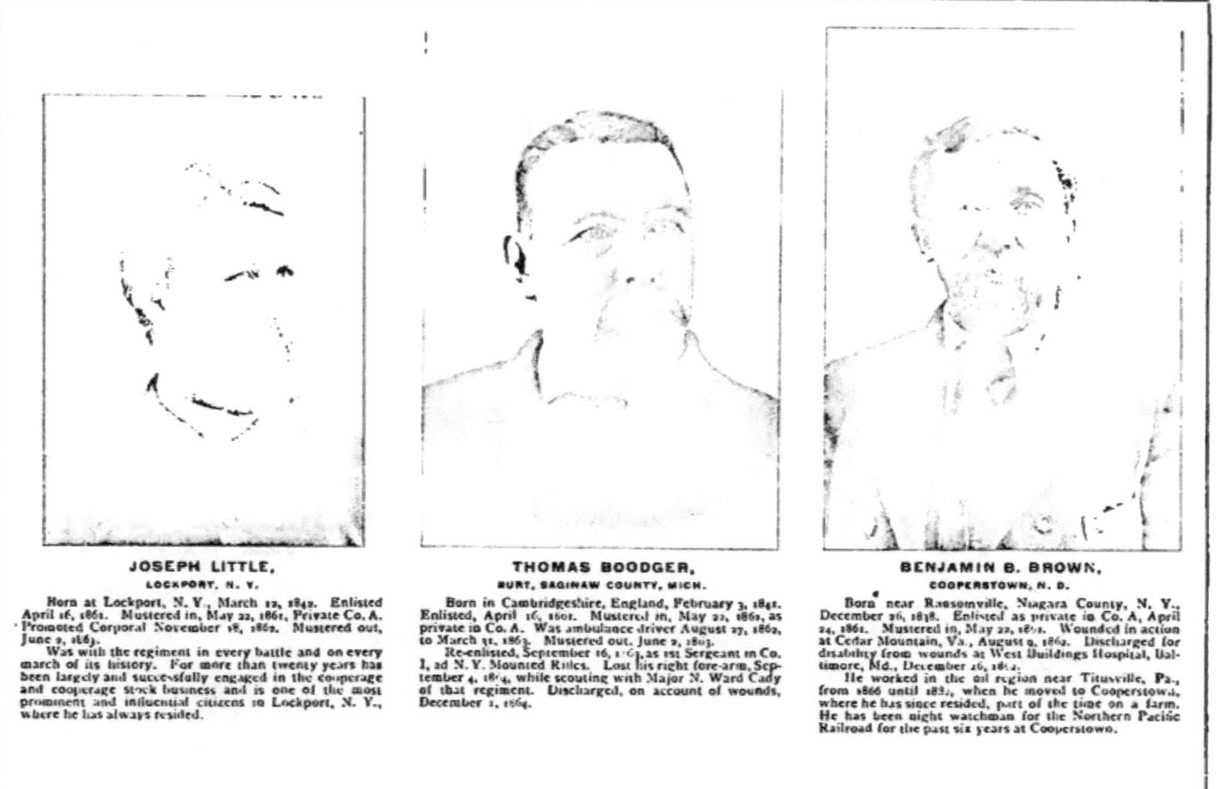

JOSEPH LITTLE,

LOCKPORT, N. Y.

Born at Lockport, N. Y., March 12, 1842. Enlisted April 16, 1861. Mustered in, May 22, 1861, Private Co. A. Promoted Corporal November 18, 1862. Mustered out, June 2, 1863.

Was with the regiment in every battle and on every march of its history. For more than twenty years has been largely and successfully engaged in the cooperage and cooperage stock business and is one of the most prominent and influential citizens in Lockport, N. Y., where he has always resided.

THOMAS BOODGER,

BURT, SAGINAW COUNTY, MICH.

Born in Cambridgeshire, England, February 3, 1841. Enlisted, April 16, 1861. Mustered in, May 22, 1861, as private in Co. A. Was ambulance driver August 27, 1862, to March 31, 1863. Mustered out, June 2, 1863.

Re-enlisted, September 16, 1863, as 1st Sergeant in Co. I, 2d N. Y. Mounted Rifles. Lost his right fore-arm, September 4, 1864, while scouting with Major N. Ward Cady of that regiment. Discharged, on account of wounds, December 1, 1864.

BENJAMIN B. BROWN,

COOPERSTOWN, N. D.

Born near Ransomville, Niagara County, N. Y., December 26, 1838. Enlisted as private in Co. A, April 24, 1861. Mustered in, May 22, 1861. Wounded in action at Cedar Mountain, Va., August 9, 1862. Discharged for disability from wounds at West Buildings Hospital, Baltimore, Md., December 26, 1862.

He worked in the oil region near Titusville, Pa., from 1866 until 1882, when he moved to Cooperstown, where he has since resided, part of the time on a farm. He has been night watchman for the Northern Pacific Railroad for the past six years at Cooperstown.

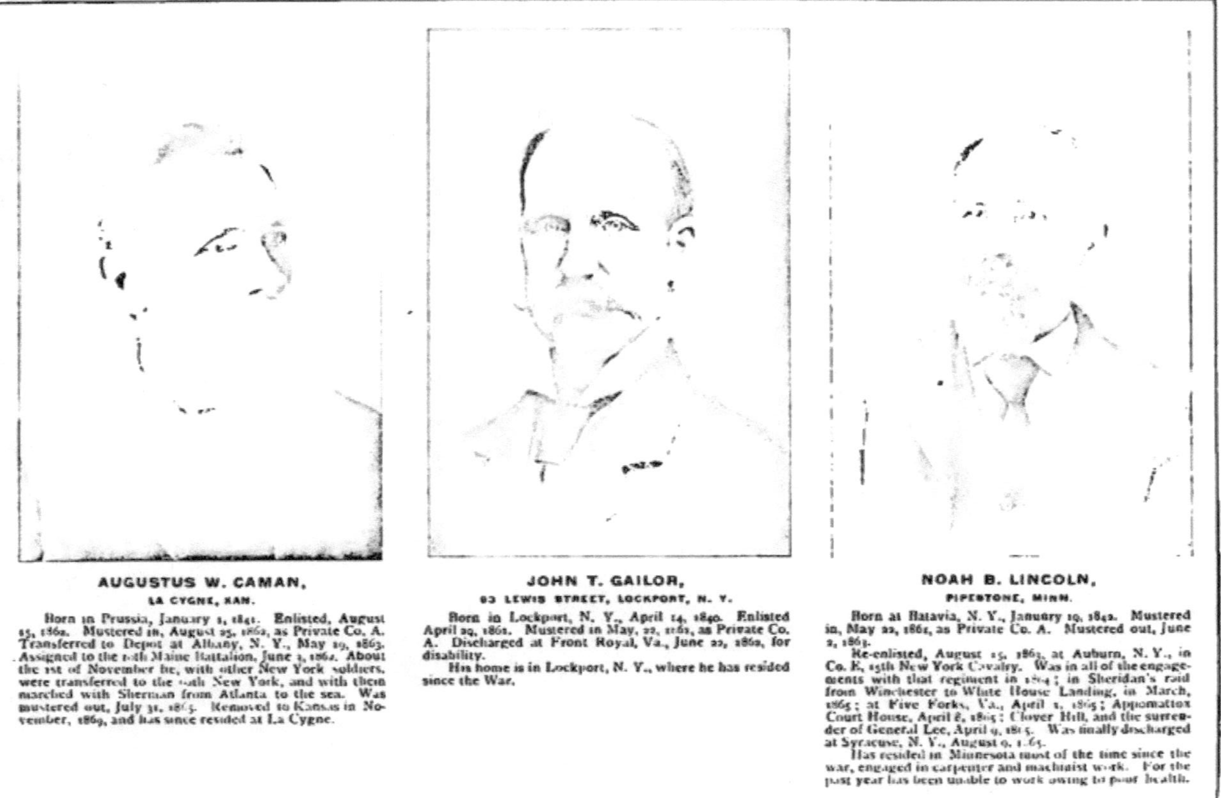

AUGUSTUS W. CAMAN,

LA CYGNE, KAN.

Born in Prussia, January 1, 1841. Enlisted, August 15, 1862. Mustered in, August 25, 1862, as Private Co. A. Transferred to Depot at Albany, N. Y., May 19, 1863. Assigned to the [illegible]th Maine Battalion, June 3, 1864. About the 1st of November he, with other New York soldiers, were transferred to the [illegible]th New York, and with them marched with Sherman from Atlanta to the sea. Was mustered out, July 31, 1865. Removed to Kansas in November, 1869, and has since resided at La Cygne.

JOHN T. GAILOR,

93 LEWIS STREET, LOCKPORT, N. Y.

Born in Lockport, N. Y., April 14, 1840. Enlisted April 29, 1861. Mustered in May, 22, 1861, as Private Co. A. Discharged at Front Royal, Va., June 22, 1862, for disability.

His home is in Lockport, N. Y., where he has resided since the War.

NOAH B. LINCOLN,

PIPESTONE, MINN.

Born at Batavia, N. Y., January 19, 1842. Mustered in, May 22, 1861, as Private Co. A. Mustered out, June 2, 1863.

Re-enlisted, August 15, 1863, at Auburn, N. Y., in Co. E, 15th New York Cavalry. Was in all of the engagements with that regiment in 1864; in Sheridan's raid from Winchester to White House Landing, in March, 1865; at Five Forks, Va., April 1, 1865; Appomattox Court House, April 8, 1865; Clover Hill, and the surrender of General Lee, April 9, 1865. Was finally discharged at Syracuse, N. Y., August 9, 1865.

Has resided in Minnesota most of the time since the war, engaged in carpenter and machinist work. For the past year has been unable to work owing to poor health.

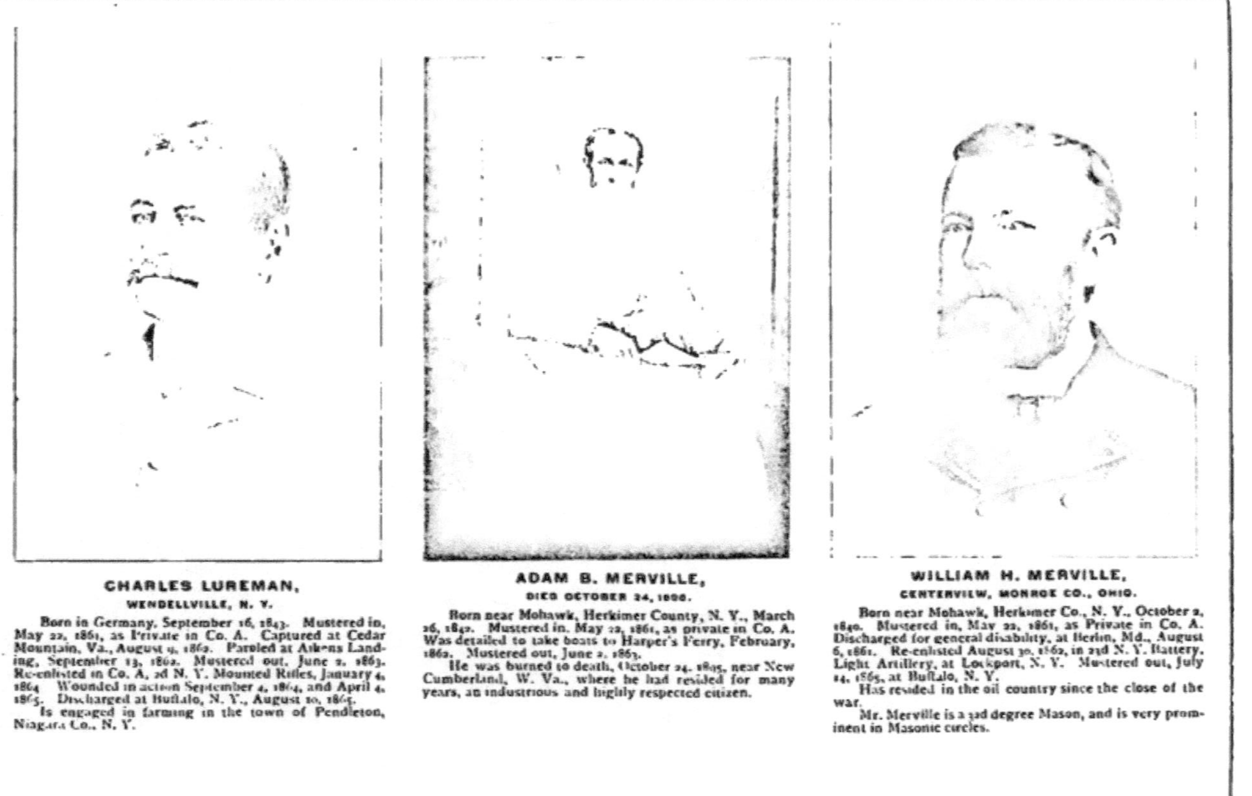

CHARLES LUREMAN,

WENDELLVILLE, N. Y.

Born in Germany, September 16, 1843. Mustered in, May 22, 1861, as Private in Co. A. Captured at Cedar Mountain, Va., August 9, 1862. Paroled at Aikens Landing, September 13, 1862. Mustered out, June 2, 1863. Re-enlisted in Co. A, 2d N. Y. Mounted Rifles, January 4, 1864. Wounded in action September 4, 1864, and April 4, 1865. Discharged at Buffalo, N. Y., August 10, 1865.

Is engaged in farming in the town of Pendleton, Niagara Co., N. Y.

ADAM B. MERVILLE,

DIED OCTOBER 24, 1895.

Born near Mohawk, Herkimer County, N. Y., March 26, 1842. Mustered in, May 22, 1861, as private in Co. A. Was detailed to take boats to Harper's Ferry, February, 1862. Mustered out, June 2, 1863.

He was burned to death, October 24, 1895, near New Cumberland, W. Va., where he had resided for many years, an industrious and highly respected citizen.

WILLIAM H. MERVILLE,

CENTERVIEW, MONROE CO., OHIO.

Born near Mohawk, Herkimer Co., N. Y., October 2, 1840. Mustered in, May 22, 1861, as Private in Co. A. Discharged for general disability, at Berlin, Md., August 6, 1861. Re-enlisted August 30, 1862, in 23d N. Y. Battery, Light Artillery, at Lockport, N. Y. Mustered out, July 14, 1865, at Buffalo, N. Y.

Has resided in the oil country since the close of the war.

Mr. Merville is a 32d degree Mason, and is very prominent in Masonic circles.

THOMAS H. PASCO,

36 VICTORIA STREET, MONTREAL, QUE.

Born at Niagara-on-the-Lake, May 26, 1840. Enlisted at Lockport, April 25, 1861. Mustered in, May 22, 1861, as private in Co. A. Was wounded and captured at Cedar Mountain, Va., August 9, 1862. Spent one month in Libby prison. Was paroled and sent to Fort Delaware, Del. Discharged for disability, January 14, 1863.

Lived in Rochester, N. Y., for a time after the war, afterward in Detroit, Mich. Is foreman in car wheel department of the C. P. R. R. at Montreal, Quebec.

LYMAN A. STICKELS,

401 SOUTH DIVISION STREET, GRAND RAPIDS, MICH.

Born at Newfane, Niagara Co., N. Y., August 19, 1843. Enlisted April 25, 1861. Mustered in, May 22, 1861, Private Co. A. Discharged for disability from typhoid fever at Sandy Hook, Md., September 22, 1862.

Went to Oil City, Pa. A year later went to Grand Rapids, Mich., where he has since resided. For the past twenty years has been in railroad work.

JOHN F. TAYLOR,

YOUNGSTOWN, N. Y.

Born at Lockport, N. Y., December 29, 1839. Mustered in, May 22, 1861, as Private in Co. A. Discharged November 8, 1862, at Albany, N. Y., for disability. Re-enlisted in 23d N. Y. Independent Battery September 24, 1864. Finally discharged July 14, 1865.

Has resided, since the war, in Western New York, working at his trade—a mason—but for the past eleven years has been in the employ of the Government as keeper of the lighthouse at Fort Niagara, at the mouth of Niagara River.

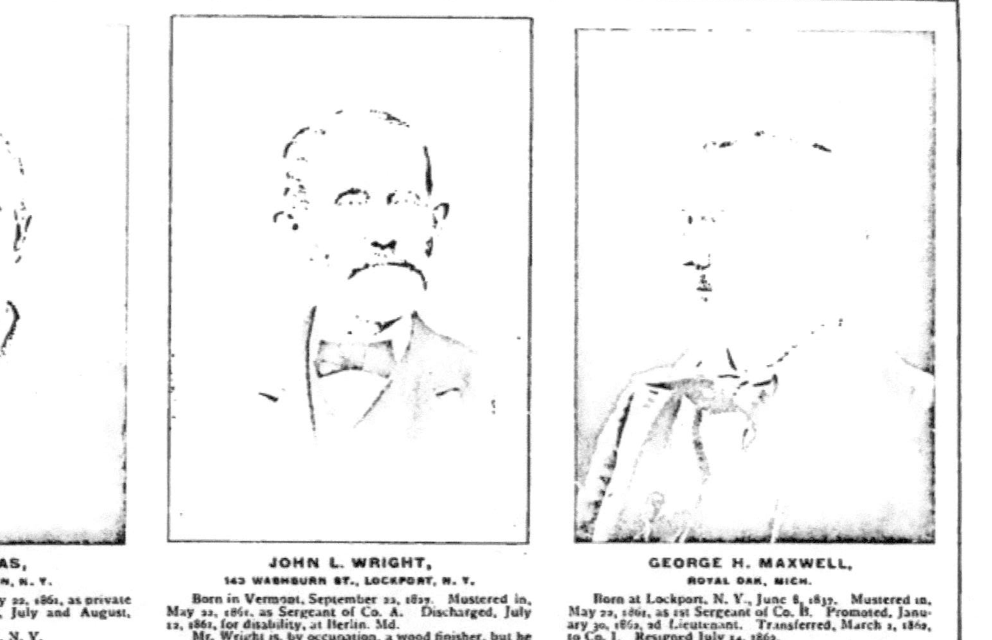

HARRY THOMAS,

45 HOLLEY ST., AUBURN, N. Y.

Born in 1842. Mustered in, May 22, 1861, as private in Co. A. Was ambulance driver, July and August, 1862. Mustered out, June 2, 1863.

Mr. Thomas' home is at Auburn, N. Y.

JOHN L. WRIGHT,

143 WASHBURN ST., LOCKPORT, N. Y.

Born in Vermont, September 22, 1837. Mustered in, May 22, 1861, as Sergeant of Co. A. Discharged, July 12, 1862, for disability, at Berlin, Md.

Mr. Wright is, by occupation, a wood finisher, but he has been unable to do any hard work for some time, as he has suffered from heart disease for many years.

GEORGE H. MAXWELL,

ROYAL OAK, MICH.

Born at Lockport, N. Y., June 8, 1837. Mustered in, May 22, 1861, as 1st Sergeant of Co. B. Promoted, January 30, 1862, 2d Lieutenant. Transferred, March 1, 1862, to Co. I. Resigned July 14, 1862.

Is a direct descendant of Hugh Maxwell, of Revolutionary fame, and his father, Dr. Henry Maxwell, was a surgeon of the war of 1812. Was appointed Deputy United States Marshal, at Suspension Bridge, after the war. His profession is the stage; and he devotes his leisure to his vineyard and poultry farm, at Royal Oak, near Detroit, Mich.

PETER B. KELCHNER,

RENFREW, PA.

Born in Turbut Township, Northumberland Co., Pa., December 31, 1831. Enlisted April 17, 1861, at Lockport, N. Y. Mustered in, May 22, 1861, as Sergeant Co. B. Promoted 1st Sergeant, March 13, 1862; 2d Lieutenant, May 6, 1863. Seriously wounded in the left thigh at the battle of Antietam, September 17, 1862. Mustered out, June 2, 1863.

Re-enlisted January 24, 1864, 1st Lieutenant Co. C., 2d Mounted Rifles. Promoted Captain Co. A, August, 1864. In command of the regiment, under Sheridan, in the pursuit of General Lee. Performed Provost duty at Buckingham Court House, Va. Mustered out of service, at Buffalo, N. Y., August 26, 1865.

Has been engaged in the oil business in Pennsylvania since 1865, with variable success.

HENRY COLTON,

DIED MARCH 12, 1895.

Born in Erie County, N. Y., January 18, 1838. Mustered in, May 22, 1861, as private in Co. B. Mustered out, June 2, 1863.

Mr. Colton was never absent from the regiment, participating in every march and battle in which it was engaged.

After his term of service expired, he returned to Niagara County, N. Y., where he was engaged in farming for a number of years — but his health failing, he was obliged to leave the farm, and moved to Pendleton Center, where he died, March 12, 1895. He was a member of C. P. Sprout Post, No. 76, G. A. R., in Lockport, N. Y.

JAMES GOGGIN,

284 PROSPECT STREET, LOCKPORT, N. Y.

Born in Port Colborne, Ontario, December 22, 1842. Removed to Lockport in 1854. Enlisted, April 18, 1861. Mustered in, May 22, 1861, as private in Co. H. Slightly wounded in left shoulder at Winchester, Va., May 25, 1862. Captured, August 18, 1862, and paroled. Promoted Corporal, January 24, 1863. Mustered out, June 2, 1863.

Mr. Goggin has resided in Lockport since the War.

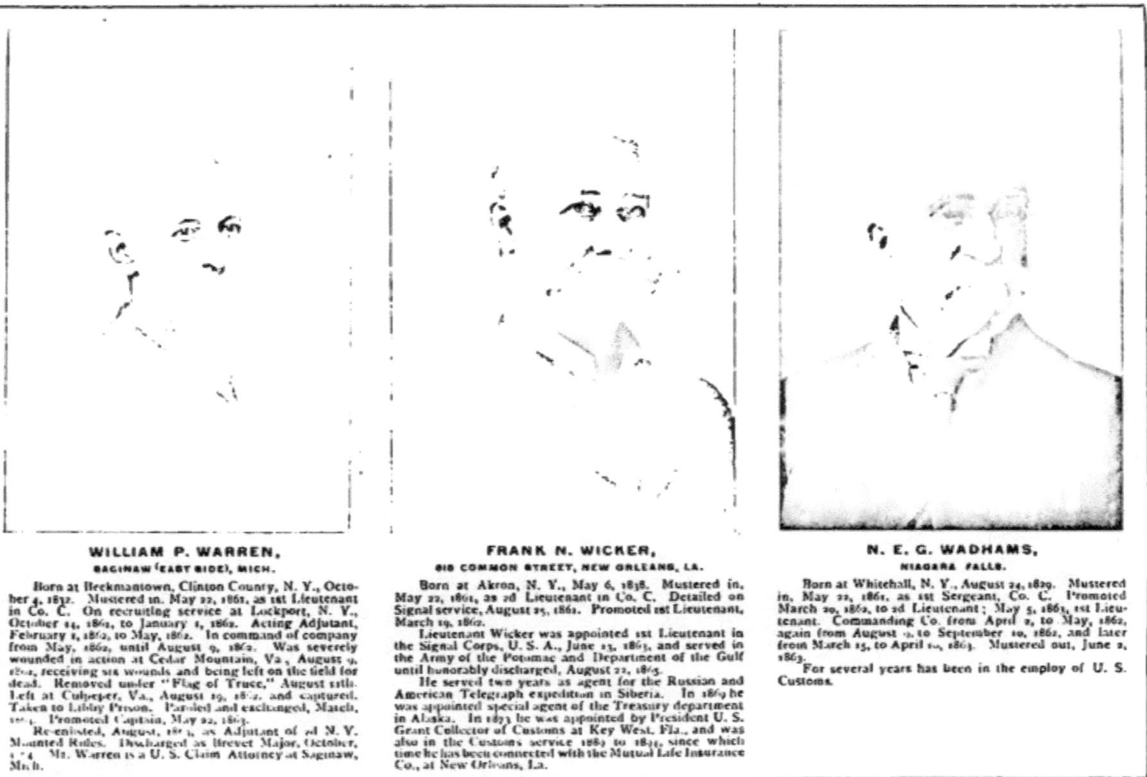

WILLIAM P. WARREN,

SAGINAW (EAST SIDE), MICH.

Born at Beekmantown, Clinton County, N. Y., October 4, 1832. Mustered in, May 22, 1861, as 1st Lieutenant in Co. C. On recruiting service at Lockport, N. Y., October 14, 1861, to January 1, 1862. Acting Adjutant, February 1, 1862, to May, 1862. In command of company from May, 1862, until August 9, 1862. Was severely wounded in action at Cedar Mountain, Va., August 9, 1862, receiving six wounds and being left on the field for dead. Removed under "Flag of Truce," August 11th. Left at Culpeper, Va., August 19, 1862, and captured. Taken to Libby Prison. Paroled and exchanged, March, [illegible]. Promoted Captain, May 22, 1863.

Re-enlisted, August, [illegible], as Adjutant of [illegible] N. Y. Mounted Rifles. Discharged as Brevet Major, October, [illegible]. Mr. Warren is a U. S. Claim Attorney at Saginaw, Mich.

FRANK N. WICKER,

815 COMMON STREET, NEW ORLEANS, LA.

Born at Akron, N. Y., May 6, 1838. Mustered in, May 22, 1861, as 2d Lieutenant in Co. C. Detailed on Signal service, August 25, 1861. Promoted 1st Lieutenant, March 19, 1862.

Lieutenant Wicker was appointed 1st Lieutenant in the Signal Corps, U. S. A., June 13, 1863, and served in the Army of the Potomac and Department of the Gulf until honorably discharged, August 22, 1865.

He served two years as agent for the Russian and American Telegraph expedition in Siberia. In 1869 he was appointed special agent of the Treasury department in Alaska. In 1873 he was appointed by President U. S. Grant Collector of Customs at Key West, Fla., and was also in the Customs service 1885 to 1891, since which time he has been connected with the Mutual Life Insurance Co., at New Orleans, La.

N. E. G. WADHAMS,

NIAGARA FALLS.

Born at Whitehall, N. Y., August 24, 1839. Mustered in, May 22, 1861, as 1st Sergeant, Co. C. Promoted March 20, 1862, to 2d Lieutenant; May 5, 1863, 1st Lieutenant. Commanding Co. from April 2, to May, 1862, again from August [illegible], to September 10, 1862, and later from March 15, to April [illegible], 1863. Mustered out, June 2, 1863.

For several years has been in the employ of U. S. Customs.

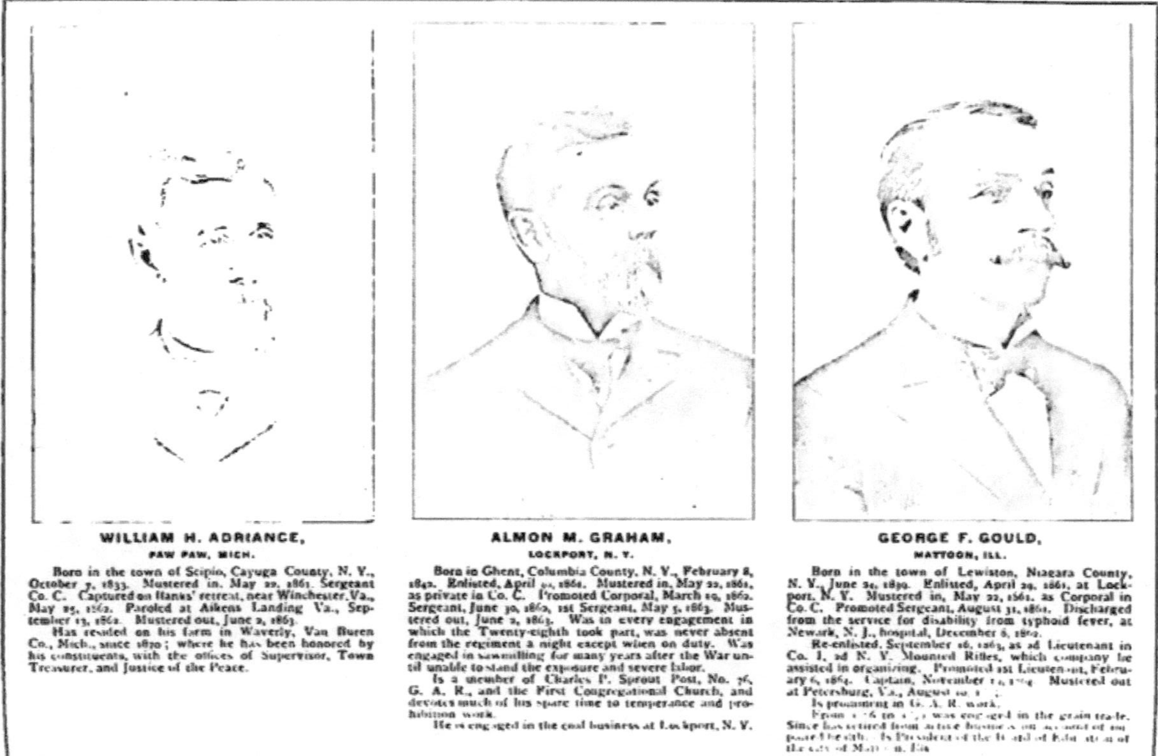

WILLIAM H. ADRIANCE,

PAW PAW, MICH.

Born in the town of Scipio, Cayuga County, N. Y., October 7, 1833. Mustered in, May 22, 1861. Sergeant Co. C. Captured on Banks' retreat, near Winchester, Va., May 25, 1862. Paroled at Aikens Landing Va., September 13, 1862. Mustered out, June 2, 1863.

Has resided on his farm in Waverly, Van Buren Co., Mich., since 1870; where he has been honored by his constituents, with the offices of Supervisor, Town Treasurer, and Justice of the Peace.

ALMON M. GRAHAM,

LOCKPORT, N. Y.

Born in Ghent, Columbia County, N. Y., February 8, 1842. Enlisted, April [illegible], 1861. Mustered in, May 22, 1861, as private in Co. C. Promoted Corporal, March 10, 1862. Sergeant, June 30, 1862, 1st Sergeant, May 5, 1863. Mustered out, June 2, 1863. Was in every engagement in which the Twenty-eighth took part, was never absent from the regiment a night except when on duty. Was engaged in sawmilling for many years after the War until unable to stand the exposure and severe labor.

Is a member of Charles P. Sprout Post, No. 76, G. A. R., and the First Congregational Church, and devotes much of his spare time to temperance and prohibition work.

He is engaged in the coal business at Lockport, N. Y.

GEORGE F. GOULD,

MATTOON, ILL.

Born in the town of Lewiston, Niagara County, N. Y., June 24, 1839. Enlisted, April 24, 1861, at Lockport, N. Y. Mustered in, May 22, 1861, as Corporal in Co. C. Promoted Sergeant, August 31, 1861. Discharged from the service for disability from typhoid fever, at Newark, N. J., hospital, December 6, 1862.

Re-enlisted, September 16, 1863, as 2d Lieutenant in Co. I, 2d N. Y. Mounted Rifles, which company he assisted in organizing. Promoted 1st Lieutenant, February 6, 1864. Captain, November [illegible]. Mustered out at Petersburg, Va., August [illegible].

Is prominent in G. A. R. work.

From [illegible] to [illegible] was engaged in the grain trade. Since has retired from active business on account of impaired health. Is President of the Board of Education of the city of Mattoon, Ill.

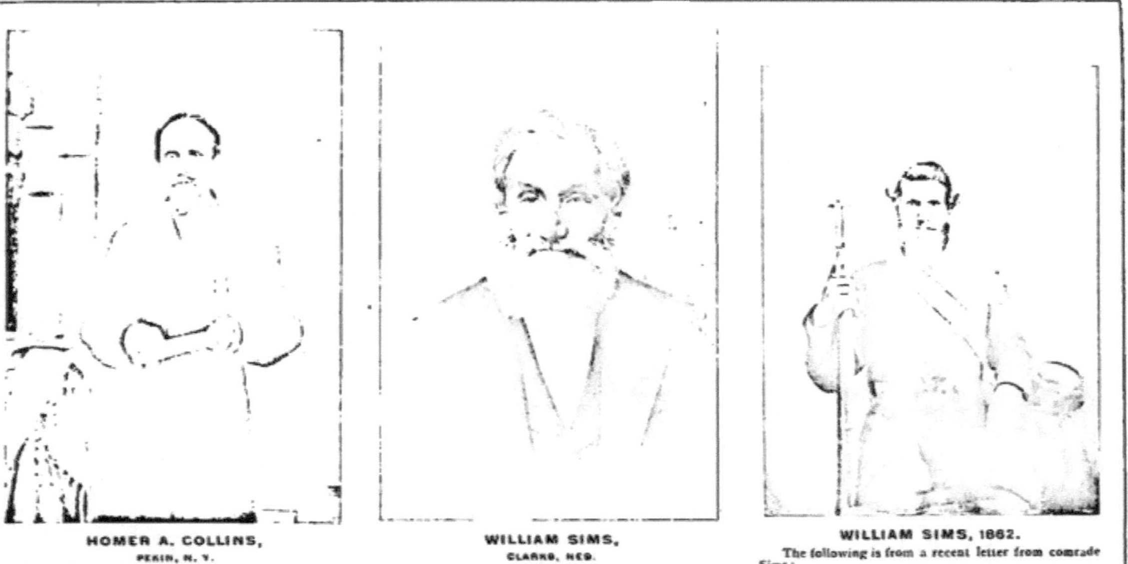

HOMER A. COLLINS,

PEKIN, N. Y.

Born in Broomfield, Ontario County, N. Y., May 29, 1838. Mustered in, May 22, 1861, as private in Co. C, having materially assisted in organizing the Company. Promoted Corporal, March [illegible], 1862. Discharged for disability at Sandy Hook, Md., December 3, 1862.

Re-enlisted in 33d N. Y. Independent Battery, Light Artillery, July, 1863. Mustered out, June [illegible]. Subsequently was appointed Brevet-Lieutenant, by Governor Fenton, "for gallant and meritorious services in the late war."

Mr. Collins was among the Sioux, Crow, Creeks and Lower Brule Indians in South Dakota, in the employment of the government, in [illegible].

His occupation is farmer. He has resided on his farm at Pekin since the war.

WILLIAM SIMS,

CLARKS, NEB.

Born in the County of Hampshire, England, April 20, 1831. Mustered in as Private in Co. C, May 22, 1861. Promoted Corporal June 30, 1861. Mustered out, June 2, 1863.

Re-enlisted in Wheeler's Independent 33d N. Y. Light Battery. Served in the [illegible]th and 18th Corps in the campaign about Petersburg, Richmond and the James River. Was promoted Corporal and Sergeant in June, 1864. Was finally mustered out at Petersburg, Va., in July, 1865.

The above is Comrade Sims the "FARMER." We have also the pleasure of seeing him as a "SOLDIER."

WILLIAM SIMS, 1862.

The following is from a recent letter from comrade Sims:

I will send you my picture that was taken in a snow storm at Woodstock, Va., March, 1862, east of the Shenandoah River, whilst in camp waiting for the bridge to be repaired, when we were after Stonewall Jackson, after Shields' fight at Winchester. I was 30 years old at the time it was taken. My hair was black as a raven, but now as white as wool. Was straight, but now bent over. I am 65 years old 20th day of next April.

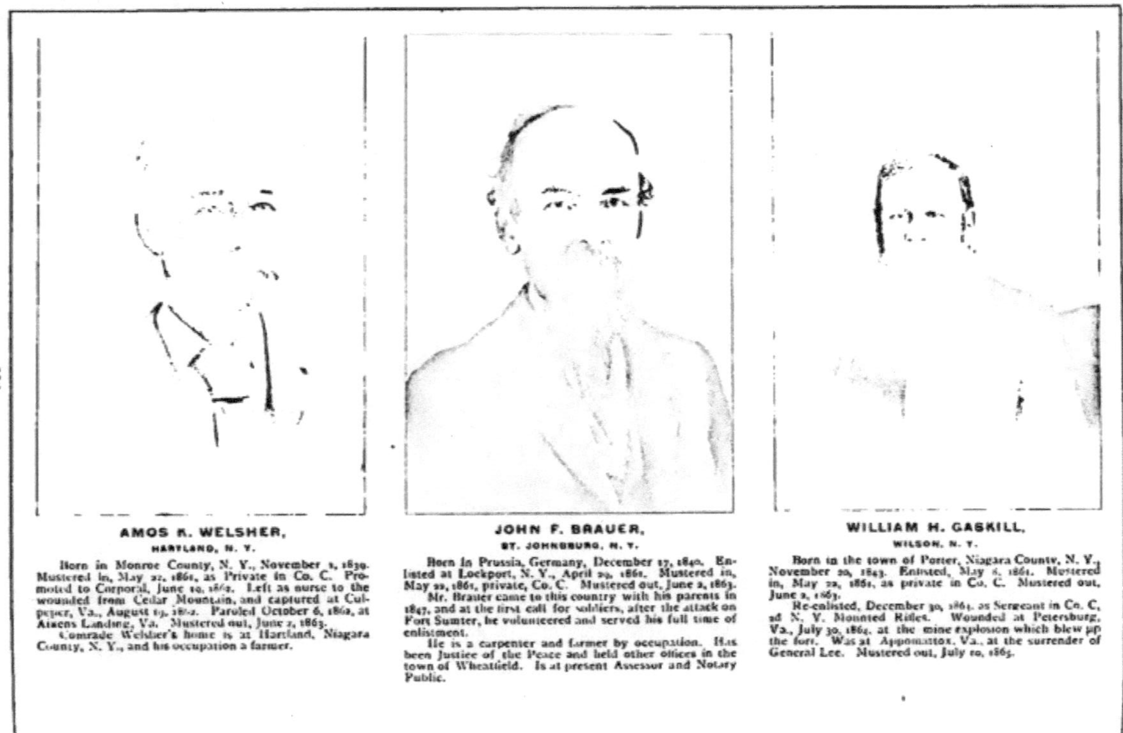

AMOS K. WELSHER,

HARTLAND, N. Y.

Born in Monroe County, N. Y., November 1, 1830. Mustered in, May 22, 1861, as Private in Co. C. Promoted to Corporal, June 10, 1862. Left as nurse to the wounded from Cedar Mountain, and captured at Culpeper, Va., August 19, 1862. Paroled October 6, 1862, at Aiken's Landing, Va. Mustered out, June 2, 1863.

Comrade Welsher's home is at Hartland, Niagara County, N. Y., and his occupation a farmer.

JOHN F. BRAUER,

ST. JOHNSBURG, N. Y.

Born in Prussia, Germany, December 17, 1840. Enlisted at Lockport, N. Y., April 29, 1861. Mustered in, May 22, 1861, private, Co. C. Mustered out, June 2, 1863.

Mr. Brauer came to this country with his parents in 1847, and at the first call for soldiers, after the attack on Fort Sumter, he volunteered and served his full time of enlistment.

He is a carpenter and farmer by occupation. Has been Justice of the Peace and held other offices in the town of Wheatfield. Is at present Assessor and Notary Public.

WILLIAM H. GASKILL,

WILSON, N. Y.

Born in the town of Porter, Niagara County, N. Y., November 20, 1843. Enlisted, May 6, 1861. Mustered in, May 22, 1861, as private in Co. C. Mustered out, June 2, 1863.

Re-enlisted, December 30, 1863, as Sergeant in Co. C, 2d N. Y. Mounted Rifles. Wounded at Petersburg, Va., July 30, 1864, at the mine explosion which blew up the fort. Was at Appomattox, Va., at the surrender of General Lee. Mustered out, July 10, 1865.

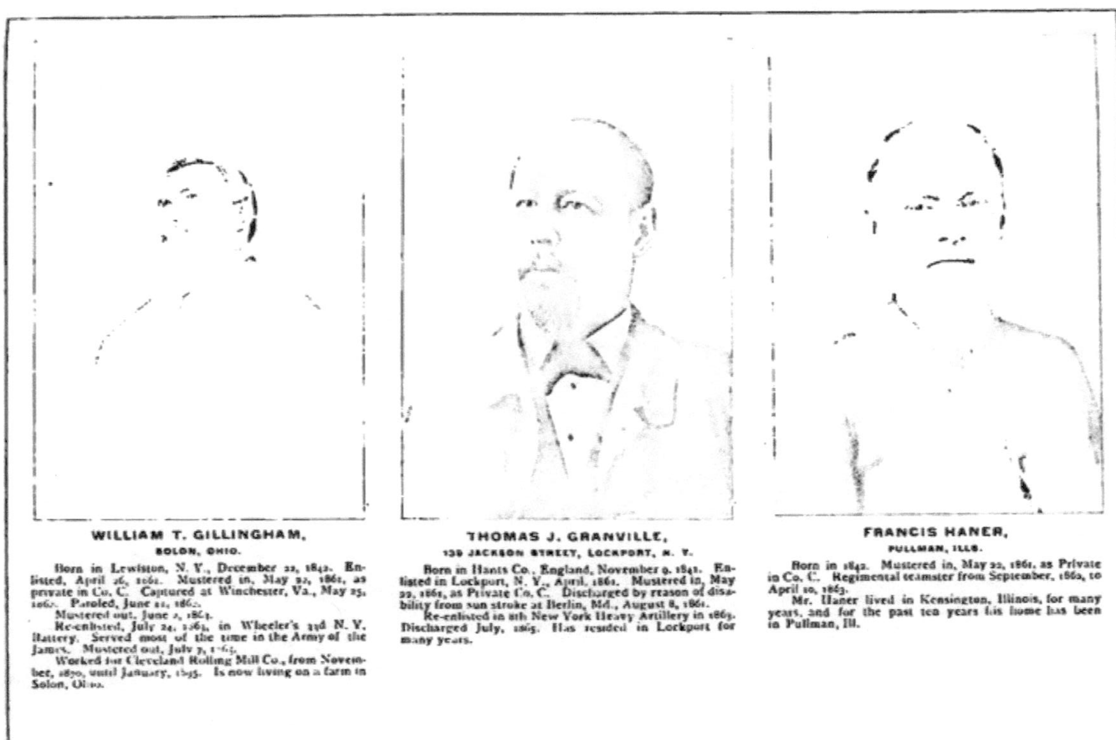

WILLIAM T. GILLINGHAM,
SOLON, OHIO.

Born in Lewiston, N. Y., December 22, 1842. Enlisted, April 26, 1861. Mustered in, May 22, 1861, as private in Co. C. Captured at Winchester, Va., May 25, 1862. Paroled, June 11, 1862.

Mustered out, June 2, 1863.

Re-enlisted, July 24, 1863, in Wheeler's 33d N. Y. Battery. Served most of the time in the Army of the James. Mustered out, July 7, 1865.

Worked for Cleveland Rolling Mill Co., from November, 1870, until January, 1895. Is now living on a farm in Solon, Ohio.

THOMAS J. GRANVILLE,
139 JACKSON STREET, LOCKPORT, N. Y.

Born in Hants Co., England, November 9, 1841. Enlisted in Lockport, N. Y., April, 1861. Mustered in, May 22, 1861, as Private Co. C. Discharged by reason of disability from sun stroke at Berlin, Md., August 8, 1861.

Re-enlisted in 8th New York Heavy Artillery in 1863. Discharged July, 1865. Has resided in Lockport for many years.

FRANCIS HANER,
PULLMAN, ILLS.

Born in 1842. Mustered in, May 22, 1861, as Private in Co. C. Regimental teamster from September, 1862, to April 10, 1863.

Mr. Haner lived in Kensington, Illinois, for many years, and for the past ten years his home has been in Pullman, Ill.

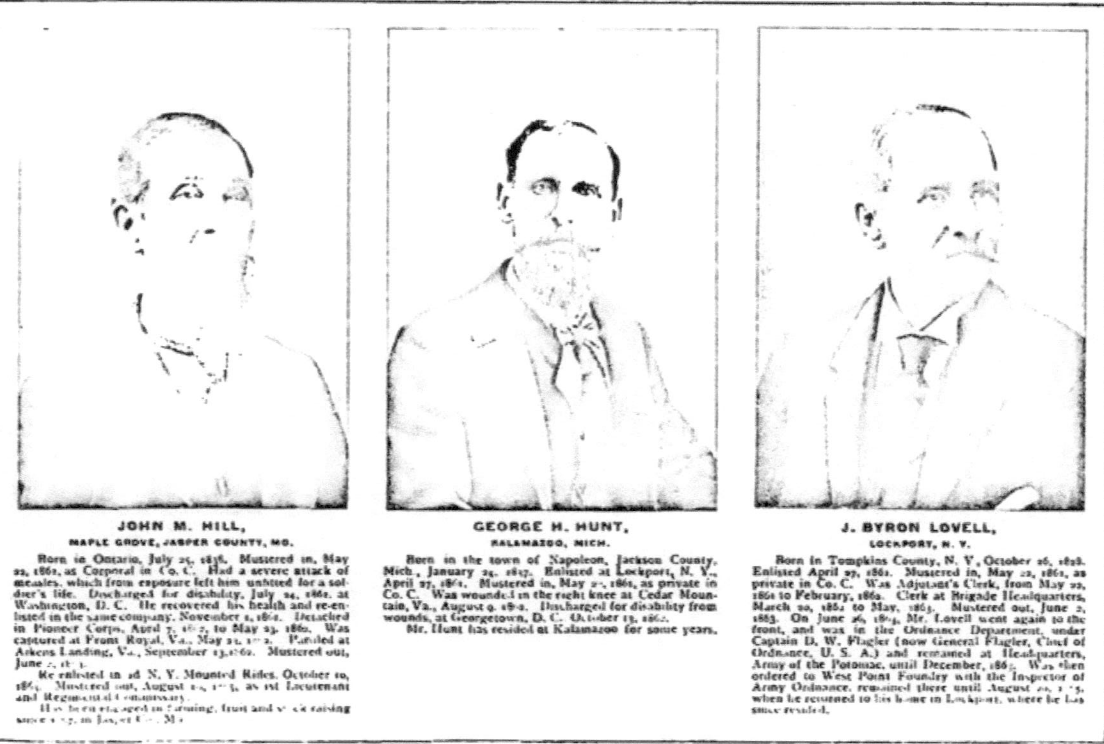

JOHN M. HILL,

MAPLE GROVE, JASPER COUNTY, MO.

Born in Ontario, July 25, 1836. Mustered in, May 22, 1861, as Corporal in Co. C. Had a severe attack of measles, which from exposure left him unfitted for a soldier's life. Discharged for disability, July 24, 1861, at Washington, D. C. He recovered his health and re-enlisted in the same company, November 1, 1861. Detached in Pioneer Corps, April 7, 1862, to May 23, 1862. Was captured at Front Royal, Va., May 23, 1862. Paroled at Aikens Landing, Va., September 13, 1862. Mustered out, June 2, 1863.

Re-enlisted in 2d N. Y. Mounted Rifles, October 10, 1864. Mustered out, August [illegible], [illegible], as 1st Lieutenant and Regimental Commissary.

Has been engaged in farming, fruit and stock raising since [illegible], in Jasper Co., Mo.

GEORGE H. HUNT,

KALAMAZOO, MICH.

Born in the town of Napoleon, Jackson County, Mich., January 24, 1837. Enlisted at Lockport, N. Y., April 27, 1861. Mustered in, May 22, 1861, as private in Co. C. Was wounded in the right knee at Cedar Mountain, Va., August 9, 1862. Discharged for disability from wounds, at Georgetown, D. C. October 13, 1862.

Mr. Hunt has resided at Kalamazoo for some years.

J. BYRON LOVELL,

LOCKPORT, N. Y.

Born in Tompkins County, N. Y., October 26, 1838. Enlisted April 27, 1861. Mustered in, May 22, 1861, as private in Co. C. Was Adjutant's Clerk, from May 22, 1861 to February, 1862. Clerk at Brigade Headquarters, March 20, 1862 to May, 1863. Mustered out, June 2, 1863. On June 26, 1864, Mr. Lovell went again to the front, and was in the Ordnance Department, under Captain D. W. Flagler (now General Flagler, Chief of Ordnance, U. S. A.) and remained at Headquarters, Army of the Potomac, until December, 1865. Was then ordered to West Point Foundry with the Inspector of Army Ordnance, remained there until August [illegible], when he returned to his home in Lockport, where he has since resided.

WILLIAM LUFF,

NORTH RIDGE, NIAGARA COUNTY, N. Y.

Born at St. Ives, England, August 10, 1842. Came to America, July 1, 1857. Enlisted, April 28, 1861. Mustered in, May 22, 1861, as private in Co. C. Detached in Ambulance Corps, October 23, 1861, to December 31, 1862. Received injuries in leg at Fairfax Station, Va., December 29, 1862. Mustered out, June 2, 1863.

Re-enlisted, December 29, 1863, in Co. C, 2d N. Y. Mounted Rifles, as Sergeant. Mustered out, August 10, 1865, at City Point, Va.

Has resided at North Ridge, N. Y., since the War, engaged in farming.

WILLIAM E. MINARD,

MARATHON, N. Y.

Born at South Yarmouth, Ontario, August 20, 1844. Enlisted December 16, 1861, as Private in Co. C. Mustered in, December 25, 1861. Mustered out, June 2, 1863.

Re-enlisted in Co. E, 49th N. Y. Served with that regiment till the close of the war. Saw the flag of truce come into the Union lines at Appomattox, when General Lee surrendered.

Has been engaged in the photographic business thirty-one years, and traveled from the Atlantic to the Pacific and Gulf of Mexico. For the past nineteen years has resided at Marathon, N. Y.

FRANK W. MORSE,

PLAINFIELD, N. J.

Born at Lockport, N. Y., May 14, 1845. Enlisted May 22, 1861, Private Co. C. Captured at Winchester, Va., May 25, 1862. Paroled at Aiken's Landing, Va., September 13, 1862. Discharged at Lockport, N.Y., June 2, 1863.

Served in U. S. Navy from 1864-66. Was Captain of the after-guard on sloop of war "Augusta," when she acted as convoy to Monitor, "Miantonomah," on her memorable trip to Europe, in 1865.

Was engaged in the oil business in Europe from 1887 to 1890. At present is Superintendent of "Garwood Land and Improvement Company," at Garwood, N. J., 17 miles from New York City. Residence, Plainfield, N. J. P. O. address, Garwood, Union county, N. J.

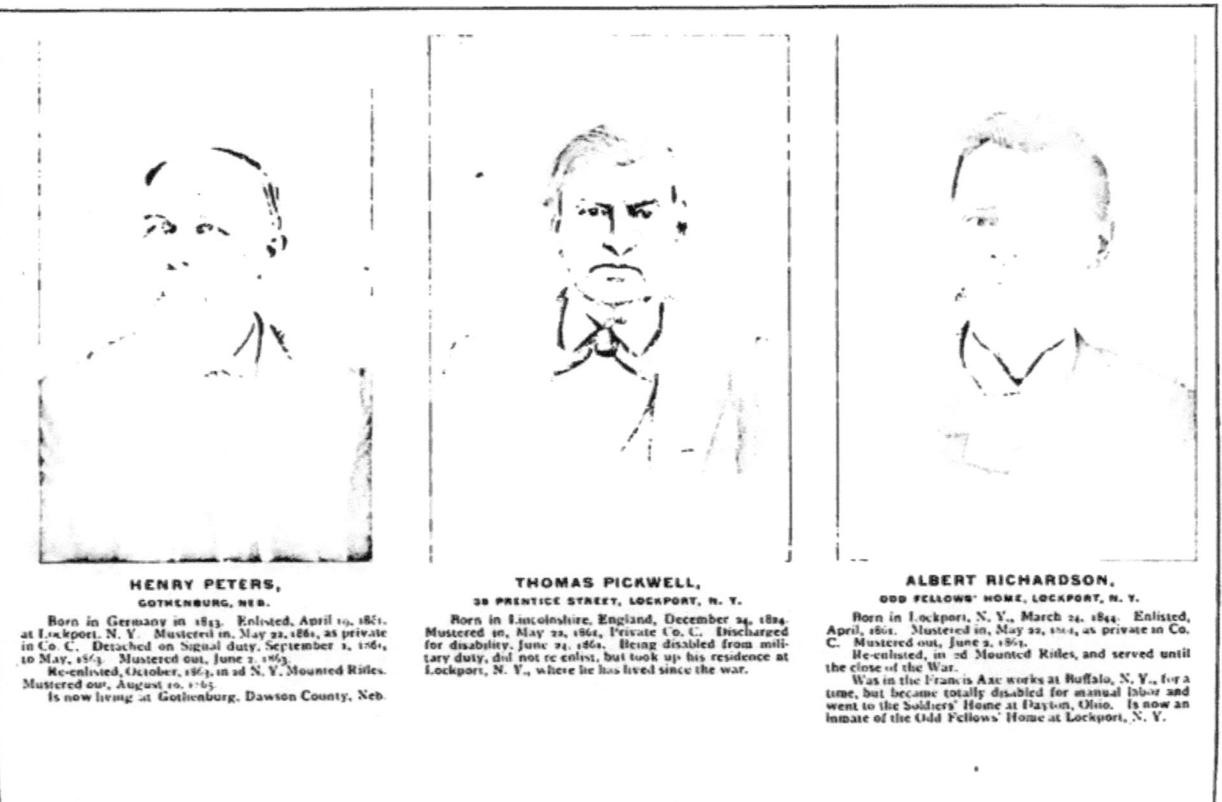

HENRY PETERS,

GOTHENBURG, NEB.

Born in Germany in 1843. Enlisted, April 19, 1861, at Lockport, N. Y. Mustered in, May 22, 1861, as private in Co. C. Detached on Signal duty, September 1, 1861, to May, 1863. Mustered out, June 2, 1863.

Re-enlisted, October, 1863, in 2d N. Y. Mounted Rifles. Mustered out, August 10, 1865.

Is now living at Gothenburg, Dawson County, Neb.

THOMAS PICKWELL,

38 PRENTICE STREET, LOCKPORT, N. Y.

Born in Lincolnshire, England, December 24, 1824. Mustered in, May 22, 1861, Private Co. C. Discharged for disability, June 24, 1861. Being disabled from military duty, did not re enlist, but took up his residence at Lockport, N. Y., where he has lived since the war.

ALBERT RICHARDSON,

ODD FELLOWS' HOME, LOCKPORT, N. Y.

Born in Lockport, N. Y., March 24, 1844. Enlisted, April, 1861. Mustered in, May 22, 1861, as private in Co. C. Mustered out, June 2, 1863.

Re-enlisted, in 2d Mounted Rifles, and served until the close of the War.

Was in the Francis Axe works at Buffalo, N. Y., for a time, but became totally disabled for manual labor and went to the Soldiers' Home at Dayton, Ohio. Is now an inmate of the Odd Fellows' Home at Lockport, N. Y.

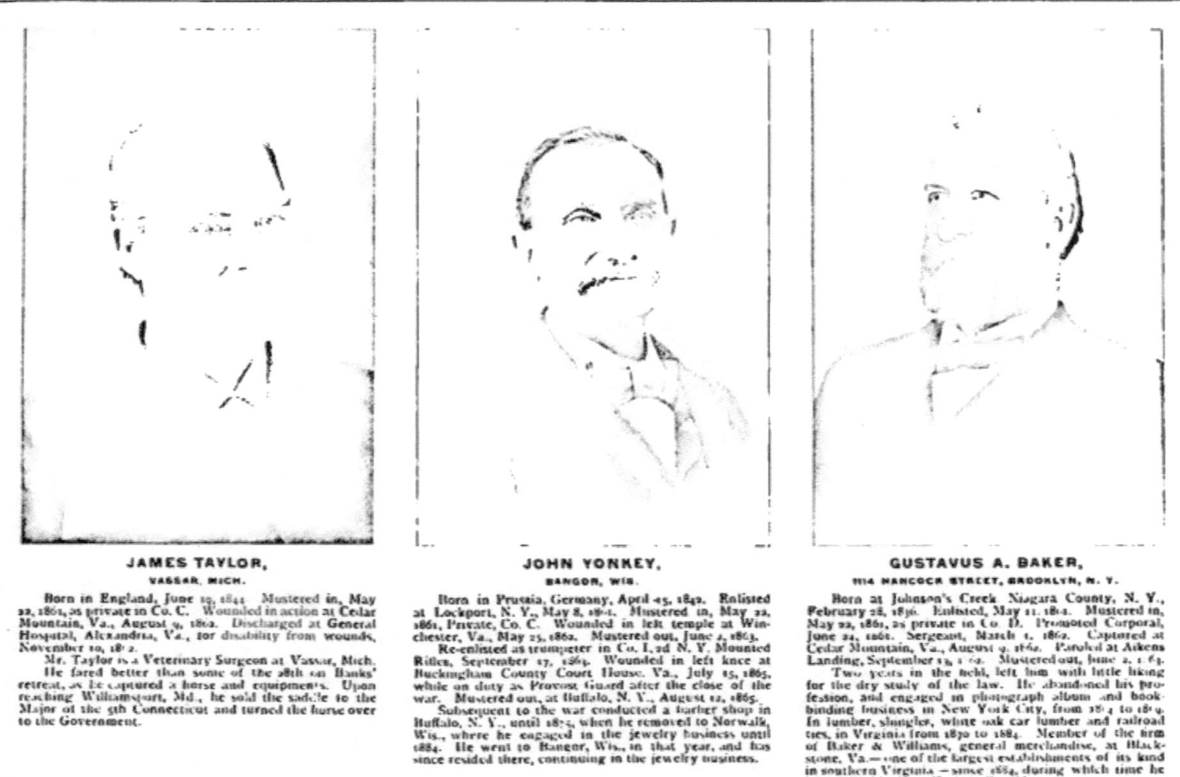

JAMES TAYLOR,

VASSAR, MICH.

Born in England, June 19, 1841. Mustered in, May 22, 1861, as private in Co. C. Wounded in action at Cedar Mountain, Va., August 9, 1862. Discharged at General Hospital, Alexandria, Va., for disability from wounds, November 10, 1862.

Mr. Taylor is a Veterinary Surgeon at Vassar, Mich.

He fared better than some of the 28th on Banks' retreat, as he captured a horse and equipments. Upon reaching Williamsport, Md., he sold the saddle to the Major of the 5th Connecticut and turned the horse over to the Government.

JOHN YONKEY,

BANGOR, WIS.

Born in Prussia, Germany, April 25, 1842. Enlisted at Lockport, N. Y., May 8, 1861. Mustered in, May 22, 1861, Private, Co. C. Wounded in left temple at Winchester, Va., May 25, 1862. Mustered out, June 2, 1863.

Re-enlisted as trumpeter in Co. I, 2d N. Y. Mounted Rifles, September 17, 1864. Wounded in left knee at Buckingham County Court House, Va., July 15, 1865, while on duty as Provost Guard after the close of the war. Mustered out, at Buffalo, N. Y., August 12, 1865.

Subsequent to the war conducted a barber shop in Buffalo, N. Y., until 1875, when he removed to Norwalk, Wis., where he engaged in the jewelry business until 1884. He went to Bangor, Wis., in that year, and has since resided there, continuing in the jewelry business.

GUSTAVUS A. BAKER,

1114 HANCOCK STREET, BROOKLYN, N. Y.

Born at Johnson's Creek, Niagara County, N. Y., February 28, 1836. Enlisted, May 11, 1861. Mustered in, May 22, 1861, as private in Co. D. Promoted Corporal, June 24, 1861. Sergeant, March 1, 1862. Captured at Cedar Mountain, Va., August 9, 1862. Paroled at Aikens Landing, September 13, 1862. Mustered out, June 2, 1863.

Two years in the field, left him with little liking for the dry study of the law. He abandoned his profession, and engaged in photograph album and book-binding business in New York City, from 1864 to 1869. In lumber, shingles, white oak car lumber and railroad ties, in Virginia from 1870 to 1884. Member of the firm of Baker & Williams, general merchandise, at Blackstone, Va.—one of the largest establishments of its kind in southern Virginia—since 1884, during which time he has resided in New York or Brooklyn.

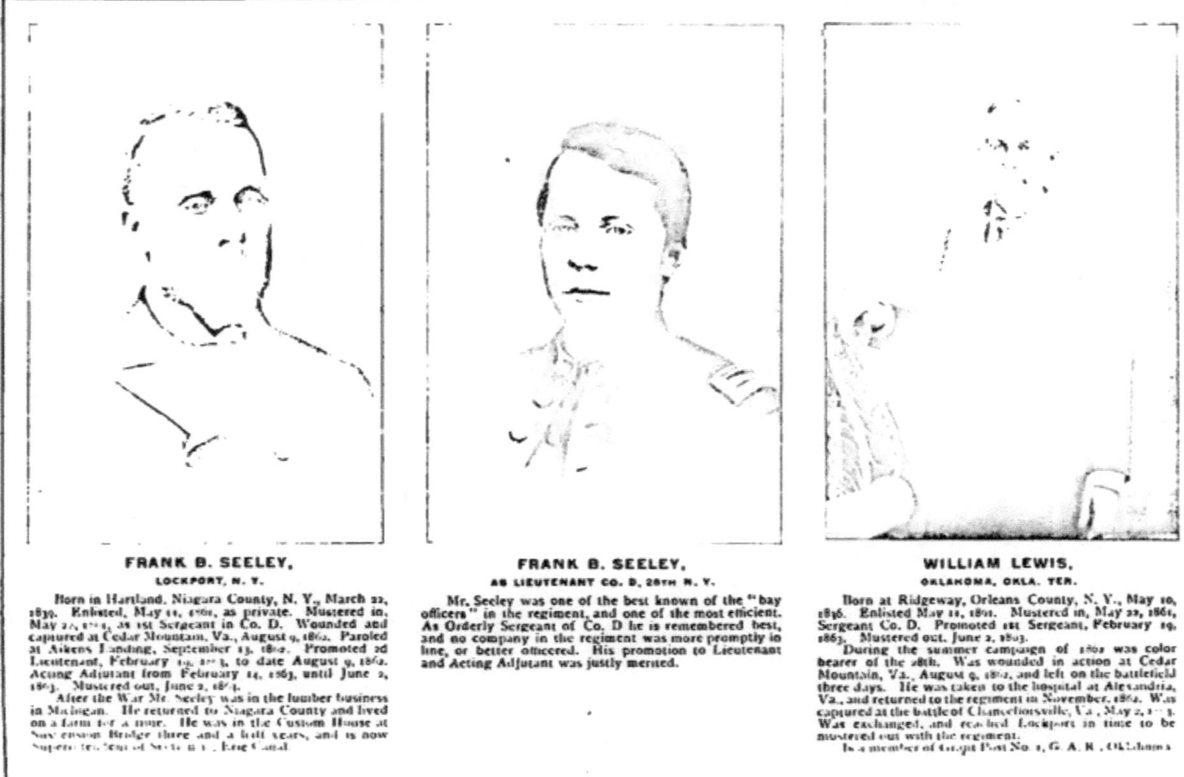

FRANK B. SEELEY,

LOCKPORT, N. Y.

Born in Hartland, Niagara County, N. Y., March 22, 1839. Enlisted, May 11, 1861, as private. Mustered in, May 22, 1861, as 1st Sergeant in Co. D. Wounded and captured at Cedar Mountain, Va., August 9, 1862. Paroled at Aikens Landing, September 13, 1862. Promoted 2d Lieutenant, February 19, 1863, to date August 9, 1862. Acting Adjutant from February 14, 1863, until June 2, 1863. Mustered out, June 2, 1863.

After the War Mr. Seeley was in the lumber business in Michigan. He returned to Niagara County and lived on a farm for a time. He was in the Custom House at Suspension Bridge three and a half years, and is now Superintendent of Section [illegible], Erie Canal.

FRANK B. SEELEY,

AS LIEUTENANT CO. D, 28TH N. Y.

Mr. Seeley was one of the best known of the "bay officers" in the regiment, and one of the most efficient. As Orderly Sergeant of Co. D he is remembered best, and no company in the regiment was more promptly in line, or better officered. His promotion to Lieutenant and Acting Adjutant was justly merited.

WILLIAM LEWIS,

OKLAHOMA, OKLA. TER.

Born at Ridgeway, Orleans County, N. Y., May 10, 1836. Enlisted May 11, 1861. Mustered in, May 22, 1861, Sergeant Co. D. Promoted 1st Sergeant, February 19, 1863. Mustered out, June 2, 1863.

During the summer campaign of 1862 was color bearer of the 28th. Was wounded in action at Cedar Mountain, Va., August 9, 1862, and left on the battlefield three days. He was taken to the hospital at Alexandria, Va., and returned to the regiment in November, 1862. Was captured at the battle of Chancellorsville, Va., May 2, 1863. Was exchanged, and reached Lockport in time to be mustered out with the regiment.

Is a member of [illegible] Post No. 1, G. A. R., Oklahoma.

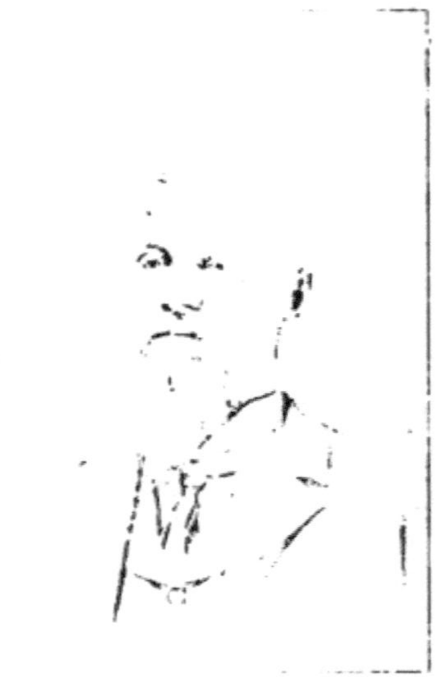

ADELBERT A. FOX,

SUNDANCE, WY.

Born in Somerset, Niagara County, N. Y., September 27, 1841. Mustered in, May 22, 1861, as Corporal in Co. D. Mustered out, June 2, 1864.

Lived near Kalamazoo, Mich., several years, in the employ of R. R. Co. as carpenter. Was a charter member of Huron Post No. [illegible], G. A. R., Department of Michigan. In 1889 removed to Wyoming, where he and his two sons have five ranches, and are engaged in farming. Has had public offices offered him, but refused, only lately accepting an appointment from the Statistician at Washington, D. C., as Township Reporter to Department of Agriculture.

BARTLEY E. SALMON,

LEAD CITY, S. D.

Born in England, June 10, 1842. Enlisted May 11, 1861. Mustered in as Private Co. D, May 22, 1861. Promoted Corporal March 4, 1862. Wounded in action at Cedar Mountain, Va., August 9, 1862. Mustered out, June 2, 1863.

Was engaged in the salt business in Saginaw, Mich., in 1863, and in the oil business in Pennsylvania from 1864 to 1869. Removed to Nebraska in 1870. Resided in Omaha and Fremont, Nebraska, until 1876, when he removed to Dakota. Has since been successfully engaged in the hardware and mining business at Lead City, S. D.

DANIEL W. AINSWORTH,

WARE, MASS.

Born in the town of Newstead, Erie County, N. Y., April 25, 1844. Mustered in, October 20, 1861, as private in Co. D. Mustered out, June 2, 1863.

Remained at home one year on account of ill health. In July, 1864, went to Illinois. In 1869 removed to Adams, Mass., and studied dentistry there and at the New York Dental College. He commenced practice in Adams, Mass. In 1871 removed to Ware, Mass., where, for more than twenty years, he has had a very successful practice in his profession. He is a prominent citizen and Grand Army comrade.

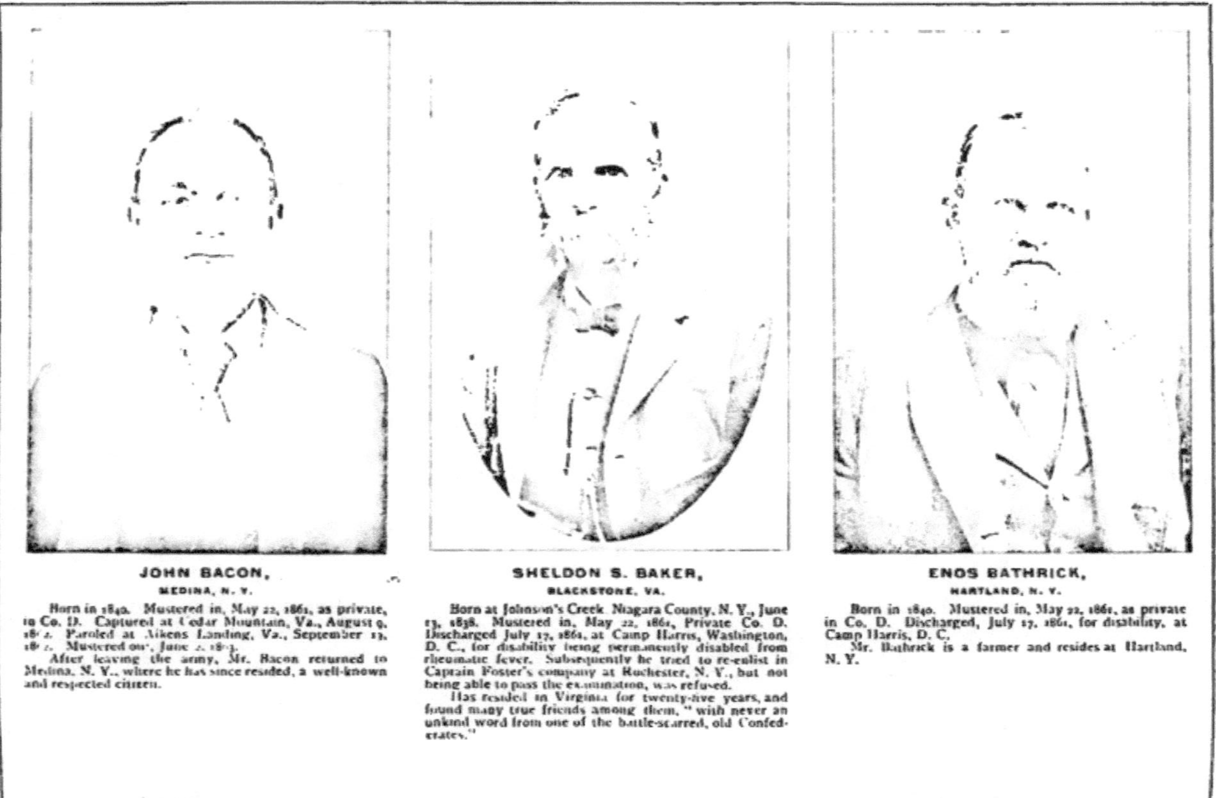

JOHN BACON,

MEDINA, N. Y.

Born in 1840. Mustered in, May 22, 1861, as private, in Co. D. Captured at Cedar Mountain, Va., August 9, 1862. Paroled at Aikens Landing, Va., September 13, 1862. Mustered out, June 2, 1863.

After leaving the army, Mr. Bacon returned to Medina, N. Y., where he has since resided, a well-known and respected citizen.

SHELDON S. BAKER,

BLACKSTONE, VA.

Born at Johnson's Creek, Niagara County, N. Y., June 13, 1838. Mustered in, May 22, 1861, Private Co. D. Discharged July 17, 1861, at Camp Harris, Washington, D. C., for disability being permanently disabled from rheumatic fever. Subsequently he tried to re-enlist in Captain Foster's company at Rochester, N. Y., but not being able to pass the examination, was refused.

Has resided in Virginia for twenty-five years, and found many true friends among them, "with never an unkind word from one of the battle-scarred, old Confederates."

ENOS BATHRICK,

HARTLAND, N. Y.

Born in 1840. Mustered in, May 22, 1861, as private in Co. D. Discharged, July 17, 1861, for disability, at Camp Harris, D. C.

Mr. Bathrick is a farmer and resides at Hartland, N. Y.

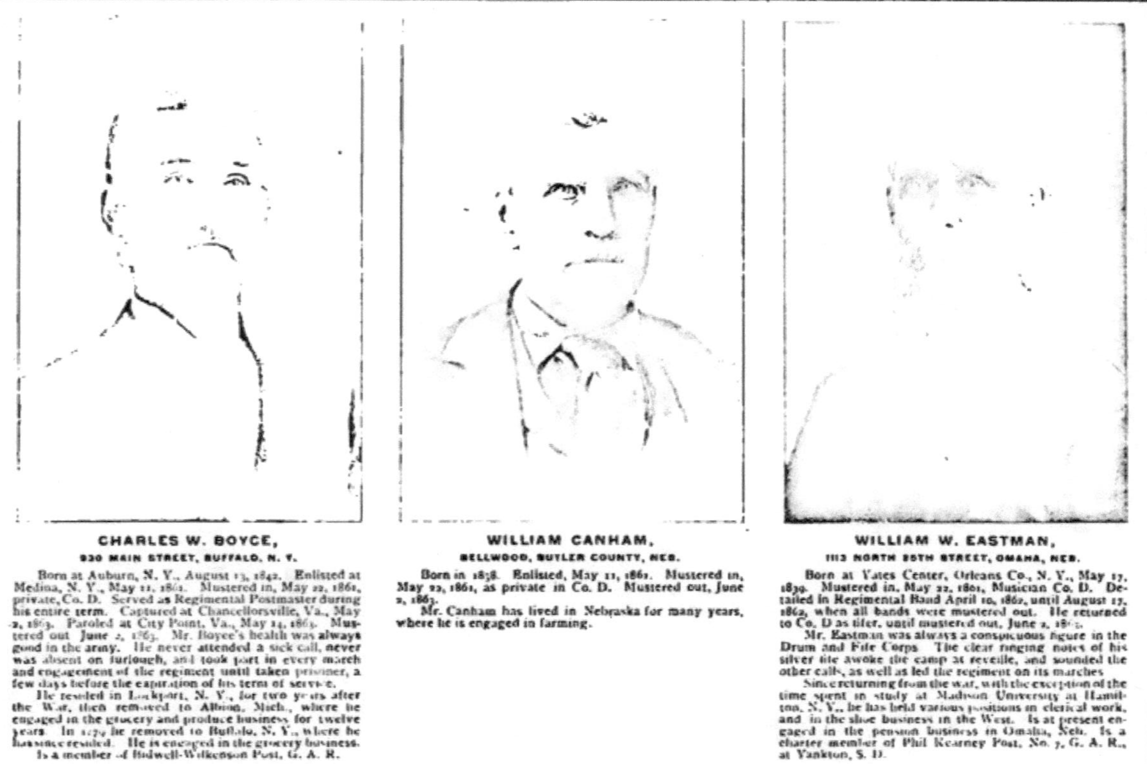

CHARLES W. BOYCE,

930 MAIN STREET, BUFFALO, N. Y.

Born at Auburn, N. Y., August 13, 1842. Enlisted at Medina, N. Y., May 11, 1861. Mustered in, May 22, 1861, private, Co. D. Served as Regimental Postmaster during his entire term. Captured at Chancellorsville, Va., May 2, 1863. Paroled at City Point, Va., May 14, 1863. Mustered out June 2, 1863. Mr. Boyce's health was always good in the army. He never attended a sick call, never was absent on furlough, and took part in every march and engagement of the regiment until taken prisoner, a few days before the expiration of his term of service.

He resided in Lockport, N. Y., for two years after the War, then removed to Albion, Mich., where he engaged in the grocery and produce business for twelve years. In 1879 he removed to Buffalo, N. Y., where he has since resided. He is engaged in the grocery business.

Is a member of Bidwell-Wilkenson Post, G. A. R.

WILLIAM CANHAM,

BELLWOOD, BUTLER COUNTY, NEB.

Born in 1838. Enlisted, May 11, 1861. Mustered in, May 22, 1861, as private in Co. D. Mustered out, June 2, 1863.

Mr. Canham has lived in Nebraska for many years, where he is engaged in farming.

WILLIAM W. EASTMAN,

1113 NORTH 25TH STREET, OMAHA, NEB.

Born at Yates Center, Orleans Co., N. Y., May 17, 1839. Mustered in, May 22, 1861, Musician Co. D. Detailed in Regimental Band April 10, 1862, until August 17, 1862, when all bands were mustered out. He returned to Co. D as fifer, until mustered out, June 2, 1863.

Mr. Eastman was always a conspicuous figure in the Drum and Fife Corps. The clear ringing notes of his silver fife awoke the camp at reveille, and sounded the other calls, as well as led the regiment on its marches.

Since returning from the war, with the exception of the time spent in study at Madison University at Hamilton, N. Y., he has held various positions in clerical work, and in the shoe business in the West. Is at present engaged in the pension business in Omaha, Neb. Is a charter member of Phil Kearney Post, No. 7, G. A. R., at Yankton, S. D.

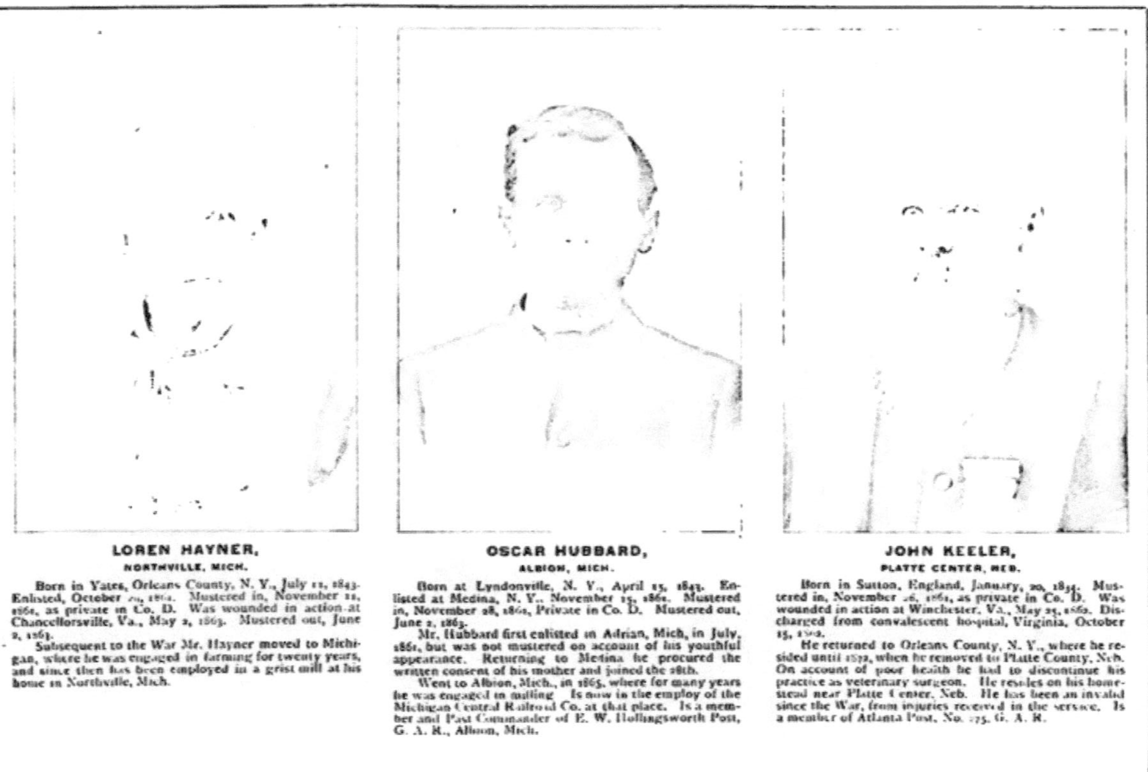

LOREN HAYNER,

NORTHVILLE, MICH.

Born in Yates, Orleans County, N. Y., July 11, 1843. Enlisted, October [illegible], 1861. Mustered in, November 11, 1861, as private in Co. D. Was wounded in action at Chancellorsville, Va., May 2, 1863. Mustered out, June 2, 1863.

Subsequent to the War Mr. Hayner moved to Michigan, where he was engaged in farming for twenty years, and since then has been employed in a grist mill at his home in Northville, Mich.

OSCAR HUBBARD,

ALBION, MICH.

Born at Lyndonville, N. Y., April 15, 1843. Enlisted at Medina, N. Y., November 15, 1861. Mustered in, November 28, 1861, Private in Co. D. Mustered out, June 2, 1863.

Mr. Hubbard first enlisted in Adrian, Mich., in July, 1861, but was not mustered on account of his youthful appearance. Returning to Medina he procured the written consent of his mother and joined the 28th.

Went to Albion, Mich., in 1865, where for many years he was engaged in milling. Is now in the employ of the Michigan Central Railroad Co. at that place. Is a member and Past Commander of E. W. Hollingsworth Post, G. A. R., Albion, Mich.

JOHN KEELER,

PLATTE CENTER, NEB.

Born in Sutton, England, January, 20, 1834. Mustered in, November 26, 1861, as private in Co. D. Was wounded in action at Winchester, Va., May 25, [illegible]. Discharged from convalescent hospital, Virginia, October 15, [illegible].

He returned to Orleans County, N. Y., where he resided until 1872, when he removed to Platte County, Neb. On account of poor health he had to discontinue his practice as veterinary surgeon. He resides on his homestead near Platte Center, Neb. He has been an invalid since the War, from injuries received in the service. Is a member of Atlanta Post, No. 275, G. A. R.

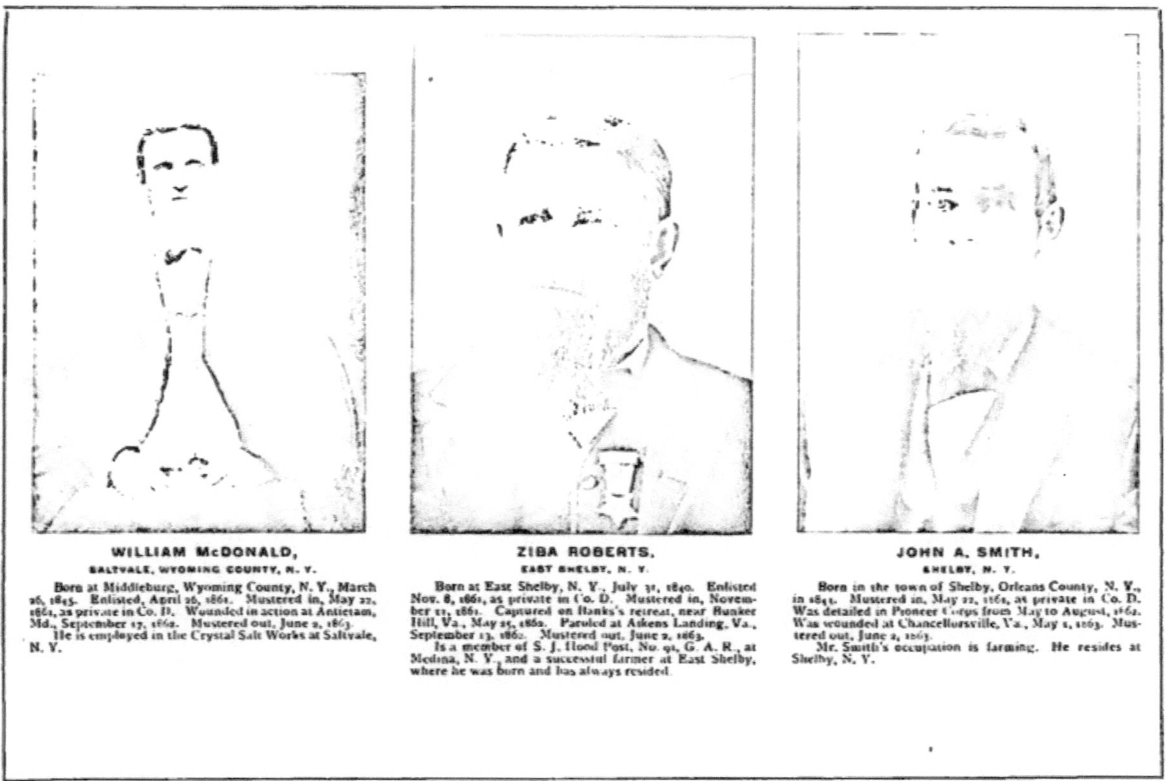

WILLIAM McDONALD,

SALTVALE, WYOMING COUNTY, N. Y.

Born at Middleburg, Wyoming County, N. Y., March 26, 1845. Enlisted, April 26, 1861. Mustered in, May 22, 1861, as private in Co. D. Wounded in action at Antietam, Md., September 17, 1862. Mustered out, June 2, 1863.

He is employed in the Crystal Salt Works at Saltvale, N. Y.

ZIBA ROBERTS,

EAST SHELBY, N. Y.

Born at East Shelby, N. Y., July 31, 1840. Enlisted Nov. 8, 1861, as private in Co. D. Mustered in, November 11, 1861. Captured on Banks's retreat, near Bunker Hill, Va., May 25, 1862. Paroled at Aikens Landing, Va., September 13, 1862. Mustered out, June 2, 1863.

Is a member of S. J. Hood Post, No. 91, G. A. R., at Medina, N. Y., and a successful farmer at East Shelby, where he was born and has always resided.

JOHN A. SMITH,

SHELBY, N. Y.

Born in the town of Shelby, Orleans County, N. Y., in 1841. Mustered in, May 22, 1861, as private in Co. D. Was detailed in Pioneer Corps from May to August, 1862. Was wounded at Chancellorsville, Va., May 1, 1863. Mustered out, June 2, 1863.

Mr. Smith's occupation is farming. He resides at Shelby, N. Y.

JOHN TUCKSON,

MONTEVIDEO, MINN.

Born in Germany, January 23, 1838. Enlisted, May 2, 1861, in Medina, N. Y. Mustered in, May 22, 1861, as private in Co. D. Wounded in action at Cedar Mountain, Va., August 9, 1862, while taking prisoners to the rear. Mustered out, June 2, 1863.

Mr. Tuckson is agent of the Minneapolis Brewing Company, at Montevideo, Minn., where he has resided for many years.

REV. WILLIAM G. WADE,

MONMOUTH, ME.

Born at Sandusky, O., May 22, 1842. Enlisted December 14, 1861. Mustered in, December 25, 1861, in Co. D. Joined the regiment at Hancock, Md. Captured on Banks' retreat near Bunker Hill, Va., May 25, 1862. Paroled at Aikens Landing, Va., September 13, 1862. Wounded in action in the right hip May 1, 1863, in the first day's battle at Chancellorsville, Va. Mustered out, June 2, 1863.

Re-enlisted as private in Battery M, 1st N. Y. Light Artillery, December 14, 1864. Joined battery at Bridgeport, Ala. Marched with Sherman to the sea. Captured at Robertsville, S. C., January 29, 1865. Mustered out, at Rochester, N. Y., August 20, 1865.

Graduated from Bangor Theological Seminary 1880. Has filled many pastorates and is now serving the fifth year with 1st Cong. Church of Monmouth, Me.

HENRY S. GULICK,

NEWARK, N. J.

Born at North Hector, N. Y., February 17, 1831. Mustered in, May 22, 1861, Sergeant Co. E. Promoted to 1st Sergeant, July 4, 1862; 2d Lieutenant, May 5, 1863. Mustered out, June 2, 1863.

Was located at Canandaigua, N. Y., after his discharge, for about five years. After which he removed to Newark, N. J., where he has since resided.

Has not been well since 1870, when he was taken with a paralytic affection, the result of a fever contracted in the service. Has also had a partial paralysis which affects his speech and his hands. He cannot write, but is able to walk. He sends his best wishes to his old comrades.

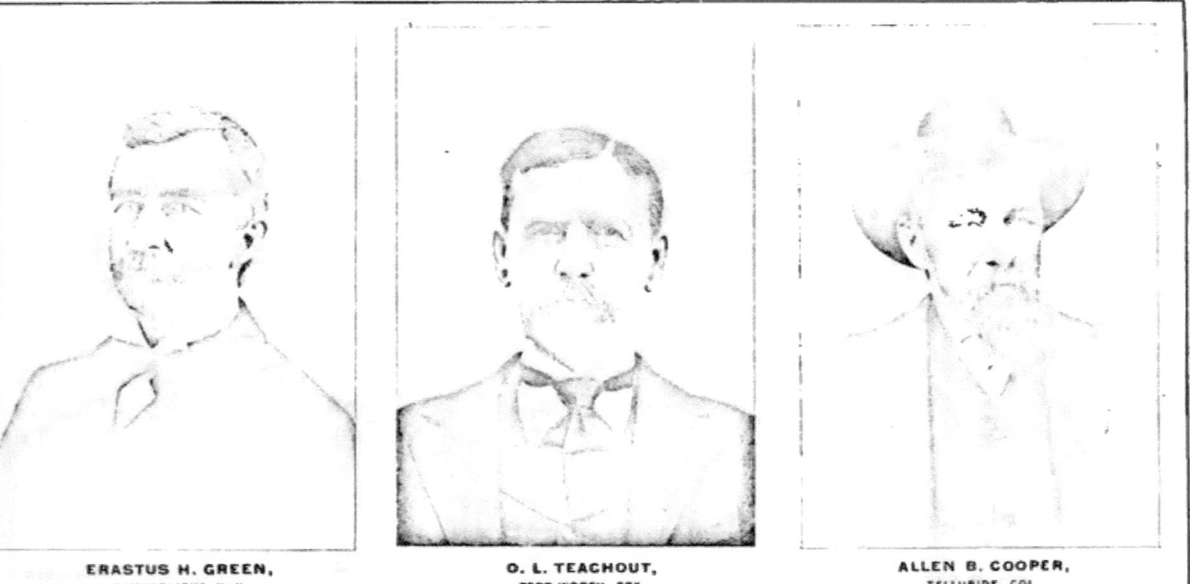

ERASTUS H. GREEN,

CANANDAIGUA, N. Y.

Born in the town of Gorham, Ontario County, N. Y., April 24, 1837. Enlisted, May 14, 1861, at Canandaigua, N. Y. Mustered in, May 22, 1861, as Sergeant in Co. E. Discharged for disability at New Market, Va., May 7, 1862.

Is now engaged in fruit culture on the East shore of Canandaigua Lake.

O. L. TEACHOUT,

FORT WORTH, TEX.

Born in Manchester, Ontario Co., N. Y., July 22, 1841. Mustered in, May 22, 1861, Private Co. E. Promoted Corporal August 26, 1861; Sergeant March 17, 1862; 1st Sergeant May 11, 1863. Was captured at Chancellorsville, Va., May 2, 1863. Paroled May 14, 1863, at City Point, Va. Mustered out, June 2, 1863.

After leaving the service lived for a number of years near Adrian, Mich., engaged in farming, and buying and selling stock. Was under-sheriff of Lenawee County, Mich., two years. Removed to Dennison, Texas, in 1879. Entered the railway mail service in 1881. November, 1888, the eleventh division railway mail service, consisting of Arkansas, Louisiana and Texas, with Indian and Oklahoma Territories, was established, and Mr. Teachout made chief clerk of the division, assistant superintendent March 2, 1889, and superintendent April 1, 1893.

ALLEN B. COOPER,

TELLURIDE, COL.

Born in Farmington, Ontario County, N. Y., September 1840. Mustered in, May 22, 1861, Private, Co. E. Mustered out, June 2, 1863.

Re-enlisted November, 1863, in Co. L, 50th N. Y. Engineers, as Private, promoted to Sergeant March, 1864. Mustered out, July, 1865.

Was employed on construction of Kansas Pacific R. R. from August, 1865, until November, 1868, in the Bridge Department on Vandalia Road, August, 1869, to July, 1870. Assistant Master of Bridges and Buildings on Atchison, Topeka & Santa Fé R. R. from 1870 to 1876. Has since been contracting and mining in Colorado, New Mexico and Arizona. Has two Quartz Mills in Telluride and one in Cochito, New Mexico.

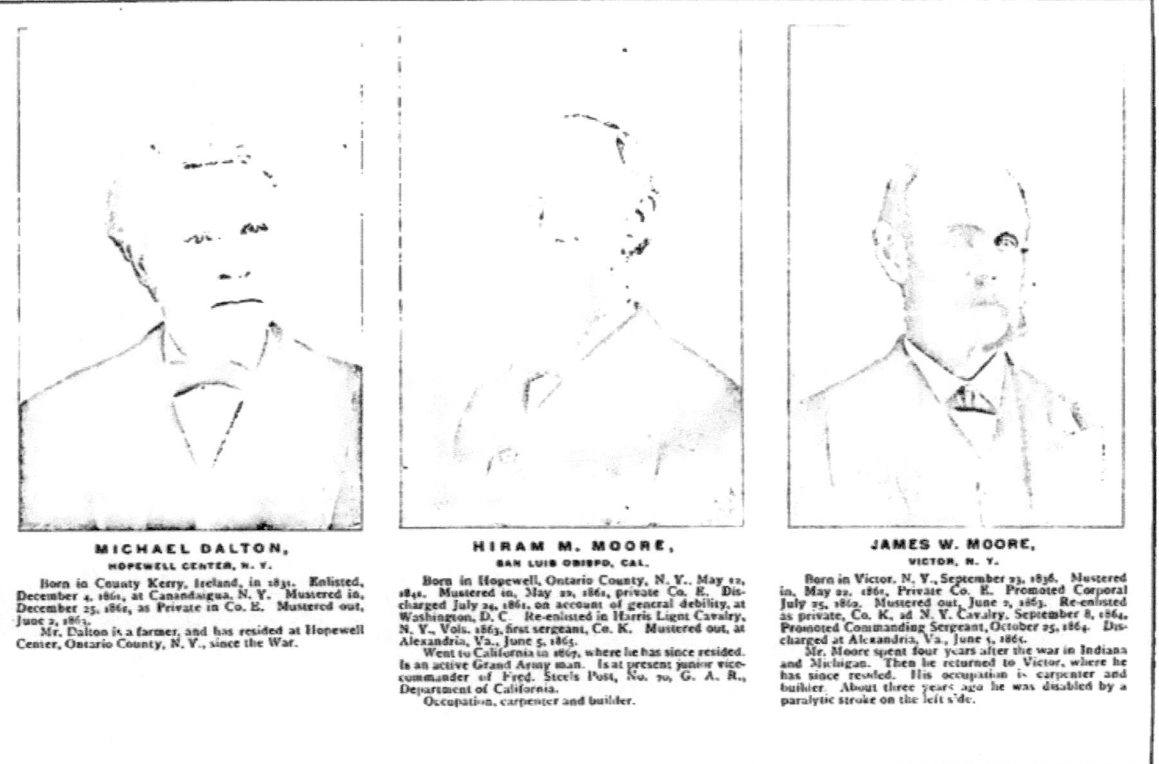

MICHAEL DALTON,

HOPEWELL CENTER, N. Y.

Born in County Kerry, Ireland, in 1831. Enlisted, December 4, 1861, at Canandaigua, N. Y. Mustered in, December 25, 1861, as Private in Co. E. Mustered out, June 2, 1863.

Mr. Dalton is a farmer, and has resided at Hopewell Center, Ontario County, N. Y., since the War.

HIRAM M. MOORE,

SAN LUIS OBISPO, CAL.

Born in Hopewell, Ontario County, N. Y., May 12, 1841. Mustered in, May 22, 1861, private Co. E. Discharged July 24, 1861, on account of general debility, at Washington, D. C. Re-enlisted in Harris Light Cavalry, N. Y., Vols. 1863, first sergeant, Co. K. Mustered out, at Alexandria, Va., June 5, 1865.

Went to California in 1867, where he has since resided. Is an active Grand Army man. Is at present junior vice-commander of Fred. Steels Post, No. 70, G. A. R., Department of California.

Occupation, carpenter and builder.

JAMES W. MOORE,

VICTOR, N. Y.

Born in Victor, N. Y., September 23, 1836. Mustered in, May 22, 1861, Private Co. E. Promoted Corporal July 25, 1862. Mustered out, June 2, 1863. Re-enlisted as private, Co. K, 2d N. Y. Cavalry, September 8, 1864. Promoted Commanding Sergeant, October 25, 1864. Discharged at Alexandria, Va., June 5, 1865.

Mr. Moore spent four years after the war in Indiana and Michigan. Then he returned to Victor, where he has since resided. His occupation is carpenter and builder. About three years ago he was disabled by a paralytic stroke on the left side.

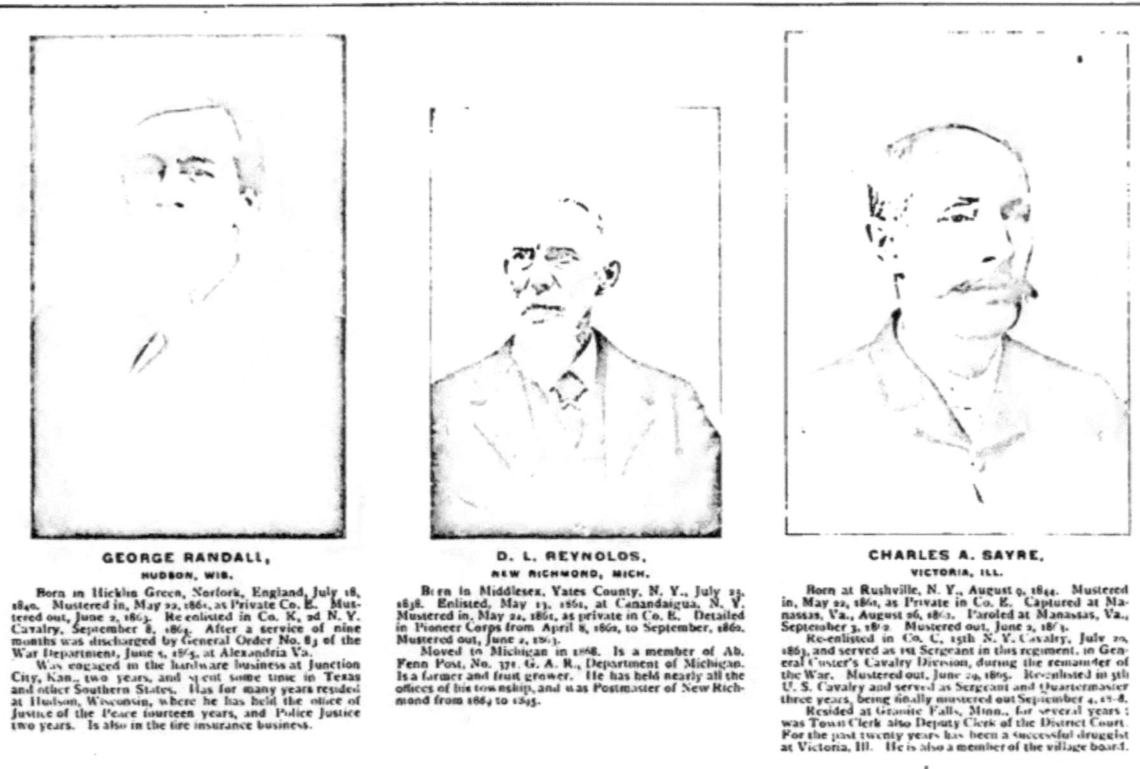

GEORGE RANDALL,

HUDSON, WIS.

Born in Hicklin Green, Norfork, England, July 18, 1840. Mustered in, May 22, 1861, as Private Co. E. Mustered out, June 2, 1863. Re enlisted in Co. K, 2d N. Y. Cavalry, September 8, 1864. After a service of nine months was discharged by General Order No. 83 of the War Department, June 5, 1865, at Alexandria Va.

Was engaged in the hardware business at Junction City, Kan., two years, and spent some time in Texas and other Southern States. Has for many years resided at Hudson, Wisconsin, where he has held the office of Justice of the Peace fourteen years, and Police Justice two years. Is also in the fire insurance business.

D. L. REYNOLDS,

NEW RICHMOND, MICH.

Born in Middlesex, Yates County, N. Y., July 23, 1838. Enlisted, May 13, 1861, at Canandaigua, N. Y. Mustered in, May 22, 1861, as private in Co. E. Detailed in Pioneer Corps from April 8, 1862, to September, 1862. Mustered out, June 2, 1863.

Moved to Michigan in 1868. Is a member of Ab. Fenn Post, No. 371, G. A. R., Department of Michigan. Is a farmer and fruit grower. He has held nearly all the offices of his township, and was Postmaster of New Richmond from 1884 to 1885.

CHARLES A. SAYRE,

VICTORIA, ILL.

Born at Rushville, N. Y., August 9, 1844. Mustered in, May 22, 1861, as Private in Co. E. Captured at Manassas, Va., August 26, 1862. Paroled at Manassas, Va., September 3, 1862. Mustered out, June 2, 1863.

Re-enlisted in Co. C, 15th N. Y. Cavalry, July 20, 1863, and served as 1st Sergeant in this regiment, in General Custer's Cavalry Division, during the remainder of the War. Mustered out, June 29, 1865. Re-enlisted in 5th U. S. Cavalry and served as Sergeant and Quartermaster three years, being finally mustered out September 4, 1868.

Resided at Granite Falls, Minn., for several years; was Town Clerk also Deputy Clerk of the District Court. For the past twenty years has been a successful druggist at Victoria, Ill. He is also a member of the village board.

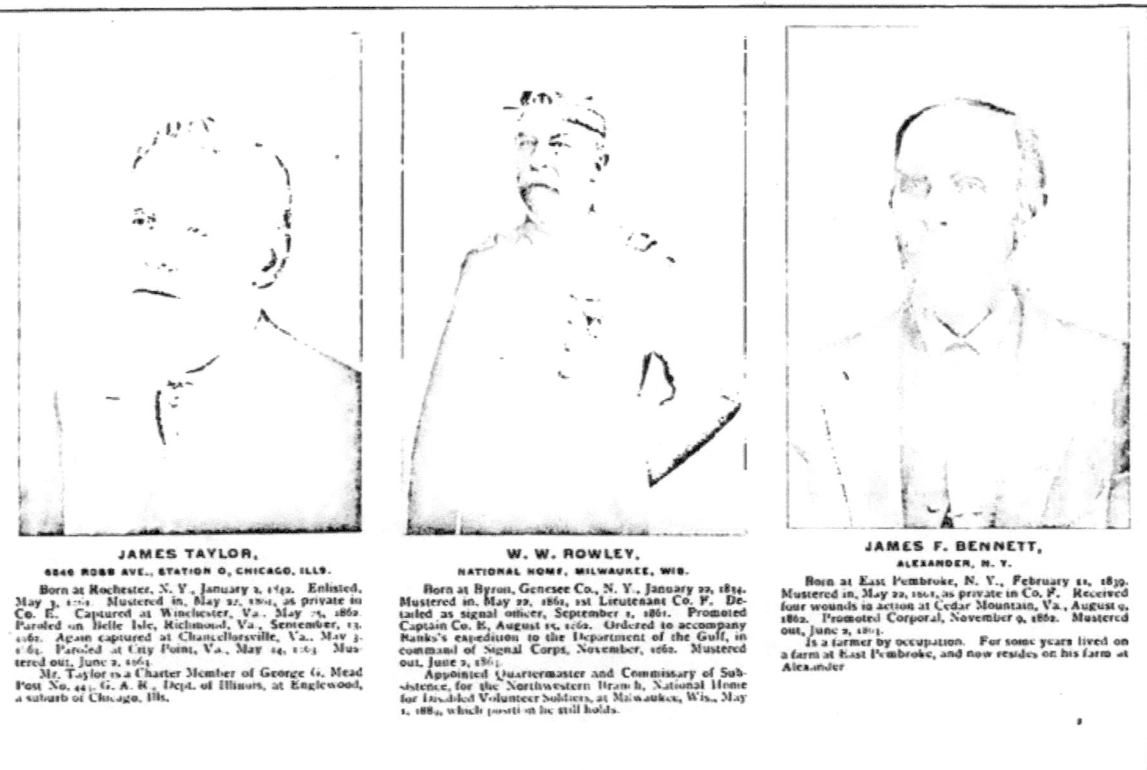

JAMES TAYLOR,

6846 ROBB AVE., STATION O, CHICAGO, ILLS.

Born at Rochester, N. Y., January 2, 1842. Enlisted, May 3, 1861. Mustered in, May 22, 1861, as private in Co. E. Captured at Winchester, Va., May 25, 1862. Paroled on Belle Isle, Richmond, Va., September, 13, 1862. Again captured at Chancellorsville, Va., May 3, 1863. Paroled at City Point, Va., May 14, 1863. Mustered out, June 2, 1863.

Mr. Taylor is a Charter Member of George G. Mead Post No. 44[illegible], G. A. R., Dept. of Illinois, at Englewood, a suburb of Chicago, Ills.

W. W. ROWLEY,

NATIONAL HOME, MILWAUKEE, WIS.

Born at Byron, Genesee Co., N. Y., January 22, 1834. Mustered in, May 22, 1861, 1st Lieutenant Co. F. Detailed as signal officer, September 1, 1861. Promoted Captain Co. B, August 15, 1862. Ordered to accompany Banks's expedition to the Department of the Gulf, in command of Signal Corps, November, 1862. Mustered out, June 2, 1863.

Appointed Quartermaster and Commissary of Subsistence, for the Northwestern Branch, National Home for Disabled Volunteer Soldiers, at Milwaukee, Wis., May 1, 1884, which position he still holds.

JAMES F. BENNETT,

ALEXANDER, N. Y.

Born at East Pembroke, N. Y., February 11, 1839. Mustered in, May 22, 1861, as private in Co. F. Received four wounds in action at Cedar Mountain, Va., August 9, 1862. Promoted Corporal, November 9, 1862. Mustered out, June 2, 1863.

Is a farmer by occupation. For some years lived on a farm at East Pembroke, and now resides on his farm at Alexander

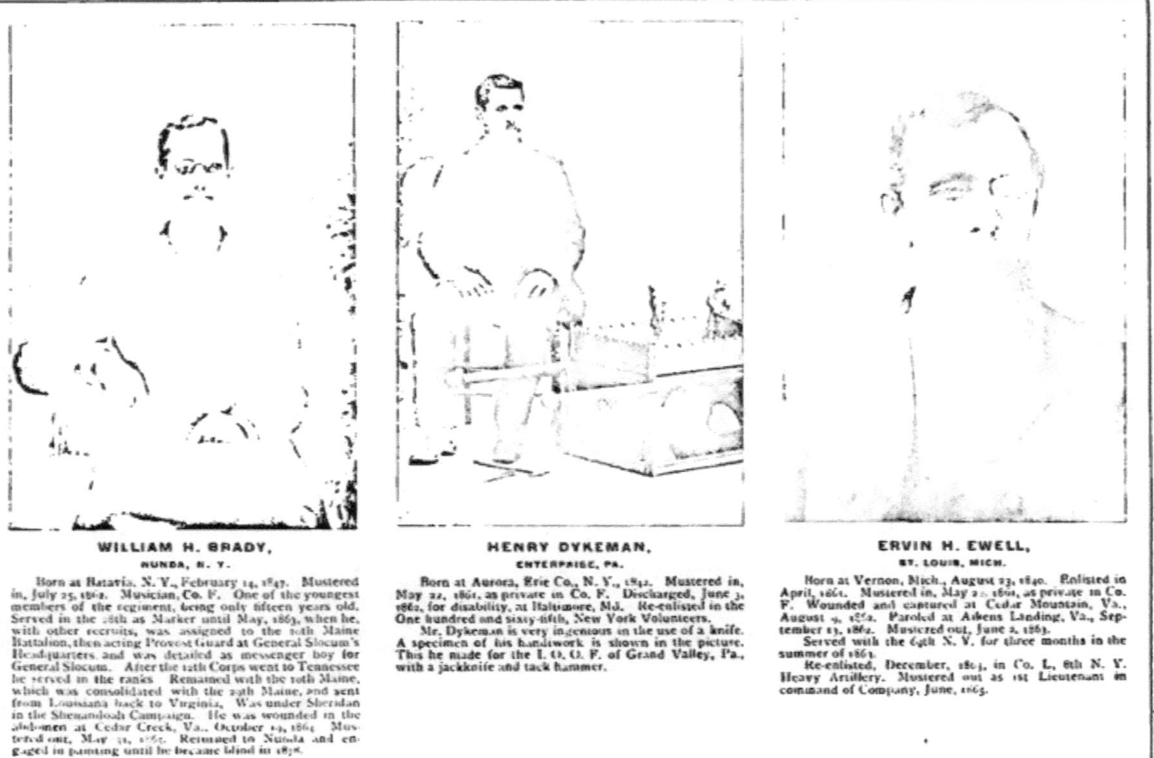

WILLIAM H. BRADY,

NUNDA, N. Y.

Born at Batavia, N. Y., February 14, 1847. Mustered in, July 25, 1862. Musician, Co. F. One of the youngest members of the regiment, being only fifteen years old. Served in the 28th as Marker until May, 1863, when he, with other recruits, was assigned to the 10th Maine Battalion, then acting Provost Guard at General Slocum's Headquarters, and was detailed as messenger boy for General Slocum. After the 12th Corps went to Tennessee he served in the ranks. Remained with the 10th Maine, which was consolidated with the 29th Maine, and sent from Louisiana back to Virginia. Was under Sheridan in the Shenandoah Campaign. He was wounded in the abdomen at Cedar Creek, Va., October 19, 1864. Mustered out, May 31, 1865. Returned to Nunda and engaged in painting until he became blind in 1878.

HENRY DYKEMAN,

ENTERPRISE, PA.

Born at Aurora, Erie Co., N. Y., 1842. Mustered in, May 22, 1861, as private in Co. F. Discharged, June 3, 1862, for disability, at Baltimore, Md. Re-enlisted in the One hundred and sixty-fifth, New York Volunteers.

Mr. Dykeman is very ingenious in the use of a knife. A specimen of his handiwork is shown in the picture. This he made for the I. O. O. F. of Grand Valley, Pa., with a jackknife and tack hammer.

ERVIN H. EWELL,

ST. LOUIS, MICH.

Born at Vernon, Mich., August 23, 1840. Enlisted in April, 1861. Mustered in, May 22, 1861, as private in Co. F. Wounded and captured at Cedar Mountain, Va., August 9, 1862. Paroled at Aikens Landing, Va., September 13, 1862. Mustered out, June 2, 1863.

Served with the 64th N. Y. for three months in the summer of 1863.

Re-enlisted, December, 1863, in Co. L, 6th N. Y. Heavy Artillery. Mustered out as 1st Lieutenant in command of Company, June, 1865.

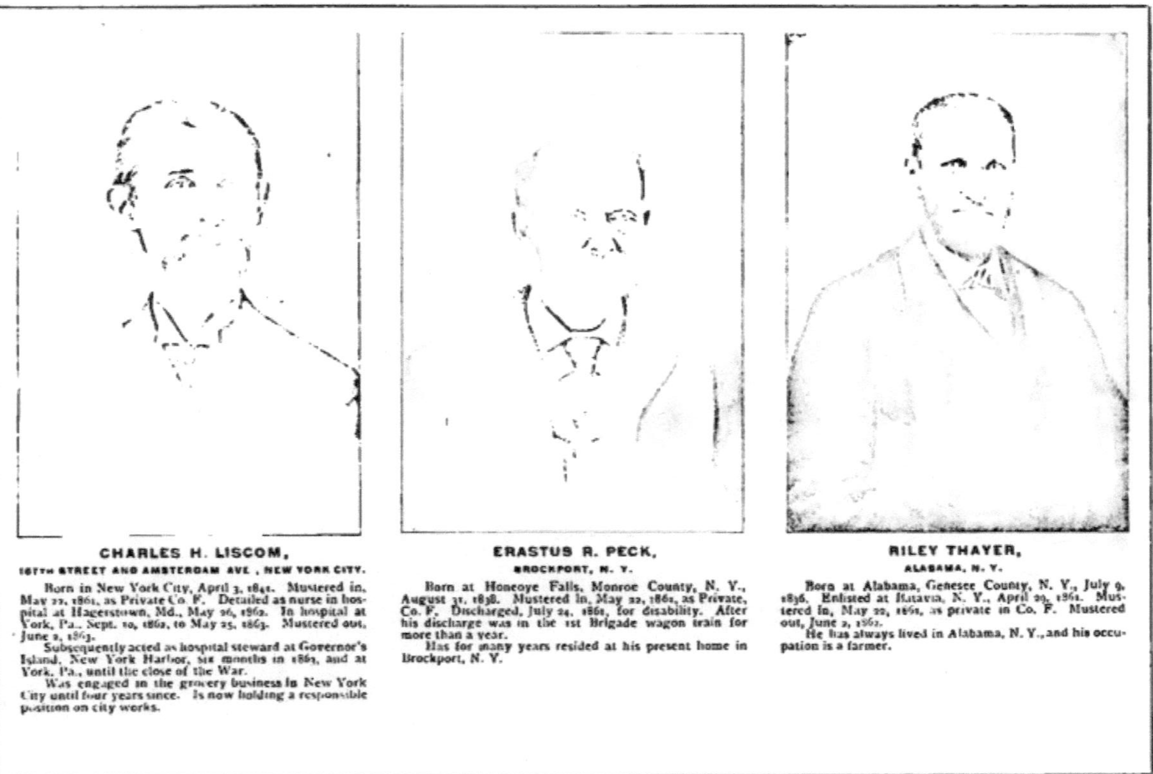

CHARLES H. LISCOM,

167TH STREET AND AMSTERDAM AVE., NEW YORK CITY.

Born in New York City, April 3, 1841. Mustered in, May 22, 1861, as Private Co. F. Detailed as nurse in hospital at Hagerstown, Md., May 26, 1862. In hospital at York, Pa., Sept. 10, 1862, to May 25, 1863. Mustered out, June 2, 1863.

Subsequently acted as hospital steward at Governor's Island, New York Harbor, six months in 1863, and at York, Pa., until the close of the War.

Was engaged in the grocery business in New York City until four years since. Is now holding a responsible position on city works.

ERASTUS R. PECK,

BROCKPORT, N. Y.

Born at Honeoye Falls, Monroe County, N. Y., August 31, 1838. Mustered in, May 22, 1861, as Private, Co. F. Discharged, July 24, 1861, for disability. After his discharge was in the 1st Brigade wagon train for more than a year.

Has for many years resided at his present home in Brockport, N. Y.

RILEY THAYER,

ALABAMA, N. Y.

Born at Alabama, Genesee County, N. Y., July 9, 1836. Enlisted at Batavia, N. Y., April 29, 1861. Mustered in, May 22, 1861, as private in Co. F. Mustered out, June 2, 1862.

He has always lived in Alabama, N. Y., and his occupation is a farmer.

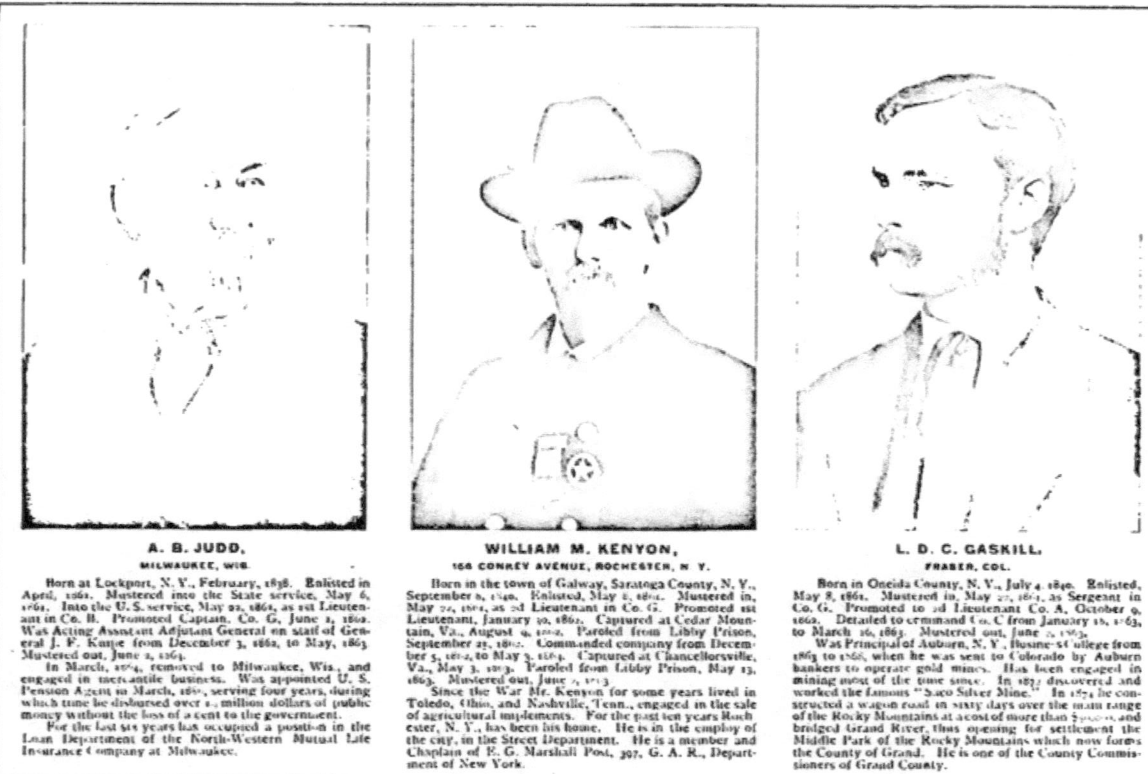

A. B. JUDD,

MILWAUKEE, WIS.

Born at Lockport, N. Y., February, 1838. Enlisted in April, 1861. Mustered into the State service, May 6, 1861. Into the U. S. service, May 22, 1861, as 1st Lieutenant in Co. B. Promoted Captain, Co. G, June 1, 1862. Was Acting Assistant Adjutant General on staff of General J. F. Knipe from December 3, 1862, to May, 1863. Mustered out, June 2, 1864.

In March, 18[illegible]4, removed to Milwaukee, Wis., and engaged in mercantile business. Was appointed U. S. Pension Agent in March, 18[illegible], serving four years, during which time he disbursed over [illegible] million dollars of public money without the loss of a cent to the government.

For the last six years has occupied a position in the Loan Department of the North-Western Mutual Life Insurance Company at Milwaukee.

WILLIAM M. KENYON,

168 CONKEY AVENUE, ROCHESTER, N. Y.

Born in the town of Galway, Saratoga County, N. Y., September [illegible], 1840. Enlisted, May [illegible], 1861. Mustered in, May 2[illegible], 1861, as 2d Lieutenant in Co. G. Promoted 1st Lieutenant, January 30, 1862. Captured at Cedar Mountain, Va., August 9, 1862. Paroled from Libby Prison, September 2[illegible], 1862. Commanded company from December 5, 1862, to May 3, 1863. Captured at Chancellorsville, Va., May 3, 1863. Paroled from Libby Prison, May 13, 1863. Mustered out, June [illegible], 1863.

Since the War Mr. Kenyon for some years lived in Toledo, Ohio, and Nashville, Tenn., engaged in the sale of agricultural implements. For the past ten years Rochester, N. Y., has been his home. He is in the employ of the city, in the Street Department. He is a member and Chaplain of E. G. Marshall Post, 397, G. A. R., Department of New York.

L. D. C. GASKILL,

FRASER, COL.

Born in Oneida County, N. Y., July 4, 1840. Enlisted, May 8, 1861. Mustered in, May 2[illegible], 1861, as Sergeant in Co. G. Promoted to 2d Lieutenant Co. A, October 9, 1862. Detailed to command Co. C from January 15, 1863, to March 26, 1863. Mustered out, June 2, 1863.

Was Principal of Auburn, N. Y., Business College from 1863 to 1866, when he was sent to Colorado by Auburn bankers to operate gold mines. Has been engaged in mining most of the time since. In 187[illegible] discovered and worked the famous "Saco Silver Mine." In 187[illegible] he constructed a wagon road in sixty days over the main range of the Rocky Mountains at a cost of more than $[illegible], and bridged Grand River, thus opening for settlement the Middle Park of the Rocky Mountains which now forms the County of Grand. He is one of the County Commissioners of Grand County.

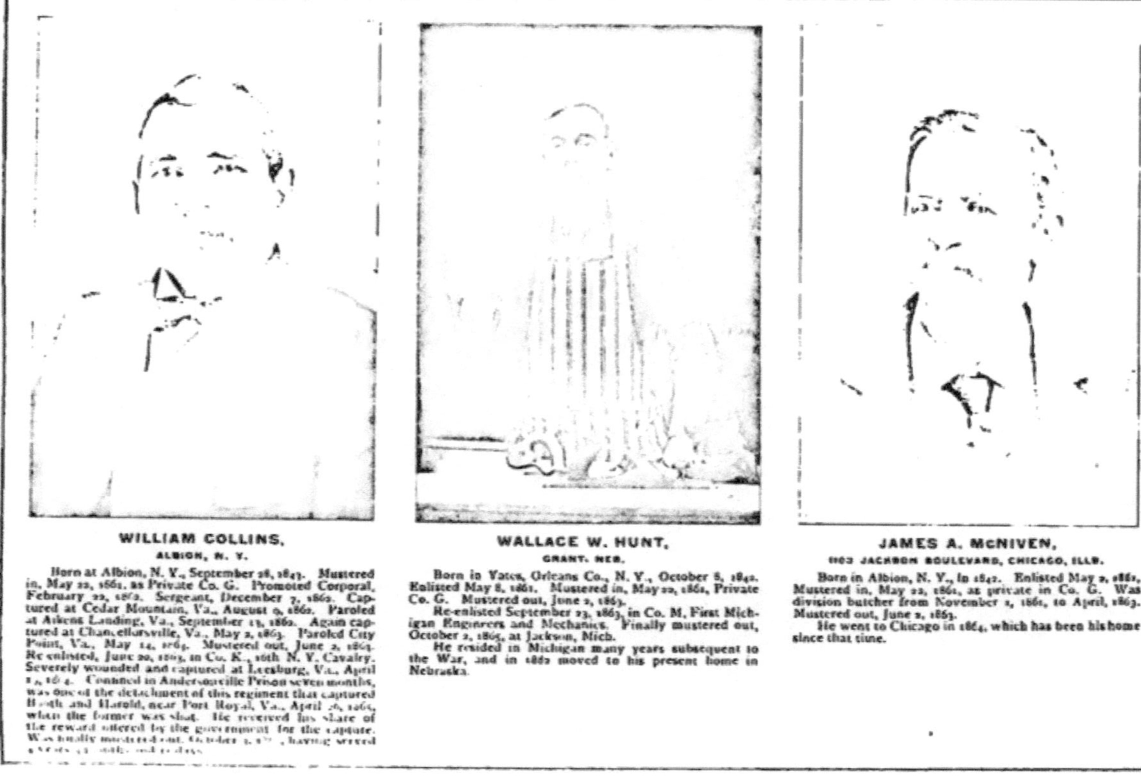

WILLIAM COLLINS,

ALBION, N. Y.

Born at Albion, N. Y., September 28, 1843. Mustered in, May 22, 1861, as Private Co. G. Promoted Corporal, February 22, 1862. Sergeant, December 7, 1862. Captured at Cedar Mountain, Va., August 9, 1862. Paroled at Aikens Landing, Va., September 13, 1862. Again captured at Chancellorsville, Va., May 2, 1863. Paroled City Point, Va., May 14, 1863. Mustered out, June 2, 1863. Re-enlisted, June 20, 1863, in Co. K., 16th N. Y. Cavalry. Severely wounded and captured at Leesburg, Va., April 1[illegible], 1864. Confined in Andersonville Prison seven months, was one of the detachment of this regiment that captured Booth and Harold, near Port Royal, Va., April 26, 1865, when the former was shot. He received his share of the reward offered by the government for the capture. Was finally mustered out, October [illegible], having served [illegible] years, [illegible] months and [illegible] days.

WALLACE W. HUNT,

GRANT, NEB.

Born in Yates, Orleans Co., N. Y., October 8, 1842. Enlisted May 8, 1861. Mustered in, May 22, 1861, Private Co. G. Mustered out, June 2, 1863.

Re-enlisted September 23, 1863, in Co. M, First Michigan Engineers and Mechanics. Finally mustered out, October 2, 1865, at Jackson, Mich.

He resided in Michigan many years subsequent to the War, and in 1882 moved to his present home in Nebraska.

JAMES A. McNIVEN,

1103 JACKSON BOULEVARD, CHICAGO, ILLS.

Born in Albion, N. Y., in 1842. Enlisted May 2, 1861, Mustered in, May 22, 1861, as private in Co. G. Was division butcher from November 1, 1861, to April, 1863. Mustered out, June 2, 1863.

He went to Chicago in 1864, which has been his home since that time.

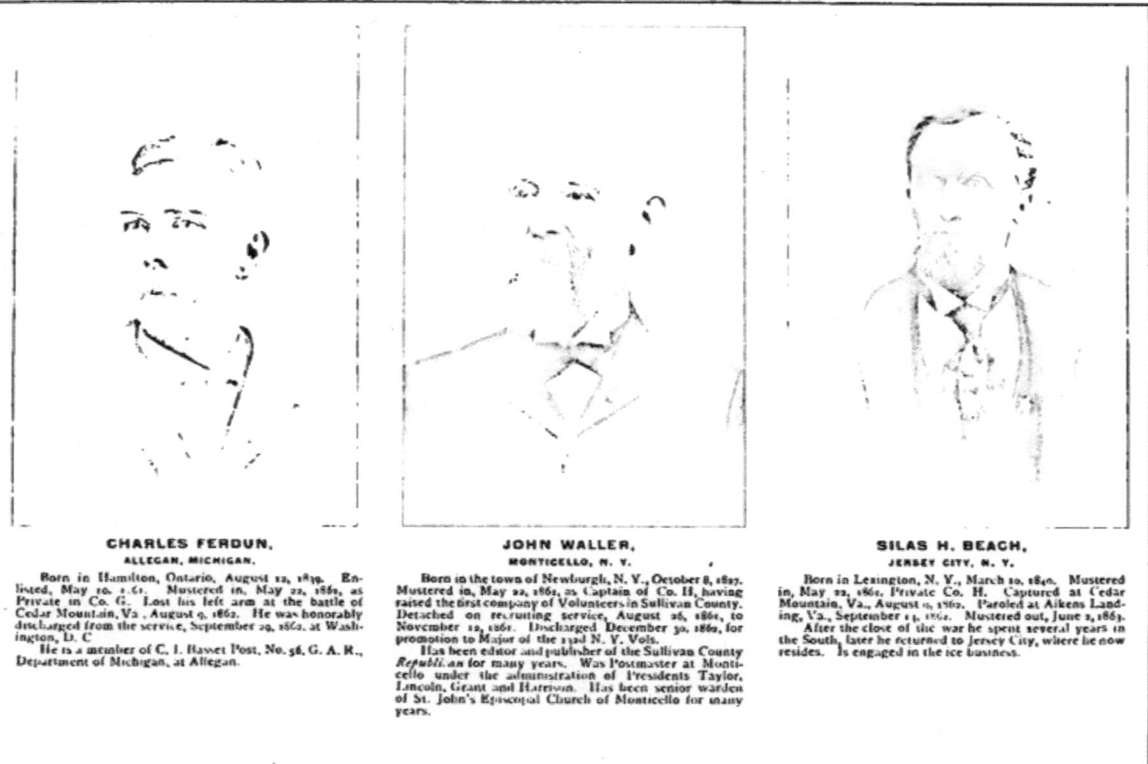

CHARLES FERDUN,

ALLEGAN, MICHIGAN.

Born in Hamilton, Ontario, August 12, 1839. Enlisted, May 10, 1861. Mustered in, May 22, 1861, as Private in Co. G. Lost his left arm at the battle of Cedar Mountain, Va., August 9, 1862. He was honorably discharged from the service, September 29, 1862, at Washington, D. C.

He is a member of C. I. Basset Post, No. 56, G. A. R., Department of Michigan, at Allegan.

JOHN WALLER,

MONTICELLO, N. Y.

Born in the town of Newburgh, N. Y., October 8, 1827. Mustered in, May 22, 1861, as Captain of Co. H, having raised the first company of Volunteers in Sullivan County. Detached on recruiting service, August 26, 1861, to November 12, 1861. Discharged December 30, 1862, for promotion to Major of the 132d N. Y. Vols.

Has been editor and publisher of the Sullivan County *Republican* for many years. Was Postmaster at Monticello under the administration of Presidents Taylor, Lincoln, Grant and Harrison. Has been senior warden of St. John's Episcopal Church of Monticello for many years.

SILAS H. BEACH,

JERSEY CITY, N. Y.

Born in Lexington, N. Y., March 10, 1840. Mustered in, May 22, 1861, Private Co. H. Captured at Cedar Mountain, Va., August 9, 1862. Paroled at Aikens Landing, Va., September 13, 1862. Mustered out, June 2, 1863.

After the close of the war he spent several years in the South, later he returned to Jersey City, where he now resides. Is engaged in the ice business.

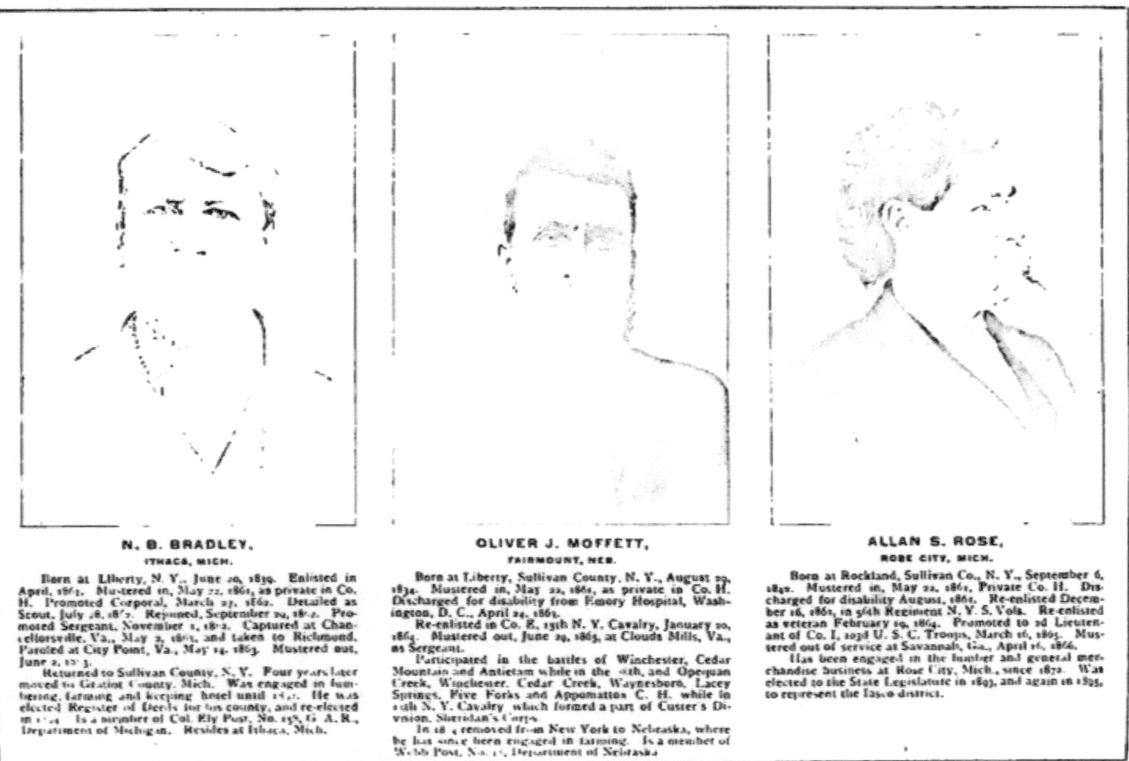

N. B. BRADLEY,

ITHACA, MICH.

Born at Liberty, N. Y., June 20, 1839. Enlisted in April, 1861. Mustered in, May 22, 1861, as private in Co. H. Promoted Corporal, March 27, 1862. Detailed as Scout, July 28, 1862. Rejoined, September 20, 1862. Promoted Sergeant, November 1, 1862. Captured at Chancellorsville, Va., May 2, 1863, and taken to Richmond. Paroled at City Point, Va., May 14, 1863. Mustered out, June 2, 1863.

Returned to Sullivan County, N. Y. Four years later moved to Gratiot County, Mich. Was engaged in lumbering, farming and keeping hotel until [illegible]. He was elected Register of Deeds for his county, and re-elected in [illegible]. Is a member of Col. Ely Post, No. 158, G. A. R., Department of Michigan. Resides at Ithaca, Mich.

OLIVER J. MOFFETT,

FAIRMOUNT, NEB.

Born at Liberty, Sullivan County, N. Y., August 29, 1834. Mustered in, May 22, 1861, as private in Co. H. Discharged for disability from Emory Hospital, Washington, D. C., April 24, 1863.

Re-enlisted in Co. E, 13th N. Y. Cavalry, January 20, 1864. Mustered out, June 29, 1865, at Clouds Mills, Va., as Sergeant.

Participated in the battles of Winchester, Cedar Mountain and Antietam while in the [illegible]th, and Opequan Creek, Winchester, Cedar Creek, Waynesboro, Lacey Springs, Five Forks and Appomattox C. H. while in 13th N. Y. Cavalry which formed a part of Custer's Division, Sheridan's Corps.

In 18[illegible] removed from New York to Nebraska, where he has since been engaged in farming. Is a member of Webb Post, No. [illegible], Department of Nebraska.

ALLAN S. ROSE,

ROSE CITY, MICH.

Born at Rockland, Sullivan Co., N. Y., September 6, 1842. Mustered in, May 22, 1861, Private Co. H. Discharged for disability August, 1861. Re-enlisted December 16, 1861, in 56th Regiment N. Y. S. Vols. Re-enlisted as veteran February 19, 1864. Promoted to 2d Lieutenant of Co. I, 103d U. S. C. Troops, March 16, 1865. Mustered out of service at Savannah, Ga., April 16, 1866.

Has been engaged in the lumber and general merchandise business at Rose City, Mich., since 1872. Was elected to the State Legislature in 1893, and again in 1895, to represent the Iosco district.

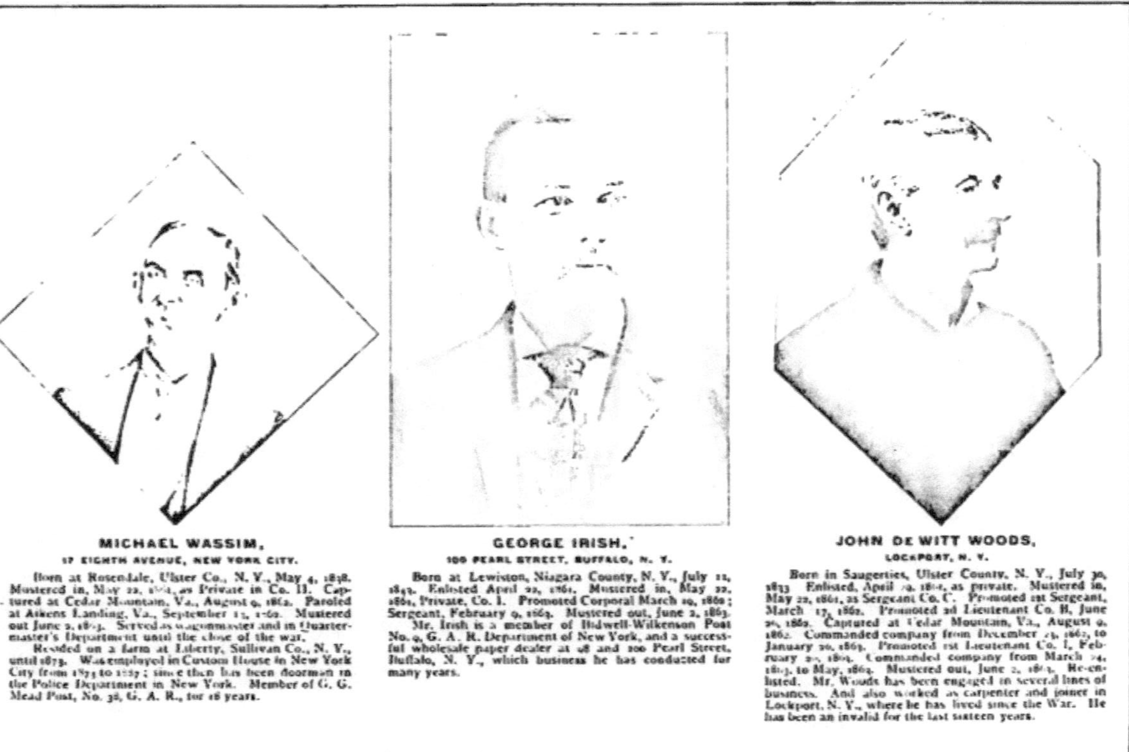

MICHAEL WASSIM,

17 EIGHTH AVENUE, NEW YORK CITY.

Born at Rosendale, Ulster Co., N. Y., May 4, 1838. Mustered in, May 22, 1861, as Private in Co. H. Captured at Cedar Mountain, Va., August 9, 1862. Paroled at Aikens Landing, Va., September 13, 1862. Mustered out June 2, 1863. Served as wagonmaster and in Quartermaster's Department until the close of the war.

Resided on a farm at Liberty, Sullivan Co., N. Y., until 1873. Was employed in Custom House in New York City from 1873 to 1887; since then has been doorman in the Police Department in New York. Member of G. G. Mead Post, No. 38, G. A. R., for 18 years.

GEORGE IRISH,

100 PEARL STREET, BUFFALO, N. Y.

Born at Lewiston, Niagara County, N. Y., July 11, 1843. Enlisted April 22, 1861. Mustered in, May 22, 1861, Private, Co. I. Promoted Corporal March 10, 1862; Sergeant, February 9, 1863. Mustered out, June 2, 1863.

Mr. Irish is a member of Bidwell-Wilkenson Post No. 9, G. A. R. Department of New York, and a successful wholesale paper dealer at 98 and 100 Pearl Street, Buffalo, N. Y., which business he has conducted for many years.

JOHN DE WITT WOODS,

LOCKPORT, N. Y.

Born in Saugerties, Ulster County, N. Y., July 30, 1833. Enlisted, April 20, 1861, as private. Mustered in, May 22, 1861, as Sergeant Co. C. Promoted 1st Sergeant, March 17, 1862. Promoted 2d Lieutenant Co. H, June 20, 1862. Captured at Cedar Mountain, Va., August 9, 1862. Commanded company from December 23, 1862, to January 20, 1863. Promoted 1st Lieutenant Co. I, February 20, 1863. Commanded company from March 24, 1863, to May, 1863. Mustered out, June 2, 1863. Re-enlisted. Mr. Woods has been engaged in several lines of business. And also worked as carpenter and joiner in Lockport, N. Y., where he has lived since the War. He has been an invalid for the last sixteen years.

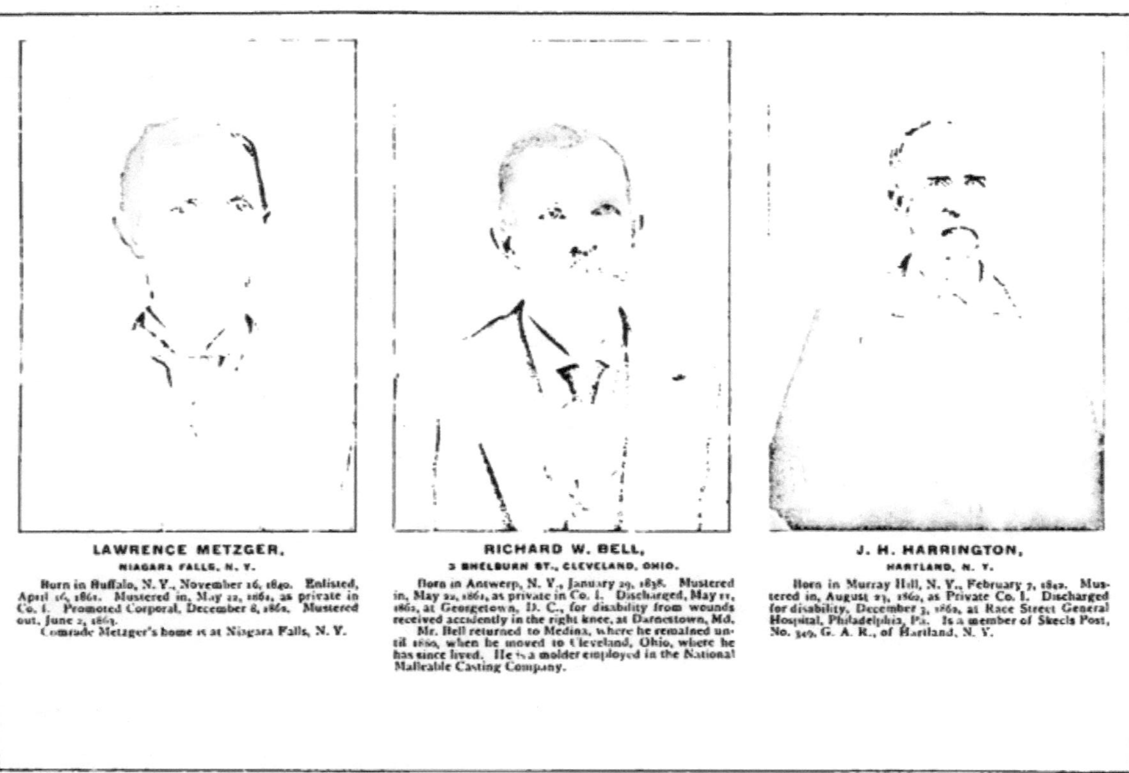

LAWRENCE METZGER,

NIAGARA FALLS, N. Y.

Born in Buffalo, N. Y., November 16, 1840. Enlisted, April 16, 1861. Mustered in, May 22, 1861, as private in Co. I. Promoted Corporal, December 8, 1862. Mustered out, June 2, 1863.

Comrade Metzger's home is at Niagara Falls, N. Y.

RICHARD W. BELL,

3 SHELBURN ST., CLEVELAND, OHIO.

Born in Antwerp, N. Y., January 29, 1838. Mustered in, May 22, 1861, as private in Co. I. Discharged, May 11, 1862, at Georgetown, D. C., for disability from wounds received accidently in the right knee, at Darnestown, Md.

Mr. Bell returned to Medina, where he remained until 1880, when he moved to Cleveland, Ohio, where he has since lived. He is a molder employed in the National Malleable Casting Company.

J. H. HARRINGTON,

HARTLAND, N. Y.

Born in Murray Hill, N. Y., February 7, 1842. Mustered in, August 23, 1862, as Private Co. I. Discharged for disability, December 3, 1862, at Race Street General Hospital, Philadelphia, Pa. Is a member of Skeels Post, No. 349, G. A. R., of Hartland, N. Y.

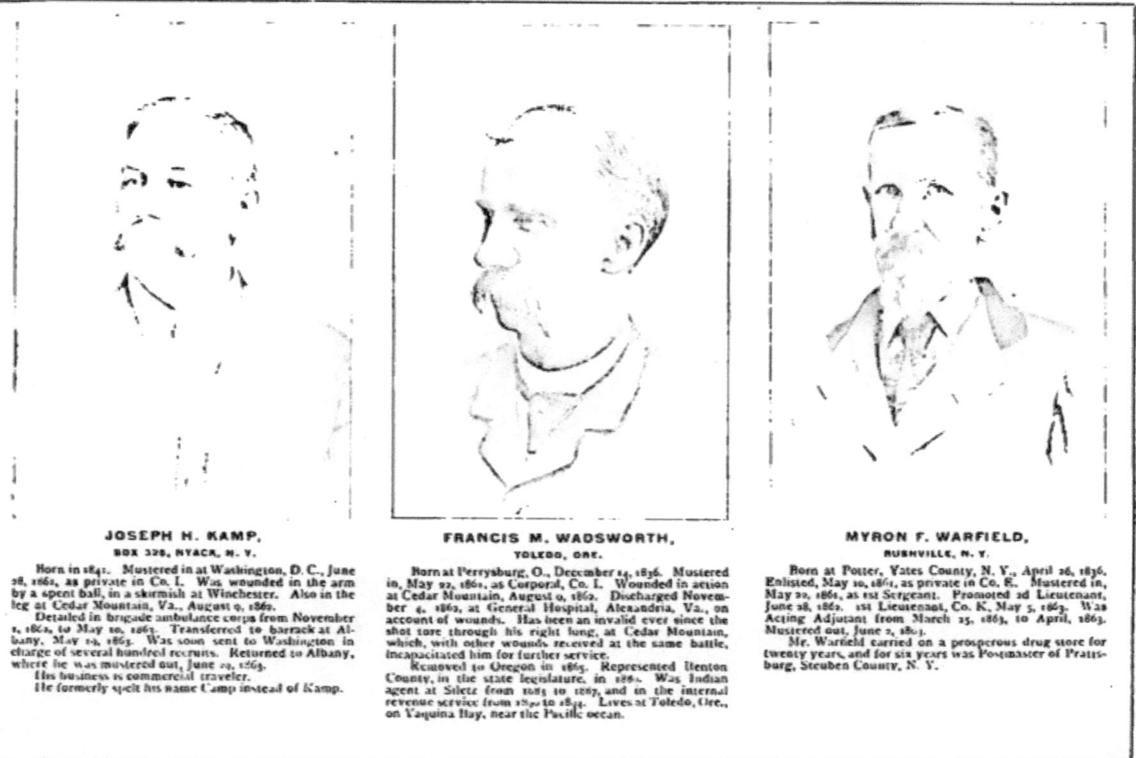

JOSEPH H. KAMP,

BOX 328, NYACK, N. Y.

Born in 1841. Mustered in at Washington, D. C., June 28, 1862, as private in Co. I. Was wounded in the arm by a spent ball, in a skirmish at Winchester. Also in the leg at Cedar Mountain, Va., August 9, 1862.

Detailed in brigade ambulance corps from November 1, 1862, to May 10, 1863. Transferred to barrack at Albany, May 14, 1863. Was soon sent to Washington in charge of several hundred recruits. Returned to Albany, where he was mustered out, June 29, 1863.

His business is commercial traveler.

He formerly spelt his name Camp instead of Kamp.

FRANCIS M. WADSWORTH,

TOLEDO, ORE.

Born at Perrysburg, O., December 14, 1836. Mustered in, May 22, 1861, as Corporal, Co. I. Wounded in action at Cedar Mountain, August 9, 1862. Discharged November 4, 1862, at General Hospital, Alexandria, Va., on account of wounds. Has been an invalid ever since the shot tore through his right lung, at Cedar Mountain, which, with other wounds received at the same battle, incapacitated him for further service.

Removed to Oregon in 1865. Represented Benton County, in the state legislature, in 1881. Was Indian agent at Siletz from 1885 to 1887, and in the internal revenue service from 1890 to 1894. Lives at Toledo, Ore., on Yaquina Bay, near the Pacific ocean.

MYRON F. WARFIELD,

RUSHVILLE, N. Y.

Born at Potter, Yates County, N. Y., April 26, 1836. Enlisted, May 10, 1861, as private in Co. E. Mustered in, May 22, 1861, as 1st Sergeant. Promoted 2d Lieutenant, June 28, 1862. 1st Lieutenant, Co. K, May 5, 1863. Was Acting Adjutant from March 25, 1863, to April, 1863. Mustered out, June 2, 1863.

Mr. Warfield carried on a prosperous drug store for twenty years, and for six years was Postmaster of Prattsburg, Steuben County, N. Y.

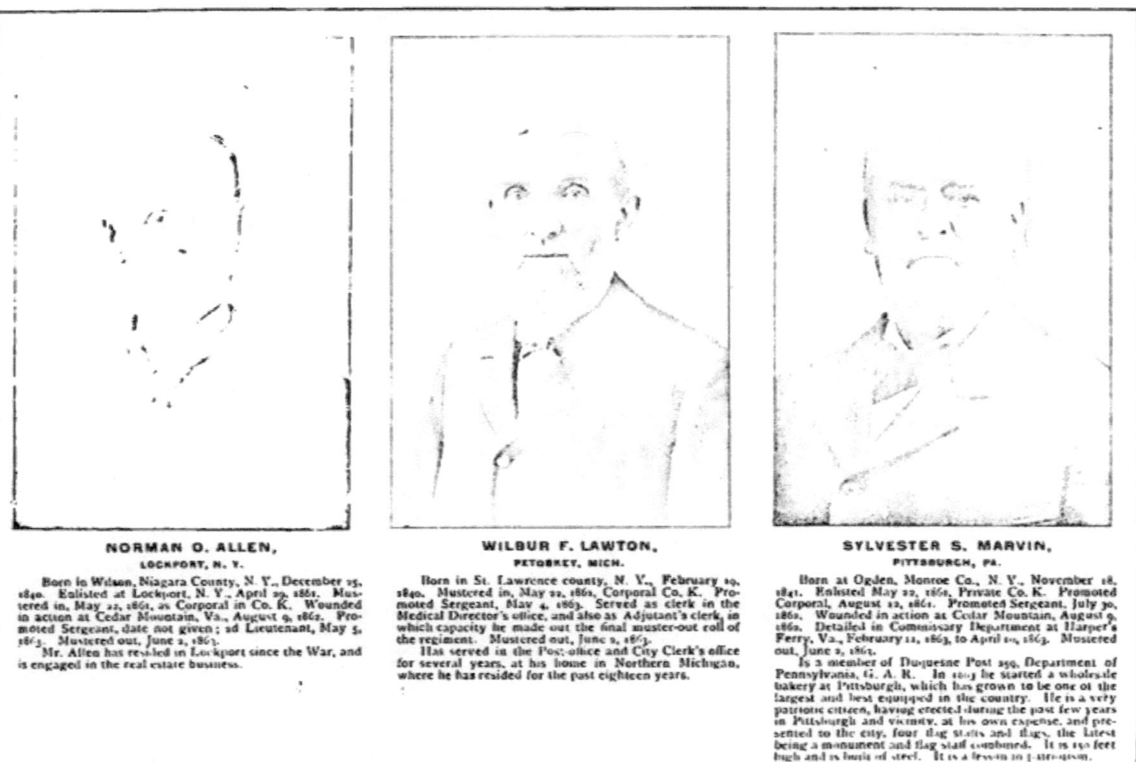

NORMAN O. ALLEN,

LOCKPORT, N. Y.

Born in Wilson, Niagara County, N. Y., December 25, 1840. Enlisted at Lockport, N. Y., April 29, 1861. Mustered in, May 22, 1861, as Corporal in Co. K. Wounded in action at Cedar Mountain, Va., August 9, 1862. Promoted Sergeant, date not given; 2d Lieutenant, May 5, 1863. Mustered out, June 2, 1863.

Mr. Allen has resided in Lockport since the War, and is engaged in the real estate business.

WILBUR F. LAWTON,

PETOSKEY, MICH.

Born in St. Lawrence county, N. Y., February 19, 1840. Mustered in, May 22, 1861, Corporal Co. K. Promoted Sergeant, May 4, 1863. Served as clerk in the Medical Director's office, and also as Adjutant's clerk, in which capacity he made out the final muster-out roll of the regiment. Mustered out, June 2, 1863.

Has served in the Post-office and City Clerk's office for several years, at his home in Northern Michigan, where he has resided for the past eighteen years.

SYLVESTER S. MARVIN,

PITTSBURGH, PA.

Born at Ogden, Monroe Co., N. Y., November 18, 1841. Enlisted May 22, 1861, Private Co. K. Promoted Corporal, August 12, 1861. Promoted Sergeant, July 30, 1862. Wounded in action at Cedar Mountain, August 9, 1862. Detailed in Commissary Department at Harper's Ferry, Va., February 11, 1863, to April [illegible], 1863. Mustered out, June 2, 1863.

Is a member of Duquesne Post 259, Department of Pennsylvania, G. A. R. In [illegible] he started a wholesale bakery at Pittsburgh, which has grown to be one of the largest and best equipped in the country. He is a very patriotic citizen, having erected during the past few years in Pittsburgh and vicinity, at his own expense, and presented to the city, four flag staffs and flags, the latest being a monument and flag staff combined. It is 150 feet high and is built of steel. It is a lesson in patriotism.

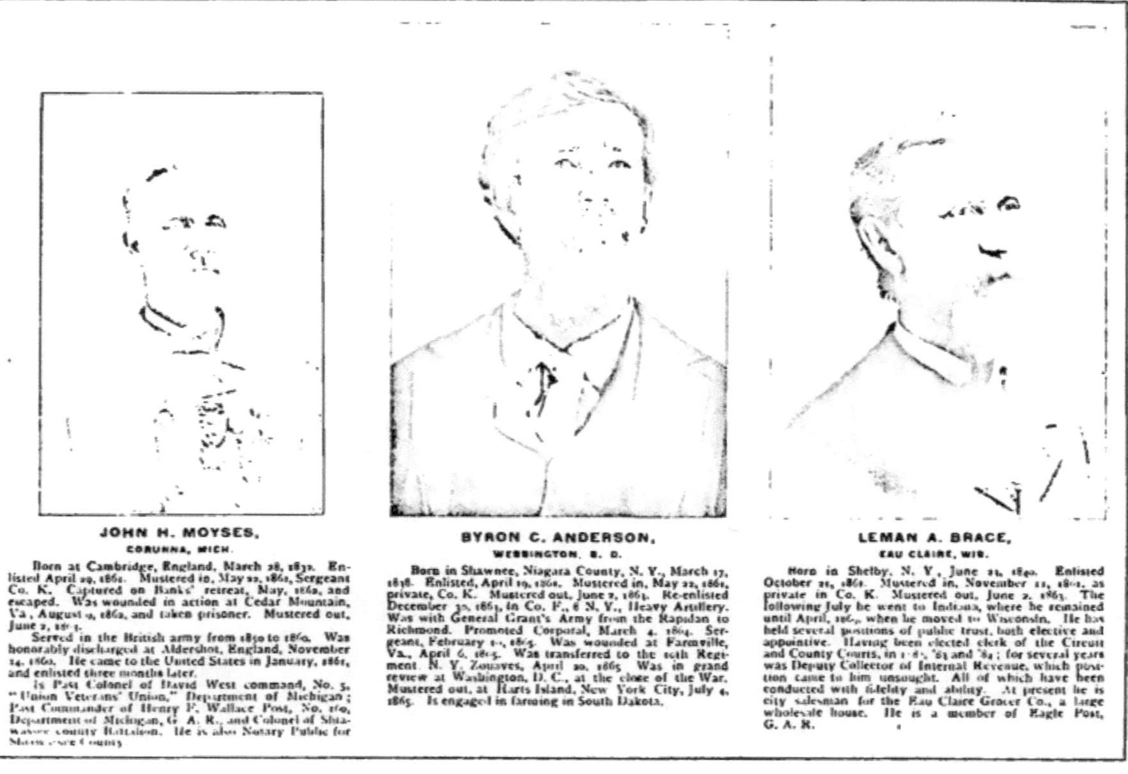

JOHN H. MOYSES,

CORUNNA, MICH.

Born at Cambridge, England, March 28, 1832. Enlisted April 29, 1861. Mustered in, May 22, 1861, Sergeant Co. K. Captured on Banks' retreat, May, 1862, and escaped. Was wounded in action at Cedar Mountain, Va., August 9, 1862, and taken prisoner. Mustered out, June 2, 1864.

Served in the British army from 1850 to 1860. Was honorably discharged at Aldershot, England, November 24, 1860. He came to the United States in January, 1861, and enlisted three months later.

Is Past Colonel of David West command, No. 5, "Union Veterans' Union," Department of Michigan; Past Commander of Henry F. Wallace Post, No. 160, Department of Michigan, G. A. R., and Colonel of Shiawassee county Battalion. He is also Notary Public for Shiawassee County.

BYRON C. ANDERSON,

WEBBINGTON, S. D.

Born in Shawnee, Niagara County, N. Y., March 17, 1838. Enlisted, April 19, 1861. Mustered in, May 22, 1861, private, Co. K. Mustered out, June 2, 1863. Re-enlisted December 30, 1863, in Co. F., 6 N. Y., Heavy Artillery. Was with General Grant's Army from the Rapidan to Richmond. Promoted Corporal, March 4, 1864. Sergeant, February 1-, 1865. Was wounded at Farmville, Va., April 6, 1865. Was transferred to the 10th Regiment N. Y. Zouaves, April 20, 1865. Was in grand review at Washington, D. C., at the close of the War. Mustered out, at Harts Island, New York City, July 4, 1865. Is engaged in farming in South Dakota.

LEMAN A. BRACE,

EAU CLAIRE, WIS.

Born in Shelby, N. Y., June 24, 1840. Enlisted October 21, 1861. Mustered in, November 11, 1861, as private in Co. K. Mustered out, June 2, 1863. The following July he went to Indiana, where he remained until April, 1867, when he moved to Wisconsin. He has held several positions of public trust, both elective and appointive. Having been elected clerk of the Circuit and County Courts, in 1882, '83 and '84; for several years was Deputy Collector of Internal Revenue, which position came to him unsought. All of which have been conducted with fidelity and ability. At present he is city salesman for the Eau Claire Grocer Co., a large wholesale house. He is a member of Eagle Post, G. A. R.

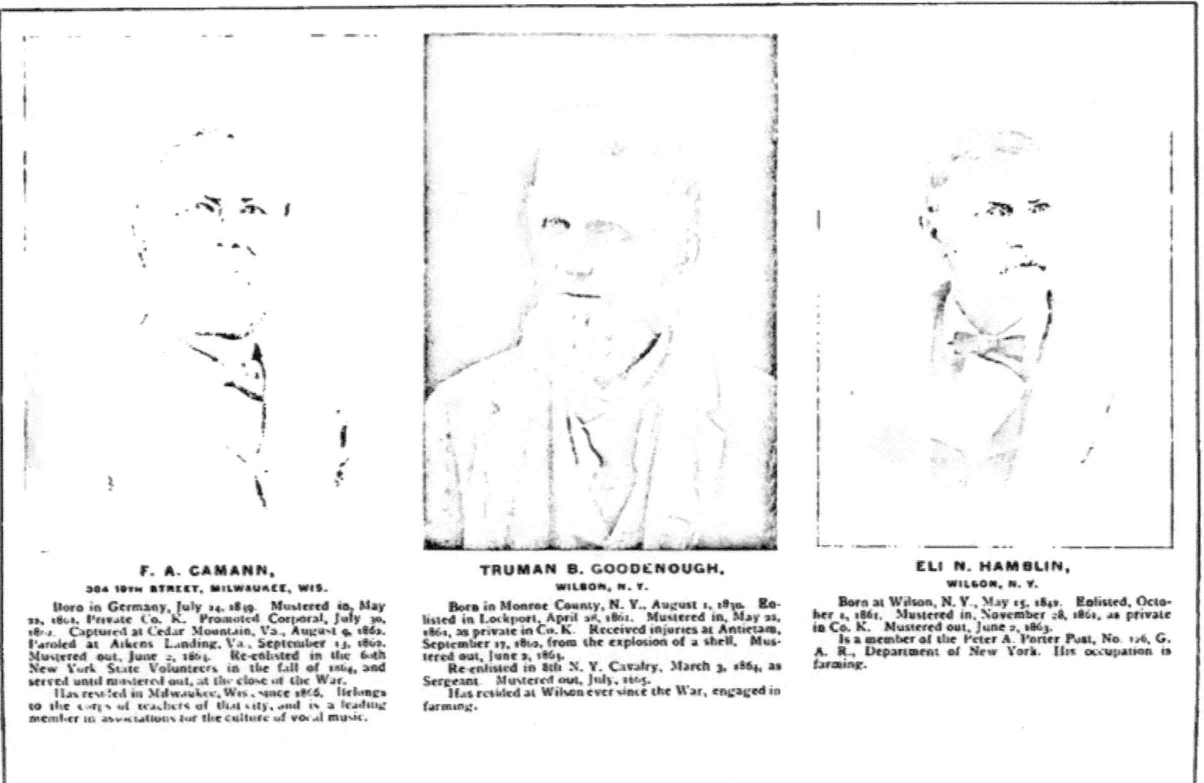

F. A. CAMANN,

304 10TH STREET, MILWAUKEE, WIS.

Born in Germany, July 24, 1839. Mustered in, May 22, 1861, Private Co. K. Promoted Corporal, July 30, 1862. Captured at Cedar Mountain, Va., August 9, 1862. Paroled at Aikens Landing, Va., September 13, 1862. Mustered out, June 2, 1863. Re-enlisted in the 6th New York State Volunteers in the fall of 1864, and served until mustered out, at the close of the War.

Has resided in Milwaukee, Wis., since 1866. Belongs to the corps of teachers of that city, and is a leading member in associations for the culture of vocal music.

TRUMAN B. GOODENOUGH,

WILSON, N. Y.

Born in Monroe County, N. Y., August 1, 1830. Enlisted in Lockport, April 28, 1861. Mustered in, May 22, 1861, as private in Co. K. Received injuries at Antietam, September 17, 1862, from the explosion of a shell. Mustered out, June 2, 1863.

Re-enlisted in 8th N. Y. Cavalry, March 3, 1864, as Sergeant. Mustered out, July, 1865.

Has resided at Wilson ever since the War, engaged in farming.

ELI N. HAMBLIN,

WILSON, N. Y.

Born at Wilson, N. Y., May 15, 1842. Enlisted, October 1, 1861. Mustered in, November 28, 1861, as private in Co. K. Mustered out, June 2, 1863.

Is a member of the Peter A. Porter Post, No. 126, G. A. R., Department of New York. His occupation is farming.

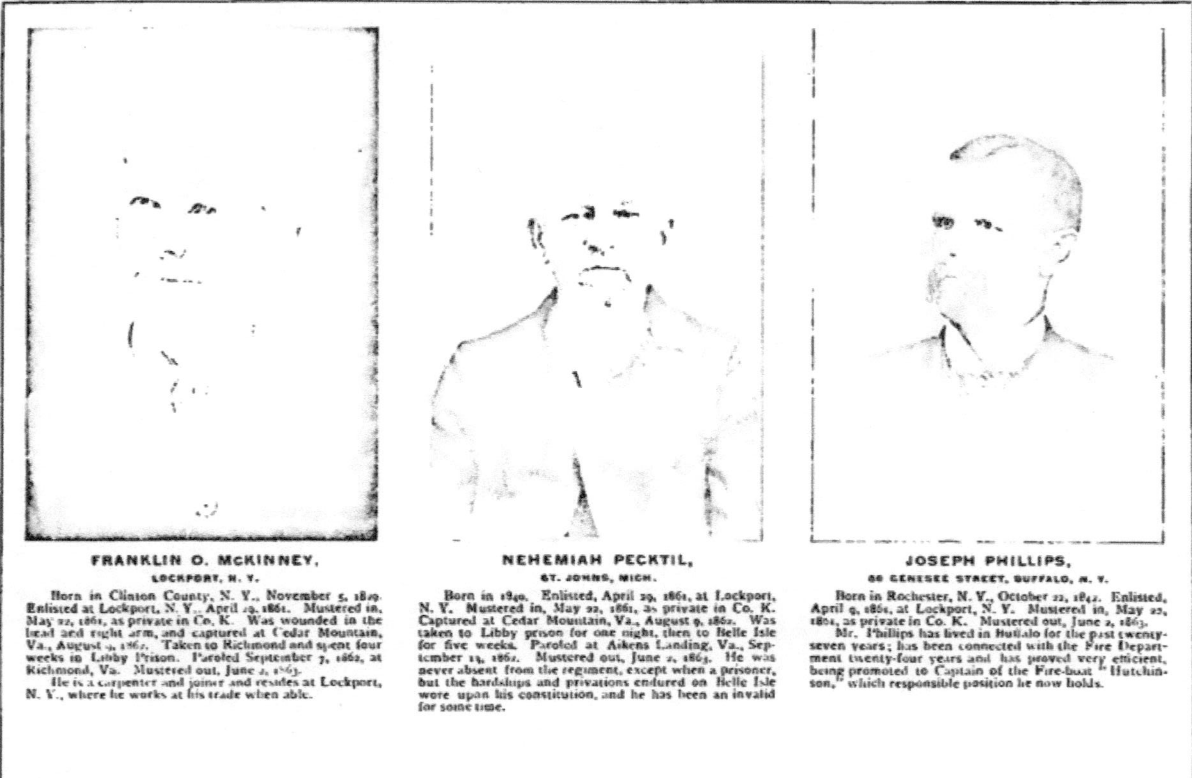

FRANKLIN O. McKINNEY,

LOCKPORT, N. Y.

Born in Clinton County, N. Y., November 5, 1829. Enlisted at Lockport, N. Y., April 29, 1861. Mustered in, May 22, 1861, as private in Co. K. Was wounded in the head and right arm, and captured at Cedar Mountain, Va., August 9, 1862. Taken to Richmond and spent four weeks in Libby Prison. Paroled September 7, 1862, at Richmond, Va. Mustered out, June 2, 1863.

He is a carpenter and joiner and resides at Lockport, N. Y., where he works at his trade when able.

NEHEMIAH PECKTIL,

ST. JOHNS, MICH.

Born in 1840. Enlisted, April 29, 1861, at Lockport, N. Y. Mustered in, May 22, 1861, as private in Co. K. Captured at Cedar Mountain, Va., August 9, 1862. Was taken to Libby prison for one night, then to Belle Isle for five weeks. Paroled at Aikens Landing, Va., September 14, 1862. Mustered out, June 2, 1863. He was never absent from the regiment, except when a prisoner, but the hardships and privations endured on Belle Isle wore upon his constitution, and he has been an invalid for some time.

JOSEPH PHILLIPS,

60 GENESEE STREET, BUFFALO, N. Y.

Born in Rochester, N. Y., October 22, 1842. Enlisted, April 9, 1861, at Lockport, N. Y. Mustered in, May 22, 1861, as private in Co. K. Mustered out, June 2, 1863.

Mr. Phillips has lived in Buffalo for the past twenty-seven years; has been connected with the Fire Department twenty-four years and has proved very efficient, being promoted to Captain of the Fire-boat "Hutchinson," which responsible position he now holds.

JOHN H. SMITH,

AURORA, ILLS.

Born at Pekin, Niagara County, N. Y., December 28, 1841. Enlisted April 29, 1861. Mustered in, May 22, 1861, as private in Co. K. Was brigade blacksmith from December, 1861, to May, 1863. Mustered out, June 2, 1863.

Soon after leaving the army Mr. Smith went to Aurora, Ills., where he has since resided, in the employ of the Chicago, Burlington & Quincy Railway Company.

AUGUST STRASBURG,

SANBORN, N. Y.

Born in Germany, December 3, 1840. Mustered in, May 22, 1861, as private in Co. K. Served in Brigade Quartermaster's department from February, 1862, to May, 1863. Mustered out, June 2, 1863.

Subsequent to the war, he lived in Grand Haven, Mich., for two years. Then returned to Niagara County, N. Y., where he has since resided.

Mr. Strasburg is a farmer by occupation.

HUGH A. JAMESON,

NORTH TONAWANDA, N. Y.

Born at Darien, Genesee County, N. Y., April 7, 1837. Enlisted April 28, 1861, at Lockport, N. Y. Mustered in, May 22, 1861, as 1st Sergeant, Co. K. On recruiting service, October and November, 1861. Mustered out, June 2, 1863.

For many years subsequent to the War Mr. Jameson was in the employ of the L. S. & M. S. R. R. Co ; and later head clerk in the Postal service, between Cincinnati and Pittsburg. He has resided in North Tonawanda for the past ten years, engaged in mercantile business. Is a member of the Willish Post, G. A. R., at Cincinnati, Ohio.

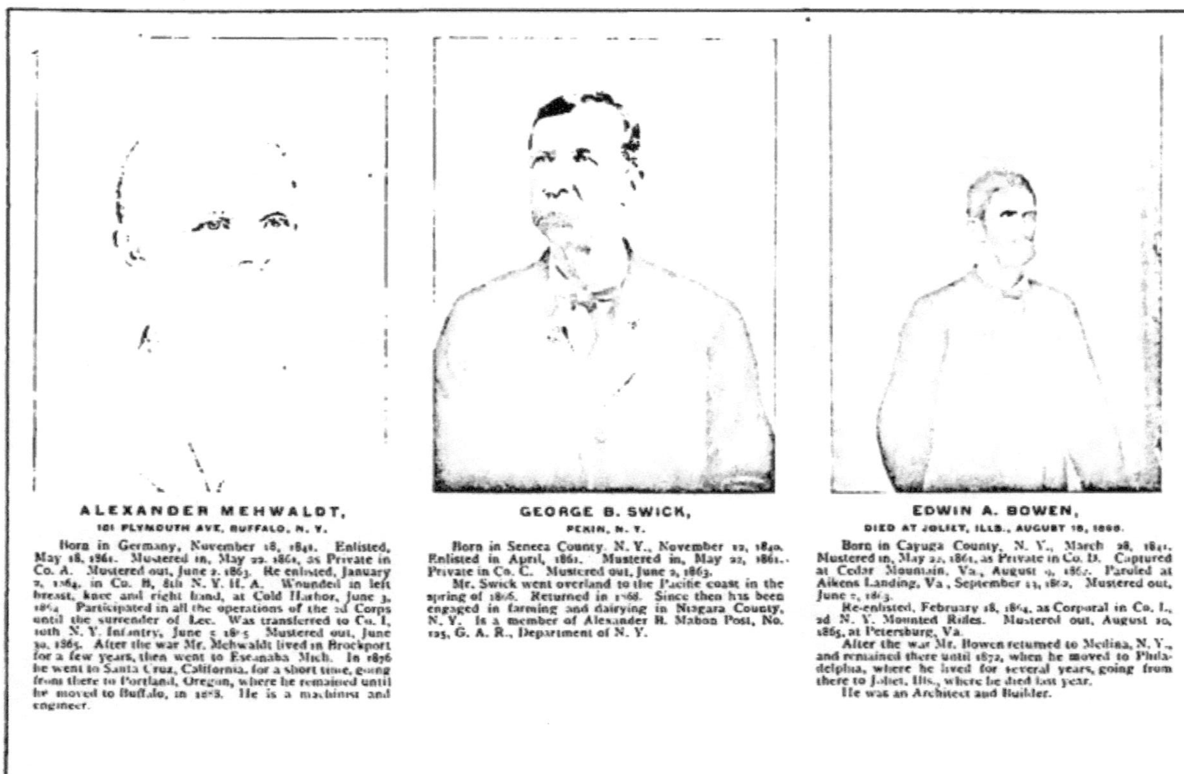

ALEXANDER MEHWALDT,

101 PLYMOUTH AVE, BUFFALO, N. Y.

Born in Germany, November 18, 1841. Enlisted, May 18, 1861. Mustered in, May 22, 1861, as Private in Co. A. Mustered out, June 2, 1863. Re enlisted, January 2, 1864, in Co. B, 8th N. Y. H. A. Wounded in left breast, knee and right hand, at Cold Harbor, June 3, 1864. Participated in all the operations of the 2d Corps until the surrender of Lee. Was transferred to Co. I, 10th N. Y. Infantry, June 5 1865. Mustered out, June 30, 1865. After the war Mr. Mehwaldt lived in Brockport for a few years, then went to Escanaba Mich. In 1876 he went to Santa Cruz, California, for a short time, going from there to Portland, Oregon, where he remained until he moved to Buffalo, in 1878. He is a machinist and engineer.

GEORGE B. SWICK,

PEKIN, N. Y.

Born in Seneca County, N. Y., November 12, 1840. Enlisted in April, 1861. Mustered in, May 22, 1861. Private in Co. C. Mustered out, June 2, 1863.

Mr. Swick went overland to the Pacific coast in the spring of 1866. Returned in 1868. Since then has been engaged in farming and dairying in Niagara County, N. Y. Is a member of Alexander R. Mabon Post, No. 125, G. A. R., Department of N. Y.

EDWIN A. BOWEN,

DIED AT JOLIET, ILLS., AUGUST 18, 1888.

Born in Cayuga County, N. Y., March 28, 1841. Mustered in, May 22, 1861, as Private in Co. D. Captured at Cedar Mountain, Va., August 9, 1862. Paroled at Aikens Landing, Va., September 13, 1862. Mustered out, June 2, 1863.

Re-enlisted, February 18, 1864, as Corporal in Co. L., 2d N. Y. Mounted Rifles. Mustered out, August 10, 1865, at Petersburg, Va.

After the war Mr. Bowen returned to Medina, N. Y., and remained there until 1872, when he moved to Philadelphia, where he lived for several years, going from there to Joliet, Ills., where he died last year.

He was an Architect and Builder.

JOHN S. CORNWELL,

YATES, ORLEANS COUNTY, N. Y.

Born May 2, 1834, in the town of Yates, N. Y. Enlisted, December 24, 1861. Mustered in, January 6, 1862, as Private in Co. D. Mustered out, June 2, 1863.

Subsequent to the War Mr. Cornwell returned to Yates, N. Y., his native place, where he has since resided on his farm. He is one of the best known and most respected citizens in the town, a man of integrity and honor, whose word is as good as his bond.

HARRY PADELFORD,

PADELFORDS, N. Y.

Born in 1832. Mustered in, May 22, 1861, as 2d Lieutenant, Co. E. Promoted, 1st Lieutenant June 8, 1862. Acting Captain, Co. G, May 29, 1862, to June 27, 1862. Mustered out, June 2, 1863

Since the War Mr. Padelford has resided at Padelfords, N. Y., for many years in the employ of the New York Central Railroad Company as station agent.

RECAPITULATION BY COMPANIES,

Showing the number of survivors in 1896, and the number of pictures printed.

Company.	Pictures of Survivors.	Comrades Who Did Not Respond.	Total Number Surviving.
Field and Staff,	5	0	5
Band, . . .	5	4	9
Company A, .	18	13	31
Company B, .	3	8	11
Company C, .	26	13	39
Company D, .	21	18	39
Company E, .	12	11	23
Company F, .	8	11	19
Company G, .	7	7	14
Company H, .	6	16	22
Company I, .	7	8	15
Company K, .	16	9	25
Survivors, .	134	118	252
Pictures of Deceased Comrades,	14		
Duplicates, .	2		
Total Number of Pictures, .	150	118	252

www.ingramcontent.com/pod-product-compliance
Lightning Source LLC
Chambersburg PA
CBHW030403230426
43664CB00007BB/729

* 9 7 8 3 3 3 7 1 2 6 1 9 3 *